高等学校英语专业教材

Selected Readings in English and American Literature

(New Edition)

新编英美文学选读

王继辉　林庆新 / 编注

中国出版集团
中译出版社

图书在版编目（CIP）数据

新编英美文学选读/王继辉，林庆新编注. —北京：中译出版社，2015.11（2022.1重印）

ISBN 978- 7- 5001- 4353- 6

I. ①新… II. ①王…②林… III. ①英语—阅读教学—高等学校—教材②英国文学—文学欣赏③文学欣赏—美国 IV. ①H319.4：I

中国版本图书馆CIP数据核字（2015）第267323号

出版发行 / 中译出版社
地　　址 / 北京市西城区新街口外大街28号普天德胜大厦主楼4层
电　　话 / （010）68359827（发行部）；53601537（编辑部）
邮　　编 / 100044
传　　真 / （010）68357870
电子邮箱 / book@ctph.com.cn
网　　址 / http://www.ctph.com.cn

责任编辑 / 范祥镇　王诗同
装帧设计 / 黄　浩

排版制作 / 陈　彬
印　　刷 / 北京玺诚印务有限公司
经　　销 / 新华书店

规　　格 / 710mm×1000mm　1/16
印　　张 / 33.5
字　　数 / 534千字
版　　次 / 2016年1月第一版
印　　次 / 2022年1月第六次

ISBN 978-7-5001-4353-6　　**定价**：68. 00元

前　言

英美文学是世界文学宝库中的一颗璀璨明珠，二者间既有传承，又各有显著特征，是英语专业学生了解英美文化，乃至世界文化极好的通识阅读材料。

英国文学自中世纪至今，已有一千五百多年异彩纷呈且文化深厚的历史。从《贝奥武甫》这部用古代英语写就的英雄史诗开始，它经历了古英语时期、中古英语时期、文艺复兴时期、王政复辟及十八世纪、浪漫主义时期、维多利亚时期以及二十世纪等各个文学发展阶段，每个阶段都分别涌现出众多代表不同流派的世界级诗人、戏剧家、小说家、散文作家。乔叟的《坎特伯雷故事集》和柯勒律治的《老舟子吟》，莎士比亚的《奥赛罗》和萧伯纳的《圣女贞德》，奥斯丁的《傲慢与偏见》和劳伦斯的《儿子与情人》，乃至约翰逊等的散文作品，无不闪耀着不列颠诸岛孕育出的文学大家们智慧的光辉。一位老师曾说过，英国文学未必能给我们带来什么实际用处，但它一定能帮助我们搁置实用性思维，回归对本质性问题的沉思，阅读英国文学的魅力也正在于此。

相比较而言，美国文学的历史虽然不很长，但也经历了新古典主义、浪漫主义、现实主义、自然主义、现代主义以及后现代主义等文学演变过程。这一部分的选文从浪漫主义时期（1800—1865）开始，因为19世纪的美国浪漫主义文学（包括超验主义文学）第一次在真正意义上体现了张扬个性、强调直觉、崇尚自然、反对清教主义教条等美国文化的独特精神。美国现实主义文学及自然主义文学（1865—1918）则关注社会现实的各个方面，尤其是社会底层的生活状态，而20世纪美国现代主义文学

（1918—1945）以“迷惘的一代”、“意象派”、“垮掉的一代”等文学潮流为代表，凸显了美国作家大量使用讽刺、幻想、黑色幽默、荒诞的写作风格。二战后美国文学呈现出空前的繁荣景象，涌现出很多具有世界影响的作家，但是，考虑到这一时期的文学作品仍处于新经典的形成过程之中，我们只选了米勒和海勒两位较早的作家。

呈现在各位朋友面前的这部《新编英美文学选读》，旨在为全国英语专业的本科生和研究生提供一个全面体验英美文学独特魅力的系统阅读机会。全书共分33个单元，按每周一个单元计，本书所提供的内容可满足大学英语专业两个学期的课程需求。考虑到英语专业本科生或研究生课程的特点，我们在每个单元中均提供了术语解释、作家介绍、作品概要、原著选读、难词注释、作品评述、课堂讨论题、推荐书目等内容。在选篇过程中，我们也着力保持了每一单元作品的相对完整性，以真实地反映作家的创作特色和思想内涵。

阅读经典文学作品是认识自我、接触社会、了解世界的重要途径。我们希望读者通过系统学习，对英美文学的演变历程、文学思潮，乃至英美社会文化的发展脉络有更为深入的理解，并藉此不断提高自己的语言能力和文学欣赏水平。

CONTENTS

Part I ENGLISH LITERATURE

Part II AMERICAN LITERATURE

SELECTED READINGS IN ENGLISH AND AMERICAN LITERATURE

PART I

English Literature

Unit 1 *Beowulf*

(Anonymous Author; Approximately 1000 CE)

A GUIDE TO LITERARY TERMINOLOGY

"Medieval English": *In historical linguistics, a study of the history of human language in general and a study of the history of one language in particular, Medieval English is not an accurate term we use. In the history of English, we name the different phases of the language as Old English (OE 499—1066), Middle English (ME 1066—1500), Modern English (ModE 1500—1800) and Present-Day English (PDE 1800-present). English in the Middle Ages is normally divided into two periods, namely the periods of Old English and Middle English.*

English took its form when the Germanic tribes invaded England which had been long inhabited by the Celtic people until about 499 when such Germanic peoples from northern Europe as Angles, Saxons and Jutes attacked England and eventually settled down there. Since the Angles were the most powerful among the tribes, their Germanic dialect called Angelisc became gradually the common language of England. Thus, English came into being.

Old English then was a highly inflectional language. That is to say, every word has many endings which determine the functions of grammar of that particular word. For instance, a noun may have various endings as it has its own cases (nominative, accusative, genitive and dative), numbers (singular and plural) and genders (masculine, feminine and neuter). So when the noun shows a particular ending, we will know the case, the number and the gender of it and therefore we understand how it functions in terms of grammar no matter where it stands in a sentence. In Old English, therefore, correct endings are a lot more important than the word order of a sentence in the transmission of its meaning. Such features of the inflectional language have become less and less outstanding ever since the so-called Middle English period which extended approximately from the Norman Conquest in 1066, when the French-speaking Normans invaded and ruled England, to the English Renaissance which started by and large from the time of Shakespeare.

NOTES ON THE WORK

Beowulf, known as the oldest epic written in the English vernacular, is one of the best folk epics in medieval Europe. Written down probably by two scribes around 1000 CE, it must have been circulated in its oral form by storytellers from one royal court gathering to another for many decades in the northern Germanic world. Although the story of the epic is mainly about the Danes and the Geats, the chief participants seem to reflect Anglo-Saxon England as well. The only manuscript that has been passed down is currently housed by the British Museum under the title "Cotton Vitllius A xv."

This medieval epic, with some 3,200 lines in length, is a long and serious narrative about kings and heroes of Denmark and Geatland with the Geatish hero Beowulf as the protagonist, who is involved in a series of actions against two monsters and a dragon that endanger the two kingdoms. Written in Old English, the poem shows the phase of the language extending from the invasion of England by the Angles, Saxons and Jutes since approximately 499 CE to the Norman Conquest in 1066 CE, and demonstrates many of the ancient Germanic poetic features, such as alliterative lines and kennings. The title of the epic was given by one of the later editors of this old work.

SYNOPSIS OF THE WORK

Beowulf, a young hero of the kingdom of Geatland hears that Hrothgar, King of Denmark, is in trouble because his great hall Heorot has been harassed by a man-like monster from wildness named Grendel. He decides to travel to Denmark and give the old king a hand. He is successful in slaying the fearful monster bare-handed in the hall only to make Grendel's mother so furious that she comes to take her revenge for her kinsman. She attacks the hall that very evening and, after snapping one of the most respected warriors among the Danes, disappears in darkness. Again, Beowulf promises to help and remove the lingering threat for the old king. He attacks the she-monster in an unnatural water lair and kills the dam with the aid of an ancient sword hanging on the wall. Thus, he completely delivers Hrothgar and his people from all their sufferings.

The third major fight happens many years later when Beowulf, having successfully ruled the Geats for some fifty years, has become an aged monarch. The trouble comes because a thief has sneaked into the hoard owned and guarded by a fierce dragon and stolen an old cup out of it. In due course, the dragon, burning with rage, devastates villages and towns of the kingdom. Beowulf, not without hesitation, decides once more to fight against the dragon for his subjects. He is not that triumphant this time and, even though the dragon is eventually slaughtered by him with the help of only one young warrior, the old king receives his fatal wound during the fight. Before he dies, he watches the treasures from the hoard, which he has won at the cost of his life and asks the young retainer with him to deliver the news of his death to his subjects, warning them about the upcoming invasion and enslavement. The story ends with a mournful funeral with people walking around Beowulf's funeral pyre wailing for the death of their old king and perhaps for the disaster they are facing.

SELECTED READINGS

Beowulf[1]

(Excerpts from the translation by Donaldson)

Then Hrothgar went out of the hall with his company of warriors, the protector of the Scyldings [1]. The war-chief would seek the bed of Wealhtheow the queen. The King of Glory — as men had learned — had appointed a hall-guard against Grendel; he had a special mission to the prince of the Danes: he kept watch against monsters.

And the man of the Geats had sure trust in his great might, the favor of the Ruler[2]. Then he took off his shirt of armor, the helmet from his head, handed his embellished sword, best of irons[3], to an attendant, bade him keep guard over his war-gear. Then the good warrior spoke some boast words before he went to his bed, Beowulf of the Geats: "I claim myself no poorer in war-strength, war works, than Grendel claims himself. Therefore I will not put him to sleep with a sword, so take away his life, though surely I might. He knows no good tools with which he might strike against me, cut my shield in pieces, though he is strong in fight. But we shall forgo the sword in the night — if he dare seek war without weapon — and then may wise God, Holy Lord, assign glory on whichever hand seems good to Him." [2]

---

1 The excerpts are taken from the modern prose version of *Beowulf* translated by Donaldson of Norton Critical Edition.

2 Ruler: Christian God.

3 irons: weapons.

The battle-brave one laid himself down, the pillow received the earl's head[4], and about him many a brave seaman lay down to hall-rest[5]. None of them thought that he would ever again seek[6] from there his dear home, people or town where he had been brought up; for they knew that bloody death had carried off far too many men in the wine-hall [3], folk of the Danes. But the Lord granted to weave for them good fortune in war, for the folk of the Weather-Geats, comfort and help that they should quite overcome their foe through the might of one man, through his sole strength: the truth has been made known that mighty God has always ruled mankind.

There came gliding in the black night the walker in darkness. The warriors slept who should hold the horned house — all but one. It was known to men that when the Ruler did not wish it the hostile creature might not drag them away beneath the shadows. But he, lying awake for the fierce foe, with heart swollen in anger awaited the outcome of the fight.

Then from the moor under the mist-hills Grendel came walking, wearing God's anger [4]. The foul ravager thought to catch some one of mankind there in the high hall. Under the clouds he moved until he could see most clearly the wine-hall, treasure-house of men, shining with gold. That was not the first time that he had caught Hrothgar's home. Never before or since in his life-days did he find harder luck, hardier hall-thanes. The creature deprived of joy came walking to the hall. Quickly the door gave way, fastened with fire-forged bands, when he touched it with his hands. Driven by evil desire, swollen with rage, he tore it open, the hall's mouth. After that the foe at once stepped onto the shining floor, advanced angrily. From his eyes came a light not fair, most like a flame. He saw many men in the hall, a band of kinsmen all asleep together, a company of war-men. Then his heart laughed: dreadful monster, he thought that before the day came

4 the earl's head: the noble man's head.
5 hall-rest: rest in the hall.
6 seek: go back to.

he would divide the life from the body of every one of them, for there had come to him a hope of full-feasting. It was not his fate that when that night was over he should feast on more of mankind.

The kinsman of Hygelac[7], mighty man, watched how the evil-doer would make his quick onslaught. Nor did the monster mean to delay it, but, starting his work, he suddenly seized a sleeping man, tore at him ravenously, bit into his bone-locks, drank the blood from his veins, swallowed huge morsels; quickly he had eaten all of the life-less one, feet and hands. He stepped closer, then felt with his arm for the brave-hearted man on the bed, reached out towards him, the foe with his hand; at once in fierce response Beowulf seized it and sat up, leaning on his own arm. Straightway the fosterer of crimes knew that he had not encountered on middle-earth [5], anywhere in this world, a harder hand-grip from another man. In mind he became frightened, in his spirit: not for that might he escape the sooner. His heart was eager to get away, he could flee to his hiding-place, seek his rabble of devils. What he met there was not such as he had ever before met in the days of his life. Then the kinsman of Hygelac, the good man, thought of his evening's speech[8], stood upright and laid firm hold on him: his fingers cracked. The giant[9] was pulling away, the earl stepped forward. The notorious one thought to move farther away, wherever he could, and flee his way from there to his fen-retreat; he knew his fingers' power to be in a hateful grip. That was a painful journey that the loathsome despoiler had made to Heorot. The retainers' hall rang with the noise — terrible drink for all the Danes, the house-dwellers [6], every brave man, the earls. Both were enraged, fury-filled, the two who meant to control the hall. The building resounded. Then was it much wonder that the wine-hall withstood them joined in fierce fight, that it did not

7 Hygelac: Beowulf's uncle, king of Geatland.

8 his evening's speech: the boasting speech Beowulf made during the welcome feast given in Heorot by King Hrothgar.

9 the giant: Gredel is described as a man-like monster massive like a giant.

fall to the ground, the fair earth-dwelling; but it was so firmly made fast with iron bands, both inside and outside, joined by skillful smith-craft. There started from the floor — as I have heard say — many a mead-bench, gold-adorned, when the furious ones fought. No wise men of the Scyldings ever before thought that any men in any manner might break it down, splendid with bright horns, have skill to destroy it, unless flame should embrace it, swallow it in fire.[7] Noise rose up, sound strange enough. Horrible fear came upon the North-Danes, upon every one of those who heard the weeping from the wall, God's enemy sing his terrible song, song without triumph — the hell-slave bewail his pain. There held him fast he who of men was strongest of might in the days of this life.

Not for anything would the protector of warriors [8] let the murderous guest[10] go off alive: he did not consider his life-days of use to any of the nations. There more than enough of Beowulf's earls[11] drew swords, old heirlooms, wished to protect the life of their dear lord, famous prince, however they might. They did not know when they entered the fight, hardy-spirited warriors, and when they thought to hew him on every side, to seek his soul, that not any of the best of irons on earth, no war-sword, would touch the evil-doer: for with a charm he had made victory-weapons useless, every sword-edge. His departure to death from the time of this life was to be wretched; and the alien spirit was to travel far off into the power of fiends. Then he who before had brought trouble of heart to mankind, committed many crimes — he was at war with God — found that his body would do him no good, for the great-hearted kinsman of Hygelac had him by the hand. Each was hateful to the other alive. The awful monster had lived to feel pain in his body, a huge wound in his shoulder was exposed, his sinews sprang apart, his bone-locks broke. Glory in battle was giv-

10 the murderous guest: Grendel.

11 earls: noble warriors.

en to Beowulf. Grendel must flee from there, mortally sick, seek his joyless home in the fen-slopes. He knew the more surely that his life's end had come, the full number of his days. For all the Danes was their wish fulfilled after the bloody fight. Thus he who had lately come from far off, wise and stout-hearted, had purged Heorot, saved Hrothgar's house from affliction. He rejoiced in his night's work, a deed to make famous his courage. The man of the Geats had fulfilled his boast to the East-Danes; so too he had remedied all the grief, the malice-caused sorrow that they had endured before, and had had to suffer from harsh necessity, no small distressed. That was clearly proved when the battle-brave man set the hand up under the curved roof — the arm and the shoulder: there all together was Grendel's grasp.

NOTES ON THE TEXT

[1] In terms of lineage, the mystical founder of the Danish royalty was Scyld, who was victorious in his constant fighting against the neighboring tribes. He soon became the most powerful king and took tributes from many peoples. Descendants from the royal line of Scyld were called Scyldings, which is the traditional way to address the sons of Scyld, just like "Johnson" was so called because the person was the son of John in the Germanic tradition and "MacMillin" the son of Millin in the Celtic tradition. Hrothgar was supposed to be the king of the Scyldings. Notice the mild sarcasm here.

[2] Removing all his war gears, Beowulf decided to wrestle with the monster bare-handed. As he boasted in his speech just before the fight, he would rather deal with Grendel by using his naked strength because he believed that success rested ultimately with God, the most glorious of kings. His confidence would be gone when he fought with the dragon as an old king.

[3] The wine hall here refers to Heorot, a great hall King Hrothgar had built in which he treated his retainers with good food and treasures as a return to their services at war time. This kind of social grouping between a lord and his retainers is what the Germanic people called "comitatus," a typical feature in the ancient Germanic culture, as is observed by the first-century Roman historian Tacitus in his account of Germanic society entitled *Germania*. Notice, at this point, that Grendel had become the actual master of the hall, at least at night.

[4] Throughout the story, Grendel is said to be the enemy of God. He is even taken as the descendant of Cain, the first murderer, according to the Christian Bible, who slaughtered his own brother Abel owing to his jealousy. Some scholars have argued that the poem used to be

a purely secular heroic work and the touches of Christian ideas were added by the scribes. Touches of this kind are referred to as "Christian coloring" by F. A. Blackburn.

[5] Medieval people, especially the ancient Germanic people, understood the cosmos as a multi-layered world, namely heavens far above us and hell down below, and human beings live in the middle, which is often referred to as Middle Earth. In Scandinavian mythology, the region is called Midgard, the place where human beings reside.

[6] Here the house-dwellers refer to the retainers of King Hrothgar. They were to serve their lord on the battlefield and to enjoy the generosity and kindness of their lord at the time of peace. The social grouping of this kind is what the Germanic people called "comitatus." What is ironic about the situation is that at this point all the glorious Danish retainers, who were supposed to fight, were all gone, only leaving Beowulf and a group of Geats behind.

[7] The poet tells us time and again that Heorot was the most brilliantly built wine-hall. As it was so firmly made with iron bands from floor to roof, nobody seemed to have power to destroy it. However, as the poet hints here that flame would eventually swallow it up, we feel that it will collapse in a huge fire. The poem anticipates on different occasions that the hall was burnt down later because of the feud between members of the royal family.

[8] The king or prince is sometimes referred to as "protector of warriors." The rather metaphorical description of this type is widely used in Old English poetry, especially in those works of the oral tradition. For instance, they would call "body" as "bone house," "sea" as "whale road," and "sun" as "sky candle." This kind of picturesque usage in Old English poetry is called "kennings."

QUESTIONS FOR DISCUSSION

1. According to the *Oxford Companion to English Literature,* an epic is supposed to be a poem that celebrates in the form of a continuous narrative the achievements of one or more heroic personages of history or tradition. Is *Beowulf* a typical epic in its classical sense?

2. *Beowulf* is basically a story about the Danes and the Geats, two ancient Germanic peoples. Why then is it taken by many scholars today as a revered English epic?

3. Even without being able to read the original Old English poem, readers of *Beowulf* should know the meaning of a few terms pertinent to an understanding of the work, namely alliterative verse, kenning, scop, comitatus, mead hall, etc. Do you understand at this point what they really mean?

4. There has been debate about whether *Beowulf* was a pagan heroic story or a Christian one. Which side are you on? Document your opinion with specific details from the text.

5. As Tolkien famously argued in 1936, it was the superhuman opposition of the heathen monsters that elevated the epic to heroic stature, and all other historical allusions were related directly to the transient grandeur of Beowulf's life and battles with the monsters. How do you understand his point?

SUGGESTED REFERENCES

Bishop, Chris. "Beowulf: The Monsters and the Comics." *Journal of the Australian Early Medieval Association* 7 (2011): 73+.

Bloomfield, Joan. "The Style and Structure of *Beowulf*." *Review of English Studies* 14.56 (1992): 390-403.

Drout, Michael D. C. "The Inheritance System in *Beowulf*." *The Journal of English and Germanic Philology* 104. 2 (1986): 199-226.

Nicholson, L. E. *An Anthology of Beowulf Criticism.* London: U of Notre Dame P, 1971.

Taylor, Paul Beekman. "The Traditional Language of Treasure in *Beowulf*." *The Journal of English and Germanic Philology* 85.2 (1986): 191-205.

Unit 2 Geoffrey Chaucer

(1340—1400)

A GUIDE TO LITERARY TERMINOLOGY

"Heroic Couplet": *A couplet refers to a pair of lines of poetry, featuring a shared rhyme of their ending words and a rhythm of iambic pentameter, that is, a line of five metrical feet with an unstressed syllable followed by a stressed one. Couplets may fall into two groups. When each line of the couplet is self-contained in structure and in meaning, it is referred to as a closed couplet, and when the structure and meaning of the first line run on without a pause to the second, it is called an enjambment.*

The forerunner responsible for its introduction to English poetry was Chaucer, the fourteenth century poet, who borrowed the form probably from French versification and, by using it a great deal in his own works, made it popular and widely used by his contemporaries. Chaucer's verse form, named later heroic couplet, was gradually perfected from the late seventeeth century to the early eighteenth, and reached a height of sophistication in the marvelous poems by John Dryden (1631-1700) and by Alexander Pope (1688—1744).

Following are two lines as a sample of a typical heroic couplet chosen from "Eloisa to Abelard" by Alexander Pope:

Then share thy pain, allow that sad relief;
Ah, more than share it, give me all thy grief.

NOTES ON THE AUTHOR

Geoffrey Chaucer, the greatest among the fourteenth-century English poets, was certainly one of the most important authors in the history of English literature. Owing to his outstanding innovativeness both in form and in content as is reflected in the Middle English narrative poem the *Canterbury Tales*, he has also been celebrated by many as father of English poetry.

Born in approximately 1340 to a prosperous and influential London vintner, he began to serve at court at a very young age. He was taken prisoner when serving in the military in France but shortly ransomed. Being later a diplomat, he traveled back and forth frequently between England and the continent. His experiences especially in France and Italy made him familiar with European humanism and thus prepared him with a keen humanist perspective for his later writings.

The uniqueness of Chaucer's times was quite outstanding since England by the end of the fourteenth century was reviving after a series of frustrating events. The Norman Conquest, for instance, and the subsequent ruling of the conquerors over the centuries only left the French-speaking aristocrats in England increasingly hostile towards their counterparts in France and thus identified themselves more with England and her culture; Black Death had caused tremendous casualty in England as well as in Europe and left the kingdom with an acute shortage of labor. The English-speaking working class had gained a better social status as a result of the social need for labor, and the language they conducted every day became more important and more widely used for different purposes of social life. This was the time when Chaucer and some of his contemporaries began to use English, instead of Latin or Norman French, for their major literary expressions.

Chaucer started his writing career close to the end of the 50s of the fourteenth century and, until his death in 1400, he had written for approximately forty years. Chaucerian scholars tend to put his works into three distinctive periods, namely the period of French influence (1359 – 1372), the period of Italian influence (1372 – 1386), and the period of his maturity (1386 – 1400), depending on the stylistic characteristics of his poetry. Chaucer's *Canterbury Tales* and the so-called "Heroic Couplets" he began to employ in his poetry are among the most outstanding contributions he made to English literature.

SYNOPSIS OF THE WORK

In April the light showers, warming sun, and gentle winds, have awakened nature from its winter sleep. Then people yearn to travel. In this charming season, people make their way from every corner of England to Canterbury to receive the blessings of "the holy blissful martyr" — St. Thomas a Becket.

One spring day at Tabard Inn in Southwark, the narrator awaits the following day when he will commence his journey to Canterbury. That evening a company of twenty-nine persons have arrived at the inn, all of whom are Canterbury pilgrims. Admitted to their company before the pilgrimage begins, the narrator takes time to describe his companions.

The Host, named Harry Bailey, decides to join the company and make the trip with them to Canterbury. He serves the company an excellent dinner after which he suggests that, to make the trip pass more pleasantly, each member of the party should tell two tales on the way to Canterbury and, on the return trip, each member of the company should tell two more tales. The man who tells the best story is to be awarded with a sumptuous dinner by other members of the party. The Host adds that, to keep the journey merry, he will be the judge of what is best for the group. All members of the company agree to his proposal.

Early in the following morning the party depart. The Host then silences the noisy group and announces that they will draw straws to see in which order the tales are told. As the Knight draws the shortest straw, he agrees to tell the first tale, and he does.

SELECTED READINGS

The Canterbury Tales

(Excerpts from the "General Prologue")

(ll. 1—42)

When that April with its showers soote [1] — soote: sweet
The draught of March has pierced to the roote,
And bathed every vein in such licour — licour: liquid
Of which power engendered is the flour; — of: by; flour: flower
When Zephirus [2] also with its sweet breeth: — breeth: breath
Has inspired in every grove and heeth — heeth: field
The tender crops, and the young sun
Has in the Ram [3] its half course run,
And small fowls make melodye,
That sleep all the night with open ye — ye: eyes
(So pricks them nature in their corages), — corages: hearts
Then folk long to go on pilgrimages,
And palmers for to seek strange strondes, — strondes: shores
To distant shrines, known in various londes;
And specially from every shire's ende

Of England to Canterbury [4] they wende, wende: go
The holy blissful martyr for to seke, seke: seek
That has helped them when they were seeke. seeke: sick
    Bifil that in that season on a day, bifil: it happened
In Southwark at the Tabard as I lay
Ready to go on my pilgrimage
To Canterbury with full devout corage. corage: feelings
At night had come into that hostelry hostelrye: inn
Well nine and twenty in a company
Of various folk, by chance yfalle yfalle: fallen
In fellowship, and pilgrims were they alle,
That toward Canterbury would ride.
The chambers and the stables were wide,
And well we were eased at best,
And shortly, when the sun was to rest,
So had I spoken with them everichon everichon: every one
That I was of their fellowship anon, anon: straightway
And made foreword early for to rise, foreword: agreement
To take our way there as I you devise. devise: tell
    But nonetheless, while I have time and space, space: opportuinity
Er that I further in this tale pace, er: before; pace: proceed
I think it in accord with reason
To tell you all the condition
Of each of them, so as it seemed to me,
And which they were, and of what degree, degree: social rank
And also in what array what they were in; array: dress
And at a knight then would I first begin.
...

(ll. 118–162)
    There was also a Nun, a Prioresse [5],

That of her smiling was very simple and coy;
Her greatest oath was but by Saint Loy [6];
And she was called madam Eglentine.
Very well she sang the service divine,
Intoned in her nose very semely; semely: seemly
And French she spoke so fair and fetisly, fetisly: elegantly
After the school of Stratford rather than at Bowe,
For French of Paris was to her unknowe. unknowe: unknown
At dinner well taught was she with alle; with alle: indeed
She let no morsel from her lips falle,
Never wet her fingers in her sauce depe; depe: deep
Well could she carry a morsel and well kepe kepe: keep
That no drop ne fell [7] upon her breast.
In courtesy was set very much her lest. lest: pleasure
Her upper lip wiped she so clean
That in her cup there was no speck seen
Of grease, when she drunk had her draughte. draughte: drink
Very seemly after her food she raughte. raughte after: reached for
And truly she was of great desport, desport: deportment
And very pleasant, and amiable of port, port: manner
And took pains to imitate cheere cheere: manners
Of court, and to be dignified in manere, in manere: in behaviour
And to be held worthy of reverence. reverence: respect
But for to speak of her conscience, conscience: moral sense
She was so charitable and so pitous pitous: compassionate
She would weep, if that she saw a mous
Caught in a trap, if it was dead or bled.
Of small hounds had she that she fed
With roasted meat, or milk and fine bread.
But sorely wept she if one of them was dead,
Or if men beat it with a switch smart; smart: smartly

And all was conscience and tender heart.
Very seemly her wimple pleated was,
Her nose well formed, her eyes gray as glass,
Her mouth very small, and moreover soft and red.
But certainly she had a fair forehead;
It was almost a span broad, I trowe; trowe: believe
For, certainly, she was not undergrowe. undergrowe: undergrown
Very elegant was her cloak, as I was war. war: aware
Of small coral about her arm she bar bar: bore
A set of beads, divided all with greene,
And on it hang a broach of gold very sheene, sheene: bright
On which there was first written a crowned A,
And after Amor vincit omnia [8]. Amor vincit omnia: Love conquers all

NOTES ON THE TEXT

[1] All Chaucer's narrative verse, except for the "Monk's Tale," is written either in rhymed couplets or in stanzas of seven lines. The language of Chaucer is what we call in historical linguistics Middle English. In order to reserve some medieval flavor of Chaucer's poetry, the following things have been done to the text: 1. Some of the Middle English words in the lines are translated into their Present-day English equivalents. 2. Word order has been changed to what we are familiar with such as "Inspired has" in Line 6. 3. Words at the end of the lines are preserved even though they appear to be foreign so that the tail rhyme is kept as what it sounds like in the original, such as "soote" ("sweet") in Line 1. 4. Some words at the tails of the lines are not given an explanation in the side gloss as they do not cause much difficulty to us even though they look different, such as "mous" ("mouse") in Line 144.

[2] Zephyrus in Greek mythology is one of the four sons of Eos and Astraeus and, like his three brothers, he is the god of one of the four winds, namely the god of the gentle west wind that blows in spring.

[3] Ram, also known as Aries in Latin, is the first sign of the zodiac in western astrology. If the sun has passed through the second half of the zodiacal sign Ram, the time is late April. The solar year has just begun with the vernal equinox.

[4] St. Thomas a Becket, who was born in approximately 1118 and died in 1170, was an English Roman Catholic martyr. Being Chancellor to Henry II after 1154, he was appointed arch-

bishop of Canterbury in 1162 but soon fell into disfavor with the king. Charged with misappropriating crown funds in 1164, Becket fled the country. Upon his return in 1170 he was embroiled in the controversy surrounding Henry's appointment of his son as archbishop of York and was murdered by four mysterious knights in the Canterbury Cathedral. He was canonized in 1173 and, ever since, pilgrims made trips to his shrine in Canterbury to receive the blessings of the holy blissful martyr, St. Thomas a Becket.

[5] An abbey in medieval England could be a monastery or a convent, and it could also be the common place for both monks and nuns. Prioress is a nun in charge of a priory or she might rank next below the abbess of an abbey.

[6] St. Loy here refers to St. Eligius, a seventh-century French clergyman. He was known for his lower-class origin and for his contribution with his own wealth to the construction of abbeys. Her choice of this oath "by Sainte Loy," the most fashionable and handsome saint known for his great courtesy, implies her secret longing for a more worldly life and also discloses her similar origin to that of the saint.

[7] The early phases of the English language, such as Old English and Middle English, are Germanic and relatively reflectional in nature as compared to Modern and Present-day English. Chaucer's language in the late medieval period still has besides others the rather archaic double negative forms.

[8] Chaucer's depiction of the Prioress is filled with subtle ironies. Here is a picture of a lady who happens to be a nun, but she never forgets that she is a lady first. The inscription on a piece of lovely jewelry, which is used both in religion and in courtly romances, shows the last touch of Chaucer's subtle irony on the prioress who longs for a worldly life.

QUESTIONS FOR DISCUSSION

1. If you are asked to compare Chaucer with any of the European authors you happen to be familiar with of more or less the same time period, how does Geoffrey Chaucer differ from him or her?

2. In terms of the poetic style Chaucer has demonstrated in his "General Prologue" to the *Canterbury Tales*, what in your opinion is the most outstanding feature? Could you support yourself?

3. Many believe that the most important single part of the *Canterbury Tales* is the "General Prologue." Do you agree? If your answer is positive, what is the basis for your judgment?

4. If you are told that Chaucer is a satirist, how would you comment on his satire? What word would you use to describe his tone? Is it mild, mocking or critical?

5. Medieval writers in Europe tended to end their works by distancing themselves from the non-Christian elements in the books they had completed and Chaucer did the same thing with his closing "Retracciouns" in which he asked forgiveness of God for his writing on worldly matters. What overall picture do you have, anyway, of Chaucer's world after reading the "General Prologue"?

SUGGESTED REFERENCES

Bowden, Muriel. *A Commentary on the "General Prologue" to the Canterbury Tales.* New York: MacMillan, 1948.

Hoy, Michael and Michael Stevens. *Chaucer's Major Tales.* New York: Schocken Books, 1983.

Kolve, V. A. *Chaucer and the Imagery of Narrative: The First Five Canterbury Tales.* Stanford: Standford UP, 1984.

Rowland, Beryl, ed. *Companion to Chaucer Studies.* Revised edition. Oxford: Oxford UP, 1979.

Stillinger, Thomas C. ed. *Critical Essays on Geoffrey Chaucer.* New York: G. K. Hll, 1998.

Unit 3 William Shakespeare

(1564 – 1616)

A GUIDE TO LITERARY TERMINOLOGY

"Tragedy": *The concept of tragedy, as general opinion holds, originates from Aristotle, the author of the* ***Poetics****, which is one of the two outstanding critical works of his various mysterious arts. The work is divided into two sections defining respectively tragedy and comedy. Although we have no idea about Aristotle's definition of comedy since the second section addressing it was lost, we are fortunate enough to have learned in great detail his theory about tragedy.*

According to Aristotle, a typical tragedy should be a drama in which events move through rapid actions to a predestined disastrous ending owing to the fact that the hero, always of a noble character, brings about his downfall by his own error which is named by Aristotle the tragic flaw. Since the noble man's fate is unavoidable, the spectators are to thrill with fear and melt to pity for what has fallen upon him. Aristotle argues that through this pity and fear the audience of a tragedy would experience a kind of purification of their emotions which is what he calls catharsis.

Although Aristotle's ***Poetics*** *has been taken, to some extent, as a touchstone of thoughts on the genre known as tragedy, we see new tragic conventions that have developed ever since the English Renaissance when the Elizabethan and Jacobean dramatists such as Shakespeare demonstrated their innovativeness and power in their production of many tragic works. Tragedy as a form also shows its relevance and timeliness in the twentieth-century works by such talented tragedians as Eugene O'Neill and Arthur Miller, the latter of whom, as a critic and playwright, convinces us with his opinion and works that a common man can be a fit subject for a tragedy.*

NOTES ON THE AUTHOR

William Shakespeare, born in Stratford-on-Avon in 1564 to a well-to-do family, received his preliminary education at a local grammar school and picked up his Latin and his little Greek. He left his family in 1586 for London and, after working for a while at odd jobs in a theater, he became an actor and very soon a writer for the stage as well. He started with revising plays written by other playwrights and then he worked on the plays of his own. Obviously talented in the profession, he soon enjoyed huge popularity as a writer of all kinds of plays such as tragedies, comedies, historicals, as well as romances. He was incredibly prolific and had completed 37 plays, 2 narrative poems and 155 sonnets before he died in 1616 at his hometown.

It is generally agreed that Shakespeare's career as a playwright falls into three periods. The first one, dating from 1590 to 1600, witnessed the appearance and production of many of his historical plays and comedies and, of course, some of his early tragedies. The period from 1601 to 1608 is seen as his second, during which he completed his major tragedies such as *Hamlet*, *Othello*, *King Lear* and *Macbeth,* almost all of which demonstrated his growing consciousness of and anxiety over the social ills of the time. From the year 1609 he began to articulate his optimistic faith in the future world with tragic-comedies and among them *The Tempest* is the most outstanding. This is usually taken as the last period of his writing career which lasted until some two years before he passed away.

Shakespeare has been considered not only as one of the greatest writers of the European Renaissance but also as probably the most outstanding dramatist of world literature. Just as Ben Jonson, his beloved friend, once rightly commented, Shakespeare is "not of an age, but for all time."

SYNOPSIS OF THE WORK

Desdemona, a Venetian senator's daughter who has secretly married Othello, a Moor in the service of the state, is wrongly accused by her husband of having an illicit sexual relationship with Cassio, Othello's lieutenant. Othello's misjudgement results from the conspiracy organized by Iago, his ensign and the villain, who manages to have convinced Othello of her guilt by letting him see Cassio in possession of a handkerchief which he gave Desdemona as a token of love shortly before their marriage. Owing to the bitter jealousy aroused in him by Iago through his wickedly designed plot, Othello decides to put his wife to death in the name of righteousness.

Othello gets into the bed chamber when Desdemona is nearly asleep. Determined to kill, he gives his wife one more kiss in darkness which wakes her up. Desdemona begs her husband for mercy even though she is innocent. As Othello has been made completed blind to the truth, he smothers her. The arrival of Emilia, Iago's wife and Desdemona's maid, makes Othello realize, too late as it is, that he has stumbled into the deadly trap set for him by Iago. Infuriated by his wife's exposure of his vicious deception, Iago kills Emilia and he himself is wounded by Othello who flies into a fit of rage at his evil and crafty scheme. Othello, having sunk to the depths of despair over his wife's death, stabs himself and, giving his beloved wife a last kiss, dies miserably.

SELECTED READINGS

The Tragedy of Othello, the Moor of Venice

(Act V, Scene ii)

The Names of the Actors

Othello, the Moor, [in the military service of Venice]
Cassio, an honorable lieutenant
Iago, [an ensign,] a villain
Roderigo, a gull'd gentleman
Desdemona, [daughter to Brabantio and] wife to Othello
Emilia, wife to Iago

Scene: Venice; a sea-port in Cyprus

Enter Othello [*with a light*] *and Desdemona in her bed* [*asleep*].

Oth. It is the cause, it is the cause, my soul; — cause: crime
Let me not name it to you, you chaste stars,
It is the cause. Yet I'll not shed her blood,
Nor scar that whiter skin of hers than snow,
And smooth as monumental alablaster. — alablaster: alabaster
Yet she must die, else she'll betray more men.
Put out the light, and then put out the light:
If I quench thee, thou flaming minister, — quench: put out

I can again thy former light restore,
Should I repent me; but once put out thy light, repent: change mind
Thou cunning'st pattern of excelling nature,
I know not where is that Promethean heat Promoethean: divine
That can thy light relume. When I have pluck'd thy rose, relume: rekindle
I cannot give it vital growth again,
It needs must wither. I'll smell thee on the tree.
[*Kisses her.*]
O balmy breath, that dost almost persuade
Justice to break her sword! One more, one more.
Be thus when thou art dead, and I will kill thee thou art: you are
And love thee after. One more, and that's the last.
So sweet was ne'er so fatal. I must weep,
But they are cruel tears. This sorrow's heavenly, cruel: unrelenting
It strikes where it doth love. She wakes. [1]

Des. Who's there? Othello?
Oth. Ay, Desdemona. ay: yes
Des. Will you come to bed, my lord?
Oth. Have you pray'd to-night, Desdemona?
Des. Ay, my lord.
Oth. If you bethink yourself of any crime crime: sin
Unreconcil'd as yet to heaven and grace,
Solicit for it straight.
Des. Alack, my lord, what may you mean by that? alack: oh
Oth. Well, do it, and be brief, I will walk by.
I would not kill thy unprepared spirit,
No, [heaven] forefend! I would not kill thy soul. forefend: forbid
Des. Talk you of killing?
Oth. Ay, I do.

Des. Then heaven
Have mercy on me!
Oth. Amen, with all my heart!
Des. If you say [so], I hope you will not kill me.
Oth. Humh!
Des. And yet I fear you; for you're fatal then
When your eyes roll so. Why I should fear I know not,
Since guiltiness I know not; but yet I feel I fear.
Oth. Think on thy sins.
Des. They are loves I bear to you.
Oth. Ay, and for that thou di'st.
Des. That death's unnatural that kills for loving.
Alas, why gnaw you so your nether lip?
Some bloody passion shakes your very frame.
These are portents; but yet I hope, I hope,
They do not point on me.

point on: point

Oth. Peace, and be still!
Des. I will so. What's the matter?
Oth. That handkerchief which I so lov'd, and gave thee,
Thou gav'st to Cassio.
Des. No, by my life and soul!
Send for the man, and ask him.
Oth. Sweet soul, take heed,
Take heed of perjury, thou art on thy death-bed. [2]
Des. Ay, but not yet to die.
Oth. [Yes,] presently:
Therefore confess thee freely of thy sin;
For to deny each article with oath
Cannot remove nor choke the strong conception
That I do groan withal. Thou art to die.

withal: in addition

Des. [Then Lord] have mercy on me!

Oth. I say, amen.
Des. And have you mercy too! I never did
Offend you in my life; never lov'd Cassio, offend: wrong
But with such general warranty of heaven warranty: approval
As I might love. I never gave him token.
Oth. By heaven, I saw my handkerchief in's hand.
O perjur'd woman, thou dost stone my heart, stone: turn to stone
And [mak'st] me call what I intend to do
A murther, which I thought a sacrifice. murther: murder
I saw the handkerchief.
Des. He found it then;
I never gave it him. Send for him hither; hither: here
Let him confess a truth.
Oth. He hath confess'd.
Des. What, my lord?
Oth. That he hath us'd thee.
Des. How? unlawfully?
Oth. Ay.
Des. He will not say so.
Oth. No — his mouth is stopp'd;
Honest Iago hath ta'en order for't. make it happen
Des. O, my fear interprets. What, is he dead?
Oth. Had all his hairs been lives, my great revenge
Had stomach for them all.
Des. Alas, he is betray'd and I undone!
Oth. Out, strumpet! Weep'st thou for him to my face?
Des. O, banish me, my lord, but kill me not!
Oth. Down, strumpet!
Des. Kill me to-morrow, let me live to-night!
Oth. Nay, [an'] you strive — strive: struggle
Des. But half an hour!

Oth. Being done, there is no pause.

Des. But while I say one prayer!

Oth. It is too late. [*Smothers her.*]

[*Des.* O Lord, Lord, Lord!]

Emil. (*At the door*, [*within*].) My lord, my lord!
What, ho! My lord, my lord!

Oth. What noise is this? Not dead? Not yet quite dead?
I that am cruel am yet merciful,
I would not have thee linger in thy pain.
So, so.

Emil. [*Within.*] What ho! My lord, my lord!

Oth. Who's there?

Emil. [*Within.*] O, good my lord, I would speak a word with you!

Oth. Yes.—'Tis Emilia.—By and by.—She's dead.
'Tis like she comes to speak of Cassio's death;
The noise was high. Hah, no more moving?
Still as the grave. Shall she come in? Were't good?
I think she stirs again. No. What's best to do?
If she come in, she'll sure speak to my wife.
My wife, my wife! What wife? I have no wife.
O insupportable! O heavy hour!
Methinks it should be now a huge eclipse
Of sun and moon, and that th'affrighted globe
Did yawn at alteration. [3]

alteration: change

Emil. [*Within.*] I do beseech you
That I may speak with you. O, good my lord!

Oth. I had forgot thee. O, come in, Emilia.—
Soft, by and by, let me the curtains draw.—
Where art thou?

[*Unlocks the door.*]

Enter Emilia.

What's the matter with thee now?

Emil. O, my good lord, yonder's foul murthers done!

Oth. What? Now?

Emil. But now, my lord.

Oth. It is the very error of the moon,

She comes more nearer earth than she was wont,

And makes men mad.

Emil. Cassio, my lord, hath kill'd a young Venetian

Call'd Roderigo.

Oth. Roderigo kill'd?And Cassio kill'd?

Emil. No, Cassio is not kill'd.

Oth. Not Cassio kill'd? Then murther's out of tune,

And sweet revenge grows harsh.

Des. O, falsely, falsely murder'd!

Emil. [O Lord], what cry is that?

Oth. That? What?

Emil. Out, and alas, that was my lady's voice.

Help, help, ho, help! O lady, speak again!

Sweet Desdemona, O sweet mistress, speak!

Des. A guiltless death I die.

Emil. O, who hath done this deed?

Des. Nobody; I myself. Farewell!

Commend me to my kind lord. O, farewell!

[*Dies.*]

Oth. Why, how should she be murd'red?

Emil. Alas! Who knows?

Oth. You [heard] her say herself, it was not I.

Emil. She said so; I must needs report the truth.

Oth. She's like a liar gone to burning hell;

’Twas I that kill’d her.

Emil. O, the more angel she,

And you the blaker devil!

Oth. She turn’d to folly, and she was a whore.

Emil. Thou dost belie her, and thou art a devil.

Oth. She was false as water.

Emil. Thou art rash as fire to say

That she was false. O, she was heavenly true!

Oth. Cassio did top her; ask thy husband else.

O, I were damn’d beneath all depth in hell

But that I did proceed upon just grounds

To this extremity. Thy husband knew it all.

Emil. My husband?

Oth. Thy husband.

Emil. That she was false to wedlock?

Oth. Ay, with Cassio. [Nay,] had she been true,

If heaven would make me such another world

Of one entire and perfect chrysolite,

I’d not have sold her for it.

chrysolite: topaz

Emil. My husband?

Oth. Ay, ’twas he that told me first; An honest man he is, and hates the slime. That sticks on filthy deeds.

Emil. My husband?

Oth. What needs this iterance, woman? I say thy husband.

Emil. O mistress, villainy hath made mocks with love! My husband say she was false?

Oth. He, woman:

I say thy husband; dost understand the word?

My friend, thy husband, honest, honest Iago.

Emil. If he say so, may his pernicious soul

Rot half a grain a day! He lies to th' heart.
She was too fond of her most filthy bargain.
Oth. Hah?
Emil. Do thy worst!
This deed of thine is no more worthy heaven
Than thou wast worthy her.
Oth. Peace, you were best.
Emil. Thou hast not half that pow'r to do me harm
As I have to be hurt. O gull, O dolt,
As ignorant as dirt! Thou hast done a deed—
I care not for thy sword, I'll make thee known,
Though I lost twenty lives. Help, help, ho, help!
The Moor hath kill'd my mistress! Murther, murther!

thine: yours

gull: dupe

Enter Montano, Gratiano, and Iago [*with others*].

Mon. What is the matter? How now, general?
Emil. O, are you come, Iago? You have done well,
That men must lay their murthers on your neck.
Gra. What is the matter?
Emil. Disprove this villain, if thou be'st a man.
He says thou toldst him that his wife was false.
I know thou didst not; thou'rt not such a villain.
Speak, for my heart is full.
Iago. I told him what I thought, and told no more
Than what he found himself was apt and true.
Emil. But did you ever tell him she was false?
Iago. I did.
Emil. You told a lie, an odious, demned lie;
Upon my soul, a lie, a wicked lie.

apt: credible

She false with Cassio? Did you say with Cassio?
Iago. With Cassio, mistress. Go to, charm your tongue.
charm: silence
Emil. I will not charm my tongue; I am bound to speak.
My mistress here lies murthered in her bed—
All. O heavens forefend!
Emil. And your reports have set the murder on.
Oth. Nay, stare not, masters, it is true indeed.
Gra. 'Tis a strange truth.
Mon. O monstrous act!
Emil. Villainy, villainy, villainy!
I think upon't, I think—I smell't—O villainy!
I thought so then—I'll kill myself for grief—
O villainy! villainy!
Iago. What, are you mad? I charge you, get you home.
Emil. Good gentlemen, let me have leave to speak.
'Tis proper I obey him; but not now.
Perchance, Iago, I will ne'er go home.
Oth. O, O, O!
[*Othello falls on the bed.*]
Emil. Nay, lay thee down and roar;
For thou hast kill'd the sweetest innocent
That e'er did lift up eye.
Oth. [*Rising.*] O, she was foul!
I scarce did know you, uncle; there lies your niece,
Whose breath, indeed, these hands have newly stopp'd.
I know this act shows horrible and grim.
Gra. Poor Desdemona! I am glad thy father's dead.
Thy match was mortal to him, and pure grief
shore: cut
Shore his old thread in twain. Did he live now,
This sight would make him do a desperate turn, [4]
turn: act

Yea, curse his better angel from his side,
And fall to reprobance. reprobance: into damnation
Oth. 'Tis pitiful; but yet Iago knows
That she with Cassio hath the act of shame
A thousand times committed. Cassio confess'd it,
And she did gratify his amorous works
With that recognizance and pledge of love recognizance: token
Which I first gave her. I saw it in his hand;
It was a handkerchief, an antique token
My father gave my mother.
Emil. O [God]! O heavenly [God]!
Iago. ['Zounds], hold your peace.
Emil. 'Twill out, 'twill out! I peace?
No, I will speak as liberal as the north: north: north wind
Let heaven and men and devils, let them all,
All, all, cry shame against me, yet I'll speak.
Iago. Be wise, and get you home.
Emil. I will not. [*Iago offers to stab Emilia.*]
Gra. Fie,
Your sword upon a woman?
Emil. O thou dull Moor, that handkerchief thou speak'st of,
I found by fortune, and did give my husband;
For often, with a solemn earnestness
[More than indeed belong'd to such a trifle],
He begg'd of me to steal't.
Iago. Villainous whore!
Emil. She give it Cassio? No, alas, I found it,
And I did give't my husband.
Iago. Filth, thou liest!
Emil. By heaven, I do not, I do not, gentlemen.
O murd'rous coxcomb, what should such a fool coxcomb: fool

Do with so good a wife?

Oth. Are there no stones in heaven
But what serves for the thunder?—Precious villain!

[*The Moor runs at Iago; Montano disarms Othello; Iago kills his wife.*]

Gra. The woman falls; sure he hath kill'd his wife.
Emil. Ay, ay! O, lay me by my mistress' side

[*Exit Iago*]

Gra. He's gone, but his wife's kill'd.
Mon. 'Tis a notorious villain. Take you this weapon
Which I have [here] recover'd from the Moor.
Come guard the door without; let him not pass,
But kill him rather. I'll after that same villain,
For 'tis a damned slave.

Exit [*with all but Othello and Emilia*].

Oth. I am not valiant neither,
But every puny whipster gets my sword.
But why should honor outlive honesty?
Let it go all.
Emil. What did thy song bode, lady?
Hark, canst thou hear me? I will play the swan,
And die in music. [*Sings.*] "Willow, willow, willow."
Moor, she was chaste; she lov'd thee, cruel Moor;

honesty: inward integrity

hark: listen

So come my soul to bliss, as I speak true;
So speaking as I think, alas, I die. [5]

Oth. I have another weapon in this chamber;
It was a sword of Spain, the ice-brook's temper—
O, here it is. Uncle, I must come forth.

Gra. [*Within.*] If thou attempt it, it will cost thee dear:
Thou hast no weapon, and perforce must suffer. perforce: necessarily

Oth. Look in upon me then and speak with me,
Or naked as I am I will assault thee. naked: unarmed

[*Enter Gratiano.*]

Gra. What is the matter?

Oth. Behold, I have a weapon;
A better never did itself sustain
Upon a soldier's thigh. I have seen the day
That with this little arm, and this good sword,
I have made my way through more impediments
Than twenty times your stop. But [O vain boast!] stop: power to stop
Who can control his fate? ' Tis not so now.
Be not afraid though you do see me weapon'd;
Here is my journey's end, here is my butt butt: goal
And very sea-mark of my utmost sail. sea-mark: beacon
Do you go back dismay'd? 'Tis a lost fear;
Man but a rush against Othello's breast,
And he retires. Where should Othello go?
Now—[*To Desdemona*] how dost thou look now?
O ill-starr'd wench,
Pale as thy smock! When we shall meet at compt, compt: Judgement Day
This look of thine will hurl my soul from heaven,
And fiends will snatch at it. Cold, cold, my girl?

Even like thy chastity.
O cursed, cursed slave! Whip me, ye devils,
From the possession of this heavenly sight!
Blow me about in winds! Roast me in sulphur!
Wash me in steep-down gulfs of liquid fire!
O Desdemona! dead, Desdemona! dead!
O, O!

Enter Lodovico, Cassio [*in a chair*], *Montano, and Iago* [*guarded*], *with Officers.*

Lod. Where is this rash and most unfortunate man?
Oth. That's he that was Othello; here I am.
Lod. Where is that viper? Bring the villain forth.
Oth. I look down towards his feet; but that's a fable. fable: lie
If that thou be'st a devil, I cannot kill thee.

[*Wounds Iago.*]

Lod. Wrench his sword from him.
Iago. I bleed, sir, but not kill'd.
Oth. I am not sorry neither, I'ld have thee live;
For in my sense, 'tis happiness to die.
Lod. O thou Othello, that was once so good,
Fall'n in the practice of a [damned] slave,
What shall be said to thee?
Oth. Why, any thing:
An honourable murderer, if you will;
For nought I did in hate, but all in honour. nought: nothing
Lod. This wretch hath part confess'd his villainy.
Did you and he consent in Cassio's death?

Oth. Ay.
Cas. Dear general, I never gave you cause.
Oth. I do believe it, and I ask your pardon.
Will you, I pray, demand that demi-devil
Why he hath thus ensnar'd my soul and body?
Iago. Demand me nothing; what you know, you know:
From this time forth I never will speak word.
Lod. What? Not to pray?
Gra. Torments will ope your lips.
Oth. Well, thou dost best.
Lod. Sir, you shall understand what hath befall'n,
Which, as I think, you know not. Here is a letter
Found in the pocket of the slain Roderigo,
And here another. The one of them imports
The death of Cassio to be undertook
By Roderigo.
Oth. O villain!
Cas. Most heathenish and most gross!
Lod. Now here's another discontented paper,
Found in his pocket too; and this it seems
Roderigo meant t'have sent this damned villain;
But that, belike, Iago in the [nick] — belike: perhaps
Came in and satisfied him.
Oth. O thou pernicious caitiff! — — caitiff: wretch
How came you, Cassio, by that handkerchief
That was my wive's?
Cas. I found it in my chamber:
And he himself confess'd it but even now,
That there he dropp'd it for a special purpose
Which wrought to his desire. — wrought to: worked toward
Oth. O fool, fool, fool!

Cas. There is besides, in Roderigo's letter,
How he upbraids Iago, that he made him
Brave me upon the watch, whereon it came — brave: defy
That I was cast; and even but now he spake
[After long seeming dead] Iago hurt him,
Iago set him on.
Lod. [*To Othello*]
You must forsake this room and go with us.
Your power and your command is taken off,
And Cassio rules in Cyprus. For this slave,
If there be any cuning cruelty
That can torment him much, and hold him long,
It shall be his. You shall close prisoner rest,
Till that the nature of your fault be known
To the Venetian state. Come, bring away.
Oth. Soft you; a word or two before you go.
I have done the state some service, and they know't—
No more of that. I pray you, in your letters,
When you shall these unlucky deeds relate,
Speak of me as I am; nothing extenuate, — extenuate: make thin
Nor set down aught in malice. Then must you speak
Of one that lov'd not wisely but too well; [6]
Of one not easily jealious, but being wrought, — wrought: worked upon
Perplexed in the extreme; of one whose hand
(Like the base [Indian]) threw a pearl away
Richer than all his tribe; of one whose subdued eyes,
Albeit unused to the melting mood, — albeit: although
Drops tears as fast as the Arabian trees
Their medicinable gum. Set you down this; — medicinable: medicinal
And say besides, that in Aleppo once,

Where a malignant and a turban'd Turk
Beat a Venetian and traduc'd the state.
I took by th'throat the circumcised dog,
And smote him—thus.

Lod. O bloody period! — period: conclusion

Gra. All that is spoke is marr'd.

Oth. [*To Des.*]
I kiss'd thee ere I kill'd thee. No way but this,
Killing myself, to die upon a kiss.
[*Falls on the bed and*] *dies.*

Cas. This did I fear, but thought he had no weapon;
For he was great of heart.

Lod. [*To Iago.*] O Spartan dog,
More fell than anguish, hunger, or the sea! — fell: cruel
Look on the tragic loading of this bed;
This is thy work. The object poisons sight, — object: spectacle
Let it be hid. Gratiano, keep the house, — keep: remain in
And seize upon the fortunes of the Moor, — seize: possess
For they succeed on you. [*To Cassio*] To you, Lord Governor,
Remains the censure of this hellish villain, — censure: sentence
The time, the place, the torture, O, enforce it!
Myself will straight aboard, and to the state
This heavy act with heavy heart relate.

NOTES ON THE TEXT

[1] This is one of the most devastating soliloquys in *Othello* which discloses the hero's minds right before he smothers Desdemona. Here his jealousy and longing for revenge are gone. Instead, he sounds calm and cold, ready to execute justice for righteousness. He is torn between his love for her and his urge for justice and he sticks without much hesitation to the latter because of his conviction that Desdemona's beauty is deceptive and it makes her

corrupted. Most ironically, the soliloquy presents Othello as an out-and-out tragic hero because he is grossly wrong in his condemnation of Desdemona in the name of righteousness without proof.

[2] As originally a man admirably self-possessed and as the master of situations, Othello uses in this harrowing episode a language extremely controlled and elevated. To respond to Desdemona's cry for the Lord to have mercy on her, the man gives a solemn "amen" and addresses her as a "sweet soul." Her pleading for mercy only makes her husband convinced that she is a perjured woman and more determined to smother her even though she begs to say one last prayer.

[3] It was commonly believed in the Elizabethan time that eclipse, accompanied by an earthquake, would be a sort of evidence in the heavens that would acknowledge the death of a person on earth. When Emilia cries from outside for Othello, the man is still convinced that he is merciful to Desdemona and he tries to make sure that she is dead before he answers Emilia.

[4] We are told here by Gratiano that Desdemona's father has been dead maybe because of the grief he felt as his daughter married the Moor. Gratiano's words certainly remind us of Desdemona who had told Emilia before she died that she herself was to blame in order to protect her husband from being charged of murder. All this, and Emilia's challenge to her husband and her mocking of the Moor's power and anguish, clearly make Desdemona's innocence and her affection for her husband outstanding.

[5] The "Willow Song" is originally sung by Desdemona to Emilia when Othello wrongs her and orders her to go to bed unattended in Act IV, Scene iii. This old song tells a story of a man who betrays his love and a girl who sighs and weeps for her lover's betrayal. Aware that she is near death, Emilia recalls Desdemona's prophetic "Willow Song" and reaffirms the innocence of her mistress.

[6] As all the details of the plot are revealed, Othello falls into great remorse. He pleads for a complete report of the whole story so that everybody has a chance to know that he is not a barbarous foreigner but an honourable general who "loved not wisely but too well." Eventually he stabs himself for throwing away blindly the most precious pearl in the world, a tragic flaw made by a righteous man, which reminds us of the Aristotalian theory of tragedy.

QUESTIONS FOR DISCUSSION

1. We are certainly moved by Emilia who recalls Desdemona's "Willow Song" before she dies. What elements in the "Willow Song" do you think parallel Emilia's as well as Desdemona's own situation?

2. Let us consider the way the Moor behaves during the last scene of Act V. How does Othello proves that he loves and regrets for what he is about to do?

3. Of all the ways that Othello considers murdering Desdemona, why does he finally decide to murder her in her bed?

4. Aristotle argues that a typical tragedy should have a tragic hero who runs into trouble because of a tragic flaw, which causes in its audience pity and fear. How do you apply his theory to your interpretation of *Othello*?

5. An eighteenth-century critic Thomas Rymer condemned *Othello* as a "bloody farce" and observed that one of the play's morals was a warning to all good wives that they should look well to their linen. Try to evaluate his idea about *Othello*. Remember to support yourself.

SUGGESTED REFERENCES

Adamson, Jane. "'Pluming up the Will': Iago's Place in the Play." *Iago.* Ed. Harold Bloom. New York: Chelsea House, 1992. 165-89.

Bevington, David. *Shakespeare.* Arlington Heights, IL: A. H. M. Pulications, 1978.

Greenblatt, Stephen. *Will in the World: How Shakespeare Became Shakespeare.* Cambridge: Oxford UP, 2004.

Shapiro, Barbra A. "Psychoanalysis and the Problem of Evil: Debating Othello in the Classroom." *American Image* 60.4 (2003): 481-99.

Wilson, Harold S. "Othello." *On the Design of Shakespearean Tragedy.* Toronto: U of Toronto P, 1957.

Unit 4 John Milton

(1608—1674)

A GUIDE TO LITERARY TERMINOLOGY

"Epic": *The term "epic" generally refers to a long poem, in an elevated tone and diction, that narrates the extraordinary experiences or achievements of one or more personages who are of national, religious or legendary significance to one particular tradition. Homer (900—750 BCE), the ancient Greek blind poet, is often taken as the origin and source of the Western European epics.*

People tend to put Western epics into two different groups, namely traditional epics and literary ones. The first group of epics, such as Homer's ***Iliad*** *and* ***Odyssey****, usually bearing the features of an oral formulaic tradition, deals with stories originating in ancient heroic times, while the second group of epics, composed by poets with self-conscious and sophisticated literary purposes, could be well represented by such works as Virgil's* ***Aeneid*** *and Milton's* ***Paradise Lost****.*

Epics of the traditional nature seem to have been prevalent too during the Middle Ages. Rather than in Latin, the epic narratives of this particular period addressing heroic experiences were delivered in such vernaculars as French, German and English. Among them are the ***Chanson de Roland****,* ***Nibelungenlied*** *and* ***Beowulf****. The first work of the three depicts a battle in the Pyrenees between Charlemagne's army and the Saracens, while the second is an account of a story derived from the war of the thirteenth century between the Burgundians and the Huns. The Anglo-Saxon poem* ***Beowulf*** *is based on the story of a number of historical figures of the sixth century including Beowulf who is said to have struggled against two monsters and one fire dragon in order to deliver the Danes and the Geats from their trouble.*

The fantasy sequel ***The Lord of the Rings*** *written in prose by J. R R. Tolkien, the famous medievalist of Oxford, represents a successful twentieth century attempt at the literary epic, and his trilogy, based on a mythology of his own and the tradition of Norse Sagas and Anglo-Saxon poetry, deals with interesting adventures in the realm of Middle Earth.*

NOTES ON THE AUTHOR

The life of John Milton is known to us in far more fullness of detail than that of any other major English poet before the eighteenth century. As he inherited the Renaissance thirst for enduring fame, he was intensely concerned to have his own image stand in the public eye as he himself conceived it.

He was born in London in 1608 to a well-to-do scrivener and composer of music. He was educated in Cambridge and began to write poems as a college student in Latin, Italian as well as English. Although his parents were both highly religious, he stayed away from civil and religious affairs in his early days and devoted himself to the study of classical literature and to the writing of poetry.

His rather short marriage with Mary Powell, the daughter of a Royalist, sympathizing Charles I, did not stop him from writing a number of pamphlets expressing his stands for individual liberty and liberty of publishing without pre-publication censorship, the most renowned tract along the line was his 1644 *Areopagitica*, a defense of the liberty of press.

His political stands and writings not only won him praises and attacks, the hard work also led him to darkness. By 1652 his eyes became almost completely blind.

Milton's fame, however, lies to us on his authorship of a number of literary works. The epic *Pradise Lost* is said to have been completed in 1663 and his last poems, *Paradise Regained* and *Samson Agonistes* had been published together in 1671 before he died quietly on November 8, 1674. By 1700 his literary works were already considered as part of the canon of English literature.

SYNOPSIS OF THE WORK

Paradise Lost, consisting of twelve books of about ten thousand lines, has been known as Milton's masterpiece and the greatest epic ever written in the English language. Based upon the Old Testament, the epic is built around two themes, namely the fall of angels and the fall of man.

The excerpts below are taken from Book IX, which provides us with the poet's interpretation of the central incident in the fall of Adam and Eve. Satan enters into a serpent and, in this form, finds Eve alone. He subtly flatters her at first, and then convinces her that he has eaten the fruit of the Tree of Knowledge and gained wisdom and speech. Gradually she is persuaded that he is telling the truth and, in due course, she eats the fruit from the tree. Eve later relates to her husband what has happened and, perceiving that she is lost, Adam decides to perish with her by eating the fruit too since he loves her too much even though he is superior to her in terms of intelligence.

The dialogue between Satan the Tempter and Eve the Tempted shows the craftiness of the former and the rather unjustified confidence of the latter in what she does and the intoxication of her mind which leads to fancy herself the equal of God. Although Eve falls through vanity and curiosity for new experience, she is not labeled in simple terms by the poet as the symbol of evil in the soul.

SELECTED READINGS

Paradise Lost

(Excerpts from Book IX)

. . .

He bolder [1] now, uncalled before her stood;
But as in gaze admiring; Oft he bowed — oft: often
His turret crest, and sleek enameled neck, — sleek: elegant
Fawning, and licked the ground whereon she trod. — fawning: flattering
His gentle dumb expression turned at length
The eye of Eve to mark his play; he glad — play: move
Of her attention gained, with serpent tongue
Organic, or impulse of vocal air,
His fraudulent temptation thus began.
Wonder not, sovereign mistress, if perhaps
Thou [2] canst, who art sole wonder, much less arm — art: are
Thy looks, the heaven of mildness, with disdain,
Displeased that I approach thee thus, and gaze
Insatiate, I thus single, nor have feared — insatiate: insatiable
Thy awful brow, more awful thus retired. [3] — brow: forehead
Fairest resemblance of thy Maker fair,

Thee all things living gaze on, all things thine
By gift, and thy celestial beauty adore
With ravishment beheld, there best beheld — ravishment: pleasure
Where universally admired; but here
In this enclosure wild, these beasts among,
Beholders rude, and shallow to discern — rude: roughly made
Half what in thee is fair, one man except,
Who sees thee? (and what is one?) who shouldst be seen
A Goddess among Gods, adored and served
By Angels numberless, thy daily train. [4] — train: a number of people
So glozed the tempter, and his proem tuned; — glozed: flattered
Into the heart of Eve his words made way,
Though at the voice much marveling; at length
Not unamazed she thus in answer spoke.
What may this mean? Language of man pronounced
By tongue of brute, and human sense expressed? — brute: animal-like
The first at least of these I thought denied
To beasts, whom God on the creation-day
Created mute to all articulate sound;
The latter I demur, for in these looks — demur: doubt
Much reason, and in these actions oft appears.
Thee, serpent, suttlest beast of all the field — field: land
I knew, but not with human voice endured; — endured: existed
Redouble then this miracle, and say, — redouble: double
How comest thou speakable of mute, and how — speakable: able to speak
To me so friendly grown above the rest
Of brutal kind, that daily are in sight? — daily: everyday
Say, for such wonder claims attention due. [5] — due: expected

To whom the guileful tempter thus replied.
Empress of this fair world, resplendent Eve, — resplendent: brilliant
Easy to me it is to tell thee all
What thou commandst, and right thou shouldst be obeyed:
I was at first as other beasts that graze — graze: eat grass
The trodden herb, of abject thoughts and low,
As was my food, nor aught but food discerned — aught: anything
Or sex, and apprehended nothing high:
Till on a day roving the field, I chanced
A goodly tree far distant to behold — goodly: massive
Laden with fruit of fairest colours mixed,
Ruddy and gold: I nearer drew to gaze; — ruddy: rosy
When from the boughs a savoury odour blowen,
Grateful to appetite, more pleased my sense — grateful: pleasing
Than smell of sweetest fennel, or the teats — fennel: fennel seeds
Of ewe or goat dropping with milk at Eve,
Unsucked of lamb or kid, that tend their play. — tend: care for
To satisfy the sharp desire I had
Of tasting those fair apples, I resolved
Not to defer; hunger and thirst at once,
Powerful persuaders, quickened at the scent
Of that alluring fruit, urged me so keen.
About the mossy trunk I wound me soon,
For high from ground the branches would require
Thy utmost reach or Adams: round the tree — Adams: Adam's
All other beasts that saw, with like desire — like: similar
Longing and envying stood, but could not reach.
Amid the tree now got, where plenty hung
Tempting so nigh, to pluck and eat my fill — nigh: near
I spared not, for such pleasure till that hour

At feed or fountain never had I found. feed: food
Sated at length, ere long I might perceive ere: before
Strange alteration in me, to degree
Of reason in my inward powers, and speech
Wanted not long, though to this shape retained. wanted: lack
Thenceforth to speculations high or deep thenceforth: from then on
I turned my thoughts, and with capacious mind capacious: capable
Considered all things visible in Heaven,
Or Earth, or Middle, [6] all things fair and good;
But all that fair and good in thy divine
Semblance, and in thy beauties heavenly ray semblance: appearance
United I beheld; no fair to thine
Equivalent or second, which compelled
Me thus, though importune perhaps, to come
And gaze, and worship thee of right declared
Sovereign of creatures, universal dame.
. . .
To whom thus Eve [replied] yet sinless. Of the fruit
Of each tree in the garden we may eat,
But of the fruit of this fair tree amidst
The garden, God hath said, ye shall not eat
Thereof, nor shall ye touch it, lest ye die. [7]
She scarce had said, though brief, when now more bold scarce: scarcely
The tempter, but with shew of zeal and love shew: show
To man, and indignation at his wrong,
New part puts on, and as to passion moved,
Fluctuates disturbed, yet comely, and in act comely: pleasant
Raised, as of some great matter to begin.
As when of old some orator renowned of old: of old days

In Athens or free Rome, where eloquence
Flourished, since mute, to some great cause addressed,
Stood in himself collected, while each part,
Motion, each act won audience ere the tongue,
Somtimes in highth began, as no delay
Of preface brooking through his zeal of right. — of right: appropriately
So standing, moving, or to highth upgrown
The tempter all impassioned thus began. — impassioned: emotional
    O sacred, wise, and wisdom-giving plant,
Mother of science, now I feel thy power
Within me clear, not only to discern
Things in their causes, but to trace the ways
Of highest agents, deemed however wise. — agents: causes
Queen of this universe, do not believe
Those rigid threats of death; ye shall not die:
How should ye? By the fruit? It gives you life
To knowledge: By the threatener? Look on me,
Me who have touched and tasted, yet both live,
And life more perfect have attaind than fate
Meant me, by venturing higher than my lot. — my lot: my fellows
Shall that be shut to man, which to the beast
Is open? Or will God incense his ire — ire: anger
For such a petty trespass, and not praise
Rather your dauntless virtue, whom the pain
Of death denounced, whatever thing death be,
Deterred not from achieving what might lead
To happier life, knowledge of good and evil;
Of good, how just? Of evil, if what is evil
Be real, why not known, since easier shunned? — shunned: avoided
God therefore cannot hurt ye, and be just;
Not just, not God; not feared then, nor obeyed:

Your fear itself of death removes the fear.
Why then was this forbidden? Why but to awe,
Why but to keep ye low and ignorant,
His worshippers; he knows that in the day
Ye eat thereof, your eyes that seem so clear,
Yet are but dim, shall perfectly be then
Opened and cleared, and ye shall be as Gods,
Knowing both good and evil as they know.
That ye should be as Gods, since I as man,
Internal man, is but proportion meet,
I of brute human, ye of human Gods.
So ye shall die perhaps, by putting off
Human, to put on Gods, death to be wished,
Though threatened, which no worse than this can bring.
And what are Gods that man may not become
As they, participating God-like food?
The Gods are first, and that advantage use
On our belief, that all from them proceeds;
I question it, for this fair earth I see,
Warmed by the sun, producing every kind,
Them nothing: If they all things, who enclosed
Knowledge of good and evil in this tree,
That whoso eats thereof, forthwith attains — whoso: whoever
Wisdom without their leave? and therein lies — leave: permission
The offence, that man should thus attain to know?
What can your knowledge hurt him, or this tree
Impart against his will if all be his? — impart: give
Or is it envy, and can envy dwell
In heavenly breasts? These, these and many more
Causes import your need of this fair fruit. — import: show importance of

Goddess humane, reach then, and freely taste.
    He ended, and his words replete with guile   replete: filled with
Into her heart too easy entrance won:
Fixed on the fruit she gazed, which to behold
Might tempt alone, and in her ears the sound
Yet rung of his persuasive words, impregnated   impregnated: filled up
With reason to her seeming, and with truth;   seeming: appearance
Meanwhile the hour of noon drew on, and woke
An eager appetite, raised by the smell
So savoury of that fruit, which with desire,
Inclinable now grown to touch or taste,
Solicited her longing eye; yet first
Pausing a while, thus to herself she mused.   mused: absorbed in thought
. . .
    Her rash hand in evil hour
Forth reaching to the fruit, she plucked, she ate:
Earth felt the wound, and nature from her seat
Sighing through all her works gave signs of woe,
That all was lost. [8] Back to the thicket slunk   slunk: moved quiety
The guilty serpent, and well might, for Eve
Intent now wholly on her taste, naught else   naught: nothing
Regarded, such delight till then, as seemed,
In fruit she never tasted, whether true
Or fancied so, through expectation high
Of knowledge, nor was God-head from her thought.   God-head: God
Greedily she ingorged without restraint,   ingorged: gorged
And knew not eating death: Satiate at length,   satiate: satisfied
And hightened as with wine, jocund and boon,   jocund: cheerful
Thus to herself she pleasingly began.
. . .

NOTES ON THE TEXT

[1] The seventeenth-century English shows words spelled differently from what we are familiar with. For instance, "bolder" in the first line of the excerpt is spelled in the original work as "boulder." To make the reading of Milton's poetry easier, the following work has been done: 1. Words have been respelled when they in their original form may cause difficulty in reading. 2. The abbreviations have been changed to the regular forms, such as "uncall'd." 3. Capitalized words such as "Crest" and "Serpent" have been regularized according to Modern English spelling convention except for words like "God" and proper names such as "Adam" and "Eve." 4. Some of the archaic spellings have been modernized. For instance, "thir" has been replaced by either "this" or "these" according to the context.

[2] The English second person pronouns in the late medieval period still showed their distinction in number, namely "thou, thy, thee" as singular forms and "ye, your, you" as plural ones, and in the thirteenth century the singular forms were very often used to refer to familiars and to address children or persons of inferior rank, while the plural forms came to be used to refer to a single person and a distinctive mark of respect in addressing a superior or a person of importance. Although the distinction was gone in Milton's time, the poet was still using it consciously in his poetry. You will notice in the excerpt that when in the dialog the second person pronouns "thou, thy, thee" are used to show the tone of friendliness and familiarity and "ye, your, you" are used to show that of solemnity and respect.

[3] We certainly notice the poet's rather mocking reference to the tradition of medieval courtly love which often shows two aristocratic lovers with the lady as the superior and the man as a pure worshiper. The female always looks down with "disdain" upon her admirer, which would make the man look at her "insatiate" and fall sick because of the impossible love. To flatter Eve in his attempt to seduce her, Satan behaves from the very beginning as a man of this kind.

[4] Satan enters the body of a sleeping serpent from its mouth and, in the shape of it, he begins his effort to destroy man. His major tactic, after surprising Eve as a talking snake, is to appeal to her vanity by flattering her. You have certainly noticed the meaning behind such expressions as "fairest resemblance" and "celestial beauty" who is "universally admired."

[5] Eve's attention is drawn by the cunning flattery of Satan and, in due course, is very much surprised by the ability of the serpent who can conduct the human language and express human ideas. This is the basis for the eventual success of Satan's evil plot.

[6] "Middle" here refers to Middle Earth, the place where human beings dwell as opposed to heaven and hell, the former of which are said in the European Christian tradition to be the world of God, the angels and the souls of those who are granted salvation, and the latter the miserable abode of devils and of the condemned souls.

[7] We are not surprised to have the second person pronoun "ye" here in Eve's speech even

though we know that the pronoun refers to Adam. Since this is the commandment given by God to Adam, "ye" represents appropriately God's tone of celestial dignity and seriousness.

[8] We have been reading Milton's version of the core event of the fall of man which, according to the poet, is at least in his *Paradise Lost* a tragedy in its classical sense, rather than just an episode of a typical epic of the European tradition. As Milton announced, he intended to change the "notes" of this intensely dramatic story to tragic. Book IX of *Paradise Lost* fills all the classical requirements of tragedy as was carefully defined by Aristotle, according to one commentator.

QUESTIONS FOR DISCUSSION

1. Although *Paradise Lost* is written in the form of an epic, it does not stick to the subject matter of the genre. Instead of glorifying war, some scholars argue, it fills all the classical requirements of tragedy. How do you comment on this?

2. What do you think are the psychological causes of the fall of man? What makes Eve liable to be tempted and to fall?

3. From the point of view of a modern woman, do you think that the treatment of woman in Milton's *Paradise Lost* is not at all justified? If this is what you want to argue for, how do you then support yourself?

4. Satan is called "the father of lies" in the Bible. Does the story of the temptation of Eve provide us with a good example of this nature?

5. An Italian epic writer once stated that the language of the epic ought to be elevated above the speech of ordinary men. Do you feel that Milton's poetry meets this language requirement?

SUGGESTED REFERENCES

Gardner, Helen. *A Reading of Paradise Lost.* New York: Oxford UP, 1965.

Geisst, C. R. *The Political Thought of John Milton.* London: MacMillan, 1984.

Lewalski, Barbara Kiefer. "The Genres of *Paradise Lost.*" *The Cambridge Companion to Milton. 2nd ed.* Ed. Dennis Danielson. Cambridge: Cambridge UP, 1999. 113-29.

Martz, Louis L., ed. *Milton: A Collection of Critical Essays.* Englewood Cliffs, NJ: Prentice-Hall, 1966.

Webber, Joan Malory. "The Politics of Poetry: Feminism and *Paradise Lost.*" *Milton Studies* 14 (1980): 3-24.

Unit 5 Jonathan Swift

(1667 – 1745)

A GUIDE TO LITERARY TERMINOLOGY

"Satire": *A satire is often defined by standard reference books as a literary form, both in verse and in prose, in which human vices, follies and shortcomings are held up to censure by means of ridicule, derision or wit. Literary satires, mild or bitter, are often meant to bring about improvement on human living conditions. Although Roman rhetoricians claimed that they were inventors of the genre, they seem to have inherited the tone and form of satire, at least partially, from the ancient Greek comedians.*

The introduction of satire to English literature is a less complicated story because Chaucer is generally considered as the first poet who used satire extensively in his writings. Although the Elizabethan times saw satirists like Thomas Lodge and John Marston who enjoyed popularity with their poems and plays with some directed against their literary rivals, the great age of English satire began with John Dryden, who became the poet laureate in 1668 and brought the English satire with his learning and wit to an unprecedented height. His use of heroic couplet followed by Alexander Pope is worth mentioning for they made it an efficient tool of expression for this particular genre. Ever since the novel became an important vehicle for social satire in the hand of such nineteenth-century authors as Charles Dickens and William Makepeace Thackeray, satire has been vigorously explored in various forms and it has been one of the most popular expression of thoughts right up to the present time.

A typical satire has a thesis and an antithesis, the former being the satirist's declared position and the latter often his implicit positive values, which should be made especially clear in the work so that those the satirist favors shall not be offended.

NOTES ON THE AUTHOR

Born in 1667, Jonathan Swift was the posthumous son of an English father who was steward of the King's Inns in Dublin. Supported financially by his uncles, he attended Trinity College in Dublin but, as he detested the curriculum and studied only what appealed to him, took his degree "by special grace." He was hired for a while by Sir William Temple, a distant relative and a renowned statesman in London, and went back to Dublin for a post in the Anglican Church.

He returned to Temple again a year later and remained in his service until 1699 when Temple died. He started his writing, prolific and vehement, during his stay with Temple.

His years after Temple's death were tough though productive. As a man of action, he was deeply involved in the politics of Ireland and produced a substantial body of prose, known as the Irish tracts. Addressing England as well as Ireland, his works showed his grave concern about the economic and political issues between the two kingdoms. As for his effort in the field of literary writing, even though he was said to be hopeless in poetry by his cousin, he was obviously considered one of the literary geniuses of the eighteenth century. Swift, a master of satire, was known for his famous literary works such as *A Tale of the Tub* (1704), *A Modest Proposal* (1729) and, of course, *Gulliver's Travels*, which was published in 1726. His deadly control of understatements and satire made his works one of the features of his times.

During his old age, he was said to be a man of an unsound mind. His infirmities and deafness cut him off from his social duties when he was 72 years of age and died in 1745 in Dublin. He donated all his property for the founding of an asylum for lunatics and incurables.

NOTES ON THE WORK

The year 1729 witnessed the first edition of *A Modest Proposal* which is Swift's most biting satire and is possibly the best work of this kind in the history of English literature. With an assumed persona of an economic projector who was versed in providing remedies, the work addresses in its own original manner the social and political ills of Ireland resulting from the English oppression as well as from natural calamities that had devastated the kingdom for three years in a row.

Shortly before the work was published, Swift expressed his grave concerns about the situation in Ireland in a letter to his friend Alexander Pope as follows: "As to this country, there have been three terrible years death of corn, and every place strowed with beggars, but dearths are common in better climates, and our evils here lie much deeper. Imagine a nation the two-thirds of whose revenues are spent out of it, and who are not permitted to trade with the other third, and where the pride of the women will not suffer them to wear their own manufactures even where they excel what come from abroad: This is the true state of Ireland in a very few words." Thus, by proposing in the mouth of the projector eating young children in order to ease the economic plight of so many in Ireland, Swift made his plea once again to the Irish that the only way to save the kingdom is to consume domestically the domestic products of Ireland.

SELECTED READINGS

A Modest Proposal[1]

FOR PREVENTING THE CHILDREN OF POOR PEOPLE IN IRELAND
AND FROM BEING A BURTHEN TO THEIR PARENTS OR COUNTRY,
AND FOR MAKING THEM BENEFICIAL TO THE PUBLIC

It is a melancholy object to those who walk through this great town[2], or travel in the country, when they see the *streets*, the *roads*, and *cabin-doors*, crowded with beggars of the female sex, followed by three, four, or six children, all in rags, and importuning[3] every passenger for an alms[4]. These mothers instead of being able to work for their honest livelihood, are forced to employ all their time in strolling, to beg sustenance for their *helpless infants*, who, as they grow up, either turn *thieves* for want of work, or leave their *dear native country to fight for the pretender in Spain*, [1] or sell themselves to the Barbados. [2]

I think it is agreed by all parties that this prodigious number of children, in the arms, or on the backs, or at the *heels of their mothers*, and frequently of their fathers, is *in the present deplorable state of the kingdom* a very great additional grievance; and therefore whoever

---

1 The excerpt is taken from the 1969 edition of the *Eighteenth-Century English Literature* edited by Geoffrey Tillotson. Some editorial work has been done such as the dropping of the historical forms of capitalization and the modernization of old spelling of some words. Italics are kept in their original state as they could hardly cause any difficulty in reading.

2 this great town: Dublin.

3 importuning: begging.

4 alms: money or food given to the poor.

could find out a fair, cheap and easy method of making these children sound, useful members of the common-wealth[5] would deserve so well of the public as to have his statue set up for a preserver of the nation.

But my intention is very far from being confined to provide only for the children of *professed beggars*; it is of a much greater extent, and shall take in the whole number of infants at a certain age who are born of parents in effect as little able to support them as those who demand our charity[6] in the streets.

As to my own part, having turned my thoughts, for many years, upon this important subject, and maturely weighed the several *schemes of other projectors*[7], I have always found them grossly mistaken in their computation. It is true a child, just dropped from it's dam[8], may be supported by her milk for a solar year [3] with little other nourishment, at most not above the value of two shillings, which the mother may certainly get, or the value in *scraps*, by her lawful occupation of begging, and it is exactly at one year old that I propose to provide for them, in such a manner, as, instead of being a charge upon their parents, or the *parish*[9], or *wanting food and raiment*[10] for the rest of their lives, they shall, on the contrary, contribute to the feeding and partly to the clothing of many thousands.

There is likewise another great advantage in my scheme: that it will prevent those *voluntary abortions*, and that horrid practice of *women murdering their bastard children*, alas! too frequent among us, sacrificing the *poor innocent babes*, I doubt[11], more to avoid the expense than the shame, which would move tears and pity in the most savage and inhuman breast.

---

5 the common-wealth: association consisting of the UK together with states that were part of the British Empire.
6 charity: help given to those in need.
7 projectors: speculators or cheats.
8 dam: female parent.
9 parish: a district with its own church and clergy.
10 raiment: clothes.
11 doubt: suspect.

The number of souls in *Ireland* being usually reckoned one million and a half, of these I calculate there may be about two hundred thousand couple whose wives are breeders, from which number I subtract thirty thousand couple who are able to maintain their own children, although I apprehend there cannot be so many under *the present distresses of the kingdom*, but this being granted, there will remain a hundred and seventy thousand breeders. I again subtract fifty thousand for those women who miscarry, or whose children die by accident or disease within the year. There only remain a hundred and twenty thousand children of poor parents annually born: the question therefore is, how this number shall be reared and provided for, which, as I have already said, under the present situation of affairs, is utterly impossible by all the methods hitherto[12] proposed, for we can *neither employ them in handicraft or agriculture*; we neither build houses (I mean in the country) nor cultivated land: [4] they can very seldom pick up a livelihood *by stealing* until they arrive at six years old, except where they are of towardly parts[13], although, I confess they learn the rudiments much earlier, during which time they can however be properly looked upon only as *probationers*[14], as I have been informed by a principal gentleman in the county of *Cavan*, who protested to me, that he never knew above one or two instances under the age of six, even in a part of the kingdom *so renowned for the quickest proficiency in that art*.

I am assured by our merchants, that a boy or a girl, before twelve years old, is no saleable commodity, and even when they come to this age, they will not yield above three pounds, or three pounds and half a crown[15] at most on the exchange, which cannot turn to account[16] either

12 hitherto: until this point in time.
13 towardly parts: ready abilities.
14 probationers: people serving in a period of training.
15 crown: a former British coin worth five shillings (25 pence).
16 turn to account: be of profit.

to the parents or kingdom, the charge of nutriment and rags having been at least four times that value.

I shall now therefore humbly propose my own thoughts, which I hope will not be liable to the least objection.

I have been assured by a very knowing American [5] of my acquaintance in London that a young healthy child well nursed is at a year old a most delicious, nourishing, and wholesome[17] food, whether *stewed, roasted, baked,* or *boiled*, and I make no doubt that it will equally serve in a *fricasie*[18], or *a ragout*[19].

I do therefore humbly offer it to public consideration that of the hundred and twenty thousand children already computed, twenty thousand may be reserved for breed, whereof only one fourth part to be males, which is more than we allow to *sheep, black-cattle*[20], or *swine*, and my reason is that these children are seldom the fruits of marriage, a circumstance not much regarded by our savages; therefore one male will be sufficient to serve *four females*. That the remaining hundred thousand may at a year old be offered in sale to the persons of quality and fortune, through the kingdom, always advising the mother to let them suck plentifully in the last month, so as to render them plump and fat for a good table. A child will make two dishes at an entertainment for friends, and when the family dines alone, the fore or hind quarter will make a reasonable dish, and seasoned with a little pepper or salt will be very good boiled on the fourth day, especially in *winter*.

I have reckoned upon a medium, that a child just born will weigh twelve pounds, and in a solar year if tolerably nursed increaseth to twenty-eight pounds.

I grant this food will be somewhat dear, [6] and therefore very

---

17 wholesome: healthy.

18 fricasie: meat cut into pieces and stewed in gravy.

19 ragout: a highly seasoned meat stew.

20 black-cattle: cows raised for beef.

proper for landlords, who, as they have already devoured most of the parents, seem to have the best title to the children.

Infants' flesh will be in season[21] throughout the year, but more plentiful in *March*, and a little before and after, for we are told by a grave author, [7] an eminent *French* physician, that *fish being a prolific diet*, there are more children born in *Roman Catholic countries* [8] about nine months after Lent[22] than at any other season; therefore reckoning a year after *Lent*, the markets will be more glutted than usual, because the number of *Popish infants* is at least three to one in this kingdom, and therefore it will have one other collateral advantage by lessening the number of *Papists*[23] among us.

I have already computed the charge of nursing a beggar's child (in which list I reckon all *cottagers*[24], *labourers,* and four fifths of the *farmers*) to be about two shillings *per annum*, rags included, and I believe no gentleman would repine to give ten shillings for the *carcass of a good fat child*, which, as I have said, will make four dishes of excellent nutritive meat, when he hath only some particular friend or his own family to dine with him. Thus the squire[25] will learn to be a good landlord, and grow popular among his tenants, the mother will have eight shillings net profit, and be fit for work till she produces another child.

Those who are more thrifty (*as I must confess the times require*) may flay the carcass; the skin of which, artificially[26] dressed, will make admirable *gloves* for *ladies*, and *summer boots for fine gentlemen.*

As to our city of *Dublin*, shambles[27] may be appointed for this purpose in the most convenient parts of it, and butchers we may be

---

21 in season: plentiful and ready to eat.
22 Lent: the period immediately before Easter during which feasting takes place.
23 Papists: Roman Catholics.
24 cottagers: tenant farmers, cottiers in Ireland.
25 squire: a country gentleman.
26 artificially: skillfully.
27 shamble: meat market, slaughterhouse.

assured will not be wanting, although I rather recommend buying the children alive, and dressing them hot from the knife, as we do *roasting pigs*.

A very worthy person, *a true lover of his country*, and whose virtues I highly esteem, was lately pleased, in discoursing on this matter, to offer a refinement upon my scheme. He said that many gentlemen of this kingdom having of late[28] destroyed their deer, he conceived that the want[29] of venison might be well supplied by the bodies of young lads and maidens, not exceeding fourteen years of age, nor under twelve, so great a number of both sexes in every country being now ready to starve for want of work and service: And these to be disposed of by their parents if alive, or otherwise by their nearest relations. But with due deference to so excellent a friend, and so deserving a patriot, I cannot be altogether in his sentiments; for as to the males, my *American* acquaintance assured me, from frequent experience, that their flesh was generally tough and lean, like that of our school-boys, by continual exercise, and their taste disagreeable, and to fatten them would not answer the charge. Then as to the females, it would, I think with humble submission[30], *be a loss to the public*, because they soon would become breeders themselves: and besides, it is not improbable that some scrupulous people might be apt to censure such a practice (although indeed very unjustly) as a little bordering upon cruelty; which, I confess, hath always been with me the strongest objection against any project, however so well intended.

But in order to justify my friend, he confessed, that this expedient was put into his head by the famous *Psalmanazar*, [9] a native of the island *Formosa*[31], who came from thence to *London*, above twen-

---

28 having of late: recently.
29 want: shortage.
30 with humble submission: respectfully.
31 Formosa: an old name of our Taiwan island used by the westerners.

ty years ago, and in conversation told my friend that in his country when any young person happened to be put to death, the executioner sold the carcass to *persons of quality*, as a prime dainty[32], and that, in his time, the body of a plump girl of fifteen who was crucified for an attempt to poison the emperor, was sold to his Imperial Majesty's *Prime Minister of State*, and other great mandarins[33] of the court, *in joints from the gibbet*, at four hundred crowns. Neither indeed can I deny that if the same use were made of several plump young girls in this town, who, without one single groat[34] to their fortunes, cannot stir abroad without a chair[35], and appear at the *play-house* and *assemblies* in foreign fineries, which they never will pay for; the kingdom would not be the worse.

Some persons of a desponding spirit are in great concern about that vast number of poor people, who are aged, diseased, or maimed, and I have been desired to employ my thoughts what course may be taken to ease the nation of so grievous an encumbrance. But I am not in the least pain upon that matter, because it is very well known, that they are every day *dying* and *rotting*, by *cold,* and *famine*, and *filth*, and *vermin*, as fast as can be reasonably expected. And as to the younger labourers, they are now in almost as hopeful a condition. They cannot get work, and consequently pine away for want of nourishment, to a degree, that if at any time they are accidentally hired to common labour, they have not strength to perform it; and thus the country and themselves are in a fair way[36] of being soon delivered from the evils to come.

I have too long digressed, and therefore shall return to my subject. I think the advantages by the proposal which I have made are

---

32 dainty: an appetizer.
33 mandarins: high-ranking courtiers.
34 groat: an old English silver coin worth four pence.
35 chair: sedan chair.
36 be in a fair way: have a good chance.

obvious and many, as well as of the highest importance.

For first, as I have already observed, it would greatly lessen *the number of Papists*, with whom we are yearly over-run, being the principal breeders of the nation, as well as our most dangerous enemies, and who stay at home on purpose with a design *to deliver the kingdom to the Pretender*[37], hoping to take their advantage by the absence of *so many good Protestants*[38], who have chosen rather to leave their country [10] than stay at home and pay tithes[39], against their conscience, to an *Episcopal curate*[40].

Secondly, the poorer tenants will have something valuable of their own, which by law may be made liable to distress[41], and help to pay their landlord's rent, their corn and cattle being already seized, and *money a thing unknown.*

Thirdly, whereas the maintenance of a hundred thousand children, from two years old, and upwards, cannot be computed at less than ten shillings apiece *per annum*, the nation's stock will be thereby increased fifty thousand pounds *per annum*[42], besides the profit of a new dish, introduced to the tables of all *gentlemen of fortune* in the kingdom, who have any refinement in taste, and the money will circulate among our selves, the goods being entirely of our own growth and manufacture.

Fourthly, the constant breeders, besides the gain of eight shillings *sterling*[43] *per annum*, by the sale of their children, will be rid of the charge of maintaining them after the first year.

Fifthly, this food would likewise bring great *custom to taverns*, where the vintners will certainly be so prudent as to procure the best

---

37 Pretender: a person who claims a right to the throne though other people disagree with him.

38 Protestants: nonconformists, who in Swift's view were bad Protestants.

39 tithe: a tenth of one's income.

40 Episcopal curate: an assistant to a bishop.

41 distress: seizure for debt.

42 per annum: per year.

43 sterling: money system of Britain based on the pound.

recipes for dressing it to perfection, and consequently have their houses frequented by all the *fine gentlemen* who justly value themselves upon their knowledge in good eating, and a skillful cook, who understands how to oblige his guests, will contrive to make it as expensive as they please.

Sixthly, this would be a great inducement to marriage, which all wise nations have either encouraged by rewards, or enforced by laws and penalties. It would increase the care and tenderness of mothers towards their children when they were sure of a settlement for life to the poor babes, provided in some sort by the public to their annual profit instead of expense, we should see an honest emulation among the married women, *which of them could bring the fattest child to the market*, men would become as fond of their wives during the time of their pregnancy, as they are now of their mares in foal, their cows in calf, or sows when they are ready to farrow, nor offer to beat or kick them (as it is too frequent a practice) for fear of a miscarriage.

Many other advantages might be enumerated: For instance, the addition of some thousand carcasses in our exportation of barreled beef; the propagation of *swine's flesh*, and improvement in the art of making good bacon, so much wanted among us by the great comparable in taste or magnificence to a well-grown, fat yearling child, which roasted whole will make a considerable figure at a *Lord Mayor's feast*[44], or any other public entertainment. But this, and many others I omit being studious of brevity.

Supposing that one thousand families in this city would be constant customers for infants' flesh, besides others who might have it at *merry-meetings*, particularly *weddings* and *christenings*[45], I compute that *Dublin* would take off annually about twenty thousand carcasses, and the rest of the kingdom (where probably they will be sold some-

44 Lord Mayor's feast: feast given by the mayor of the city of London.
45 christening: a Christian ceremony in which a baby is officially named.

what cheaper) the remaining eighty thousand.

I can think of no one objection, that will possibly be raised against this proposal, unless it should be urged that the number of people will be thereby much lessened in the kingdom. This I freely own, and was indeed one principal design in offering it to the world. I desire the reader will observe that I calculate my remedy f*or this one individual kingdom of IRELAND, and for no other that ever was, is, or, I think, ever can be upon earth. Therefore let no man talk to me of other expedients: Of taxing our absentees at five shillings a pound: Of using neither clothes, nor household furniture, except what is of our own growth and manufacture: Of utterly rejecting the materials and instruments that promote foreign luxury: Of curing the expensiveness of pride, vanity, idleness, and gaming in our women: Of introducing a vein of parsimony*[46]*, prudence, and temperance: Of learning to love our country, wherein we differ even from LAPLANDERS, and the inhabitants of TOPINAMBOO*[47]*: Of quitting our animosities and factions, nor act any longer like the Jews, who were murdering one another at the very moment their city was taken: [11] Of being a little cautious not to sell our country and consciences for nothing: Of teaching landlords to have at least one degree of mercy toward their tenants. Lastly of putting a spirit of honesty, industry, and skill into our shop-keepers, who, if a resolution could now be taken to buy only our native goods, would immediately unite to cheat and exact*[48]* upon us in the price, the measure, and the goodness, nor could ever yet be brought to make one fair proposal of just dealing, though often and earnestly invited to it.*

Therefore, I repeat, let no man talk to me of these and the like expedients till he hath at least some glimpse of hope, that there will

46 parsimony: unwillingness to spend money.
47 Topinamboo: a district in Brazil.
48 exact: impose.

ever be some hearty and sincere attempt to put them in practice.

But as to my self, having been wearied out for many years with offering vain, idle, visionary thoughts, and at length utterly despairing of success, I fortunately fell upon this proposal, which as it is wholly new, so it hath something solid and real, of no expense and little trouble, full in our own power, and whereby we can incur no danger in *disobliging England*. For this kind of commodity will not bear exportation, the flesh being of too tender a consistence to admit a long continuance in salt, *although perhaps I could name a country*[49]*, which would be glad to eat up our whole nation without it.*

After all, I am not so violently bent upon my own opinion as to reject any offer, proposed by wise men, which shall be found equally innocent, cheap, easy, and effectual. But before something of that kind shall be advanced in contradiction to my scheme, and offering a better, I desire the author or authors will be pleased maturely to consider two points. *First*, as things now stand, how they will be able to find food and raiment for a hundred thousand useless mouths and backs. And *secondly*, there being a round million of creatures in human figure, throughout this kingdom, whose whole subsistence put into a common stock would leave them in debt two millions of pounds *sterling* adding those, who are beggars by profession, to the bulk of farmers, cottagers, and labourers with their wives and children, who are beggars in effect; I desire those *politicians*[50], who dislike my overture[51], and may perhaps be so bold to attempt an answer, that they will first ask the parents of these mortals, whether they would not at this day think it a great happiness to have been sold for food at a year old, in the manner I prescribe, and thereby have avoided such a perpetual scene of misfortunes, as they have since gone through, by

49 a country: England.
50 politicians: people who are good at using situations in an organization for their own interests.
51 overture: suggestion.

the *oppression of landlords*, the impossibility of paying rent without money or trade, the want of common sustenance, with neither house nor clothes to cover them from the inclemencies of the weather, and the most inevitable prospect of entailing the like, or greater miseries upon their breed forever.

I profess in the sincerity of my heart that I have not the least personal interest in endeavouring to promote this necessary work, having no other motive than the *public good of my country, by advancing our trade, providing for infants, relieving the poor, and giving some pleasure to the rich*. I have no children, by which I can propose to get a single penny; the youngest being nine years old, and my wife past child-bearing.

NOTES ON THE TEXT

[1] Spain, supported by France, had military collisions with England even before 1739 in its scrambling for commercial and political interests both in North America and in Europe. Spain and France in due course took Ireland as their major recruiting ground in their wars against England.

[2] Barbados, the easternmost island of the West Indies, had been a British colony since the early 1600s and had been one of the destinies of many impoverished Irish people in their effort to flee from home because of natural disasters. The West Indian plantation owners forced them to provide unpaid labor at least for a period of time by paying for their transportation.

[3] The persona shows here his alarming precision in his description of things. A solar year is a period of time the earth takes to go around the sun once, approximately 365.25 days.

[4] The English control over Ireland caused the outstanding reduction of the Irish farmland owing to the crying need for pastures of the English woolen industry.

[5] During the years of colonization, English took Americans as a prototype of barbarism and treated them with open contempt. Notice the author's sarcasm here.

[6] Well versed in wordplay, Swift employs the word "dear" here for its two meanings, namely "expensive" and "precious."

[7] Swift here talks about Francois Rebelais, a noted French author whose dates are 1494—1553.

[8] The Roman Catholic countries refer to those states who are related to the Roman Catholic Church, the western part of the Christian Church seated in Rome with Pope as its supreme leader, as opposed to the eastern branch of the Christian Church which is known as the Or-

thodox or Eastern Orthodox Church.

[9] George Psalmanazar (c. 1679 – 1763) is an eighteenth-century French author who was known for his writings during his days on Taiwan, called *Formosa*, the name given to the island by the early Portugese colonialists.

[10] The landlords wrenched from Ireland but spent in England. This was one of the grievous burdens Ireland had to bear at the time.

[11] Swift here talks about the sack of Jerusalem in 70 CE by the Roman legions led by Emperor Titus (39 – 81), originally named Flavius Sabinus Vespasianus. He was also known for the construction of the Roman Colosseum.

QUESTIONS FOR DISCUSSION

1. One of the features of Swift's satire is its understatements which make what he describes sound less important and serious. Could you find some examples of this nature in his *A Modest Proposal*?

2. The general opinion among the critics is that Swift had in mind a larger liberation, not merely political, but a freeing of the human mind from error and the human spirit from baseness. How do you comment on the opinion?

3. Henry Fielding, one of the contemporaries of Swift, once argued that the satirist should be regarded as a physician, rather than an enemy. With what you have read in mind, do you think Swift's satire is that affirmative and constructive? If so, how do you support yourself?

4. *A Modest Proposal* has been considered as a masterpiece of ironic logic among the English satires. Could you make a list of what he proposed in the tract which you could label as ironic?

5. The speaker in *A Modest Proposal* is a fictional character rather than the author himself. The speaker's failure to distinguish when he refers to human babies as being "dropped" from their "dam" makes it perfectly clear. Could you find more examples of this kind from the text?

SUGGESTED REFERENCES

Atkins, G. Douglas. *Swift's Satires on Modernism: Battlegrounds of Reading and Writing.* New York: Palgrave MacMillan, 2013.

Ferguson, Oliver W. "The Last Proposals." *Jonathan Swift: A Collection of Critical Essays.* Ed. Claude Rawson. Englewood Cliffs, NJ: Prentice-Hall, 1995. 280-90.

Rawson, Claude. "'Indians' and Irish: Montaigne, Swift, and the Cannibal Question." *Modern Language*

Quarterly 53 (1992): 299-363.

---. "A Reading of 'A Modest Proposal'." *Augustan Worlds: Essays in Honour of A. R. Humphreys.* Eds. J. C. Hilson, et al. Leicester: Leicester UP, 1978.

Rosenheim, Edward W. *Swift and the Satirist's Art.* Chicago: U of Chicago P, 1963.

Unit 6 Samuel Johnson

(1709—1784)

A GUIDE TO LITERARY TERMINOLOGY

"Patronage": *Literary patronage originally refers to the support of a man of wealth in the form of financial help to a man of letters who is supposed, in return, to dedicate his work to the supporter known as his patron. Even though Samuel Johnson once sarcastically defined a patron as "a wretch who supports with insolence, and is paid with flattery," individual patronage often functioned as direct inspirations for many great works in the history of English literature. Among the most celebrated patrons of arts are John of Gaunt, a powerful supporter to Geoffrey Chaucer who wrote the famous elegy* ***Book of the Duchess*** *for the death of his wife, and Sir George Howland, better known as Beaumont, the benefactor of William Wordsworth who proclaimed that some of his best poems were composed under the shade of his groves. Even Johnson who boasted with pride to his biographer that he had lived more independently by literature than anybody else, he never freed himself from worries over the question of patronage. As Jacob Leed estimated, among the essays he contributed to the* ***Ramblers****, one fifth deal directly with the matter and many others take up the central issues involved in patronage.*

The eighteenth century saw the high watermark of the English patronage and also witnessed a remarkable shifting of the benefactors from men of individual wealth to men of professional power or commercial interest. Library owners, periodical editors and book sellers became important financial sources for authors of literary works. As a result of this significant change, men of letters in England depended more and more heavily upon the public resources for subsistence.

NOTES ON THE AUTHOR

Samuel Johnson was born at Lichfield in 1708 to a local bookseller. He spent fourteen months at Pembroke College, Oxford, but did not take a degree there. His father died in 1731 and he seemed to have made his life by writing soon after that. He published poems, long and short, and essays addressing various issues both in politics and literature. He contributed articles regularly and sometimes solely to such periodicals as the *Rambler* and the *Adventurer*, and he wrote the very first major dictionary in the English language, which was published in 1755. Among his writings were many famous pieces such as his powerful letter to Lord

Chesterfield, his wise preface to the *Dictionary*, let alone his brilliant biographical "Lives of the Poets" and lives of many other well-known figures such as Cheynel and Browne. Besides his learning, he was also known for his wit, humor and sturdy common sense as are reflected in his conversations and all this was faithfully recorded by his biographer, James Boswell in his celebrated masterpiece *Life of Johnson*. He died at his house in Bolt Court in 1784 and was buried in Westminster Abbey. A monument was erected to him in St. Paul's Cathedral in memory of this great man with a kind heart which was sometimes concealed under a gruff exterior.

NOTES ON THE WORK

The occasion for the famous letter was the appearance in *The World* of two articles written by Philip Dormer Stanhope, fourth Earl of Chesterfield (1694—1773). The two articles he published to commend Johnson's *Dictionary* which was about to be published, aroused but disgust and bitterness in the heart of Johnson, because of Chesterfield's trifling monetary acknowledgment and silence on the subject after Johnson had dedicated seven years earlier the "Plan of the *Dictionary*" to him. As Johnson expected more help from him according to the customs of patronage in the eighteenth century which was not forthcoming, Johnson took Chesterfield's pose of his patron as a presumptuous gesture.

As a commentator once observed, one of the glories of the eighteenth century is certainly that its wars were relatively bloodless and that its great men, though they may have acquiesced in a harsh social and economic system, seldom exhibited the ferocity characteristic of many ages — including those most inclined to boast of their civilization. Chesterfield did not respond Johnson's bitterness with hostility. Instead, he articulated his admiration for the eloquence of his opponent, and Johnson never overpublicized his victory and, as he hardly exploited the letter, the text of it was all but lost.

SELECTED READINGS

A Letter to the Right Honourable the Earl of Chesterfield[1]

February 7, 1755

My Lord[2]

I have been lately informed, by the proprietor[3] of *The World* [1] that two papers, in which my *Dictionary* is recommended to the public, were written by your Lordship. To be so distinguished is an honour which, being very little accustomed to favours from the great, I know not well how to receive, or in what terms to acknowledge.

When upon some slight encouragement I first visited your Lordship, I was overpowered, like the rest of mankind, by the enchantment of your address[4]; and I could not forbear to wish that I might boast myself "*le vainqueur du vainqueur de la terre*" [2]; that I might obtain that regard for which I saw the world contending; but I found my attendance so little encouraged, that neither pride nor modesty would suffer me to continue it. When I had once addressed your Lordship in public, I had exhausted all the art of pleasing which a retired and uncourtly[5] scholar can possess. I had done all that I could; and no man is well pleased to have his all neglected, be it ever so little.

Seven years, my Lord, have now passed, since I waited in your outward rooms[6], or was repulsed from your door, during which time I have been pushing on my work through difficulties, of which it is useless to complain, and have brought it, at last, to the verge of publication, without one act of assistance, one word of encouragement, or one smile of favour

---

1 Selections of Unit 6 are from *The Reader's Johnson: A Representative Selection from His Writings*, edited by C. H. Conley and published by American Book Company in 1940.
2 My lord: a title of respect used when speaking to a male member of nobility.
3 proprietor: owner of a business.
4 address: a formal speech.
5 uncourtly: not flattering.
6 outward rooms: antechamber.

[3]. Such treatment I did not expect, for I never had a Patron[7] before.

The shepherd in Virgil grew at last acquainted with Love, and found him a native of the rocks [4].

Is not a Patron, my Lord, one who looks with unconcern on a man struggling for life in the water and, when he has reached ground, encumbers him with help? The notice which you have been pleased to take of my labours, had it been early, had been kind; but it has been delayed till I am indifferent, and cannot enjoy it; till I am solitary, and cannot impart it; till I am known, and do not want[8] it. I hope it is no very cynical asperity not to confess obligations where no benefit has been received, or to be unwilling that the public should consider me as owing that to a Patron, which Providence[9] has enabled me to do for myself.

Having carried on my work thus far with so little obligation to any favourer of learning, I shall not be disappointed though I should conclude it, if less be possible, with less; for I have been long wakened from that dream of hope, in which I once boasted myself with so much exultation, my Lord,

your Lordship's most humble

most obedient servant,

Sam. Johnson.

NOTES ON THE TEXT

[1] *The World* was a periodical that appeared regularly from 1753 to 1756 to which Chesterfield frequently contributed articles.

[2] This is the first line of "Alaric," a poem written by Georges de Scudéry, brother of Madeleine de Scudéry (1607—1701), a popular French writer of heroic romances in the seventeenth century. Georges de Scudéry, known as a dramatic poet, collaborated with his sister in her earlier romances. The line means "the Conqueror of the Conqueror of the World," and "Le vainqueur" refers to Alaric the Goth who conquered Rome.

[3] Johnson was very careful with his word choice. The parallel structure here and elsewhere

7 Patron: a person who gives money or support to artists or writers.

8 want: need.

9 Providence: God or fate that is supposed to control what happens to people.

in this famous letter demonstrates the charm of Johnson's elegant and poignant prose style.

[4] The passage here refers to Virgil's *Eclogues* or *Bucolics*, which is an imitation of the pastoral works of Theocritus (310? — 250? BCE), the great Greek pastoral poet. Borrowing his thrust from the pastorals, Johnson makes powerfully his point that Chesterfield's untimely "love" arouses in effect but misery and disgust in his heart. The line was translated by Dryden as "I know thee, Love; in Desarts thou wert bred."

QUESTIONS FOR DISCUSSION

1. Johnson's letter to Chesterfield, sent to him some four months before the publication of the *Dictionary*, has been said to be the climax of the whole story. Do you know why?

2. Considering the tone of the whole letter, what words would you use to describe Johnson in terms of his personality?

3. Although the letter is filled up with bitterness and disgust, it is obviously one of the perfect examples of Johnson's mastery of wit and humor. Could you discuss the letter along this line?

4. As a magnificent piece of rhetoric, the letter undoubtedly demonstrates its outstanding strength in terms of its language. Comment on the special features of Johnson's language.

5. Johnson once observed that a poor man had no honor. Does the event, marking the end of the age of patronage, supports what he believed in?

NOTES ON THE WORK

Johnson's two-volume *Dictionary of the English Language*, published in 1755, is by no means the first one even in English as it is often said to be, since it is proceeded by Nathaniel Bailey's *Universal Etymological Dictionary*, besides a couple of other minor ones, which had not only been published 34 years before but also had more entries than Johnson's. His *Dictionary*, however, represents one of the two great landmarks in English lexicographical history, the second of which is the *Oxford English Dictionary* of the late nineteenth century, the greatest, perhaps, of any modern language.

The fame of Johnson's work, author's wilful effort to regulate the English language in usage and thus to keep his mother tongue from deteriorating, does not lie in its glossing of one word in terms of the other. Instead, it lies in the precision of its definitions, which were elegantly formulated and richly illustrated with copious quotations from the entire range of English literature. Shades of meaning of words were also exemplified with the quotations even though some words, as shown in his *Dictionary*, were not always objectively done. An interesting example of this kind is his definition of the word "Oats" which is "a grain which in England is generally given to horses, but in Scotland supports the people." It is often taken, however, as an instance of his wit and wisdom.

The principles laid down by Johnson in his *Dictionary*, needless to say, exerted tremendous influence on English lexicography for more than a century. Even though it is no longer authoritative to modern readers, the *Dictionary* and the preface he wrote to the work, in terms of its fair judgment of language, are still considered masterpieces of particular literary and linguistic interest.

SELECTED READINGS

A Preface to the *Dictionary*

(Selections)

It is the fate of those who toil at the lower employments of life, to be rather driven by the fear of evil than attracted by the prospect of good; to be exposed to censure[1] without hope of praise; to be disgraced by miscarriage or punished for neglect, where success would have been without applause and diligence without reward.

Among these unhappy mortals is the writer of dictionaries, whom mankind have considered not as the pupil[2] but the slave of science, the pioneer of literature, doomed only to removed rubbish and clear obstructions from the paths through which learning and genius press forward to conquest and glory, without bestowing a smile on the humble drudge that facilitates their progress. Every other author may aspire to praise; the lexicographer can only hope to escape reproach, and even this negative recompense has been yet granted to very few.

1 censure: strong disapproval or criticism.
2 pupil: scholar.

I have, notwithstanding[3] this discouragement, attempted a dictionary of the English language, which, while it was employed in the cultivation of every species of literature, has itself been hitherto neglected, suffered to spread under the direction of chance into wild exuberance, resigned to the tyranny of time and fashion, and exposed to the corruptions of ignorance and caprices of innovation.

When I took the first survey of my undertaking, I found our speech copious without order and energetic without rules. Wherever I turned my view, there was perplexity to be disentangled and confusion to be regulated; choice was to be made out of boundless variety without any established principle of selection; adulterations were to be detected without a settled test of purity; and modes of expression to be rejected or received without the suffrages[4] of any writers of classical reputation or acknowledged authority.

...

Thus I have laboured by settling the orthography[5], displaying the analogy, regulating the structures, and ascertaining the signification[6] of English words to perform all the parts of a faithful lexicographer. But I have not always executed my own scheme or satisfied my own expectations. The work, whatever proofs of diligence and attention it may exhibit, is yet capable of many improvements. The orthography which I recommend is still controvertible; the etymology which I adopt is uncertain and perhaps frequently erroneous; the explanations are sometimes too much contracted and sometimes too much diffused; the significations are distinguished rather with subtilty than skill, and the attention is harassed with unnecessary minuteness.

The examples are too often injudiciously truncated and perhaps sometimes, I hope very rarely, alleged in a mistaken sense; for in mak-

3 notwithstanding: in spite of.
4 suffrages: judgments.
5 orthography: spelling system.
6 signification: expression.

ing this collection I trusted more to memory than in a state of disquiet and embarrassment memory can contain, and purposed to supply at the review what was left incomplete in the first transcription.

Many terms appropriated to particular occupations, though necessary and significant, are undoubtedly omitted; and of the words most studiously considered and exemplified many senses have escaped observation.

Yet these failures, however frequent, may admit extenuation and apology. To have attempted much is always laudable, even when the enterprise is above the strength that undertakes it. To rest below his own aim is incident to everyone whose fancy is active and whose views are comprehensive; nor is any man satisfied with himself because he has done much but because he can conceive little. When first I engaged in this work, I resolved to leave neither words nor things unexamined, and pleased myself with a prospect of the hours which I should revel away in feasts of literature, with the obscure recesses of northern learning which I should enter and ransack, the treasures with which I expected every search into those neglected mines to reward my labour, and the triumph with which I should display my acquisitions to mankind. When I had thus inquired into the original of words, I resolved to show likewise my attention to things; to pierce deep into every science, to inquire the nature of every substance of which I inserted a name, to limit every idea by a definition strictly logical, and exhibit every production of art or nature in an accurate description, that my book might be in place of all other dictionaries, whether appellative or technical. But these were the dreams of a poet doomed at last to wake a lexicographer. I soon found that it is too late to look for instruments when the work calls for execution, and that whatever abilities I had brought to my task with those I must finally perform it. To deliberate whenever I doubted, to inquire whenever I was ignorant would have protracted the undertaking without end and perhaps without much improvement; for I did not find by my first experiments that what I had not of my own was easily to be obtained. I saw that one inquired only gave occasion to another, that book referred to book, that to search was not always to find, and to find was not always to be informed; and what thus to pursue perfection was, like the first inhabitants of Arcadia, to chase the sun, which when they had reached the hill where he seemed to rest, was still beheld at the same distance from them. [1]

I then contracted my design, determining to confide in myself and no longer to solicit auxiliaries which produced more encumbrance than assistance. By this I obtained at least one advantage, that I set limits to my work, which would in time be ended though not completed.

Despondency has never so far prevailed as to depress me to negligence; some faults will at last appear to be the effects of anxious diligence and persevering activity. The nice and subtle ramifications of meaning were not easily avoided by a mind intent upon accuracy and convinced of the necessity of disentangling combinations and separating similitudes. Many of the distinctions which to common readers appear useless and idle, will be found real and important by men versed in the school philosophy, without which no dictionary can ever be accurately compiled or skillfully examined.

Some senses, however, there are which, though not the same, are yet so nearly allied that they are often confounded. Most men think indistinctly and therefore cannot speak with exactness; and, consequently, some examples might be indifferently put to either signification. This uncertainty is not to be imputed to me, who do not form but register[7] the language; who do not teach men how they should think but relate how they have hitherto expressed their thoughts.

The imperfect sense of some examples I lamented but could not

7 register: to standardize in form of writing.

remedy, and hope they will be compensated by innumerable passages selected with propriety and preserved with exactness, some shining with sparks of imagination and some replete with treasures of wisdom.

The orthography and etymology, though imperfect, are not imperfect for want of care but because care will not always be successful and recollection or information come too late for use.

...

Care will sometimes betray to the appearance of negligence. He that is catching opportunities which seldom occur will suffer those to pass by unregarded which he expects hourly to return; he that is searching for rare and remote things will neglect those that are obvious and familiar. Thus many of the most common and cursory words have been inserted with little illustration, because in gathering the authorities, I forbore to copy those which I thought likely to occur whenever they were wanted. It is remarkable that in reviewing my collection I found the word SEA unexemplified.

Thus it happens that in things difficult there is danger from ignorance, and in things easy from confidence; the mind, afraid of greatness and disdainful of littleness, hastily withdraws herself from painful searches and passes with scornful rapidity over tasks not adequate to her powers; sometimes too secure for caution and again too anxious for vigorous effort; sometimes idle in a plain path and sometimes distracted in labyrinths and dissipated by different intentions.

A large work is difficult because it is large, even though all its parts might singly be performed with facility; where there are many things to be done, each must be allowed its share of time and labour, in the proportion only which it bears to the whole; nor can it be expected that the stones which form the dome of a temple should be squared and polished like the diamond of a ring.

Of the event of this work, for which, having laboured it with so much application, I cannot but have some degree of parental fondness, it is natural to form conjectures. Those who have been persuaded to think well of my design, will require that it should fix our language, and put a stop to those alterations which time and chance have hitherto been suffered to make in it without opposition. With this consequence I will confess that I have indulged expectation which neither reason nor experience can justify. When we see men grow old and die at a certain time one after another, from century to century, we laugh at the elixir[8] that promises to prolong life to a thousand years; and with equal justice may the lexicographer be derided, who, being able to produce no example of a nation that has preserved their words and phrases from mutability, shall imagine that his dictionary can embalm his language, and secure it from corruption and decay, that it is in his power to change sublunary nature, and clear the world at once from folly, vanity, and affectation.

With this hope, however, academies [2] have been instituted to guard the avenues of their languages, to retain fugitives, and repulse intruders. But their vigilance and activity have hitherto been vain; sounds are too volatile and subtile for legal restraints; to enchain syllables, and to lash the wind are equally the undertakings of pride unwilling to measure its desires by its strength. The French language has visibly changed under the inspection of the Academy; [3] the style of Amelot's translation of Father Paul is observed by Le Courayer to be *un peu passé*; [4] and no Italian will maintain that the diction of any modern writer is not perceptibly different from that of Boccace, [5] Machiavel, [6] or Caro. [7]

Total and sudden transformations of a language seldom happen; conquests and migrations are now very rare; but there are other causes of change, which, though slow in their operation and invisible in

---

8 elixir: a magical potion supposedly able to make people live forever.

their progress, are perhaps as much superior to human resistance as the revolutions[9] of the sky or intumescence of the tide. Commerce, however necessary, however lucrative, as it depraves the manners, corrupts the language; they that have frequent intercourse with strangers, to whom they endeavour to accommodate themselves, must in time learn a mingled dialect, like the jargon which serves the traffickers[10] on the Mediterranean and Indian coasts. This will not always be confined to the exchange, the warehouse, or the port, but will be communicated by degrees to other ranks of the people, and be at last incorporated with the current speech.

There are likewise internal causes equally forcible. The language most likely to continue long without alteration would be that of a nation raised a little, and but[11] a little, above barbarity, secluded from strangers, and totally employed in procuring the conveniences of life; either without books or, like some of the Mahometan countries, [8] with very few: men thus busied and unlearned, having only such words as common use requires, would perhaps long continue to express the same notions by the same signs. But no such constancy can be expected in a people polished by arts and classed by subordination, where one part of the community is sustained and accommodated by the labour of the other. Those who have much leisure to think, will always be enlarging the stock of ideas; and every increase of knowledge, whether real or fancied, will produce new words or combinations of words. When the mind is unchained from necessity, it will range after convenience; when it is left at large in the fields of speculation, it will shift opinions; as any custom is disused, the words that expressed it must perish with it; as any opinion grows popular, it will innovate speech in the same proportion as it alters practice.

9 revolutions: movements of celestial bodies.

10 traffickers: traders.

11 but: only.

NOTES ON THE TEXT

[1] Inhabitants of the ancient Greek region Arcadia were called Arcadians. They were once looked upon as uncivilized and doltish people.

[2] Johnson decided to compile his *Dictionary* as he was inspired by *Accademia della Crusca*, the Italian dictionary published in 1612, and by the French dictionary of the *Academie francaise* which had been published in 1694.

[3] Academies were set up in France and in Italy for regulating their native tongues and maintaining the standards of literature. Projects of dictionary writing also resulted from the establishment of such academies as part of the same effort.

[4] Amelot de la Houssaye, a seventeenth-century translator, turned Paolo Sarpi's *Istoria del concilio di Trento* from Latin into French in 1619, and his unfaithful translation was superseded in 1736 by the translation of Pierre Francois le Courayer, canon regular and librarian of the Abbey of Ste. Genevieve, Paris.

[5] Giovanni Boccaccio, the most known novelist and poet in the fourteenth-century Italy and the author of *Decameron*, shares with Petrarch the honor of shaping Italian into a modern literary language.

[6] Niccolo Machiavelli was a Florentine statesman and political philosopher and his dates were 1469—1527. He was especially known for his writings on history and philosophy and his best work, *Il Principe*, a treatise on despotic government, was translated into English in 1640.

[7] Annibale Caro, an Italian writer of the sixteenth century, translated Virgil's *Aeneid* into Italian and became well known for the quality of the language used in his translation.

[8] Mahometan countries, also known as Muhammadan countries, are those Arabic countries whose people believe in Islam.

QUESTIONS FOR DISCUSSION

1. Inspired greatly by the dictionaries both in Italian and in French, Johnson finally decided to prepare a dictionary in English too. How do you compare Johnson's original intention with that of the Italian and French lexicographers as is indicated in his preface to the *Dictionary*?

2. Johnson's "Preface to the *Dictionary*" reflects the change of his attitude toward language in general and English in particular. Describe briefly Johnson's idea about language change.

3. One of Johnson's well-known playful definitions is that of "lexicographer," which goes "a writer of dictionaries, a harmless drudge." With your knowledge of Johnson's intention, plan and work of the project, how do you understand his interesting definition, especially the latter part of it?

4. How did Johnson understand the nature of the language and the outer and inner elements that may cause the change of it?

5. As Johnson eventually indicated, language is a living thing, always changing. Old words die and new words come in. Some sentence structures gradually fall out of use and others push their way in. As an English major, could you give details to support the idea that English is changing?

SUGGESTED REFERENCES

DeMaria, Jr., Robert. *Johnson's Dictionary and the Language of Learning.* Chapel Hill: Np, 1986.

Leed, Jacob. "Johnson and Cheseterfield: 1946—1947." *Studies in Burke and His Time* 12 (1970): 677-90.

Reddick, Allen. *The Making of Johnson's Dictionary, 1746—1773.* Cambridge: Cambridge UP, 1990.

Sledd, James H. and Gwin J. Kolb. *Dr. Johnson's Dictionary.* Chicago: U of Chicago P, 1955.

Wimsatt, Jr., W. K. "Johnson's Dictionary." *New Light on Dr. Johnson.* Ed. F. W. Hilles. New Haven: Yale UP, 1959. 65-90.

Unit 7 William Blake

(1757—1827)

A GUIDE TO LITERARY TERMINOLOGY

"Meter": *"Meter," a measured arrangement of words in poetry, is the term we can hardly afford not to know if we are serious in reading poems. Lines of poetry usually follow a specific metrical pattern based on the natural rhythms of one particular language in which these lines are formed. The so-called accentual verse, for instance, is typical in the poetic lines of Germanic languages which are different in origin from Romance tongues whose versification features syllable counting rather than the counting of stresses. Thus, lines in Old English poetry are formed with such distinctive stresses and, as typical English words almost always accentuate their first syllables, Old English verse is reinforced by head-rhymes which are called, to use a more scholarly term, alliteration.*

Therefore, accentual-syllabic is the normal metrical pattern of English verse which, with its unique combination of Germanic stress counting and Romance syllable counting, shows lines of fixed numbers of alternating stressed and unstressed syllables. We often describe the meter of English poetic lines as iambic pentameter, which means lines of ten syllables or five iambic feet, with each foot being composed of an unstressed syllable followed by a stressed one.

NOTES ON THE AUTHOR

Born into a petty proprietor's family in London, William Blake never had a chance to receive a normal education. He became an apprentice to an engraver in 1772, the seven-year experience of which made him a book illustrator as well as publisher. His poetic talent in poetry was not really noticed until his *Songs of Innocence* was written, engraved and published all by himself in 1789, the very first collection of poems in which he first showed the mystical cast of his mind.

As a precursor of Romanticism hostile to all of the dominant tendencies of the Neoclassical period, he produced volumes of poems including *The Songs of Innocence* and *The Songs of Experience*, which shocked his contemporaries with two widely different views of human life and soul. The brightness of the earlier collection is followed by a sense of appalling and profound gloom and mystery as is reflected in the poems of the latter volume. His attitude of revolt against authorities was first of all developed in his marriage with no benediction whatsoever from his parents and significantly reinforced as is reflected in his later writings denying the reality of matter as well as authorities of all kinds.

With his extraordinary talent for engraving, Blake illustrated many works besides his own and thus revealed his greatness as an artist as well as a poet even though he lived childless and poor, enchanted with his life-long mystical visions while laboring on his poetry and engraving. He died quietly in 1827.

SYNOPSIS OF THE WORK

The Songs of Innocence and *The Songs of Experience* are two volumes of poems produced and beautifully illuminated respectively in 1789 and in 1794 by William Blake, which at least partially contributed to his tremendous success as the very first full-fledged Romantic poet in England. As two companion collections, his poems in the two separate volumes reflect perfectly the poet's desire to make them as a logical whole, namely an expression of the totality of the human situation. With parallelism and opposition, the two volumes not only celebrate the simple joys of childhood but also touch upon the limits of these joys.

Poems in *The Songs of Innocence* follow by and large the tradition of Christian poetry for children, even though they from time to time demonstrate a touch of mockery typical in his apparently pastoral lyricism, just as he later observes, "Innocence dwells with Wisdom, but never with Ignorance."

Poems in *The Songs of Experience*, on the other hand, do show an expression of the poet's understanding of the loss of innocence and his contemplation of the mystery and complexity of human life. The articulation of his idea, however, shows his consideration of the linkage between the two phases of human life, as is clearly expressed in the title with which Blake issued both parts, namely *Songs of Innocence and of Experience*: *Shewing the Two Contrary States of the Human Soul*. As one commentator observes, most of the poems in either book are not to be apprehended without their matching "contraries" in the other. The two volumes of poems enjoy full support from each other.

SELECTED READINGS

Poems from *The Songs of Innocence*[1]

Holy Thursday

'Twas on a Holy Thursday, [1] their innocent faces clean,
The children walking two & two, in red & blue & green, — in school uniform
Grey-headed beadles walk'd before, with wands as white as snow, — beadle: priest
Till into the high dome of Paul's [2] they like Thames' waters flow.

O what a multitude they seem'd, these flowers of London town!
Seated in companies they sit with radiance all their own.
The hum of multitudes was there, but multitudes of lambs,
Thousands of little boys & girls raising their innocent hands.

Now like a mighty wind they raise to heaven the voice of song,
Or like harmonious thundering the seats of Heaven among.
Beneath them sit the aged men, wise guardians of the poor;
Then cherish pity, lest you drive an angel from your door.

The Lamb

Little Lamb, who made thee?
Dost thou know who made thee? [3]
Gave thee life, & bid thee feed
By the stream & o'er the mead; — mead: an alcoholic drink
Gave thee clothing of delight,

1 The poems in Unit 7 are taken from the 1969 edition of *Eighteenth-Century English Literature* edited by Geoffrey Tillotson, et. al. published by Harcourt Brace Jovanovich, Publishers, and other sources.

Softest clothing, wooly, bright;
Gave thee such a tender voice,
Making all the vales rejoice? vale: valley
Little Lamb, who made thee?
Dost thou know who made thee?

Little Lamb, I'll tell thee,
Little Lamb, I'll tell thee:
He is called by thy name,
For he calls himself a Lamb. Lamb: Jesus Christ
He is meek, & he is mild;
He became a little child.
I a child, & thou a lamb,
We are called by his name.
Little Lamb, God bless thee!
Little Lamb, God bless thee! [4]

The Chimney Sweeper [5]

When my mother died I was very young,
And my father sold me while yet my tongue
Could scarcely cry "weep! weep! weep!" weep: sweep
So your chimneys I sweep, & in soot I sleep.

There's little Tom Dacre, who cried when his head,
That curl'd like a lamb's back, was shav'd: so I said
"Hush, Tom! never mind it, for when your head's bare
You know that the soot cannot spoil your white hair." white: blond

And so he was quiet, & that very night,
As Tom was a-sleeping, he had such a sight!

That thousands of sweepers, Dick, Joe, Ned, & Jack,
Were all of them lock'd up in coffins of black.

And by came an Angel who had a bright key,
And he open'd the coffins & set them all free;
And down a green plain leaping, laughing, they run,
And wash in a river, and shine in the Sun.

Then naked & white, all their bags left behind, bags: for holding soot
They rise upon clouds and sport in the wind; sport: play
And the Angel told Tom, if he'd be a good boy,
He'd have God for his father, & never want joy. want: lack

And so Tom awoke; and we rose in the dark,
And got with our bags & our brushes to work.
Tho' the morning was cold, Tom was happy & warm;
So if all do their duty they need not fear harm. [6]

Poems from *The Songs of Experience*

Holy Thursday

Is this a holy thing to see
In an rich and fruitful land,
Babes reduc'd to misery,
Fed with cold and usurious hand?

Is that trembling cry a song?
Can it be a song of joy?
And so many children poor?
It is a land of poverty!

And their sun does never shine,
And their fields are bleak & bare,
And their ways are fill'd with thorns:
It is eternal winter there.

For where-e'er the sun does shine,
And where-e'er the rain does fall,
Babe can never hunger there,
Nor poverty the mind appall.

The Tyger

Tyger! Tyger! burning bright
In the forests of the night,
What immortal hand or eye
Could frame thy fearful symmetry? [7]

symmetry: perfect design

In what distant deeps or skies
Burnt the fire of thine eyes?
On what wings dare he aspire?
What the hand dare sieze the fire?

deep: sea

And what shoulder, & what art,
Could twist the sinews of thy heart?
And when thy heart began to beat,
What dread hand? & what dread feet?

What the hammer? what the chain?
In what furnace was thy brain?
What the anvil? what dread grasp
Dare its deadly terrors clasp?

When the stars threw down their spears,
And water'd heaven with their tears,
Did he smile his work to see?
Did he who made the Lamb make thee?

Tyger! Tyger! burning bright
In the forests of the night,
What immortal hand or eye,
Dare frame thy fearful symmetry? [8]

London

I wander thro' each charter'd street, charter' d: monopolized
Near where the charter'd Thames does flow,
And mark in every face I meet
Marks of weakness, marks of woe.

In every cry of every Man,
In every Infant's cry of fear,
In every voice, in every ban ban: curse
The mind-forg'd manacles I hear. manacles: shackles

How the Chimney-sweeper's cry
Every black'ning Church appalls; [9]
And the hapless Soldier's sigh
Runs in blood down Palace walls.

But most thro' midnight streets I hear
How the youthful Harlot's curse
Blasts the new born Infant's tear,
And blights with plagues the Marriage hearse. [10]

NOTES ON THE TEXT

[1] Holy Thursday, also known as Ascension Day, is the fortieth day after Easter, observed in the Anglican Church in commemoration of the Last Supper of Jesus Christ. Thousands of children from the charity schools of London, who were orphans and very often abandoned children, would march to a service at St. Paul's Cathedral on this day according to an old local tradition.

[2] St. Paul's Cathedral was built in 604, which, dedicated to St. Paul, has overlooked the City of London ever since.

[3] The form of questions and answers at the beginning of "The Lamb" shows the poet's conscious imitation of catechism often used in children's poems for religious instruction.

[4] Lamb as a highly symbolic image may stand for youth, beauty and unspoiled pleasures. It is also a symbol of Jesus Christ in Christian iconography, which stands for mercy and the presence of the divine.

[5] The employment of young children in the dangerous and health-destroying chimney sweeping was obviously the violation of an Act of Parliament passed in 1788 in England which was intended to limit the working hours of the workers and to prohibit the employment of children who were younger than eight years old.

[6] Although the poem depicts the miserable life of those young chimney sweepers, the poet does not change the gentle tone of *The Songs of Innocence*. By representing children as comforted by heavenly visions and assurances of future happiness, the poet seems to argue that the essential innocence of childhood can triumph over all odds.

[7] The problem of the rhyme here and also of the last stanza, namely the rhyming of "eye" with "symmetry," results from the pronunciation of the syllable in the dialect of English Blake conducted.

[8] The image of tiger shows an essential difference both in mood and in content from the previous collection. The poet's exploration of the deep mystery of creation and the extraordinary complexity of life seems to tell us the loss of innocence as is reflected in the image of the tiger, which shows terror and beauty at the same time, forming a sharp contrast with that of the lamb in *The Songs of Innocence*.

[9] The heartlessness of London, growing black with time and pollution, is cruelly exposed in this short but shocking poem. The heart-stirring cry of a young chimney sweeper provides us with an unutterably sad comment on the appalling failure of the Church which is supposed to promote decency and morality.

[10] The last two lines of the poem probably imply the horrifying venereal disease of the time that prostitutes spread, causing the blindness of the newborn and the death of the newly-weds.

QUESTIONS FOR DISCUSSION

1. It is generally accepted that Blake tries to explore the loss of innocence in the two volumes of poems we have cited in Unit 7. Could you give some details from the so-called companion poems to support this argument?

2. A well-known critic prefers not to discuss "what" a poem means but "how" a poem means. Access this judgment by using the terrifying but beautiful symbol Blake has created in "The Tyger."

3. In Blake's poetry, innocent young children appear to know a happiness untouched by doubts, but adults discover that life does consist of endless merriment. How does this judgment apply to our understanding of the two poems both entitled "Holy Thursday"?

4. The poet in "The Tyger" poses two similar questions respectively in the first stanza and in the last one. There is, however, a difference in wording, namely "could change thy fearful symmetry" and "dare frame thy fearful symmetry." What do you think the poet has in mind when he changes his wording?

5. You may not be, at this point, quite familiar with the term "Romanticism" which, in the history of English literature, could be understood as an opposition to Neoclassical period characterized by a regard for reason and form. Blake is known as the first full-fledged Romantic. Do a bit of research and try to explain why people say so.

6. Now that you know what an iambic pentameter is, could you analyze one of the poems by Blake and see in what way it follows or does not follow the metrical form?

SUGGESTED REFERENCES

Damon, S. Foster. *William Blake: His Philosophy and Symbols.* Whitefish: Kessinger Publishing, 2006.

Gleckner, Robert F. "'The Lamb' and 'The Tyger' — How Far with Blake?" *The English Journal* 51.8 (1962): 536-43.

Hirsch, E. D., Jr. *Innocence and Experience: An Introduction to Blake.* New Haven and London: Yale UP, 1964.

Larrissy, Edward. *Blake and Modern Literature.* Basingstoke: Palgrave MacMillan, 2006.

Miner, Paul. "Blake's 'Tyger' as Miltonic Beast." *Studies in Romanticism* 47.4 (2008): 479-505.

Unit 8 William Wordsworth

(1770－1850)

A GUIDE TO LITERARY TERMINOLOGY

"Lake Poets": *Cumbria of England, charming for its lake-strewn valleys, covers an area of 2,243 square kilometers known as the English Lake District. In point of fact, the region gained its fame when such poets as Samuel Taylor Coleridge, Robert Southey, William Wordsworth and sometimes De Quincey were attached to it. These poets were later named Lake Poets or Lakers since they lived one way or another in the Lake District at the beginning of the nineteenth century. Although two of the four, namely Southey and Wordsworth, were Poets Laureate, they were confusingly grouped since Southey and De Quincey do not seem to have subscribed in their views or work to the poetic theories of such romantic poets as Coleridge and Wordsworth who co-authored the famous* ***Lyrical Ballads****.*

The Lake School, another term that refers to this group of poets, seems to have appeared for the first time in the ***Edinburgh Review*** *of August 1817. The expression and a couple of others related to the Lake District were not always taken as that of proper respect by the contemporaries. Lord Byron, for instance, referred slightingly to "all the Lakers" in his dedication to* ***Don Juan*** *and De Quincey even denied the existence of such a "school" in his recollections of the Lake Poets.*

NOTES ON THE AUTHOR

William Wordsworth was born to a lawyer's family in 1770 in Cockermouth of West Cumberland, a scenic place of the Lake District. His parents died when he was young, leaving him rather poor and unhappy in his young days. He attended school at Hawkshead where he developed his abiding love of nature in the beautiful surroundings. In 1787, he went to Cambridge and graduated from the university without distinction.

The fall of the Bastille and the thoughts of the French Revolution exerted great influence upon Wordsworth, but the establishment of the Jacobin dictatorship and the British declaration of war against France in 1793 made his republican enthusiasm recede and give place to his political conservatism. Leading a life as a poet under the influence of his friends, he met Coleridge in his native Lake District and their long-standing friendship led them to the co-authorship of the famous *Lyrical Ballads* in 1798, a landmark of the English romantic poetry.

Most of Wordsworth's best known poems were composed between 1797 and 1807, works that expressed in deliberate simplicity his understanding of nature and the truth of ordinary life. He lived long with undying fame and substantial income and succeeded Robert Southey eventually as Poet Laureate in 1843 even though his mind power was considerably deteriorating. He passed away at Rydal Mount in 1850 at the age of eighty.

NOTES ON THE WORK

The *Lyrical Ballads*, from which the three pieces of this unit are chosen, is a collection of poems contributed by both Wordsworth and his lifelong friend Coleridge. Opening their book with Coleridge's "The Rime of the Ancient Mariner" and closing it with Wordsworth's "Lines Composed a Few Miles above Tintern Abbey," the two poets carried out their experiment on poetry with themes related to everyday issues of true importance and with a language "really used by men," which is an outstanding revolt from the conventional theme and diction of artificial literature of the day in an effort to drag poetry to the right track. We see, therefore, poetic pieces in the collection expressing well the poets' rather religious feelings for Nature in a natural and simple language, which, as is generally believed, marks the beginning of the English Romantic period.

The year 1798 saw the publication of the first edition of the *Lyrical Ballads* and, owing to the nature of experimentation, it took time before the public accepted their way of writing poetry. To explain what their poetry was aiming at, Wordsworth wrote his well-known essay entitled "Observations" and had the book published in 1800 as its second edition with the essay as well as his name in it. Two years later, they further enlarged the work with an appendix of poetic diction and published it for the third time. The two poets' consistent effort, not unexpectedly, only aroused greater bitterness of their contemporaries. Like the two great poets who were unmoved in spite of the hostility of the critics, the *Lyrical Ballads* remains to be a strong manifestation of the basic principles of Romanticism in the history of English literature.

SELECTED READINGS

Poems from *Lyrical Ballads with a Few Other Poems*

To My Sister

It is the first mild day of March:
Each minute sweeter than before,
The redbreast sings from the tall larch
That stands beside our door.

redbreast: linnet

There is a blessing in the air,
Which seems a sense of joy to yield
To the bare trees, and mountains bare,
And grass in the green field.

My sister! ('tis a wish of mine)
Now that our morning meal is done,
Make haste, your morning task resign;
Come forth and feel the sun.

Edward will come with you; — and, pray,
Put on with speed your woodland dress;
And bring no book; for this one day
We'll give to idleness.

Edward: a child

No joyless forms shall regulate
Our living calendar:
We from to-day, my Friend, will date
The opening of the year.

Love, now a universal birth,
From heart to heart is stealing,
From earth to man, from man to earth:
— It is the hour of feeling.

One moment now may give us more
Than years of toiling reason:
Our minds shall drink at every pore
The spirit of the season. [1]

pore: a minute opening of a leaf

Some silent laws our hearts will make,
Which they shall long obey:
We for the year to come may take
Our temper from to-day.

And from the blessed power that rolls
About, below, above,
We'll frame the measure of our souls:
They shall be tuned to love.

Then come, my Sister! come, I pray,
With speed put on your woodland dress;
And bring no book: for this one day
We'll give to idleness.

Expostulation and Reply [2]

expostulation: questioning

"Why, William, on that old grey stone,
Thus for the length of half a day,
Why, William, sit you thus alone,

And dream your time away?

"Where are your books? — that light bequeathed
To Beings else forlorn and blind!
Up! up! and drink the spirit breathed
From dead men to their kind.

forlorn: unlikely to succeed

"You look round on your Mother Earth,
As if she for no purpose bore you;
As if you were her first-born birth,
And none had lived before you!"

One morning thus, by Esthwaite lake,
When life was sweet, I knew not why,
To me my good friend Matthew spake, [3]
And thus I made reply:

spake: spoke

"The eye — it cannot choose but see;
We cannot bid the ear be still;
Our bodies feel, where'er they be,
Against or with our will.

"Nor less I deem that there are Powers
Which of themselves our minds impress;
That we can feed this mind of ours
In a wise passiveness. [4]

"Think you, 'mid all this mighty sum
Of things for ever speaking,
That nothing of itself will come,
But we must still be seeking?

" — Then ask not wherefore, here, alone,
Conversing as I may,
I sit upon this old grey stone,
And dream my time away."

wherefore: for what reason

conversing: communing

The Tables Turned:
An Evening Scene on the Same Subject

Up! up! my Friend, and quit your books;
Or surely you'll grow double:
Up! up! my Friend, and clear your looks;
Why all this toil and trouble?

double: double over

The sun, above the mountain's head,
A freshening luster mellow
Through all the long green fields has spread,
His first sweet evening yellow.

Books! 'tis a dull and endless strife:
Come, hear the woodland linnet,
How sweet his music! on my life,
There's more of wisdom in it.

linnet: a small red-breast finch

And hark! how blithe the throstle sings!
He, too, is no mean preacher:
Come forth into the light of things,
Let Nature be your Teacher.

hark: listen; throstle: song thrush

She has a world of ready wealth,
Our minds and hearts to bless —

Spontaneous wisdom breathed by health,
Truth breathed by cheerfulness.

One impulse from a vernal wood
May teach you more of man,
Of moral evil and of good,
Than all the sages can. [5]

vernal: of spring season

Sweet is the lore which Nature brings;
Our meddling intellect
Mis-shapes the beauteous forms of things: —
We murder to dissect.

meddling: interfering

beauteous: beautiful

Enough of Science and of Art;
Close up those barren leaves;
Come forth, and bring with you a heart
That watches and receives.

leaves: pages

NOTES ON THE TEXT

[1] These lines of "To My Sister" are an early expression of Wordsworth's idea of "wise passiveness," which is one of the favorite doctrines of Romantic poets such as him who emphasized the importance of nature rather than intellectual efforts in the process of learning.

[2] According to the poet's 1798 Advertisement to the *Lyrical Ballads*, the poem "Expostulation and Reply" originated in a conversation between two close friends who debated on the merits of nature and books. The use of the device of overstatement in the rallying may not reflect accurately the idea of Wordsworth about the issue, as some scholars have argued.

[3] The friend who blamed the poet for idling away his time without reading was William Hazlitt (1778—1830) even though he was given the name of Matthew. Hazlitt, a contemporary of Wordsworth, was a prolific man of letters. His relations with the poets including Wordsworth are described in his essay "My First Acquaintance with Poets." As he was in actuality quite quarrelsome and unamiable, it is nothing unexpected that he was chosen as part of the poem.

[4] Wordsworth formulated this famous phrase "wise passiveness" and put it into use here for the very first time. It is said to be one of his important ideas that marked the turning point of

Wordsworth from the Neoclassical beliefs.

[5] The stanza in "The Tables Turned," the companion piece of the previous poem, may give us an idea of the kind of shock that people might have experienced when they first read the lines of this revolutionary poet.

The Solitary Reaper [6]

Behold her, single in the field, behold: see
Yon solitary Highland Lass! yon: yonder; Highland: NW Scotland
Reaping and singing by herself;
Stop here, or gently pass!
Alone she cuts and binds the grain
And sings a melancholy strain;
O listen! for the vale profound vale: valley
Is overflowing with the sound.

No nightingale did ever chant
More welcome notes to weary bands
Of travellers in some shady haunt, haunt: a place one visits frequently
Among Arabian sands; [7]
A voice so thrilling ne'er was heard
In spring-time from the cuckoo-bird,
Breaking the silence of the seas
Among the farthest Hebrides. [8]

Will no one tell me what she sings? — [9]
Perhaps the plaintive numbers flow numbers: musical notes
For old, unhappy, far-off things,
And battles long ago;
Or is it some more humble lay, lay: narrative poem
Familiar matter of to-day?

Some natural sorrow, loss, or pain,
That has been, and may be again?

Whate'er the theme, the maiden sang
As if her song could have no ending;
I saw her singing at her work,
And o'er the sickle bending; —
I listened, motionless and still;
And, as I mounted up the hill,
The music in my heart I bore,
Long after it was heard no more.

NOTES ON THE TEXT

[1] Wordsworth mentions in a note to the poem in 1807 that the subject of the poem was not taken from his own experience, but suggested by a passage in Thomas Wilkinson's *Tours to the British Mountains*. As the passage he had seen goes, "[I] passed a female who was reaping alone: she sang in Erse [the Goidelic language of Scotland] as she bended over her sickle; the sweetest human voice I ever heard; her strains were tenderly melancholy, and felt delicious, long after they were heard no more."

[2] Romantic poets, such as Wordsworth, are known for their special interests in far-away lands and, therefore, their poems are very often dotted with exotic touches. Phrases like "no nightingale" and "Arabian sands" thus give us a flavor of Orientalism of Romantic poetry.

[3] The Hebrides, an island group off the western and northwestern coasts of Scotland, were originally inhabited by the Celts and were conquered by Scandinavians who ruled the islands until 1266. The Hebrides passed to the kingdom of Scotland in the sixteenth century after the actual control of the islands for some three hundred years by a series of Scottish chieftains.

[4] The Highland lass was singing in Erse, which is also known as Scotish Gaelic, a Goidelic language of Scotland. Wordsworth obviously did not understand the young reaper's language.

QUESTIONS FOR DISCUSSION

1. "To My Sister" in the *Lyrical Ballads* is supposed to be an early expression of Wordsworth's emphasis on the so-called "wise passiveness" in life, which marked his turning away from Neoclassical beliefs. Could you relate the details of the poem to the poet's favorite doctrine?

2. According to the poet, "Expostulation and Reply" arose out of his conversation with a friend, named in the poem Matthew, who was somewhat unreasonbly attached to modern books of moral philosophy. How would you respond as a modern reader to his friend's questioning if the challenge had fallen upon you?

3. The poet claims in the third poem of this unit that nature may teach people more of evil and good than all the sages do. Comment on his argument by relating the experiences of your own and, perhaps, of your friends.

4. Although the *Lyrical Ballads* was mainly known for such pieces like Coleridge's famous "The Rime of the Ancient Mariner" and Wordsworth's "Tintern Abbey" which winds up the volume, short poems such as the three mentioned above, as many commentators say, contribute a lot to the greatness of the volume. Do you agree with the judgment? If the answer is positive, how could you support yourself?

5. Wordsworth is a poet with an immense range of interests and one who is constantly challenging our habitual ways of seeing things, rather than a simple man who "wandered lonely as a cloud" and looked at "golden daffodils." Along this line of argument, do you think his "The Solitary Reaper" has the power to force us to look at the world afresh? If you think so, how would you argue for your belief?

SUGGESTED REFERENCES

Bloom, Harold, ed. *Bloom's Modern Critical Views: William Wordsworth.* Updated ed. New York: Infobase Publishing, 2007.

Dykstra, Scott. "Wordsworth's 'Solitaries' and the Problem of Literary Reference." *ELH* 63.4 (1996): 893-928.

Gaskell, Ronald. *Wordsworth's Poem of the Mind: An Essay on* ***The Prelude***. Edinburgh: Edinburgh UP, 1991.

Heaney, Seamus. "'Apt Admonishment': Wordsworth as an Example." *The Hudson Review* 61.1 (2008): 19-33.

Heffernan, James A. W. "Wordsworth's London: The Imperial Monster." *Studies in Romanticism* 37.3 (1998): 421-43.

Unit 9 Samuel Taylor Coleridge

(1772—1834)

A GUIDE TO LITERARY TERMINOLOGY

"Ballad": *Originated in Medieval Europe, ballad as a form of narrative folk song has been preserved as musical and literary forms up to our modern times. Both standard ballads, also known as folk ballads, and literary ballads written by known authors in conscious imitation of the old traditional ones, usually tell a compact tale in the form of stanzas, each of which, normally speaking, consists of four or six lines with four or three stresses on each line, rhyming a b a b. To prolong highly charged moments during the performance, a typical ballad features frequent repetitions of key words and lines, in forms of refrains or stock descriptive phrases. As ballads thrived in oral forms enriched gradually by the singers during their performances, each of the traditional ones would show a characteristic variation, an evidence of instantaneous narration coming freshly out of the memory of the singer at each performance.*

The narrative of ballads usually focuses on such themes as supernatural happenings, apocryphal legends, historical disasters, heroic exploits, tragedies of unfortunate lovers and so forth. The deeds of outlaws often graphically narrated are also one of the favorite themes of traditional ballads. Coleridge's "The Rime of the Ancient Mariner," perhaps the finest "literary" ballad in English literature, represents an eighteenth- and nineteenth-century vogue for traditional balladry stimulated perhaps by the publication in 1765 of Thomas Percy's ***Reliques of Ancient English Poetry****, a renowned collection of old ballads, sonnets, historical songs and metrical romances.*

NOTES ON THE AUTHOR

Samuel Taylor Coleridge was born in 1772 to the vicar of Ottery St. Mary, Devon and, as his father was learned, he lived in a world of books and ideas from a very young age. He started his school years in Christ's Hospital, a charity school in London, when his father passed away in 1782. As one of his friends recalled, his school days were not quite pleasant to him, but he read widely in classical as well as English authors. He did not attend Cambridge long because he was enlisted for an unknown reason in the military for a while. He was soon discharged and went back to the campus of Oxford. He became acquainted with

Robert Southey and the two, influenced by the American War of Independence and the French Revolution, worked on "Pantisocracy," a sort of communist society targeting on the sharing of power by all.

He got to know Wordsworth and developed a deep friendship with him in 1797. This event marked the beginning of frequent exchange of ideas between the two great Romantic writers and their communication of enthusiasm led up to the publication of their collaborated masterpiece, the *Lyrical Ballads*, in the following year in which his famous "The Rime of the Ancient Mariner," an admirable experiment in the ballad manner and a psychologically profound study of guilt, of remorse, and of the nature of evil, was included.

As he grew older, he was constantly troubled with unhappy marriage and ill-health in addition to his addiction to opium, only the public acceptance of his eminence as a thinker leaving him with some happiness. As he wrote profusely on various subjects during his later years, he has been known also to later generations as an outstanding provocative critic charged with the spirit of Romanticism. He died in 1834.

SYNOPSIS OF THE WORK

As the narrative goes, the ancient mariner detains forcibly a young man on his way to a wedding feast to listen to his chilling story concerning a storm that carried his ship to the seas of the Antarctic. Drawn towards the South Pole, the sailors were terrified to find that they were surrounded by ice over the high seas isolated utterly from the world of living things. The appearance of an albatross, at this point of time, made the crew overjoyed but the sea bird was shot presently by the ancient mariner with his cross-bow. A curse for his act of cruelty fell on the ship which, as it was in due course driven northward to the Equator, was suddenly becalmed in the torrid sea. The crew was once again terrified when they saw a skeleton-ship approaching them and all of the mariner's shipmates died, one after another, as a result of the grisly dice game that took place on the ship, only leaving the mariner hopelessly alive with his physical agony and consciousness of guilt. His realization of the sacredness of life in his terrible loneliness eventually released him from the intense agony he had been suffering. The spell thus broke and the ship was brought back to England. The ancient mariner, conscious of his evil-doing and the salvation of God, became for penance an eternal wanderer throughout the world and, by telling the horrifying story of his wanton shooting of the bird and the mysterious consequences of his deviant behavior, taught with his personal experience love for and reverence toward the creatures of God.

SELECTED READING

The Rime of the Ancient Mariner [1]

Part I

It is an ancient Mariner, — ancient: old; mariner: sailor
And he stoppeth one of three.
"By thy long grey beard and glittering eye, — thy: your
Now wherefore stopp'st thou me? — wherefore: why; thou: you

The Bridegroom's doors are opened wide,
And I am next of kin;
The guests are met, the feast is set
May'st hear the merry din." — din: noise

He holds him with his skinny hand,
"There was a ship," quoth he. — quoth: says
"Hold off! unhand me, grey-beard loon!" — loon: crazy man
Eftsoons his hand dropt he. — efsoons: at once

He holds him with his glittering eye —
The Wedding-Guest stood still, [2]
And listens like a three years' child:
The Mariner has his will.

The Wedding-Guest sat on a stone:

He cannot choose but hear;
And thus spake on that ancient man,
The bright-eyed Mariner. spake: spoke

"The ship was cheered, the harbour cleared,
Merrily did we drop
Below the kirk, below the hill, kirk: church
Below the lighthouse top.

The Sun came up upon the left,
Out of the sea came he! he: the sun
And he shone bright, and on the right
Went down into the sea.

Higher and higher every day,
Till over the mast at noon — " [3]
The Wedding-Guest here beat his breast,
For he heard the loud bassoon.

The bride hath paced into the hall,
Red as a rose is she;
Nodding their heads before her goes
The merry minstrelsy.

The Wedding-Guest he beat his breast,
Yet he cannot choose but hear;
And thus spake on that ancient man,
The bright-eyed Mariner.

"And now the *storm-blast* came, and he he: storm-blast
Was tyrannous and strong:

He struck with his o'ertaking wings,
And chased us south along.
With sloping masts and dipping prow, — prow: front of the ship
As who pursued with yell and blow
Still treads the shadow of his foe,
And forward bends his head,
The ship drove fast, loud roared the blast,
And southward aye we fled. — aye: still

And now there came both mist and snow,
And it grew wondrous cold:
And ice, mast-high, came floating by,
As green as emerald.

And through the drifts the snowy clifts
Did send a dismal sheen: — sheen: a soft shine
Nor shapes of men nor beasts we ken — — ken: know
The ice was all between.

The ice was here, the ice was there,
The ice was all around:
It cracked and growled, and roared and howled,
Like noises in a swound! — swound: swoon

At length did cross an Albatross, — albatross: a large seabird
Thorough the fog it came; — thorough: through
As if it had been a Christian soul,
We hailed it in God's name.

It ate the food it ne'er had eat, — eat: eaten
And round and round it flew.

The ice did split with a thunder-fit;
The helmsman steered us through!

And a good south wind sprung up behind;
The Albatross did follow,
And every day, for food or play,
Came to the mariners' hollo! hollo: hollow, emptiness

In mist or cloud, on mast or shroud, shroud: rope supporting the mast
It perched for vespers nine; vespers: church evening service
Whiles all the night, through fog-smoke white,
Glimmered the white Moon-shine."

"God save thee, ancient Mariner!
From the fiends, that plague thee thus!
Why look'st thou so?" — With my cross-bow
I shot the *albatross*. [4]

Part II

The Sun now rose upon the right: [5]
Out of the sea came he,
Still hid in mist, and on the left
Went down into the sea.

And the good south wind still blew behind,
But no sweet bird did follow,
Nor any day for food or play
Came to the mariners' hollo!

And I had done a hellish thing,
And it would work 'em woe:
For all averred, I had killed the bird
That made the breeze to blow.
Ah wretch! said they, the bird to slay,
That made the breeze to blow!

'em: other sailors

aver: declare

wretch: a disliked person

Nor dim nor red, like God's own head,
The glorious Sun uprist:
Then all averred, I had killed the bird
That brought the fog and mist.
'Twas right, said they, such birds to slay,
That bring the fog and mist. [6]

The fair breeze blew, the white foam flew,
The furrow followed free;
We were the first that ever burst
Into that silent sea.

Down dropt the breeze, the sails dropt down,
'Twas sad as sad could be;
And we did speak only to break
The silence of the sea!

All in a hot and copper sky,
The bloody Sun, at noon,
Right up above the mast did stand,
No bigger than the Moon.

copper: reddish brown

Day after day, day after day,
We stuck, nor breath nor motion;

As idle as a painted ship
Upon a painted ocean.

Water, water, every where,
And all the boards did shrink;
Water, water, every where,
Nor any drop to drink.

The very deep did rot: O Christ! deep: ocean
That ever this should be!
Yea, slimy things did crawl with legs
Upon the slimy sea.

About, about, in reel and rout
The death-fires danced at night; [7]
The water, like a witch's oils,
Burnt green, and blue and white.

And some in dreams assured were
Of the Spirit that plagued us so;
Nine fathom deep he had followed us
From the land of mist and snow.

And every tongue, through utter drought,
Was withered at the root;
We could not speak, no more than if
We had been choked with soot.

Ah! well a-day! what evil looks
Had I from old and young!
Instead of the cross, the Albatross

About my neck was hung.

Part III

There passed a weary time. Each throat
Was parched, and glazed each eye. parched: dried up
A weary time! a weary time!
How glazed each weary eye,
When looking westward, I beheld
A something in the sky.

At first it seemed a little speck,
And then it seemed a mist;
It moved and moved, and took at last
A certain shape, I wist. wist: knew

A speck, a mist, a shape, I wist!
And still it neared and neared:
As if it dodged a water-sprite, sprite: elf
It plunged and tacked and veered. veer: change directions suddenly

With throats unslaked, with black lips baked,
We could not laugh nor wail;
Through utter drought all dumb we stood!
I bit my arm, I sucked the blood,
And cried, A sail! a sail!

With throats unslaked, with black lips baked,
Agape they heard me call: agape: wide open
Gramercy! They for joy did grin, Gramercy: Thank God

And all at once their breath drew in,
As they were drinking all.

See! see! (I cried) she tacks no more!
Hither to work us weal; weal: good
Without a breeze, without a tide,
She steadies with upright keel!
The western wave was all a-flame.
The day was well nigh done! well nigh: almost
Almost upon the western wave
Rested the broad bright Sun;
When that strange shape drove suddenly
Betwixt us and the Sun. betwixt: between

And straight the Sun was flecked with bars,
(Heaven's Mother send us grace!)
As if through a dungeon-grate he peered
With broad and burning face.

Alas! (thought I, and my heart beat loud)
How fast she nears and nears!
Are those *her* sails that glance in the Sun,
Like restless gossamers? gossamer: fine thread of a spider

Are those *her* ribs through with the Sun
Did peer, as through a grate?
And is that Woman all her crew?
Is that a *death*? and are there two?
Is *death* that woman's mate?

Her lips were red, *her* looks were free,

Her locks were yellow as gold:
Her skin was as white as leprosy,
The Night-mare *life-in-death* was she,
Who thicks man's blood with cold.

The naked hulk alongside came,
And the twain were casting dice; twain: two
"The game is done! I've won! I've won!"
Quoth she, and whistles thrice.

The Sun's rim dips; the stars rush out:
At one stride comes the dark;
With far-heard whisper, o'er the sea,
Off shot the spectre-bark.

We listened and looked sideways up! sideways: towards
Fear at my heart, as at a cup,
My life-blood seemed to sip!
The stars were dim, and thick the night,
The steersman's face by his lamp gleamed white;
From the sails the dew did drip —
Till clomb above the eastern bar clomb: climbed
The horned Moon, with one bright star
Within the nether tip. [8] nether: lower

One after one, by the star-dogged Moon, one after one: one after another
Too quick for groan or sigh,
Each turned his face with a ghastly pang,
And cursed me with his eye.

Four times fifty living men,

(And I heard nor sigh nor groan)
With heavy thump, a lifeless lump,
They dropped down one by one.

dropped down: died

The souls did from their bodies fly, —
They fled to bliss or woe!
And every soul, it passed me by,
Like the whizz of my *cross-bow*!

Part IV

"I fear thee, ancient Mariner!
I fear thy skinny hand!
And thou art long, and lank, and brown,
As is the ribbed sea-sand.

I fear thee and thy glittering eye,
And thy skinny hand, so brown." —
Fear not, fear not, thou Wedding-Guest!
This body dropt not down.

Alone, alone, all, all alone,
Alone on a wide wide sea!
And never a saint took pity on
My soul in agony.

The many men, so beautiful!
And they all dead did lie:
And a thousand thousand slimy things
Lived on; and so did I.

I looked upon the rotting sea,
And drew my eyes away;
I looked upon the rotting deck,
And there the dead men lay.

I looked to Heaven, and tried to pray;
But or ever a prayer had gusht,
A wicked whisper came, and made
My heart as dry as dust.

I closed my lids, and kept them close,
And the balls like pulses beat;
For the sky and the sea, and the sea and the sky
Lady like a load on my weary eye,
And the dead were at my feet.

The cold sweat melted from their limbs,
Nor rot nor reek did they:
The look with which they looked on me
Had never passed away.

reek: give bad smell

An orphan's curse would drag to Hell
A spirit from on high;
But oh! more horrible than that
Is the curse in a dead man's eye!
Seven days, seven nights, I saw that curse,
And yet I could not die.

The moving Moon went up the sky,
And no where did abide:
Softly she was going up,

And a star or two beside —

Her beams bemocked the sultry main,
Like April hoar-frost spread;
But where the ship's huge shadow lay,
The charmed water burnt always
A still and awful red.

main: ocean

Beyond the shadow of the ship,
I watched the water-snakes:
They moved in tracks of shining white,
And when they reared, the elfish light
Fell off in hoary flakes.

Within the shadow of the ship
I watched their rich attire:
Blue, glossy green, and velvet black,
They coiled and swam; and every track
Was a flash of golden fire.

O happy living things! no tongue
Their beauty might declare:
A spring of love gushed from my heart,
And I blessed them unaware:
Sure my kind saint took pity on me,
And I blessed them unaware.

The self-same moment I could pray;
And from my neck so free
The Albatross fell off, and sank
Like lead into the sea.

the self-same: the very same

Part V

Oh sleep! it is a gentle thing,
Beloved from pole to pole!
To Mary Queen the praise be given!
She sent the gentle sleep from Heaven,
That slid into my soul.

The silly buckets on the deck,
That had so long remained,
I dreamt that they were filled with dew;
And when I awoke, it rained.

My lips were wet, my throat was cold,
My garments all were dank; — dank: damp and cold
Sure I had drunken in my dreams,
And still my body drank.

I moved, and could not feel my limbs:
I was so light — almost
I thought that I had died in sleep,
And was a blessed ghost.

And soon I heard a roaring wind:
It did not come anear; — anear: near
But with its sound it shook the sails,
That were so thin and sere. — sere: whithered

The upper air burst into life!
And a hundred fire-flags sheen, — sheen: shone
To and fro they were hurried about!

And to and fro, and in and out,
The wan stars danced between. wan: pale

And the coming wind did roar more loud,
And the sails did sigh like sedge;
And the rain poured down from one black cloud;
The Moon was at its edge.

The thick black cloud was cleft, and still
The Moon was at its side:
Like waters shot from some high crag,
The lightning fell with never a jag,
A river steep and wide.

The loud wind never reached the ship,
Yet now the ship moved on!
Beneath the lightning and the Moon
The dead men gave a groan.

They groaned, they stirred, they all uprose,
Nor spake, nor moved their eyes;
It had been strange, even in a dream,
To have seen those dead men rise.

The helmsman steered, the ship moved on;
Yet never a breeze up-blew;
The mariners all 'gan work the ropes,
Where they were wont to do;
They raised their limbs like lifeless tools —
We were a ghastly crew.

The body of my brother's son
Stood by me, knee to knee:
The body and I pulled at one rope,
But he said nought to me.

"I fear thee, ancient Mariner!"
Be calm, thou Wedding-Guest!
'Twas not those souls that fled in pain,
Which to their corses came again,
But a troop of spirits blest:

corses: corpses

blest: blessed

For when it dawned — they dropped their arms,
And clustered round the mast;
Sweet sounds rose slowly through their mouths,
And from their bodies passed.

Around, around, flew each sweet sound,
Then darted to the Sun;
Slowly the sounds came back again,
Now mixed, now one by one.

Sometimes a-dropping from the sky
I heard the sky-lark sing;
Sometimes all little birds that are,
How they seemed to fill the sea and air
With their sweet jargoning!

jargoning: chirping

And now 'twas like all instruments,
Now like a lonely flute;
And now it is an angel's song,
That makes the Heavens be mute.

It ceased; yet still the sails made on
A pleasant noise till noon,
A noise like of a hidden brook
In the leafy month of June,
That to the sleeping woods all night
Singeth a quiet tune.

Till noon we quietly sailed on,
Yet never a breeze did breathe:
Slowly and smoothly went the ship,
Moved onward from beneath.

Under the keel nine fathom deep,
From the land of mist and snow,
The spirit slid: and it was he
That made the ship to go.
The sails at noon left off their tune,
And the ship stood still also.

The Sun, right up above the mast,
Had fixed her to the ocean:
But in a minute she 'gan stir,
With a short uneasy motion —
Backwards and forwards half her length
With a short uneasy motion.

Then like a pawing horse let go,
She made a sudden bound:
It flung the blood into my head,
And I fell down in a swound. swound: swoon

How long in that same fit I lay,
I have not to declare;
But ere my living life returned,
I heard and in my soul discerned
Two voices in the air.

I...declare: I cannot say

"It is he?" quoth one, "Is this the man?
By him who died on cross,
With his cruel bow he laid full low
The harmless Albatross.

The spirit who bideth by himself
In the land of mist and snow,
He loved the bird that loved the man
Who shot him with his bow."

The other was a softer voice,
As soft as honey-dew:
Quoth he, "The man hath penance done,
And penance more will do."

Part VI

FIRST VOICE

"But tell me, tell me! speak again,
Thy soft response renewing —
What makes that ship drive on so fast?
What is the *ocean* doing?"

SECOND VOICE

"Still as a slave before his lord,
The *ocean* hath no blast;
His great bright eye most silently
Up to the Moon is cast —

If he may know which way to go;
For she guides him smooth or grim.
See, brother, see! how graciously
She looketh down on him."

FIRST VOICE

"But why drives on that ship so fast,
Without or wave or wind?"

SECOND VOICE

"The air is cut away before,
And closes from behind.

Fly, brother, fly! more high, more high!
Or we shall be belated:
For slow and slow that ship will go,
When the Mariner's trance is abated."

I woke, and we were sailing on
As in a gentle weather:
'Twas night, calm night, the moon was high;
The dead men stood together.

All stood together on the deck,
For a charnel-dungeon fitter: [9]
All fixed on me their stony eyes,
That in the Moon did glitter.

The pang, the curse, with which they died,
Had never passed away:
I could not draw my eyes from theirs,
Nor turn them up to pray.

And now this spell was snapt: once more
I viewed the ocean green,
And looked far forth, yet little saw
Of what had else been seen —

Like one, that on a lonesome road
Doth walk in fear and dread,
And having once turned round walks on,
And turns no more his head;
Because he knows, a frightful fiend
Doth close behind him tread.

But soon there breathed a wind on me,
Nor sound nor motion made:
Its path was not upon the sea,
In ripple or in shade.

It raised my hair, it fanned my cheek
Like a meadow-gale of spring —
It mingled strangely with my fears,
Yet it felt like a welcoming.

Swiftly, swiftly flew the ship,
Yet she sailed softly too:
Sweetly, sweetly blew the breeze —
On me alone it blew.

Oh! dream of joy! is this indeed
The light-house top I see?
Is this the hill? is this the kirk?
Is this mine own countree?

We drifted o'er the harbour-bar,
And I with sobs did pray —
O let me be awake, my God!
Or let me sleep always.

The harbour-bay was clear as glass,
So smoothly it was strewn!
And on the bay the moonlight lay,
And the shadow of the Moon.

The rock shone bright, the kirk no less,
That stands above the rock:
The moonlight steeped in silentness
The steady weathercock.

weathercock: weathervane

And the bay was white with silent light,
Till rising from the same,
Full many shapes, that shadows were,
In crimson colours came.

A little distance from the prow

Those crimson shadows were:
I turned my eyes upon the deck —
Oh, Christ! what saw I there!

Each corse lay flat, lifeless and flat,
And, by the holy rood!
A man all light, a seraph-man,
On every corse there stood.

rood: crucifix

seraph: angel associated with light

This seraph-band, each waved his hand:
It was a heavenly sight!
They stood as signals to the land,
Each one a lovely light;

This seraph-band, each waved his hand,
No voice did they impart —
No voice; but oh! the silence sank
Like music on my heart.

But soon I heard the dash of oars,
I heard the Pilot's cheer;
My head was turned perforce away
And I saw a boat appear.

perforce: necessarily

The Pilot and the Pilot's boy,
I heard them coming fast:
Dear Lord in Heaven! it was a joy
The dead men could not blast.

I was a third — I heard his voice:
It is the Hermit good!

He singeth loud his godly hymns
That he makes in the wood.
He'll shrieve my soul, he'll wash away
The Albatross's blood.

Part VII

This Hermit good lives in that wood
Which slopes down to the sea.
How loudly his sweet voice he rears!
He loves to talk with marineres
That come from a far countree.

He kneels at morn, and noon, and eve —
He hath a cushion plump:
It is the moss that wholly hides
The rotted old oak-stump.

The skiff-boat neared: I heard them talk, skiff-boat: light rowing boat
"Why, this is strange, I trow! trow: think
Where are those lights so many and fair,
That signal made but now?"

"Strange, by my faith!" the Hermit said —
"And they answered not our cheer!
The planks looked warped! and see those sails,
How thin they are and sere! sere: whithered
I never saw aught like to them,
Unless perchance it were perchance: by some chance

Brown skeletons of leaves that lag
My forest-brook along;
When the ivy-tod is heavy with snow,
And the owlet whoops to the wolf below,
That eats the she-wolf's young."

ivy-tod: ivy bush

owlet: young owl

"Dear Lord! it hath a fiendish look —
(The Pilot made reply)
I am a-feared" — "Push on, push on!"
Said the Hermit cheerily.

The boat came closer to the ship,
But I nor spake nor stirred;
The boat came close beneath the ship,
And straight a sound was heard.

Under the water it rumbled on,
Still louder and more dread:
It reached the ship, it split the bay;
The ship went down like lead.

Stunned by that loud and dreadful sound,
Which sky and ocean smote,
Like one that hath been seven days drowned
My body lay afloat;
But swift as deams, myself I found
Within the Pilot's boat.

smote: hit with hard blows

Upon the whirl, where sank the ship,
The boat spun round and round;
And all was still, save that the hill

Was telling of the sound.

I moved my lips — the Pilot shrieked
And fell down in a fit;
The holy Hermit raised his eyes,
And prayed where he did sit.

I took the oars: the Pilot's boy,
Who now doth crazy go,
Laughed loud and long, and all the while
His eyes went to and fro.
"Ha! Ha!" quoth he, "full plain I see,
The Devil knows how to row."

And now, all in my own countree,
I stood on the firm land!
The Hermit stepped forth from the boat,
And scarcely he could stand.

"O shrieve me, shrieve me, holy man!" shrieve: shrive
The Hermit crossed his brow. crossed: made a sign of cross
"Say quick," quoth he, "I bid thee say —
What manner of man art thou?" art thou: are you

Forthwith this fame of mine was wrenched
With a woful agony, woful: woeful
Which forced me to begin my tale;
And then it left me free.

Since then, at an uncertain hour,
That agony returns:

And till my ghastly tale is told,
This heart within me burns.

I pass like night, from land to land;
I have strange power of speech;
That moment that his face I see,
I know the man that must hear me:
To him my tale I teach.
What loud uproar bursts from the door!
The wedding-guests are there:
But in the garden-bower the bride
And bride-maids singing are:
And hark the little vesper bell,
Which biddeth me to prayer!

O Wedding-Guest! this soul hath been
Alone on a wide wide sea:
So lonely 'twas, that God himself
Scarce seemed there to be.

O sweeter than the marriage-feast,
'Tis sweeter far to me,
To walk together to the kirk
With a goodly company! —

kirk: church

To walk together to the kirk,
And all together pray,
While each to his great Father bends,
Old men, and babes, and loving friends
And youths and maidens gay!

Farewell, farewell! but this I tell
To thee, thous Wedding-Guest!
He prayeth well, who loveth well
Both man and bird and beast.

He prayeth best, who loveth best
All things both great and small;
For the dear God who loveth us,
He made and loveth all.
The Mariner, whose eye is bright,
Whose beard with age is hoar, — hoar: hoary
Is gone: and now the Wedding-Guest
Turned from the bridegroom's door.

He went like one that hath been stunned,
And is of sense forlorn:
A sadder and a wiser man,
He rose the morrow morn.

NOTES ON THE TEXT

[1] Wordsworth once told one of his friends, Rev. Alexander Dyce, in approximately 1834 that Coleridge and he planned to write poems for a monthly periodical intending to collect some money for an excursion they planned to make together. Coleridge's "Ancient Mariner," one of the poems of this project, was based on a strange dream a friend had told him, in which that friend fancied he saw a skeleton ship with figures in it. Wordsworth contributed to the poem the idea of shooting an albatross. As the poem was too long to be published in the magazine, they decided later to include it in their *Lyrical Ballads*.

[2] We are told here that the wedding guest was enchanted by the extraordinary expression of the old sailor and, as if under his spell, could hardly move but wait for the next of his mysterious tale.

[3] The detailed description of the movement of the sun shows that the ship had reached the equator.

[4] Responding to the questioning over the cause by the wedding guest of his grim look, the old

sailor told him bluntly he had shot the bird with neither explanation nor comment. The whole story sounds extremely mysterious since it started with an impulsive and unmotivated act.

[5] The ship had rounded Cape Horn, the southernmost point of South America, and headed north into the Pacific Ocean.

[6] The crew changed their opinion of the old sailor for the same reason they had had when they accused him of shooting the sea bird. There was no standard whatsoever of good or evil at work. They leaped to their reaction and became his accomplices in the crime without thinking about the heart of the matter.

[7] Saint Elmo, a fourth-century Italian martyr, was held as the patron saint especially by the Mediterranean sailors. The death-fires, also called death-lights, were electric discharges on the mast which were believed by the sailors to be omens of death. A spirit had followed the ship.

[8] One star covered up part of the moon so that it appeared like a horn, a phenomenon which was believed by the sailors that something evil was about to happen to them.

[9] Charnel-dungeon here refers to a vault, also called charnel house, in which bones or bodies of the dead were placed in the old days.

QUESTIONS FOR DISCUSSION

1. One of the commentators was impressed by the details Coleridge gave in the "Ancient Mariner" about the polar and the equatorial regions. Could you map approximately the route of the sail as has been described by the poet in the mysterious tale?

2. It is often said that Coleridge's tale of the old sailor discloses, among other things, the nature of evil. What do you think of this judgment? If you happen to agree with the opinion, could you support yourself with details from the poem?

3. The old sailor eventually made himself a self-conscious wanderer right after he was released from the awful punishment and the ship was brought back to England. Why do you think he did so?

4. In his autobiography *Biographia Literaria*, Coleridge recalled that his conversations with Wordsworth were often concerned about the power of poetry which excited the sympathy of the reader by a faithful adherence to the truth of nature. In what way do you think the theme of his "Ancient Mariner" fits into their belief?

5. Mrs. Barbauld, a poet and a contemporary of Coleridge, openly accused the "Ancient Mariner" of "having no moral" and Coleridge responded to her criticism by saying that the poem had but "too much" moral. Which side are you on if you are asked to take a side in the debate?

SUGGESTED REFERENCES

Barth, J. Robert. *Romanticism and Transcendence: Wordsworth, Coleridge, and the Religious Imagination.* Columbia: U of Missouri P, 2003.

Fogle, Richard H. *Romantic Poets and Prose Writers.* New York: Appleton-Meredith, 1967.

Jackson, J. R. *Poetry of the Romantic Period.* London: Routledge and Kegan Paul, 1980.

McCann, Jerome. *The Romantic Ideology: A Critical Investigation.* Chicago: Chicago UP, 1983.

Wu, Ducan, ed. *A Companion to Romanticism.* Malden: Blackwell Publishers, 1998.

Unit 10 Jane Austen

(1775—1817)

A GUIDE TO LITERARY TERMINOLOGY

"Novel": *Although the term "novellae" was first used in the sixteenth century to describe the short tales from works like Boccaccio's* ***Decameron****, novel as an independent literary genre found its development and popularity in the seventeenth-century England. The down-to-earth attitude of the long prose narratives, depicting the experiences of ordinary people, fit the taste of the rising middle class in the Protestant England and, with the constant explorations of various themes and styles, types of novels such as the Gothic, romantic, realist and historical soon came into the province of English literature.*

Ever since the time when novel became a means of literary expression, the genre has steadily developed in England and has long dominated the scene of literature. Such important authors as Daniel Defoe, Samuel Richardson, Henry Fielding, Jane Austen and Charles Dickens employed the form in their careers of writing and gained their worldwide fame with it. Some twentieth-century novelists like James Joyce, however, were not satisfied with the realm of their fictional exploration and tended to examine in their works the complex and fragmentary quality of human experience. Their effort as a result made novels a considerable departure from convention and, to some extent, their works seem to have gone beyond the comprehension of ordinary readership. Like epics in Western literature, novels of the twentieth-century England seem to have fallen into two distinctive categories, namely the popular novels and the "literary" ones. It is said that works like those by Graham Greene and many others tried to bridge the gap between the two.

NOTES ON THE AUTHOR

Jane Austen was the sixth child born in 1775 to George Austen, the rector of Steventon in Hampshire who, prosperous and cultivated, taught his daughter to read and write at her young age. Jane Austen seems to have started writing as a teenager and her first book, *Love and Friendship*, was completed when she was only fourteen years of age. Her life, like the provincial surroundings of her homeplace in the south, was quiet and eventless. She never married, but her personal charm and elegance make us believe that most probably there were love passages in her life even though no evidence seems to have substantially verified this. Her lively and affectionate family, however, provided her with a stimulating environment that enabled Jane Austen to produce her incisive and elegant novels. Her six completed works include *Sense and Sensibility*, *Mansfield Park, Emma*, *Northanger Abbey*, *Persuasion* and, of course, *Pride and Prejudice* whose early form was titled *First Impressions*. Although all her works were published anonymously, her authorship became known right after the publication of *Pride and Prejudice*. Jane Austen died in 1817 at Winchester and was buried in Winchester Cathedral, leaving her last manuscript *Sanditon* unfinished.

Jane Austen is known for her ingenious subtlety of observation. We can hardly fail to notice in any of her novels the deep penetration and heart-felt delicacy even though their focus is always restricted to a quiet and prosperous middle-class circle of life. Indeed, Jane Austen's fiction never deals with extremes of wealth and poverty, neither class conflicts of her times are touched upon. It is the seemingly monotonous provincial life as is depicted with her outstanding skill in humorous and charming characterization that gave the English novel its new depth and elegance and, as some commentators observed, brought the English novel to the stage of its maturity.

SYNOPSIS OF THE WORK

Charles Bingley moved into the neighborhood of the Bennets. Being wealthy and single, Bingley chose Jane among the five daughters of the Bennet family for courtship and they soon fell in love with each other. As the rumor went, Darcy, one of Bingley's friends, was responsible for the later separation of Bingley and Jane because he thought the relationship was improper.

Mr. Collins paid a visit to the Bennet family and, intending to choose a wife from the Bennet girls, proposed to Elizabeth. Being rejected, he turned his affections to Charlotte, a friend of Elizabeth's and they entered into marriage.

During Elizabeth's visit to Charlotte, she was frequently invited to the house of Lady Catherine de Bourgh who was Darcy's aunt. There Darcy met Elizabeth and was attracted to her. However, Elizabeth got to know soon that Darcy was the conspirator who destroyed her sister's happiness with Bingley. So, when Darcy proposed to her, she refused him for the reasons that shocked Darcy. To respond to the wrong accusations from Elizabeth, he wrote a letter to her explaining what had happened. His detailed explanations eventually changed Elizabeth's attitude towards him.

Months later, Elizabeth unexpectedly met Darcy at his estate and his exceptional politeness and warmth made Elizabeth believe that he was still in love with her. Her sister Lydia at this point elopped with Mr. Wickham and this event brought Elizabeth to grief for she suspected that Darcy would no longer like to keep in touch with her because of her sister's disgraceful conduct.

Lydia and Mr. Wickham were soon found and they got into marriage by a clergyman. Elizabeth was happy to hear that Darcy was responsible for finding the couple and for arranging the wedding at his own expense and, what is more, Bingley returned to Jane who happily accepted his proposal.

To verify the rumor that Elizabeth had been engaged with Darcy, Lady Catherine paid a visit to the Bennets and, as she tried to dissuade Elizabeth from any future attachments to Darcy, her suggestion was rejected by the young lady. She was so irritated that she stopped by at London in order to inform Darcy of Elizabeth's impoliteness which led Darcy to believe that he had hope to court Elizabeth over again. So he went to Elizabeth and made his proposal for the second time. His offer was accepted.

SELECTED READING

Pride and Prejudice

(Chapters I and II)

Chapter I

It is a truth universally acknowledged, that a single man in possession of a good fortune must be in want of a wife.

However little known the feelings or views of such a man may be on his first entering a neighbourhood, this truth is so well fixed in the minds of the surrounding families, that he is considered as the rightful property of some one or other of their daughters.

"My dear Mr. Bennet," said his lady to him one day, "have you heard that Netherfield Park[1] is let at last? "

Mr. Bennet replied that he had not.

"But it is," returned she; "for Mrs. Long has just been here, and she told me all about it."

Mr. Bennet made no answer.

"Do not you want to know who has taken it?" cried his wife impatiently.

"*You* want to tell me, and I have no objection to hearing it."

This was invitation enough.

"Why, my dear, you must know, Mrs. Long says that Netherfield is taken by a young man of large fortune from the north of England; that he came down on Monday in a chaise and four[2] to see the place, and was so much delighted with it, that he agreed with Mr. Morris[3] immediately; that he is to take possession before Michaelmas[4], and some of his servants are to be in the house by the end of next week."

"What is his name? "

"Bingley."

"Is he married or single? "

"Oh! Single, my dear, to be sure! A single man of large fortune; four or five thousand a year. What a fine thing for our girls!"

"How so? How can it affect them?"

"My dear Mr. Bennet," replied his wife, "how can you be so tiresome! You must know that I am thinking of his marrying one of them."

"Is that his design in settling here? "

"Design! Nonsense, how can you talk so! But it is very likely that he *may* fall in love with one of them, and therefore you must visit him as soon as he comes."

---

1 Netherfield Park: an estate in the neighborhood of the house of the Bennets.
2 a chaise and four: a carriage drawn by four horses for transportation.
3 Mr. Morris: an estate agent.
4 Michaelmas: A Christian feast which is observed on the 29th of September in honor of the archangel Michael.

"I see no occasion for that.[5] You and the girls may go, or you may send them by themselves, which perhaps will be still better, for as you are as handsome as any of them, Mr. Bingley might like you the best of the party."

"My dear, you flatter me. I certainly *have* had my share of beauty, but I do not pretend to be anything extraordinary now. When a woman has five grown-up daughters, she ought to give over thinking of her own beauty."

"In such cases, a woman has not often much beauty to think of."

"But, my dear, you must indeed go and see Mr. Bingley when he comes into the neighbourhood."

"It is more than I engage for,[6] I assure you."

"But consider your daughters. Only think what an establishment[7] it would be for one of them. Sir William and Lady Lucas are determined to go, merely on that account, for in general, you know, they visit no newcomers. Indeed you must go, for it will be impossible for *us* to visit him if you do not." [1]

"You are over-scrupulous, surely. I dare say Mr. Bingley will be very glad to see you; and I will send a few lines by you to assure him of my hearty consent to his marrying whichever he chooses of the girls: though I must throw in a good word for my little Lizzy[8]."

"I desire you will do no such thing. Lizzy is not a bit better than the others; and I am sure she is not half so handsome as Jane[9], nor half so good-humoured as Lydia[10]. But you are always giving *her* the preference."

"They have none of them much to recommend them," replied he, "they are all silly and ignorant, like other girls; but Lizzy has some-

5 I see no reason for that.
6 It is more than I can promise.
7 establishment: arrangement.
8 Lizzy: shortened form for Elizabeth, Mr. Bennet's second daughter.
9 Jane: Mr. Bennet's eldest daughter.
10 Lydia: Mr. Bennet's youngest daughter.

thing more of quickness than her sisters."

"Mr. Bennet, how can you abuse your own children in such a way! You take delight in vexing me. You have no compassion on my poor nerves."

"You mistake me, my dear. I have a high respect for your nerves. They are my old friends. I have heard you mention them with consideration these twenty years at least."

"Ah! You do not know what I suffer."

"But I hope you will get over it, and live to see many young men of four thousand a year come into the neighbourhood."

"It will be no use to us, if twenty such should come, since you will not visit them."

"Depend upon it, my dear, that when there are twenty, I will visit them all."

Mr. Bennet was so odd a mixture of quick parts[11], sarcastic humour, reserve, and caprice, that the experience of three-and-twenty years had been insufficient to make his wife understand his character. *Her* mind was less difficult to develop[12]. She was a woman of mean understanding, little information, and uncertain temper. When she was discontented, she fancied herself nervous. The business of her life was to get her daughters married; its solace was visiting and news.

Chapter II

Mr. Bennet was among the earliest of those who waited on[13] Mr. Bingley. He had always intended to visit him, though to the last always assuring his wife that he should not go; and till the evening after the visit was paid she had no knowledge of it. It was then disclosed

11 parts: talent, individual endowment or ability.

12 develop: come gradually to light; understand.

13 wait on: visit.

in the following manner: — Observing his second daughter employed in trimming a hat, he suddenly addressed her with,

"I hope Mr. Bingley will like it, Lizzy."

"We are not in a way to know *what* Mr. Bingley likes," said her mother resentfully, "since we are not to visit."

"But you forget, mamma," said Elizabeth, "that we shall meet him at the assemblies[14], and that Mrs. Long has promised to introduce him."

"I do not believe Mrs. Long will do any such thing. She has two nieces of her own. She is a selfish, hypocritical woman, and I have no opinion[15] of her."

"No more have I," said Mr. Bennet, "and I am glad to find that you do not depend on her serving you."

Mrs. Bennet deigned not to make any reply, but, unable to contain herself, began scolding one of her daughters.

"Don't keep coughing so, Kitty[16], for Heaven's sake! Have a little compassion on my nerves. You tear them to pieces."

"Kitty has no discretion in her coughs," said her father, "she times them ill."[17]

"I do not cough for my own amusement," replied Kitty fretfully. "When is your next ball to be, Lizzy?"

"To-morrow fortnight."[18]

"Aye, so it is," cried her mother, "and Mrs. Long does not come back till the day before; so it will be impossible for her to introduce him, for she will not know him herself."

"Then, my dear, you may have the advantage of your friend, and introduce Mr. Bingley to *her*."

---

14 the assemblies: the balls.
15 opinion: high opinion.
16 Kitty: shortened form for Catherine, Mr. Bennet's fourth daughter.
17 She coughs at a wrong time.
18 To-morrow fortnight: the day after fourteen days; the day after two weeks.

"Impossible, Mr. Bennet, impossible, when I am not acquainted with him myself; how can you be so teasing?"

"I honour your circumspection. A fortnight's acquaintance is certainly very little. One cannot know what a man really is by the end of a fortnight. But if *we* do not venture[19] somebody else will; and after all, Mrs. Long and her nieces must stand their chance; and, therefore, as she will think it an act of kindness, if you decline the office[20], I will take it on myself."

The girls stared at their father. Mrs. Bennet said only, "Nonsense, nonsense!"

"What can be the meaning of that emphatic exclamation?" cried he. "Do you consider the forms of introduction, and the stress that is laid on them, as nonsense? I cannot quite agree with you *there*. What say you, Mary[21]? For you are a young lady of deep reflection, I know, and read great books and make extracts."

Mary wished to say something very sensible, but knew not how.

"While Mary is adjusting her ideas," he continued, "let us return to Mr. Bingley."

"I am sick of Mr. Bingley," cried his wife.

"I am sorry to hear *that*; but why did not you tell me so before? If I had known as much[22] this morning I certainly would not have called on him. It is very unlucky; but as I have actually paid the visit, we cannot escape the acquaintance now."

The astonishment of the ladies was just what he wished; that of Mrs. Bennet perhaps surpassing the rest; though, when the first tumult of joy was over, she began to declare that it was what she had expected all the while.

"How good it was in you, my dear Mr. Bennet! But I knew I

---

19 But if we do not venture to introduce Mr. Bingley to her…

20 office: service; help.

21 Mary: Mr. Bennet's third daughter.

22 If I had known that you were sick of Mr. Bingley…

should persuade you at last. I was sure you loved your girls too well to neglect such an acquaintance. Well, how pleased I am! And it is such a good joke, too, that you should have gone this morning and never said a word about it till now."

"Now, Kitty, you may cough as much as you choose," said Mr. Bennet; and, as he spoke, he left the room, fatigued with the raptures of his wife.

"What an excellent father you have, girls!" said she, when the door was shut. "I do not know how you will ever make him amends for his kindness; or me either[23], for that matter. At our time of life it is not so pleasant, I can tell you, to be making new acquaintance every day; but for your sakes, we would do anything. Lydia, my love, though you *are* the youngest, I dare say Mr. Bingley will dance with you at the next ball."

"Oh!" said Lydia stoutly, "I am not afraid; for though I *am* the youngest, I'm the tallest."

The rest of the evening was spent in conjecturing how soon he would return Mr. Bennet's visit, and determining when they should ask him to dinner.

NOTES ON THE TEXT

[1] As the etiquette of the time required, the male head of a family was to pay the first visit to a newly-moved-in neighbor. It would have been a shocking breach of etiquette for a mother and her daughters to call first.

23 Or make me amends either.

QUESTIONS FOR DISCUSSION

1. As one argument goes, Darcy and Elizabeth are the crucial characters, he in his pride, she in her prejudice, and vice versa, and all about them are ranged a variety of characters who represent degrees and kinds of the same deficiencies of character and vision. Could you analyze along this line the characters you have read in the first two chapters?

2. Mr. and Mrs. Bennet and their daughters appear to be different in terms of their respective personalities. In what way does the author distinguish for us those interesting characters in the first two chapters of *Pride and Prejudice*?

3. It is generally held that the novel is a comic and complex study of self-importance and egotism as these are absorbed from a society whose morality and values are derived from the economics of class. Do you agree with the judgement? Support yourself with details from your reading.

4. Jane Austen as an eighteenth-century novelist is known for her gentle humor and mild satire. Could you cite any instances from the two chapters to show the feature of her humor or satire or, perhaps, a blend of the two?

5. Novels in general terms may fall into two different catagories: those interested in a precise definition of theme, dramatizing a special quality of their potential world of subject, and those interested in a complete account of the subject, dramatizing the quantity of their world of subject. Which category do you think *Pride and Prejudice* belongs to?

SUGGESTED REFERENCES

Bonaparte, Felicia. "Conjecturing Possibilities: Reading and Misreading Texts in Jane Austen's *Pride and Prejudice*." *Studies in the Novel* 37.2 (2005):141-61.

Greenfield, Susan. "The Absent-Minded Heroine: Or, Elizabeth Bennet Has a Thought." *Eighteenth-Century Studies* 39.3 (2006): 337-50.

Hirsch, Gordon. "Shame, Pride and Prejudice: Jane Austen's Psychological Sophistication." *Mosaic* 25.1 (1992): 63-78.

Stasio, Michael and Kathryn Duncan. "An Evolutionary Approach to Jane Austen: Prehistoric Preferences in *Pride and Prejudice*." *Studies in the Novel* 39.2 (2007): 133-46.

Wylie, Judith. "Dancing in Chains: Feminist Satire in *Pride and Prejudice*." *Persuations: The Jane Austen Journal* 22 (2000): 62-74.

Unit 11 Charles Dickens

(1812—1870)

A GUIDE TO LITERARY TERMINOLOGY

"Characterization": *We are now talking about the characterization in novels. As we all know, novels fall into two categories, namely those that emphasize incidents and those that focus on characters. The former group of novels shows interest in the dramatic unity of action and the climax of it while the latter is interested, by and large, in the incidents that may throw light upon the characters of the whole narrative. Charles Dickens, as a writer of the narratives of the second type,is well versed in the characterization through multiple incidents as is shown in all his novels but, perhaps,* ***A Tale of Two Cities****.*

As one critic observes, a character in a novel is a person who is taken by its reader as being endowed with particular moral, intellectual, and emotional qualities by inferences from what the person says and the way he says it, and from what he does. In 1927, E. M. Forster further differentiated in his own terms the flat characters from the round ones. A flat character, according to Forster, is presented without much individualizing details whereas a round character is a lot more complex in temperament and motivation and, more often than not, is presented with particularities in terms of his personality. A character of the latter type, therefore, is difficult to describe with any adequacy and, as in real life, often has the quality to surprise his readers.

NOTES ON THE AUTHOR

Charles Dickens, a great nineteenth-century novelist, completed in his life time fourteen major works of fiction, the first of which, entitled *Pickwick Papers*, was written between 1836 and 1837 and the last, *Our Mutual Friend*, completed between 1864 and 1865. As is well known, most of his novels were published in installment in monthly numbers. *David Copperfield*, a typical serialized work of this kind, had been done in 18 monthly parts appearing from May of 1849 to November of 1850, with some thirty pages in every monthly issue, each of which totaled around 20,000 words. The whole work ended with a long last number of 48 pages.

The plot of the novel is expectedly unsophisticated. Essentially autobiographical, the story of David Copperfield, told chronologically in the first person, is a somewhat veiled life story of the novelist himself and, of course, a successful mingling of facts with fiction. As the story proceeds with its first chapter headed "I Am Born" and its final one "A Last Retrospect," we see the growth of David from a rejected orphan to a renowned author. Dickens once commented that he liked this novel best among all his books. As the novel is an outstanding study of characters written with the novelist's heart's blood, it has always been considered, along with *Pickwick Papers*, the favorite of readers of all time.

SYNOPSIS OF THE WORK

The episode from Chapter XXIX of *David Copperfield* is an intense study of characters, typical of Dickens's best work. Of special interest here is the depiction of Rosa Dartle, Mrs. Steerforth's companion and a rather neurotic admirer of James Steerforth, even though he did not seem to know it for sure.

Rosa Dartle was a quick-tempered woman and was in love with James, a man who had good manners and a hidden selfish heart. Unwilling to speak outright, she kept seeking information about James from David, who had just arrived for a visit to the Steerforths, in a habitually indirect manner. Her conversation, indicating her innermost suspicion and resentment of all that were between her and James, hinted not only her affection for an obviously wrongly chosen man but also some kind of bitterness and hatred for people, even for James. And, of course, the conversation made everybody uncomfortable.

To start with, Miss Dartle kept questioning David concerning the possible secret activities of James during his long absence even though she knew no details at all. She then shrewdly hinted to Mrs. Steerforth that serious quarrels would occur between the mother and her beloved son spoiled by her over-indulgence. Finally, she made a scene as she burst into a fit of anger and left her company as a result obviously of her feelings for the man she loved but found it hard to trust. In return, she won James's rather scornful comment on her behind her back: "She brings everything to a grindstone and sharpens it, as she has sharpened her own face and figure these years past. …She is all edge."

SELECTED READINGS

David Copperfield

(An excerpt from Chapter XXIX)

...

Mrs. Steerforth was pleased to see me, and so was Rosa Dartle. I was agreeably surprised to find that Littimer was not there [1], and that we were attended by a modest little parlor maid[1], with blue ribbons in her cap, whose eye it was much more pleasant, and much less disconcerting, to catch by accident, than the eye of that respectable man. But what I particularly observed, before I had been half an hour in the house, was the close and attentive watch Miss Dartle kept upon me; and the lurking manner in which she seemed to compare my face with Steerforth's, and Steerforth's with mine, and to lie in wait for[2] something to come out between the two. So surely as I looked towards her, did I see that eager visage[3], with its gaunt black eyes and searching brow, intent on mine; or passing suddenly from mine to Steerforth's; or comprehending both of us at once. In this lynxlike scrutiny she was so far from faltering when she saw I observed it, that at such a time she only fixed her piercing look upon me with a more intent expression still. Blameless as I was, and knew that I was, in reference to any wrong she could possibly suspect me of, I shrunk before her strange eyes, quite unable to endure their hungry luster.

All day, she seemed to pervade the whole house. If I talked to Steerforth in his room, I heard her dress rustle in the little gallery[4] outside. When he and I engaged in some of our old exercises on the lawn behind the house, I saw her face pass from window to window,

---

1 parlor maid: a female servant who serves food at the dinner table.
2 lie in wait for...: hide and wait for a chance to attack.
3 visage: face.
4 gallery: a passage outside the room.

like a wandering light, until it fixed itself in one, and watched us. When we all four went out walking in the afternoon, she closed her thin hand on my arm like a spring, to keep me back, while Steerforth and his mother went on out of hearing; and then spoke to me.

"You have been a long time," she said, "without coming here. Is your profession really so engaging and interesting as to absorb your whole attention? I ask because I always want to be informed, when I am ignorant. Is it really, though?"

I replied that I liked it well enough, but that I certainly could not claim so much for it.

"Oh! I am glad to know that, because I always like to be put right when I am wrong," said Rosa Dartle. "You mean it is a little dry, perhaps?"

"Well," I replied; "perhaps it *was* a little dry."

"Oh! And that's a reason why you want relief and change — excitement, and all that?" said she. "Ah! Very true! But isn't it a little — Eh? — for him? I don't mean you."

A quick glance of her eye towards the spot where Steerforth was walking, with his mother leaning on his arm, showed me whom she meant; but beyond that, I was quite lost. And I looked so, I have no doubt.

"Don't it — I don't say that it *does*, mind I want to know — don't it rather engross him? Don't it make him, perhaps, a little more remiss[5] than usual in his visits to his blindly doting — eh?" With another quick glance at them, and such a glance at me as seemed to look into my innermost thoughts [2].

"Miss Dartle," I returned, "pray[6] do not think — "

"I don't!" she said. "Oh dear me, don't suppose that I think anything! I am not suspicious. I only ask a question. I don't state any

---

5 remiss: negligence.

6 pray: please.

opinion. I want to found an opinion[7] on what you tell me. Then, it's not so? Well! I am very glad to know it."

"It certainly is not the fact," said I, perplexed, "that I am accountable for Steerforth's having been away from home longer than usual — if he has been; which I really don't know at this moment, unless I understand it from you. I have not seen him this long while, until last night". [3]

"No?"

"Indeed, Miss Dartle, no!"

As she looked full at me, I saw her face grow sharper and paler, and the marks of the old wound lengthen out until it cut through the disfigured lip, and deep into the nether lip, and slanted down the face. There was something positively awful[8] to me in this, and in the brightness of her eyes, as she said, looking fixedly at me:

"What is he doing?"

I repeated the words, more to myself than her, being so amazed.

"What is he doing?" she said, with an eagerness that seemed enough to consume her like a fire. "In what is that man assisting him, who never looks at me without an inscrutable falsehood in his eyes?[4] If you are honorable and faithful, I don't ask you to betray your friend. I ask you only to tell me, is it anger, is it hatred, is it pride, is it restlessness, is it some wild fancy, is it love, *what is it*, what is leading him?"

"Miss Dartle," I returned, "How shall I tell you, so that you will believe me, that I know of nothing in Steerforth different from what there was when I first came here? I can think of nothing. I firmly believe there is nothing. I hardly understand even what you mean."

As she still stood looking fixedly at me, a twitching or throbbing, from which I could not dissociate the idea of pain, came into that cruel

---

7 found an opinion: to form an opinion.

8 positively: very.

mark; and lifted up the corner of her lip as if with scorn, or with a pity that despised its object. She put her hand upon it hurriedly — a hand so thin and delicate, that when I had seen her hold it up before the fire to shade her face, I had compared it in my thoughts to fine porcelain — and saying, in a quick, fierce, passionate way, "I swear you to secrecy about this!" said not a word more.

Mrs. Steerforth was particularly happy in her son's society[9], and Steerforth was, on this occasion, particularly attentive and respectful to her. It was very interesting to me to see them together, not only on account of their mutual affection, but because of the strong personal resemblance between them, and the manner in which what was haughty or impetuous in him was softened by age and sex, in her, to a gracious dignity. I thought, more than once, that it was well[10] no serious cause of division had ever come between them; or two such natures[11] — I ought rather to express it, two such shades of the same nature — might have been harder to reconcile than the two extremest opposites in creation. The idea did not originate in my own discernment, I am bound to confess, but in a speech of Rosa Dartle's.

She said at dinner:

"Oh, but do tell me, though, somebody because I have been thinking about it all day, and I want to know."

"You want to know what, Rosa?" returned Mrs. Steerforth. "Pray, pray, Rosa, do not be mysterious."

"Mysterious!" she cried. "Oh! really? Do you consider me so?"

"Do I constantly entreat you," said Mrs. Steerforth, "to speak plainly, in your own natural manner?"

"Oh! then this is *not* my natural manner?" she rejoined. "Now you must really bear with[12] me, because I ask for information. We

9 society: company.

10 well: reasonable; sensible.

11 natures: beings that live in the natural world.

12 bear with...: be patient with....

never know ourselves."

"It has become a second nature," said Mrs. Steerforth, without any displeasure; "but I remember, — and so must you, I think, — when your manner was different, Rosa; when it was not so guarded, and was more trustful."

"I am sure you are right," she returned; "and so it is that bad habits grow upon one! Really? Less guarded and more trustful? How *can* I, imperceptibly, have changed, I wonder! Well, that's very odd! I must study to regain my former self."

"I wish you would," said Mrs. Steerforth, with a smile.

"Oh! I really will, you know!" she answered. "I will learn frankness from — let me see — from James[13]."

"You cannot learn frankness, Rosa," said Mrs. Steerforth quickly — for there was always some effect of sarcasm in what Rosa Dartle said, though it was said, as this was, in the most unconscious manner in the world — "in a better school." [5]

"That I am sure of," she answered, with uncommon fervor. "If I am sure of anything, of course, you know, I am sure of that."

Mrs. Steerforth appeared to me to regret having been a little nettled; for she presently said, in a kind tone:

"Well, my dear Rosa, we have not heard what it is that you want to be satisfied about?"

"That I want to be satisfied about?" she replied, with provoking coldness. "Oh! It was only whether people, who are like each other in their moral constitution — is that the phrase?"

"It's as good a phrase as another," said Steerforth.

"Thank you: — whether people, who are like each other in their moral constitution, are in greater danger than people not so circumstanced, supposing any serious cause of variance to arise

13 James: Steerforth.

between them, of being divided angrily and deeply?"

"I should say yes," said Steerforth.

"Should you?" she retorted. "Dear me! Supposing then, for instance — any unlikely thing will do for a supposition — that you and your mother were to have a serious quarrel."

"My dear Rosa," interposed Mrs. Steerforth, laughing good-naturedly, "suggest some other supposition! James and I know our duty to each other better, I pray Heaven!"

"Oh!" said Miss Dartle, nodding her head thoughtfully. "To be sure. *That* would prevent it? Why, of course it would. Exactly. Now, I am glad I have been so foolish as to put the case, for it is so very good to know that your duty to each other would prevent it! Thank you very much."

One other little circumstance connected with Miss Dartle I must not omit; for I had reason to remember it thereafter, when all the irremediable past was rendered plain. During the whole of this day, but especially from this period of it, Steerforth exerted himself with his utmost skill, and that was with his utmost ease, to charm this creature into a pleasant and pleased companion. That he should succeed, was no matter of surprise to me. That she should struggle against the fascinating influence of his delightful art — delightful nature I thought it then — did not surprise me either; for I knew that she was sometimes jaundiced and perverse. I saw her features and her manner slowly change; I saw her look at him with growing admiration; I saw her try, more and more faintly, but always angrily, as if she condemned a weakness in herself, to resist the captivating power that he possessed; and finally, I saw her sharp glance soften, and her smile become quite gentle, and I ceased to be afraid of her as I had really been all day, and we all sat about the fire, talking and laughing together, with as little reserve as if we had been children.

Whether it was because we had sat there so long, or because Steerforth was resolved not to lose the advantage he had gained, I do not know; but we did not remain in the dining room more than five minutes after her departure. "She is playing her harp," said Steerforth softly at the drawing-room door, "and nobody but my mother has heard her do that, I believe, these three years." He said it with a curious smile, which was gone directly; and we went into the room and found her alone.

"Don't get up," said Steerforth (which she had already done); "my dear Rosa, don't! Be kind for once, and sing us an Irish song."

"What do you care for an Irish song?" she returned.

"Much!" said Steerforth. "Much more than for any other. Here is Daisy, too, loves music from his soul. Sing us an Irish song, Rosa! And let me sit and listen as I used to do."

He did not touch her, or the chair from which she had risen, but sat himself near the harp. She stood beside it for some little while, in a curious way, going through the motion of playing it with her right hand, but not sounding it. At length she sat down, and drew it to her with one sudden action, and played and sang.

I don't know what it was, in her touch or voice, that made that song the most unearthly[14] I have ever heard in my life, or can imagine. There was something fearful in the reality of it. It was as if it had never been written, or set to music, but sprung out of the passion within her, which found imperfect utterance in the low sounds of her voice, and crouched again when all was still. I was dumb[15] when she leaned beside the harp again, playing it, but not sounding it, with her right hand.

A minute more, and this had roused me from my trance: — Steerforth had left his seat, and gone to her, and had put his arm

---

14 unearthly: strange.

15 dumb: unable to speak.

laughingly about her, and had said, "Come, Rosa, for the future we will love each other very much!" And she had struck him, and had thrown him off with the fury of a wild cat, and had burst out of the room.

"What is the matter with Rosa?" said Mrs. Steerforth, coming in.

"She has been an angel, mother," returned Steerforth, "for a little while; and has run into the opposite extreme, since, by way of compensation."

"You should be careful not to irritate her, James. Her temper has been soured, remember, and ought not to be tried."

Rosa did not come back; and no other mention was made of her, until I went with Steerforth into his room to say good night. Then he laughed about her, and asked me if I had ever seen such a fierce little piece of incomprehensibility.

I expressed as much of my astonishment as was then capable of expression, and asked if he could guess what it was that she had taken so much amiss, so suddenly.

"Oh, Heaven knows," said Steerforth. "Anything you like — or nothing! I told you she took everything, herself included, to a grindstone, and sharpened it. She is an edge tool[16], and required great care in dealing with. She is always dangerous. Good night!"

"Good night!" said I, "my dear Steerforth! I shall be gone before you wake in the morning. Good night!"

He was unwilling to let me go; and stood, holding me out with a hand on each of my shoulders, as he had done in my own room.

...

16 edge tool: a tool with a cutting edge.

NOTES ON THE TEXT

[1] Littimer was Steerforth's manservant who was very close to him. David did not like him because of his involvement in Steerforth's seduction of Em'ly and because of his haughty manners. He was eventually trapped and was put behind bars. Note the tone of David here.

[2] Miss Dartle suspected that James had been fooling around or even had an affair with some woman even though she was not at all sure of the matter.

[3] David had been an admirer of James ever since his school days. His surface polish and good manners deceived everyone who did not know him well, including David. Notice, David here tried to explain to Miss Dartle that he did not know what was going on and, what is more, he seemed to say that what was in Miss Dartle's mind could not have happened.

[4] Rosa Dartle, quick-tempered and in love, felt suspicious of James as well as manservant Littimer even though she did not speak out her suspicion directly. She was at this point trying to get something out of David.

[5] Mrs. Steerforth, a highly possessive woman, loved her son so much that she could hardly accept any comment or feeling unfavorable to James who was obviously spoiled by the over-indulgence and smothering affection of this kind.

QUESTIONS FOR DISCUSSION

1. Dickens' concern with social vulgarity coexisting with his basic optimism for the Victorian era is said to have appeared in its purest form in the semi-autobiographical *David Copperfield*. Do you agree? If yes, support yourself.

2. Dickens turned to be more and more critical about the inhuman aspect of the Victorian industrial society and, more often than not, his comic spirit became very satirical after *David Copperfield*. Could you detect anything from the episode of the same tone?

3. The author is known for his skill of characterization. David Copperfield is of course one of the important works of this type. Are you impressed by any of the characters in the passage? Tell you classmates why you are.

4. As Rosa Dartle had secret affection for James, she expressed her feelings in a very special way. Could you describe your understanding of the details in her speech?

SUGGESTED REFERENCES

Chesterton, Gilbert Keith. *Charles Dickens*. New York: Schochen Books, 1965.

Ley, J. W. T. *The Dickens Circle*. London: Chapman and Hall, 1919.

Pearson, Hesketh. *Dickens: His Character, Comedy, and Career*. New York: Harper and Brothers, 1949.

Van Ghent, Dorothy. *The English Novel: Form and Function*. New York: Holt, Rinehart and Winston, 1953.

Unit 12 Emily Brontë

(1818—1848)

A GUIDE TO LITERARY TERMINOLOGY

"Satanic Hero": *The rapt attention to the inner nature of human experiences is one of the notable features of thoughts during the Romantic period. Such constant exploration of the inwardness enabled the poets and novelists to discover the core of darkness and violence in every man and their understanding of its universality geared their minds, in the late eighteenth and the early nineteenth century, to the direction of creating a new type of fictional character, the so-called Satanic hero, which is an outstanding figure of strength and creativity and, at the same time, a marvelous creature of black thoughts and of rebellious passion.*

Along this line, the early nineteenth-century literary criticism began to re-evaluate the theme of such classics as Milton's ***Paradise Lost****. As compared with traditional biblical account, Satan was generally understood during this period of time as the dominating figure in Milton's work in spite of his hideous intention and more and more taken as a true hero owing to the justifiable causes that led him to plotting the fall of man. "The reason Milton wrote in fetters when he wrote of Angels and God, and at liberty when of Devils and Hell," as William Blake, one of the earliest Romantics, observed, "is because he was a true Poet and of the Devil's party without knowing it." Shelley agreed with him by saying that Milton's Devil as a moral being was far superior to his God.*

As a novelist and a thinker of the same period, Emily Brontë made her Heathcliff an embodiment of the force of evil in human conflicts and, because principal human conflicts were those between individuals and the dark universe, Heathcliff, ferocious as he was, looked like the negative of a photograph. Everything that should be dark concerning Heathcliff was light and everything that should be light turned out to be dark, as one commentator noted. In the end, we feel sympathetic to Heathcliff even though he devastates us with his cruelty and ruthlessness.

NOTES ON THE AUTHOR

In her *Biographical Notice*, Charlotte Brontë wrote: "I have never seen her parallel in anything. Stronger than a man, simpler than a child, her nature stood alone." She was talking about her beloved and talented sister, Emily Brontë, who had died of illness in 1848 like her two other sisters of the seven in the Brontë family.

Emily Brontë was born in Thornton, Yorkshire in 1820 as the sixth child to the family of a poor country clergyman of Irish origin. Her mother died when she was young. Four of the sisters were sent to a charity school, two of whom died owing, as it is said, to the maltreatment they received in it. Emily began to write with her sisters soon after they left the charity school and their father unknowingly gave them a chance to show their talent for writing in 1826 as he returned from a trip to Leeds with some toys, among which was a set of wooden soldiers. His children, inspired by the toys, created with their extraordinary imaginations two rival kingdoms, Angria and Gondal. Charlotte and Branwell became the historians of Angria while Emily and Anne started composing a complex history of Gondal. It was for the history that Emily proved herself well versed in poetry writing.

The year 1845 was another important point of time for the Brontë sisters, for they got together once more in that year and, during the gathering, the sisters discovered that they had been writing constantly in private. It took them some time of discouragement while writing poetry to turn their minds to the writing of fiction. Charlotte published her *Jane Eyre* in 1847, which was almost immediately followed by the publications of Emily's *Wuthering Heights* and Anne's *Agnes Grey.* And they all got their works properly signed with their own names when Charlotte managed to clarify the mystery of authorship in 1850 as the second edition of *Wuthering Heights* got out of press, posthumously because Emily Brontë, a quiet poet and an outstanding novelist, had passed away some two years before.

SYNOPSIS OF THE WORK

Narrated by Mr. Lockwood, a new tenant at Thrushcross Grange, a house set in a well-landscaped park in the valley, the story begins with Mr. Earnshaw who brought an orphan from the slums of Liverpool to his old and bleak house, called Wuthering Heights because it was located on the moor and was constantly buffeted by wild winds. He named the child after his dead son Heathcliff. Fierce resentment of his own son Hindley made Heathcliff's early life degrading and miserable. Even though his daughter Catherine treated Heathcliff well and developed passionate love for him, Heathcliff hated the Earnshaw family and

Catherine's decision to marry Edgar Linton from the civilized Grange in the valley made him in despair and run away in hatred.

Three years later, Heathcliff returned to the house, with wealth and determination to destroy both Earnshaw and Linton families. His passion for Catherine and unwelcome visits to her only drove Catherine to death when she was giving birth to a daughter. He then seduced Edgar's sister Isabella and forced her into marriage with him. He maltreated both his wife and Hareton, the son of Hindley, in order to take his revenge for the wrongs their families were supposed to be responsible for and later he lured with his influence young Cathy, the daughter of Linton and Catherine, and forced another unhappy marriage between her and his own sickly and repulsive son who died soon. After his son's death, Cathy fell in love with Hareton and they eventually got married happily when hatred-ridden Heathcliff was dying.

The story ends with a sad tale told by a young shepherd who claimed that he had seen the ghosts of the dead Heathcliff and Catherine walking together on the moor.

The following selection, Chapter XV of the novel, describes the pathetic scene of the final meeting between Heathcliff and Catherine just before the latter's death.

SELECTED READINGS

Wuthering Heights

(Chapter XV)

Another week over, and I [1] am so many days nearer health, and spring! I have now heard all my neighbour's[1] history, at different sittings[2], as the housekeeper[3] could spare time from more important occupations. I'll continue it in her own words, only a little condensed. She is, on the whole, a very fair narrator, and I don't think I could improve her style.

1 The neighbor here refers to Mr. Heathcliff.

2 at different sittings: during their different conversations.

3 the housekeeper: Nelly Dean, Catherine's servant.

In the evening, she said — the evening of my visit to the Heights[4] — I knew, as well as if I saw him, that Mr. Heathcliff was about the place; [2] and I shunned going out, because I still carried his letter[5] in my pocket, and didn't want to be threatened or teased any more. I had made up my mind not to give it till my master went somewhere, as I could not guess how its receipt would affect Catherine. The consequence was that it did not reach her before the lapse of three days. The fourth was Sunday, and I brought it into her room after the family were gone to church. There was a man-servant left to keep the house with me, and we generally made a practice of locking the doors during the hours of service[6]; but on that occasion the weather was so warm and pleasant that I set them wide open, and, to fulfil my engagement[7], as I knew who would be coming, I told my companion that the mistress wished very much for some oranges, and he must run over to the village and get a few, to be paid for on the morrow. He departed, and I went upstairs.

Mrs. Linton sat in a loose, white dress, with a light shawl over her shoulders, in the recess of the open window, as usual. Her thick, long hair had been partly removed[8] at the beginning of her illness, and now she wore it simply combed in its natural tresses over her temples and neck. Her appearance was altered, as I had told Heathcliff; but when she was calm, there seemed unearthly beauty in the change. The flash of her eyes had been succeeded by a dreamy and melancholy softness; they no longer gave the impression of looking at the objects around her; they appeared always to gaze beyond, and far beyond — you would have said out of this world. Then the paleness of her face — its haggard aspect having vanished as she recovered flesh — and the

---

4 The author here refers to the visit to Wuthering Heights a week before.

5 his letter: the letter Heathcliff had asked Nelly to deliver to her mistress.

6 service: Church service.

7 engagement: Nelly had engaged to carry Heathcliff's letter to Catherine and to arrange a meeting between them.

8 removed: cut off.

peculiar expression arising from her mental state, though painfully suggestive of their causes, added to the touching interest which she awakened,[9] and — invariable to me, I know, and to any person who saw her, I should think — refuted more tangible proofs of convalescence, and stamped her as one doomed to decay.

A book lay spread on the sill before her, and the scarcely perceptible wind fluttered its leaves at intervals. I believe Linton had laid it there, for she never endeavoured to divert herself with reading, or occupation of any kind, and he would spend many an hour in trying to entice her attention to some subject which had formerly been her amusement. She was conscious of his aim, and in her better moods endured his efforts placidly, only showing their uselessness by now and then suppressing a wearied sigh, and checking him at last with the saddest of smiles and kisses. At other times, she would turn petulantly away, and hide her face in her hands, or even push him off angrily; and then he took care to let her alone, for he was certain of doing no good.

Gimmerton chapel[10] bells were still ringing, and the full, mellow flow of the beck in the valley came soothingly on the ear. It was a sweet substitute for the yet absent murmur of the summer foliage, which drowned that music about the Grange when the trees were in leaf. At Wuthering Heights it always sounded on quiet days following a great thaw or a season of steady rain. And of Wuthering Heights Catherine was thinking as she listened — that is, if she thought or listened at all; but she had the vague, distant look I mentioned before, which expressed no recognition of material things either by ear or eye.

"There's a letter for you, Mrs. Linton," I said, gently inserting it in one hand that rested on her knee. "You must read it immediately, because it wants an answer. Shall I break the seal?" "Yes," she an-

9 It made her all the more touching.

10 Gimmerton chapel: the chapel in the neighborhood of Thrushcross Grange.

swered, without altering the direction of her eyes. I opened it; it was very short. "Now," I continued, "read it." She drew away her hand, and let it fall. I replaced it in her lap, and stood waiting till it should please her to glance down; but that movement was so long delayed that at last I resumed, —

"Must I read it, ma'am? It is from Mr. Heathcliff."

There was a start and a troubled gleam of recollection, and a struggle to arrange her ideas. She lifted the letter, and seemed to peruse it, and when she came to the signature she sighed; yet still I found she had not gathered its import, for, upon my desiring to hear her reply, she merely pointed to the name, and gazed at me with mournful and questioning eagerness.

"Well, he wishes to see you," said I, guessing her need of an interpreter. "He's in the garden by this time, and impatient to know what answer I shall bring."

As I spoke I observed a large dog lying on the sunny grass beneath raise its ears as if about to bark, and then, smoothing them back, announce, by a wag of the tail, that some one approached whom it did not consider a stranger. Mrs. Linton bent forward and listened breathlessly. The minute after a step traversed the hall. The open house was too tempting for Heathcliff to resist walking in. Most likely he supposed that I was inclined to shirk my promise, and so resolved to trust to his own audacity. With straining eagerness Catherine gazed towards the entrance of her chamber. He did not hit the right room directly. She motioned me to admit him, but he found it out ere I could reach the door, and in a stride or two was at her side, and had her grasped in his arms.

He neither spoke nor loosed his hold for some five minutes, during which period he bestowed more kisses than ever he gave in his life before, I dare say; but then my mistress had kissed him first, and I plainly saw that he could hardly bear, for downright agony, to look into her face. The same conviction had stricken him as me, from the instant he beheld her, that there was no prospect of ultimate recovery there; she was fated, sure to die.

"Oh Cathy! Oh my life! How can I bear it?" was the first sentence he uttered, in a tone that did not seek to disguise his despair. And now he stared at her so earnestly that I thought the very intensity of his gaze would bring tears into his eyes; but they burned with anguish — they did not melt.

"What now?" said Catherine, leaning back and returning his look with a suddenly clouded brow. Her humour was a mere vane for constantly varying caprices. "You and Edgar have broken my heart, Heathcliff! And you both come to bewail the deed to me, as if *you* were the people to be pitied! I shall not pity you, not I. You have killed me — and thriven on it, I think. How strong you are! How many years do you mean to live after I am gone?"

Heathcliff had knelt on one knee to embrace her. He attempted to rise, but she seized his hair and kept him down.

"I wish I could hold you," she continued bitterly, "till we were both dead! I shouldn't care what you suffered. I care nothing for your sufferings. Why shouldn't *you* suffer? I do! Will you forget me? Will you be happy when I am in the earth? Will you say twenty years hence, 'That's the grave of Catherine Earnshaw. I loved her long ago, and was wretched to lose her; but it is past. I've loved many others since. My children are dearer to me than she was, and at death, I shall not rejoice that I am going to her; I shall be sorry that I must leave them!' Will you say so, Heathcliff?"

"Don't torture me till I'm as mad as yourself," cried he, wrenching his head free, and grinding his teeth.

The two, to a cool spectator, made a strange and fearful picture. Well might Catherine deem that heaven would be a land of exile to her, unless with her mortal body she cast away her mortal character also. Her present countenance had a wild vindictiveness in its white cheek, and a bloodless lip and scintillating eye; and she retained in her closed fingers a portion of the locks she had been grasping. As to her companion, while raising himself with one hand, he had taken her arm with the other, and so inadequate was his stock of gentleness to the requirements of her condition that on his letting go I saw four distinct impressions left blue in the colourless skin.

"Are you possessed with a devil," he pursued savagely, "to talk in that manner to me when you are dying? Do you reflect that all those words will be branded in my memory, and eating deeper eternally after you have left me? You know you lie to say I have killed you; and, Catherine, you know that I could as soon forget you as my existence![11] Is it not sufficient for your infernal selfishness that, while you are at peace, I shall writhe in the torments of hell?"

"I shall not be at peace," moaned Catherine, recalled to a sense of physical weakness by the violent, unequal throbbing of her heart, which beat visibly and audibly under this excess of agitation. She said nothing further till the paroxysm was over, then she continued more kindly, —

"I'm not wishing you greater torment than I have, Heathcliff. I only wish us never to be parted; and should a word of mine distress you hereafter, think I feel the same distress underground, and for my own sake, forgive me! Come here and kneel down again! You never harmed me in your life. Nay, if you nurse anger, that will be worse to remember than my harsh words. Won't you come here again? Do!"

Heathcliff went to the back of her chair, and leant over, but not so far as to let her see his face, which was livid with emotion. She bent round to look at him. He would not permit it. Turning abruptly, he walked to the fire-place, where he stood, silent, with his back towards us. Mrs. Linton's glance followed him suspiciously. Every movement

11 I forget you just as easily as I forget myself.

woke a new sentiment in her. After a pause and a prolonged gaze, she resumed, addressing me in accents of indignant disappointment, —

"Oh, you see, Nelly, he would not relent a moment to keep me out of the grave. *That* is how I'm loved! Well, never mind. That is not *my* Heathcliff. I shall love mine yet, and take him with me; he's in my soul. And," added she, musingly, "the thing that irks me most is this shattered prison[12], after all. I'm tired of being enclosed here. I'm wearying to escape into that glorious world[13], and to be always there — not seeing it dimly through tears, and yearning for it through the walls of an aching heart, but really with it and in it. Nelly, you think you are better and more fortunate than I, in full health and strength. You are sorry for me. Very soon that will be altered. I shall be sorry for *you*. I shall be incomparably beyond and above you all. I *wonder* he won't be near me!" She went on to herself. "I thought he wished it.[14] Heathcliff dear, you should not be sullen now. Do come to me, Heathcliff."

In her eagerness she rose and supported herself on the arm of the chair. At that earnest appeal he turned to her, looking absolutely desperate. His eyes, wide and wet, at last flashed fiercely on her; his breast heaved convulsively. An instant they held asunder,[15] and then how they met I hardly saw, but Catherine made a spring, and he caught her, and they were locked in an embrace from which I thought my mistress would never be released alive — in fact, to my eyes, she seemed directly insensible. He flung himself into the nearest seat, and on my approaching hurriedly to ascertain if she had fainted, he gnashed at me, and foamed like a mad dog, and gathered her to him with greedy jealousy. I did not feel as if I were in the company of a creature of my own species. It appeared that he would not understand,

12 this shattered prison: She took the world as a prison.
13 that glorious world: the next world.
14 I thought he would not like to be near me.
15 They kept themselves away from each other.

though I spoke to him, so I stood off, and held my tongue, in great perplexity.

A movement of Catherine's relieved me a little presently. She put up her hand to clasp his neck, and bring her cheek to his as he held her; while he, in return, covering her with frantic caresses, said wildly, —

"You teach me how cruel you've been — cruel and false. *Why* did you despise me? *Why* did you betray your own heart, Cathy? I have not one word of comfort. You deserve this. You have killed yourself.[16] Yes, you may kiss me, and cry, and wring out my kisses and tears; they'll blight you — they'll damn you. You loved me; then what *right* had you to leave me? What right — answer me — for the poor fancy you felt for Linton? Because misery, and degradation, and death, and nothing that God or Satan could inflict would have parted us, *you*, of your own will, did it. I have not broken your heart — *you* have broken it; and in breaking it you have broken mine. So much the worse for me, that I am strong. Do I want to live? What kind of living will it be when you — Oh God! Would *you* like to live with your soul in the grave?"

"Let me alone! Let me alone!" sobbed Catherine. "If I've done wrong, I'm dying for it. It is enough! You left me too; but I won't upbraid you. I forgive you. Forgive me."

"It is hard to forgive, and to look at those eyes, and feel those wasted hands," he answered. "Kiss me again, and don't let me see your eyes. I forgive what you have done to me. I love *my* murderer — but *yours*! How can I?"

They were silent — their faces hid against each other, and washed by each other's tears. At least, I suppose the weeping was on both sides, as it seemed Heathcliff *could* weep on a great occasion like this.

I grew very uncomfortable, meanwhile, for the afternoon wore

16 Heathcliff is referring to Catherine's unhappy marriage with Edgar Linton.

fast away, the man whom I had sent off returned from his errand, and I could distinguish by the shine of the westering sun up the valley, a concourse thickening outside Gimmerton chapel porch.

"Service is over," I announced. "My master will be here in half an hour."

Heathcliff groaned a curse, and strained Catherine closer. She never moved.

Ere long I perceived a group of the servants passing up the road towards the kitchen wing. Mr. Linton was not far behind. He opened the gate himself, and sauntered slowly up, probably enjoying the lovely afternoon that breathed as soft as summer.

"Now he is here," I exclaimed. "For Heaven's sake, hurry down! You'll not meet any one on the front stairs. Do be quick, and stay among the trees till he is fairly in."

"I must go, Cathy," said Heathcliff, seeking to extricate himself from his companion's arms. "But if I live, I'll see you again before you are asleep. I won't stray five yards from your window."

"You must not go!" she answered, holding him as firmly as her strength allowed. "You shall not, I tell you."

"For one hour," he pleaded earnestly.

"Not for one minute," she replied.

"I *must* — Linton will be up immediately," persisted the alarmed intruder.

He would have risen, and unfixed her fingers by the act; she clung fast, gasping. There was mad resolution in her face.

"No!" she shrieked. "Oh, don't, don't go. It is the last time! Edgar will not hurt us. Heathcliff, I shall die! I shall die!"

"Damn the fool! There he is," cried Heathcliff, sinking back into his seat. "Hush, my darling! Hush, hush, Catherine! I'll stay. If he shot me so, I'd expire with a blessing on my lips."

And there they were fast again.[17] I heard my master mounting the stairs. The cold sweat ran from my forehead; I was horrified.

"Are you going to listen to her ravings?" I said, passionately. "She does not know what she says. Will you ruin her, because she has not wit to help herself? Get up! You could be free instantly. That is the most diabolical deed that ever you did. We are all done for[18], master, mistress, and servant."

I wrung my hands and cried out, and Mr. Linton hastened his step at the noise. In the midst of my agitation I was sincerely glad to observe that Catherine's arms had fallen relaxed, and her head hung down.

"She's fainted or dead," I thought; "so much the better. Far better that she should be dead, than lingering a burden and a misery-maker to all about her."

Edgar sprang to his unbidden guest, blanched with astonishment and rage. What he meant to do, I cannot tell. However, the other stopped all demonstrations, at once, by placing the lifeless-looking form in his arms.

"Look there!" he said. "Unless you be a fiend, help her first; then you shall speak to me!"

He walked into the parlour, and sat down. Mr. Linton summoned me, and with great difficulty, and after resorting to many means, we managed to restore her to sensation; but she was all bewildered. She sighed, and moaned, and knew nobody. Edgar, in his anxiety for her, forgot her hated friend. I did not. I went, at the earliest opportunity, and besought him to depart, affirming that Catherine was better, and he should hear from me in the morning how she passed the night.

"I shall not refuse to go out of doors," he answered, "but I shall stay in the garden; and, Nelly, mind you keep your word tomorrow. I

---

17 They held each other fast in arms again.

18 done for: ruined.

shall be under those larch trees. Mind! or I pay another visit, whether Linton be in or not."

He sent a rapid glance through the half-open door of the chamber, and, ascertaining that what I stated was apparently true, delivered the house of his luckless presence.

NOTES ON THE TEXT

[1] I: The author employs in the work the multiple narrator and the work starts with the narration of Mr. Lockwood, Mr. Heathcliff's tenant at Thrushcross. The first person singular pronoun here refers to Mr. Lockwood.

[2] I knew, as well as if I saw him, that Mr. Heathcliff was about the place: Heathcliff told Nelly during her visit to the Heights that he had been prowling about Thrushcross Grange in the hope that he would get a chance to break in and talk to Catherine.

QUESTIONS FOR DISCUSSION

1. As one of the commentators says, Emily was not unworldly, not so unadapted to the practical business of life as her sister once suggested she was. With Chapter XV you have read in mind, how would you respond to the comment? Remember to give details to support yourself.

2. We do know that Emily Brontë was different from such authors as Jane Austen who represented man's struggle as essentially a social one. Do you agree if we say that she saw the principal human conflict as one between the individual and the dark in her novel? Could you support yourself if you say yes or no?

3. Emily Brontë was a master of language in her exploration of human heart. Does the passionate last meeting of Heathcliff and Cathy in Chapter XV exemplify Emily's ability of this kind?

4. The general opinion among the critics is that Heathcliff is a powerful figure not only because he is rooted in the traditions of his own time, from which he draws strength, but also because he makes a universal statement about man's nature, which continues to strike readers today as remarkably fresh and modern. Do you think so?

5. Dobell speaks of *Wuthering Heights* as "the unformed writing of a giant's hand: the 'large utterance' of a baby god." Although you have only read one chapter of

the whole work, you must have been impressed or disappointed by it. Discuss how you feel in general terms about the novel.

SUGGESTED REFERENCES

Gold, Linda. "Catherine Earnshaw: Mother and Daughter." *English Journal* 74.3 (1985): 68-73.

Homans, Margaret. "Repression and Sublimation of Nature in *Wuthering Heights.*" *PMLA* 93.1 (1978): 9-19.

Matthews, John T. "Framing in *Wuthering Heights.*" *Texas Studies in Literature and Language* 27.1 (1985): 25-61.

Michie, Elsie. "From Simianized Irish to Oriental Despots: Heathcliff, Rochester, and Racial Difference." *Novel* 25 (1992): 125-40.

Pike, Judith E. "'My Name Was Isabella Linton': Converture, Domestic Violence, and Mrs. Heathcliff's Narrative in *Wuthering Heights.*" *Nineteenth-Century Literature* 64.3 (2009): 347-83.

Unit 13 Thomas Hardy

(1840－1928)

A GUIDE TO LITERARY TERMINOLOGY

"Narrator": *Narrator, a term frequently used in the analysis of narrative forms, finds its origin in* ***Morphology of the Folktale****, the founding work of narratology written by Vladimir Propp, a Russian narratologist, in 1928. As different narratological approaches pursue different questions, the analysis of narrator is targeted for an understanding of how a story is told and who the story teller really is. Codified by P. Lubbock in his* ***The Craft of Fiction*** *as the "narrative point of view," the approach focuses on the narrator's specific features of his narration in literary fictions. Some scholars have demonstrated in their explorations such outstanding differences between real narrators and implied ones, and between reliable narrators and untrust-worthy ones. The most comprehensive analyses of the various kinds of narrators are given in the works of the French narratologist Gerard Genette, especially in his* ***Figures III****, which was published in 1972 and parts of the work were translated in 1980 into English known as* ***Narrative Discourse****.*

As for the narrator in Thomas Hardy's ***Tess of the d'Urbervilles****, we are certainly impressed by his rather astonishing feature of omniscience. He is a man who seems to know everything about most of the characters in the story, always ready to disclose their secret thoughts, hidden motives and inner-most feelings about their surroundings, people and events they are confronted with. The narrator, for instance, frequently explains, justifies and comments on Tess's actions as if everything about her was under his control.*

NOTES ON THE AUTHOR

Being the eldest of four children, Thomas Hardy was born in 1840 into the family of a mason in Stinsford of Dorset, England. As his parents were well educated, though low on the social register, he received decent education from a very early age and he is said to have started reading before he could walk. Hardy displayed his keen interest in and remarkable talent for music and literature when quite young and, soon after his graduation from King's College, Cambridge, he turned all his attention from architecture, his major and successful profession for some time, to novel and poetry writing. Complicated plots and exciting stories of his novels soon gained him a rapid rise to prominence as a realistic or, to some

Chinese critics, a naturalist author.

His fictions fall by and large into three groups, namely romances and fantasies, novels of ingenuity and novels of character and environment as are categorized and termed by Hardy himself. His most frequently read and examined works such as *The Return of the Native*, *The Mayor of Casterbridge*, *Jude the Obscure* and, of course, *Tess of the d'Urbervilles* belong to the third group and are regarded by most of his critics as the summit of his stark realism or naturalism. His most outstanding works, however, were by no means well received at first. Controversies and often hostile attacks, while making Hardy known worldwide, forced him eventually to abandon novel writing in 1897. He concentrated in the last couple of decades of his life on short stories and poetry.

The year 1928 witnessed the death of this great man and, as a mark of honor, he was buried in Westminster Abbey and his heart was sent back in a separate casket to his hometown and was buried there.

SYNOPSIS OF THE WORK

Tess was informed by his father, a poor country pedlar, that their family were descendants of an ancient noble one called d'Urberville. In order to claim kin with the local distinctive family bearing the name, she visited them and met Alec, the son of the family and the latter seduced her. Tess gave birth to a child which died before long and, in disgrace, she left home and became a dairymaid on a distant farm. There, she met Angel, the young master of the farm and the son of a clergyman, and they soon fell in love with each other. Determined to be Angel's faithful wife, Tess disclosed her unhappy experience with Alec right after the wedding and her confession of the affair drove Angel in despair. He abandoned his newly-wed wife and left England for Brazil. Desperate in her effort to support her mother and her younger sisters and brothers as her father had passed away at this point, Tess could not help but going back to Alec and became his mistress. Angel gradually realized his mistake and, with true repentance for his own guilt, he decided to return to England and go back to his deserted wife. He found Tess with difficulty only to know that she had lived with Alec. Tess convinced herself that Alec had ruined her over again and stabbed him in a fit of despair. Thus, the two lovers reunited and spent the last few days together while trying to escape from the upcoming punishment. Tess was arrested one morning at the Stonehenge after a period of concealment which was panicking but halcyon. She was tried and hanged in due course in the name of justice.

Chapters given below describe the highly pathetic scenes of the meeting between Tess and Angel, the inevitable murder and the last heart-rending moments of the two before justice falls upon Tess.

SELECTED READINGS

Tess of the d'Urbervilles: A Pure Woman Faithfully Presented

(Chapters 55 and 56; Chapter 58)

Chapter LV

At eleven o'clock that night, having secured a bed at one of the hotels and telegraphed his address to his father immediately on his arrival, he walked out into the streets of Sandbourne. It was too late to call on or inquire for any one, and he reluctantly postponed his purpose till the morning. But he could not retire to rest just yet.

This fashionable watering-place[1], with its eastern and its western stations, its piers, its groves of pines, its promenades, and its covered gardens, was, to Angel Clare, like a fairy place suddenly created by the stroke of a wand, and allowed to get a little dusty. An outlying eastern tract of the enormous Egdon Waste was close at hand, yet on the very verge of that tawny piece of antiquity such a glittering novelty as this pleasure city had chosen to spring up. Within the space of a mile from its outskirts every irregularity of the soil was prehistoric, every channel an undisturbed British trackway; not a sod having been turned there since the days of the Caesars [1]. Yet the exotic had grown here, suddenly as the prophet's gourd; and had drawn hither Tess.

1 watering-place: a seaside resort.

By the midnight lamps he went up and down the winding ways of this new world in an old one, and could discern between the trees and against the stars the lofty roofs, chimneys, gazebos[2], and towers of the numerous fanciful residences of which the place was composed. It was a city of detached mansions; a Mediterranean lounging-place on the English Channel; and as seen now by night it seemed even more imposing than it was.

The sea was near at hand, but not intrusive; it murmured, and he thought it was the pines; the pines murmured in precisely the same tones, and he thought they were the sea.

Where could Tess possibly be, a cottage-girl, his young wife, amidst all this wealth and fashion? The more he pondered the more he was puzzled. Were there any cows to milk here? There certainly were no fields to till. She was most probably engaged to do something in one of these large houses; and he sauntered along, looking at the chamber-windows and their lights going out one by one; and wondered which of them might be hers.

Conjecture was useless, and just after twelve o'clock he entered and went to bed. Before putting out his light he re-read Tess's impassioned letter [2]. Sleep, however, he could not, — so near her, yet so far from her — and he continually lifted the window-blind and regarded the backs of the opposite houses, and wondered behind which of the sashes she reposed at that moment.

He might almost as well have sat up all night. In the morning he arose at seven, and shortly after went out, taking the direction of the chief post-office. At the door he met an intelligent postman coming out with letters for the morning delivery.

"Do you know the address of a Mrs. Clare?" asked Angel.

The postman shook his head.

---

2 gazebos: summer houses.

Then, remembering that she would have been likely to continue the use of her maiden name, Clare said —

"Or a Miss Durbeyfield?"

"Durbeyfield?"

This also was strange to the postman addressed.

"There's visitors coming and going every day, as you know, sir," he said; "and without the name of the house 'tis impossible to find 'em." [3]

One of his comrades[3] hastening out at that moment, the name was repeated to him.

"I know no name of Durbeyfield; but there is the name of d'Urberville at The Herons," said the second.

"That's it!" cried Clare, pleased to think that she had reverted to the real pronunciation. "What place is The Herons?"

"A stylish lodging-house[4]. 'Tis all lodging-houses here, bless 'ee."

Clare received directions how to find the house, and hastened thither, arriving with the milkman. The Herons, though an ordinary villa, stood in its own grounds, and was certainly the last place in which one would have expected to find lodgings, so private was its appearance. If poor Tess was a servant here, as he feared, she would go to the back-door to that milkman, and he was inclined to go thither also. However, in his doubts he turned to the front, and rang.

The hour being early, the landlady herself opened the door. Clare inquired for Teresa[5] d'Urberville or Durbeyfield.

"Mrs. d'Urberville?"

"Yes."

Tess, then, passed as a married woman, and he felt glad, even though she had not adopted his name.

---

3 comrades: fellow workers.

4 lodging-house: a house in which apartments can be rented.

5 Teresa: Tess.

"Will you kindly tell her that a relative is anxious to see her?"

"It is rather early. What name shall I give, sir?"

"Angel."

"Mr. Angel?"

"No; Angel. It is my Christian name. She'll understand."

"I'll see if she is awake."

He was shown into the front room — the dining-room — and looked out through the spring curtains at the little lawn, and the rhododendrons and other shrubs upon it. Obviously, her position was by no means so bad as he had feared, and it crossed his mind that she must somehow have claimed and sold the jewels to attain it. He did not blame her for one moment [4]. Soon his sharpened ear detected footsteps upon the stairs, at which his heart thumped so painfully that he could hardly stand firm. "Dear me! what will she think of me, so altered as I am!" he said to himself; and the door opened.

Tess appeared on the threshold — not at all as he had expected to see her — bewilderingly otherwise, indeed. Her great natural beauty was, if not heightened, rendered more obvious by her attire. She was loosely wrapped in a gray-white cashmere dressing-gown embroidered in half-mourning tints, and she wore slippers of the same hue. Her neck rose out of a frill of down, and her well-remembered cable of dark-brown hair was partially coiled up in a mass at the back of her head and partly hanging on her shoulder — the evident result of haste.

He held out his arms, but they had fallen again to his side; for she had not come forward, remaining still in the opening of the doorway. Mere yellow skeleton that he was now, he felt the contrast between them, and thought his appearance distasteful to her.

"Tessie!"[6] he said, huskily, "can you forgive me for going away? Can't you — come to me? How do you get to be — like this? "

6 Tessie: Tess's name of endurement.

"It is too late!" she said, her voice sounding hard through the room, and her eyes shining unnaturally.

"I did not think rightly of you — I did not see you as you were," [5] he continued to plead. "I have learnt to since, dearest Tessis mine!"

"Too late, too late!" she said, waving her hand in the impatience of a person whose tortures cause every instant to seem an hour. "Don't come close to me, Angel! No — you must not. Keep away!"

"But don't you love me, my dear wife, because I have been so pulled down by illness? You are not so fickle — I am come on purpose for you — my mother and father will welcome you now!"

"Yes — oh yes, yes! But I say, I say, it is too late!" She almost shrieked. She seemed like a fugitive in a dream, who tried to move away, but could not. "Don't you know all — don't you know it? Yet how do you come here if you do not know? "

"I inquired here and there, and I found the way."

"I waited and waited for you!" she went on, her tones suddenly resuming their old fluty pathos. "But you did not come, and I wrote to you, and you did not come! He kept on saying you would never come any more, and that I was a foolish woman. He was very kind to me, and to mother, and to all of us after father's death. He — "

"I don't understand."

"He has won me — back to him."

Clare looked at her keenly, then, gathering her meaning, flagged like one plague-stricken, and his glance sank; it fell on her hands, which, once rosy, were now white and delicate.

She continued —

"He is upstairs...I hate him now, because — he told me a lie — that you would not come again; and you *have* come. These clothes are what he has put upon me; I didn't care what he did wi'[7] me. But will

7 wi': with.

you go away, Angel, please, and never come any more!"

They stood fixed, their baffled hearts looking out of their eyes with a joylessness pitiful to see. Both seemed to implore something to shelter them from reality.

"Ah — it is my fault!" said Clare. But he could not get on. Speech was as inexpressive as silence. But he had a vague consciousness of one thing, though it was not clear to him till later; that his original Tess had spiritually ceased to recognise the body before him as hers — allowing it to drift, like a corpse upon the current, in a direction dissociated from its living will.

A few instants passed, and he found that Tess was gone. His face grew colder and more shrunken as he stood, concentrated on the moment, and a minute or two after he found himself in the street, walking along, he did not know whither.

Chapter LVI

Mrs. Brooks, the lady who was the householder at The Herons, and owner of all the handsome furniture, was not a person of an unusually curious turn of mind [6]. She was too deeply materialised, poor woman, by her long and enforced bondage to that arithmetical demon Profit-and-Loss, to retain much curiosity for its own sake, and apart from possible lodgers' pockets. Nevertheless, the visit of Angel Clare to her well-paying tenants, Mr. and Mrs. d'Urberville, was sufficiently exceptional in point of time and manner to reinvigorate the feminine proclivity which had been stifled down as useless save in its bearings on the letting trade.

Tess had spoken to her husband from the doorway, without entering the dining-room, and Mrs. Brooks, who stood within the partly -closed door of her own sitting-room at the back of the passage, could hear fragments of the conversation — if conversation it could be called — between those two wretched souls. She heard Tess re-ascend the stairs to the first floor[8], and the departure of Clare, and closing of the front door behind him. Then the door of the room above was shut, and Mrs. Brooks knew that Tess had re-entered her apartment. As the young lady was not fully dressed, Mrs. Brooks knew that she would not emerge again for some time.

She accordingly ascended the stairs softly, and stood at the door of the front room — a drawing-room, connected with the room immediately behind it (which was a bedroom) by folding-doors in the common manner. This first floor, containing Mrs. Brooks's best apartments, had been taken by the week by the d'Urbervilles. The back room was now in silence; but from the drawing-room there came sounds.

All that she could at first distinguish of them was one syllable, continually repeated in a low note of moaning, as if it came from a soul bound to some Ixionian wheel [7] —

"O — O — O!"

Then a silence, then a heavy sigh, and again —

"O — O — O!"

The landlady looked through the keyhole. Only a small space of the room inside was visible, but within that space came a corner of the breakfast-table, which was already spread for the meal, and also a chair beside. Over the seat of the chair Tess's face was bowed, her posture being a kneeling one in front of it; her hands were clasped over her head, the skirts of her dressing-gown and the embroidery of her night-gown flowed upon the floor behind her, and upon the chair, and her stockingless feet, from which the slippers had fallen, protruded upon the carpet. It was from her lips that came the murmur of unspeakable despair.

---

8 the first floor: the second floor.

Then a man's voice[9] from the adjoining bedroom —

"What's the matter?"

She did not answer, but went on in a tone which was a soliloquy rather than an exclamation, and a dirge[10] rather than a soliloquy. Mrs. Brooks could catch only a portion:

"And then my dear, dear husband came home to me…and I did not know it!...And you had used your cruel persuasion upon me…you did not stop using it — no — you did not stop! My little sisters and brothers and my mother's needs — they were the things you moved me by…and you said my husband would never come back — never; and you taunted me, and said what a simpleton I was to expect him. And at last I believed you and gave way!...And then he came back! Now he is gone. Gone a second time, and I have lost him now forever…and he will not love me the littlest bit ever any more — only hate me!...Oh yes, I have lost him now — again because of — you!" In writhing, with her head on the chair, she turned her face towards the door, and Mrs. Brooks could see the pain upon it; and that her lips were bleeding from the clench of her teeth upon them, and that the long lashes of her closed eyes stuck in wet tags to her cheeks. She continued: "And he is dying — he looks as if he is dying!...And my sin will kill him and not kill me!...Oh, you have torn my life all to pieces…made me victim, a caged wretch!...My own true husband will never, never — O Heaven — I can't bear this! — I cannot!"

There were more and sharper words from the man; then a sudden rustle; she had sprung to her feet. Mrs. Brooks, thinking that the speaker was coming to rush out of the door, hastily retreated down the stairs.

She need not have done so, however, for the door of the sitting-room was not opened. But Mrs. Brooks felt it unsafe to watch on the landing again, and entered her own parlour below.

---

9 a man's voice: Alec d'Urberville's voice.

10 dirge: a lament for the dead.

She could hear nothing through the floor, although she listened intently, and thereupon went to the kitchen to finish her interrupted breakfast. Coming up presently to the front room on the ground floor she took up some sewing, waiting for her lodgers to ring that she might take away the breakfast, which she meant to do herself, to discover what was the matter if possible. Overhead, as she sat, she could now hear the floor-boards slightly creak, as if some one were walking about, and presently the movement was explained by the rustle of garments against the banisters, the opening and the closing of the front door, and the form of Tess passing to the gate on her way into the street. She was fully dressed now in the walking-costume of a well-to-do young lady in which she had arrived, with the sole addition that over her hat and black feathers a veil was drawn.

Mrs. Brooks had not been able to catch any word of farewell, temporary or otherwise, between her tenants at the door above. They might have quarreled, or Mr. d'Urberville might still be asleep, for he was not an early riser.

She went into the back room which was more especially her own apartment, and continued her sewing there. The lady lodger did not return, nor did the gentleman ring his bell. Mrs. Brooks pondered on the delay, and on what probable relation the visitor who had called so early bore to the couple upstairs. In reflecting she leant back in her chair.

As she did so her eyes glanced casually over the ceiling till they were arrested by a spot in the middle of its white surface which she had never noticed there before. It was about the size of a wafer when she first observed it, but it speedily grew as large as the palm of her hand, and then she could perceive that it was red. The oblong white ceiling, with this scarlet blot in the midst, had the appearance of a gigantic ace of hearts[11].

Mrs. Brooks had strange qualms of misgiving. She got upon the

11 heart: one of the four suits in a pack of playing cards.

table, and touched the spot in the ceiling with her fingers. It was damp, and she fancied that it was a blood stain.

Descending from the table, she left the parlour and went upstairs, intending to enter the room overhead, which was the bed-chamber at the back of the drawing-room. But, nerveless woman as she had now become, she could not bring herself to attempt the handle. She listened. The dead silence within was broken only by a regular beat.

Drip, drip, drip.

Mrs. Brooks hastened downstairs, opened the front door, and ran into the street. A man she knew, one of the workmen employed at an adjoining villa, was passing by, and she begged him to come in and go upstairs with her; she feared something had happened to one of her lodgers. The workman assented, and followed her to the landing.

She opened the door of the drawing-room, and stood back for him to pass in, entering herself behind him. The room was empty; the breakfast — a substantial repast of coffee, eggs, and a cold ham — lay spread upon the table untouched, as when she had taken it up, excepting that the carving knife was missing. She asked the man to go through the folding-doors into the adjoining room.

He opened the doors, entered a step or two, and came back almost instantly with a rigid face. "My good God, the gentleman in bed is dead! I think he has been hurt with a knife — a lot of blood has run down upon the floor!"

The alarm was soon given, and the house which had lately been so quiet resounded with the tramp of many footsteps, a surgeon among the rest. The wound was small, but the point of the blade had touched the heart of the victim, who lay on his back, pale, fixed, dead, as if he had scarcely moved after the infliction of the blow. In a quarter of an hour the news that a gentleman who was a temporary visitor to the town had been stabbed in his bed, spread through every street and villa of the popular watering-place.

Chapter LVIII

The night was strangely solemn and still. In the small hours[12] she whispered to him the whole story of how he had walked in his sleep with her in his arms across the Froom stream, at the imminent risk of both their lives, and laid her down in the stone coffin at the ruined abbey[13]. He had never known of that till now [8].

"Why didn't you tell me next day?" he said. "It might have prevented much misunderstanding and woe."

"Don't think of what's past!" said she. "I am not going to think outside of now. Why should we! Who knows what to-morrow has in store?"

But it apparently had no sorrow. The morning was wet and foggy, and Clare, rightly informed that the caretaker[14] only opened the windows on fine days, ventured to creep out of their chamber, and explore the house, leaving Tess asleep. There was no food on the premises, but there was water, and he took advantage of the fog to emerge from the mansion, and fetch tea, bread, and butter from a shop in a little place two miles beyond, as also a small tin kettle and spirit-lamp, that they might get fire without smoke. His re-entry awoke her; and they breakfasted on what he had brought.

They were indisposed to stir abroad, and the day passed, and the night following, and the next, and next; till, almost without their being aware, five days had slipped by in absolute seclusion, not a sight or sound of a human being disturbing their peacefulness, such as it was. The changes of the weather were their only events, the birds of the New Forest their only company. By tacit consent they hardly once spoke of any incident of the past subsequent to their wedding-day.

---

12 small hours: the early hours of the morning after midnight.

13 ruined abbey: a deserted building which used to be occupied by a community of monks.

14 caretaker: the person employed to look after the house.

The gloomy intervening time seemed to sink into chaos, over which the present and prior times closed as if it never had been. Whenever he suggested that they should leave their shelter, and go forwards towards Southampton or London, she showed a strange unwillingness to move.

"Why should we put an end to all that's sweet and lovely!" she deprecated. "What must come will come." And, looking through the shutter-chink: "All is trouble outside there; inside here content."

He peeped out also. It was quite true; within was affection, union, error forgiven: outside was the inexorable.

"And — and," she said, pressing her cheek against his; "I fear that what you think of me now may not last. I do not wish to outlive your present feeling for me. I would rather not. I would rather be dead and buried when the time comes for you to despise me, so that it may never be known to me that you despised me."

"I cannot ever despise you."

"I also hope that. But considering what my life has been I cannot see why any man should, sooner or later, be able to help despising me. ...How wickedly mad I was! Yet formerly I never could bear to hurt a fly or a worm, and the sight of a bird in a cage used often to make me cry."

They remained yet another day. In the night the dull sky cleared, and the result was that the old caretaker at the cottage awoke early. The brilliant sunrise made her unusually brisk; she decided to open the contiguous mansion immediately, and to air it thoroughly on such a day. Thus it occurred that, having arrived and opened the lower rooms before six o'clock, she ascended to the bedchambers, and was about to turn the handle of the one wherein they lay. At that moment she fancied she could hear the breathing of persons within. Her slippers and her antiquity[15] had rendered her progress a noiseless one so far, and she made for instant retreat; then, deeming that her hearing might have deceived her, she turned anew to the door and softly tried the handle. The lock was out of order, but a piece of furniture had been moved forward on the inside, which prevented her opening the door more than an inch or two. A stream of morning light through the shutter-chink fell upon the faces of the pair, wrapped in profound slumber, Tess's lips being parted like a half-opened flower near his cheek. The caretaker was so struck with their innocent appearance, and with the novelty of Tess's gown hanging across a chair, her silk stocking beside it, the pretty parasol, and the other habits in which she had arrived because she had none else, that her first indignation at the effrontery of tramps and vagabonds gave way to a momentary sentimentality over this genteel elopement, as it seemed. She closed the door, and withdrew as softly as she had come, to go and consult with her neighbours on the odd discovery.

Not more than a minute had elapsed after her withdrawal when Tess woke, and then Clare. Both had a sense that something had disturbed them, though they could not say what; and the uneasy feeling which it engendered grew stronger. As soon as he was dressed he narrowly scanned the lawn through the two or three inches of shutter-chink.

"I think we will leave at once," said he. "It is a fine day. And I cannot help fancying somebody is about the house. At any rate, the woman will be sure to come to-day."

She passively assented, and, putting the room in order, they took up the few articles that belonged to them, and departed noiselessly. When they had got into the Forest she turned to take a last look at the house.

"Ah, happy house — good-bye!" she said. "My life can only be question of a few weeks. Why should we not have stayed there?"

---

15 antiquity: her old age.

"Don't say it, Tess! We shall soon get out of this district altogether. We'll continue our course as we've begun it, and keep straight north. Noboday will think of looking for us there. We shall be looked for at the Wessex ports if we are sought at all. When we are in the north we will get to a port and away."

Having thus persuaded her, the plan was pursued, and they kept a bee-line northward.[16] Their long repose at the manor-house lent them walking-power now; and towards mid-day they found that they were approaching the steepled city of Melchester, which lay directly in their way. He decided to rest her in a clump of trees during the afternoon, and push onward under cover of darkness. At dusk Clare purchased food as usual, and their night march began, the boundary between Upper and Mid-Wessex being crossed about eight o'clock.

To walk across country without much regard to roads was not new to Tess, and she showed her old agility in the performance. The intercepting city, ancient Melchester, they were obliged to pass through in order to take advantage of the town bridge for crossing a large river that obstructed them. It was about mid-night when they went along the deserted streets, lighted fitfully by the few lamps, keeping off the pavement that it might not echo their footsteps. The graceful pile of cathedral architecture rose dimly on their left hand, but it was lost upon them now. Once out of the town, they followed the turnpike-road, which after a few miles plunged across an open plain.

Though the sky was dense with cloud, a diffused light from some fragment of a moon had hitherto helped them a little. But the moon had now sunk, the clouds seemed to settle almost on their heads, and the night grew as dark as a cave. However, they found their way along, keeping as much on the turf as possible that their tread might not resound, which it was easy to do, there being no hedge or fence

16 They walked straight northwards.

of any kind. All around was open loneliness and black solitude, over which a stiff breeze blew.

They had proceeded thus gropingly two or three miles further when on a sudden Clare became conscious of some vast erection close in his front, rising sheer from the grass. They had almost struck themselves against it.

"What monstrous place is this?" said Angel.

"It hums," said she. "Hearken[17]!"

He listened. The wind, playing upon the edifice, produced a booming tune, like the note of some gigantic one-stringed harp. No other sound came from it, and lifting his hand and advancing a step or two, Clare felt the vertical surface of the structure. It seemed to be of solid stone, without joint or moulding. Carrying his fingers onward, he found that what he had come in contact with was a colossal rectangular pillar; by stretching out his left hand he could feel a similar one adjoining. At an indefinite height overhead something made the black sky blacker, which had the semblance of a vast architrave uniting the pillars horizontally. They carefully entered beneath and between; the surfaces echoed their soft rustle; but they seemed to be still out-of-doors. The place was roofless. Tess drew her breath fearfully, and Angel, perplexed, said —

"What can it be?"

Feeling sideways, they encountered another towering pillar, square and uncompromising as the first; beyond it another and another. The place was all doors and pillars, some connected above by continuous architraves.

"A very Temple of the Winds," he said.

The next pillar was isolated; others composed a trilithon; others were prostrate, their flanks forming a causeway wide enough for a car-

17 hearken: listen.

riage; and it was soon obvious that they made up a forest of monoliths grouped upon the grassy expanse of the plain. The couple advanced further into this pavilion of the night till they stood in its midst.

"It is Stonehenge!" [9] said Clare.

"The heathen temple, you mean?"

"Yes. Older than the centuries; older than the d'Urbervilles. Well, what shall we do, darling? We may find shelter further on."

But Tess, really tired by this time, flung herself upon an oblong slab that lay close at hand, and was sheltered from the wind by a pillar. Owing to the action of the sun during the preceding day, the stone was warm and dry, in comforting contrast to the rough and chill grass around, which had damped her skirts and shoes.

"I don't want to go any further, Angel," she said, stretching out her hand for his. "Can't we bide here?"

"I fear not. This spot is visible for miles by day, although it does not seem so now."

"One of my mother's people was a shepherd hereabouts, now I think of it. And you used to say at Talbothays that I was a heathen. So now I am at home."

He knelt down beside her outstretched form, and put his lips upon hers.

"Sleepy, are you, dear? I think you are lying on an altar". [10]

"I like very much to be here," she murmured. "It is so solemn and lonely — after my great happiness — with nothing but the sky above my face. It seems as if there were no folk in the world but we two; and I wish there were not — except 'Liza-Lu[18]."

Clare thought she might as well rest here till it should get a little lighter, and he flung his overcoat upon her, and sat down by her side.

18 'Liza-Lu: Eliza Louisa, the Durbeyfield's second child. She was twelve years of age at the beginning of the story.

"Angel, if anything happens to me, will you watch over 'Liza-Lu for my sake?" she asked, when they had listened a long time to the wind among the pillars.

"I will."

"She is so good and simple and pure. O, Angel — I wish you would marry her if you lose me, as you will do shortly. O, if you would!"

"If I lose you I lose all! And she is my sister-in-law." [11]

"That's nothing, dearest. People marry sister-laws[19] continually about Marlott; and 'Liza-lu is so gentle and sweet, and she is growing so beautiful. O I could share you with her willingly when we are spirits! If you would train her and teach her, Angel, and bring her up for your own self! ...She has all the best of me without the bad of me; and if she were to become yours it would almost seem as if death had not divided us. ...Well, I have said it. I won't mention it again."

She ceased, and he fell into thought. In the far north-east sky he could see between the pillars a level streak of light. The uniform concavity of black cloud was lifting bodily like the lid of a pot, letting in at the earth's edge the coming day, against which the towering monoliths and trilithons began to be blackly defined.

"Did they sacrifice to God here?" asked she.

"No," said he.

"Who to?"

"I believe to the sun. That lofty stone set away by itself is in the direction of the sun, which will presently rise behind it."

"This reminds me, dear," she said. "You remember you never would interfere with any belief of mine before we were married? But I knew your mind all the same, and I thought as you thought — not

19 sister-laws: sister-in-laws.

from any reasons of my own, but because you thought so. Tell me now, Angel, do you think we shall meet again after we are dead? I want to know."

He kissed her to avoid a reply at such a time.

"O, Angel — I fear that means no!" said she, with a suppressed sob. "And I wanted so to see you again — so much, so much! What — not even you and I, Angel, who love each other so well?"

Like a greater than himself, to the critical question at the critical time he did not answer; and they were again silent. In a minute or two her breathing became more regular, her clasp of his hand relaxed, and she fell asleep. The band of silver paleness along the east horizon made even the distant parts of the Great Plain appear dark and near; and the whole enormous landscape bore that impress of reserve, taciturnity, and hesitation which is usual just before day. The eastward pillars and their architraves stood up blackly against the light, and the great flame-shaped Sun-stone beyond them; and the Stone of Sacrifice midway. Presently the night wind died out, and the quivering little pools in the cup-like hollows of the stones lay still. At the same time something seemed to move on the verge of the dip eastward — a mere dot. It was the head of a man approaching them from the hollow beyond the Sun-stone. Clare wished they had gone onward, but in the circumstances decided to remain quiet. The figure came straight towards the circle of pillars in which they were.

He heard something behind him, the brush of feet. Turning, he saw over the prostrate columns another figure; then before he was aware, another was at hand on the right, under trilithon, and another on the left. The dawn shone full on the front of the man westward, and Clare could discern from this that he was tall, and walked as if trained. They all closed in with evident purpose. Her story then was true! Springing to his feet, he looked around for a weapon, loose stone, means of escape, anything. By this time the nearest man was upon him.

"It is no use, sir," he said. "There are sixteen of us on the Plain, and the whole country is reared."

"Let her finish her sleep!" he implored in a whisper of the men as they gathered round.

When they saw where she lay, which they had not done till then, they showed no objection, and stood watching her, as still as the pillars around. He went to the stone and bent over her, holding one poor little hand; her breathing now was quick and small, like that of a lesser creature than a woman. All waited in the growing light, their faces and hands as if they were silvered, the remainder of their figures dark, the stones glistening green-grey, the Plain still a mass of shade. Soon the light was strong, and a ray shone upon her unconscious form, peering under her eyelids and waking her.

"What is it, Angel?" she said, starting up. "Have they come for me?"

"Yes, dearest," he said. "They have come."

"It is as it should be," she murmured. "Angel, I am almost glad — yes, glad! This happiness could not have lasted. It was too much. I have enough; and now I shall not live for you to despise me!"

She stood up, shook herself, and went forward, neither of the men having moved.

"I am ready," she said quietly.

NOTES ON THE TEXT

[1] Julius Caesar, a general of the Roman Empire, invaded Britain with his powerful legions in 55 BCE and Britain was eventually conquered by Emperor Claudius in 43 CE. Under the Roman rule of some 400 years, highways, castles, temples, towns and even a "Great Wall" were built in England.

[2] After Tess and Angel parted, she was constantly harassed by Alec who intended to marry her. Tess wrote Angel then a long letter demonstrating how devoted she still was to him and how strong a temptation she was confronted with only to beg Angel to come back to her.

[3] As words in the conversation show, Hardy had a sensitive ear for the rustic features of his characters' dialect which, even though impressive to his contemporaries, may not mean much to modern readers.

[4] Angel's godmother had left to his wife-to-be some diamonds as a mark of affection for her godson Angel. Extremely devastated by Tess's disclosure of her past experience with Alec, Angel took back the jewels from his newly-wed wife and left them to a banker for safekeeping before his departure from Tess.

[5] Angel was here referring, with remorse and shame, to his brutal desertion of Tess just a few days after their wedding because of Tess's honest disclosure of her painful experience with Alec.

[6] The author tells us at the beginning of this chapter that the landlady was by no means an overly curious person. Therefore, as the occurrence is described as being witnessed by her, it is not a bit doubtful to us. We trust her judgment.

[7] Ixion is in Greek mythology a treacherous king of Lapithae, who murdered his own father and attempted to rape Hera, wife of Zeus, the supreme god, and was punished by being bound to a perpetually revolving wheel in the infernal region called Hades.

[8] Angel, overcome with a feeling of utter despair, walked in his sleep one night into Tess's room, wrapped his wife in a sheet, carried her to a nearby old church and laid her in an empty stone coffin. Tess led him back to the house and to his bed without waking up her greatly troubled husband and, what is more, without telling him about the whole occurence the following morning.

[9] The Stonehenge is a group of massive stones standing in a circle on Salisbury Plain in south-western England. The arrangement of the stones suggests that the Stonehenge was probably used by people during the Stone Age as a religious center and, since the morning sunlight on Mid-Summer's Day (24th of June) forms a straight beam through the center, it is believed to have been used also by the ancients as an astronomical observatory.

[10] The Stonehenge scene is extremely memorable with its significance of prediction. Tess, lying on an altar of this heathen temple which is supposed to have been used in the ancient times for sacrifices to the sun, would be arrested, at the end of her last moments, and would be led to her death, a sacrifice to the modern guardians of social law and morals.

[11] We are told throughout the story that Angel was not comfortable with his clerical family because his rather emancipated thinking had alienated him from their single-minded approach to life. However, as his response to Tess's suggestion of marrying her sister shows, he was by no means freed from his constantly denied conventional training.

QUESTIONS FOR DISCUSSION

1. Hardy calls *Tess of the d'Urbervilles* one of his Wessex novels, the name of the seven kingdoms of Anglo-Saxon Britain, which may leave us with a touch of pessimism. He is said, however, to have demonstrated throughout his works a grave concern for truth, a higher characteristic of philosophy than pessimism or even optimism. With the chapters you have read in mind, how do you comment on the theme of his works in general?

2. The philosophical comments and the explicit intrusion of the author's opinion are very often outstanding in the narration of Tess's bitter experiences. Identify examples of this nature and explain how each of them functions in the author's articulation of the theme of his work.

3. As one commentator once observes, no novel by Hardy expresses better than *Tess* his belief that the most pervasive source of pain is man's unconcern of a universe which makes and breaks man. In what way do you think that Tess's sad experience illustrates Hardy's bitter comment on the fate of human life?

4. Hardy says in the novel that the president of the immortals sports with man, the idea that underlines the author's skillful handling of plot in the novel. Analyze the use of coincidences in the chapters you have read and discuss in what way they make the story attractive.

5. Tess is obviously a somewhat elusive character under the pen of this master story-teller, so complex that it often makes its readers uncertain about what the author wants to convey to them through her characterization. How would you summarize, if you are asked to, the author's general attitude toward Tess?

SUGGESTED REFERENCES

Davis, William A. Jr. "The Rape of Tess: Hardy, English Law, and the Case for Sexual Assault." *Nineteenth-Century Literature* 52.2 (1997): 221-31.

Jeanette, Shumaker. "Breaking with the Conventions: Victorian Confession Novels and Tess of the *d'Urbervilles*." *English Literature in Transition 1880-1920* 27(1994): 445-62.

Lida, Bushloper. "Hardy's *Tess of the d'Urbervilles*." *Twentieth-Century Literary Criticism* 229 (1994): 222-25.

Richard, Carpenter. "*Tess of the d'Urbervilles*." *Twentieth-Century Literary Criticism* 143 (2004): 124-38.

Tom, Nash. "*Tess of the d'Urbervilles*: The Symbolic Use of Folklore." *Twentieth-Century Literary Criticism* 229 (1998): 38-48.

Unit 14 William Butler Yeats

(1865—1939)

A GUIDE TO LITERARY TERMINOLOGY

"Rhyme": *We all have the experience, when reading poetry, that we are attracted by the harmonious sound of words. The pleasantness appealing to our ears is created by two commonly used techniques in poetry writing, namely "rhyme" and "meter." As "meter" has been discussed previously, we will just focus on "rhyme" in this unit.*

Words with final syllables sounding identical or similar at the end of two poetic lines echoing one another are words rhyming with each other. If the lines of a stanza follow a specific pattern of sounding, they fall into a scheme of end rhyme.

Poems that strictly follow conventional patterns of rhymes are said to stick to "true rhymes" of which there are three kinds, namely masculine rhyme, in which two words end with the same vowel-consonant combination, such as stand/land, feminine rhyme, or double rhyme, in which two syllables rhyme, such as profession/discretion, and trisyllabic rhyme, in which three syllables rhyme with each other, such as patinate/latinate.

The standard way to mark the pattern of rhyme is to give the same letter to those lines that rhyme. For instance, we may describe a four line stanza as "abab," which means that Line 1 and Line 3 rhyme with each other whereas Line 2 and Line 4 show the same sound with their ending syllables.

NOTES ON THE AUTHOR

William Butler Yeats was born in 1865 in Dublin, Ireland. He moved with his parents to London when he was only two years old and stayed in the city for quite a few years since his father decided to give up his legal work and practice there his artistic talent as a portrait painter. After they returned to Ireland, his father made the second decision for his son and this time the old man sent him to a school of art at the age for college because he did not want to run the risk of spending too much money on the education of his son who did not seem to have performed well in his high school days. Instead of becoming an artist, however, Yeats made a choice of his own and began to write poetry. He had already published several poems in Dublin when he was only nineteen years of age.

All his life, Yeats was struggling to establish in him a sense of appropriate identity with his native country and his strong Irish nationalism only ended up with extraordinary bitterness towards the politics and religion of Ireland. His complicated feelings found their expression profusely, with anger of a poet, in his lyrics and in his other writings as well. So far as the style and techinique of his poetry are concerned, even though they varied with the passage of time during his writing career of some fifty years, he continued to explore three major themes, namely love, politics and religion. His poetry changed in its diction, but its aristocratic dignity of mysticism and its apocalyptic nature never cease to exist as the authoritative and powerful soul of his poetry. As a prolific and versatile writer, he wrote and published, during the period of some fifty years, twenty-six plays, four books of philosophy and literary criticism, a considerable number of short stories and, of course, many volumes of poems, lyrical as well as narrative and dramatic. He was awarded the Nobel Prize for Literature in 1923 for his outstanding contribution to English literature and World literature as well.

During the last few years of his life, poor health bothered the aged poet, but he never retired from writing. He had completed his last work *The Herne's Egg* in 1938 shortly before he passed away in the same year at Roquebrune, France. In 1948, his ashes were taken back to his hometown and buried in a quiet Protestant churchyard at Drumcliffe.

NOTES ON THE WORKS

Yeats is a poet, a playwright, as well as a rather fruitful essayist, but his lyric poetry represents obviously his greatest achievement and has been most frequently read and studied. His long career as a poet extended for over fifty year.

So far as the theme is concerned, his poetic works could be put into four groups which fall also by and large into four time periods. During the first few years when he published his earliest poems including the famous piece titled "The Lake Isle of Innisfree," his works show a style of lushness and sonority, addressing his genuine passion for the mythical heroes and lovers and the beautiful Irish countryside. As he published his *The Wind among the Reeds* in 1899, his poetry showed more or less the same concern about love, politics and religion, but his poetic diction demonstrated a significant shift from its rich stateliness to a sparer and more conversational tone, sounding like a person talking to his old friend. During the first decade of the twentieth century, the time when Yeats schooled himself to strengthen his "personal utterance" and to portray in his lyrics real characters such as his friends and acquaintances although larger than life in the form of a rather mythic stature, he kept his style even leaner and sparer as compared with that of his previous lyrics. One of the monumental works published during this period was the renowned 1914 *Responsibilities*. Then came his old age as he himself announced in a poem called "Sailing to Byzantium" printed in *The Tower* in 1928 when the poet was sixty-three years of age. A sense of urgency to address larger issues of history and human destiny can be clearly noticed, and his artistic intention to make his "unaging intellect" and poetry part of the "holy fire" and of the "artifice of eternity" tends to be openly stated in many of his rather prophetic poems.

SELECTED READINGS

The Lake Isle of Innisfree[1]

I will arise and go now, and go to Innisfree,
And a small cabin build there, of clay and wattles made;
Nine bean rows will I have there, a hive for the honey bee,
And live alone in the bee-loud[2] glade.
And I shall have some peace there, for peace comes dropping slow,
Dropping from the veils of the morning[3] to where the cricket sings;
There midnight's all a-glimmer, and noon a purple glow,
And evening full of the linnet's[4] wings.
I will arise and go now, for always night and day
I hear lake water lapping with low sounds by the shore;
While I stand on the roadway, or on the pavements gray,
I hear it in the deep heart's core.

1 Innisfree: Island in Lough Gill, which is in Sligo County in NW Ireland.
2 bee-loud: loud with the buzzes of bees.
3 veils of the morning: the morning haze.
4 linnet: small brown songbirds.

QUESTIONS FOR DISCUSSION

1. This is one of Yeats's most famous early lyrics, very popular in Ireland during Yeats's lifetime. How does the poem appeal to you as a Chinese college student? Are the details in nature attractive to city dwellers like you?

2. The speaker is nostalgic for a remote wood and lake in Sligo at the northwest coast of Ireland and he wants to go there the way Thoreau went to Walden. How does the speaker express his intense feelings?

To a Child Dancing in the Wind

Dance there upon the shore;
What need have you to care
For wind or water's roar?
And tumble out your hair
That the salt drops[5] have wet;
Being young you have not known
The fool's triumph,[6] nor yet
Love lost as soon as won,
Nor the best labourer dead
And all the sheaves[7] to bind.
What need have you to dread
The monstrous crying of wind?

QUESTIONS FOR DISCUSSION

1. Rhyme and meter are often crucial in verse writing in order to make the lines more appealing to our ears. We have quoted a couple of passages at the beginning of this unit in order to give you a general definition of rhyme and meter in English poetry. Could you analyze and describe the pattern of rhyme the above poem follows?

---

5 salt drops: drops of sea water.
6 The triumph is meaningless.
7 sheaves: bundles of corn or barley stalks tied up after the crops are reaped.

2. Poets use different schemes of rhyme and meter for their poetry and they very often break the rules for special technical purposes. You must be able at this point to identify in the above poem the lines that do not follow the general pattern of rhyming. Would you be able to explain why they don't?

To a Friend Whose Work Has Come to Nothing

Now all the truth is out,
Be secret[8] and take defeat
From any brazen[9] throat,
For how can you compete,
Being honour bred, with one
Who, were it proved he lies,
Were neither shamed in his own
Nor in his neighbours' eyes?
Bred to a harder thing
Than Triumph, turn away
And like a laughing string
Whereon mad fingers play
Amid a place of stone,
Be secret and exult,
Because of all things known
That is most difficult.

QUESTIONS FOR DISCUSSION

1. During the first decade of the twentieth century, Yeats began to write in his poems about actual events and people he knew. The lyric above was one of this kind. As one commentator once observed, this is a poem of "savage consolation." Why do you think he said so?

8 Be secret: keep your mouth shut.
9 brazen: impudent or shameless.

2. Yeats was trying to find a new way of expressing his thoughts in his lyrics during this period of time. Compare the poem above with "The Lake Isle of Innisfree" and comment on the styles of the two pieces. Is this one written in Yeats' middle period different in style from his earlier lyrics?

A Prayer for Old Age

God guard me from those thoughts men think
In the mind alone;
He that sings a lasting song
Thinks in a marrow-bone;
From all that makes a wise old man
That can be praised of all[10];
O what am I that I should not seem
For the song's sake a fool?
I pray — for fashion's word is out
And prayer comes round again —
That I may seem, though I die old,
A foolish, passionate man.

QUESTIONS FOR DISCUSSION

1. The speaker mentions that there are men who "think in the mind alone" and there are men who "think in a marrow-bone." What do you think the speaker exactly means by them?

2. The speaker prays in the poem that he would rather seem a foolish and passionate old man than a wise old one that can be praised of all. Could you explain his attitude?

10 of all: of all the people.

SUGGESTED REFERENCES

Cowell, Raymond. *Critics on Yeats.* Coral Gables, FL: U of Miami P, 1971.

Howes, Marjorie. *Yeats's Nations: Gender, Class, and Irishness.* London: Cambridge UP, 1998.

Moore, Virgina. *The Unicorn: William Butler Yeats' Search for Reality.* New York: Octagon Books, 1973.

Purdy, Dwight Hilliard. *Biblical Echo and Alusion in the Poetry of W. B. Yeats: Poetics and the Art of God.* Pennsylvania: Bucknell UP, 1994.

Ross, David. *Critical Companion to William Butler Yeats: A Literary Reference to His Life and Work.* New York: Facts on File, 2008.

Unit 15 James A. A. Joyce

(1882—1941)

A GUIDE TO LITERARY TERMINOLOGY

"Stream of Consciousness": *Based on William James's description of the continuous impressions and thoughts in the human mind, as is termed by the philosopher "stream of consciousness" in his 1890 work **Principles of Psychology**, May Sinclair applied this coined term some two decades later to literary criticism in his review of D. Richardson's novel sequence **Pilgrimage**. Sinclair's remarkable comments on the recording of fragmentary interior monologs in Richardson's work made it a popular literary method and the representative technique used by such innovative literary masters as James Joyce, Virginia Woolf and William Faulkner in their novels.*

*Compared with Richardson or the French novelist Edouard Dujardin, Joyce is better known for his brilliant use of the stream of consciousness as he was trying to record the natural flow of impressions and memories through the minds of the characters in his fiction. He demonstrated unprecedentedly almost all the possibilities of this new method with the unpunctuated final chapter of his **Ulysses**, so brilliantly done that it became soon an accepted part of the literary repertoire of the modernist novelists worldwide. One could certainly notice the tendency in Joyce's early works also of his deliberate recording of what goes on in the minds of various characters. "The Boarding House" in **Dubliners**, for instance, represents his attractive verbalization of the process of continuous thought, in addition to speeches, of quite a few of his lively characters, which contributes a great deal to the overdue recognition of this short-story series.*

NOTES ON THE AUTHOR

James Joyce, born at Rathgar, Dublin in 1882, witnessed during his young days the downhill movement of his rather genteel family into somewhat poverty along with the depression of the Irish economy. As he showed an outstanding talent for reading among the ten children of the family, his parents managed to give him a fairly good education, first at a Jesuit school and then at University College in Dublin. His early well-guided and extensive reading aroused in him burning interest in both language and literature and, impatient with the intolerant atmosphere of Irish Catholicism at his home town, he chose to stay abroad almost all his life time and to make a living by teaching English while writing poems and novels.

The initial effort he made during the first few years of his writing career did not seem to have freed him from frustration and poverty, but the publication of his *Ulysses* in 1922 eventually brought him international fame. The development of "stream of consciousness" in his fiction, seeking to depict thoughts and feelings in the minds of his characters, and his thematic concentration on sexuality of human life plunged his works into the depths of decades-long controversy and raised them finally to the heights of the most definitive modernist fiction after the works by Joseph Conrad. Indeed, Joyce has been greatly admired even to the present day for the unique form and structure of his novels, especially of the later ones. The novelist himself was conscious, however, of the erudite feature of his fiction, too difficult perhaps for common readers to deal with. As he once wisely observed, it might take the whole life of a serious reader to read and understand such of his books as *Ulysses* and *Finnegans Wake.*

Joyce had never returned to Ireland since 1905 when he settled down with his wife in Trieste, and he died in Zurich on January 13, 1941.

NOTES ON THE WORK

Known as one of the most important sets of short stories ever written in the English language, *Dubliners* as a volume demonstrates its dramatic artistry with a carefully designed narrative pattern of childhood, adolescence, maturity, old age and finally death which becomes the haunting theme of the last story entitled "The Dead." Joyce intended with the rather photographic realism of each of the stories to provide his readers with "a chapter of the moral history of Ireland" setting in Dublin because, as the novelist sees it, the city is the center of paralysis, social and moral, of the country, of the world and, what is more, of all human experiences.

"The Boarding House," selected from *Dubliners*, is a sophisticated account of the premarital intimate relationship between Polly, a "wisely innocent" nineteen-year-old girl, and Mr. Doren, an unmarried young man in his mid-thirties with a well-paid job in town. The young man was forced to make reparation for his affair with Polly as a result of the deliberate entrapment of the girl's mother Mrs. Mooney, a calculating owner of the boarding house who had long been suspected to run her business with sexual exploitation. The story is by no means attractive because of its plot. Rather, what is noteworthy about it are its innovative description of the train of thoughts and feelings of the characters and, with a vivid and accurate language, its artistic synthesis of the narrator's ironic diagnosis and his humanistic sympathy.

SELECTED READINGS

The Boarding House

Mrs. Mooney was a butcher's daughter. She was a woman who was quite able to keep things to herself: a determined woman. She had married her father's foreman and opened a butcher's shop near Spring Gardens. But as soon as his father-in-law was dead Mr. Mooney began to go to the devil[1]. He drank, plundered the till[2], ran head-long into debt. It was no use making him take the pledge[3]: he was sure to break out again a few days after. By fighting his wife in the presence of customers and by buying bad meat he ruined his business. One night he went for his wife with the cleaver and she had to sleep in a neighbour's house.

After that they lived apart. She went to the priest and got a separation from him [1] with care of the children. She would give him neither money nor food nor house-room; and so he was obliged to enlist himself as a sheriff's man. He was a shabby stooped little drunkard with a white face and a white moustache and white eyebrows, pencilled above his little eyes, which were pink-veined and raw; and all day long he sat in the bailiff's room, waiting to be put on a job. Mrs. Mooney, who had taken what remained of her money out of the butcher business and set up a boarding house in Hardwicke Street,

---

1 go to the devil: He felt depraved.
2 till: small drawer for money in the shop.
3 take the pledge: take an oath not to do it any more.

was a big imposing woman. Her house had a floating population made up of tourists from Liverpool and the Isle of Man and, occasionally, *artistes*[4] from the music halls[5]. Its resident population was made up of clerks from the city. She governed the house cunningly and firmly, knew when to give credit, when to be stern and when to let things pass. All the resident young men spoke of her as *The Madam* [2].

Mrs. Mooney's young men paid fifteen shillings a week for board and lodgings (beer or stout[6] at dinner excluded). They shared in common tastes and occupations and for this reason they were very chummy with one another. They discussed with one another the chances of favourites and outsiders[7]. Jack Mooney, the Madam's son, who was clerk to a commission agent in Fleet Street, had the reputation of being a hard case[8]. He was fond of using soldiers' obscenities; usually he came home in the small hours. When he met his friends he had always a good one[9] to tell them and he was always sure to be on to a good thing — that is to say, a likely horse or a likely *artiste*. He was also handy with the mits[10] and sang comic songs. On Sunday nights there would often be a reunion in Mrs. Mooney's front drawing-room. The music-hall *artistes* would oblige; and Sheridan played waltzes and polkas and vamped accompaniments. Polly Mooney, the Madam's daughter, would also sing. She sang:

I'm a... naughty girl.
You needn't sham:
You know I am.[11]

---

4 artistes: popular touring performers.
5 music hall: a location for pop entertainment involving singing, dancing and comedies.
6 stout: a kind of strong, dark beer brewed with roasted malt or barley.
7 Favourites and outsiders are terms in horse-racing, the former referring to the horses that will possibly win the race and the latter referring to those that will not.
8 hard case: a person hard to deal with.
9 a good one: a dirty story.
10 handy with the mits: good with the fists and inclined to use them.

Polly was a slim girl of nineteen; she had light soft hair and a small full mouth. Her eyes, which were grey with a shade of green through them, had a habit of glancing upwards when she spoke with anyone, which made her look like a little perverse madonna [3]. Mrs. Mooney had first sent her daughter to be a typist in a corn-factor's[12] office but, as disreputable sheriff's man used to come every other day to the office, asking to be allowed to say a word to his daughter, she had taken her daughter home again and set her to do housework. As Polly was very lively the intention was to give her the run of the young men. Besides, young men like to feel that there is a young woman not very far away. Polly, of course, flirted with the young men but Mrs. Mooney, who was a shrewd judge, knew that the young men were only passing the time away: none of them meant business. Things went on so for a long time and Mrs. Mooney began to think of sending Polly back to typewriting when she noticed that something was going on between Polly and one of the young men. She watched the pair and kept her own counsel [4].

Polly knew that she was being watched, but still her mother's persistent silence could not be misunderstood. There had been no open complicity between mother and daughter, no open understanding but, though people in the house began to talk of the affair, still Mrs. Mooney did not intervene. Polly began to grow a little strange in her manner and the young man was evidently perturbed. At last, when she judged it to be the right moment, Mrs. Mooney intervened. She dealt with moral problems as a cleaver deals with meat: and in this case she had made up her mind.

It was a bright Sunday morning of early summer, promising heat, but with a fresh breeze blowing. All the windows of the boarding house were open and the lace curtains ballooned gently towards the

---

11 a song with much interest in sexual matters.

12 corn-factor: a trader in corn.

street beneath the raised sashes. The belfry of George's Church[13] sent out constant peals and worshippers, singly or in groups, traversed the little circus before the church, revealing their purpose by their self-contained demeanour no less than by the little volumes in their gloved hands[14]. Breakfast was over in the boarding house and the table of the breakfast-room was covered with plates on which lay yellow streaks of eggs with morsels of bacon-fat and bacon-rind.

Mrs. Mooney sat in the straw arm-chair and watched the servant Mary remove the breakfast things. She made Mary collect the crusts and pieces of broken bread to help to make Tuesday's bread-pudding. When the table was cleared, the broken bread collected, the sugar and butter safe under lock and key, she began to reconstruct the interview which she had had the night before with Polly. Things were as she had suspected: she had been frank in her questions and Polly had been frank in her answers. Both had been somewhat awkward, of course. She had been made awkward by her not wishing to receive the news in too cavalier a fashion or to seem to have connived and Polly had been made awkward not merely because allusions of that kind always made her awkward but also because she did not wish it to be thought that in her wise innocence she had divined the intention behind her mother's tolerance.

Mrs. Mooney glanced instinctively at the little gilt clock on the mantelpiece as soon as she had become aware through her revery that the bells of George's Church had stopped ringing. It was seventeen minutes past eleven: she would have lots of time to have the matter out with Mr. Doran[15] and then catch short twelve[16] at Marlborough

---

13 George's Church: a Protestant church of Ireland.

14 As the habit of the Protestants, they wear gloves when holding prayer books in hands during church services.

15 Mr. Doran: The name in the Irish language indicates that the man is a stranger to the community.

16 short twelve: the shortest cathedral service of the day held at noon at the side altar.

Street. She was sure she would win. To begin with she had all the weight of social opinion on her side: she was an outraged mother. She had allowed him to live beneath her roof, assuming that he was a man of honour, and he had simply abused her hospitality. He was thirty-four or thirty-five years of age, so that youth could not be pleaded as his excuse; nor could ignorance be his excuse since he was a man who had seen something of the world. He had simply taken advantage of Polly's youth and inexperience: that was evident. The question was: What reparation would he make?

There must be reparation made in such case. It is all very well for the man: he can go his ways as if nothing had happened, having had his moment of pleasure, but the girl has to bear the brunt. Some mothers would be content to patch up such an affair for a sum of money; she had known cases of it. But she would not do so. For her only one reparation could make up for the loss of her daughter's honour: marriage.

She counted all her cards again before sending Mary up to Mr. Doran's room to say that she wished to speak with him. She felt sure she would win. He was a serious young man, not rakish or loud-voiced like the others. If it had been Mr. Sheridan or Mr. Meade or Bantam Lyons her task would have been much harder. She did not think he would face publicity. All the lodgers in the house knew something of the affair; details had been invented by some. Besides, he had been employed for thirteen years in a great Catholic wine-merchant's office and publicity would mean for him, perhaps, the loss of his job. Whereas if he agreed all might be well. She knew he had a good screw[17] for one thing and she suspected he had a bit of stuff[18] put by.

Nearly the half-hour! She stood up and surveyed herself in the pier-glass. The decisive expression of her great florid face satisfied

17 screw: salary.
18 stuff: savings.

her and she thought of some mothers she knew who could not get their daughters off their hands. [5]

Mr. Doran was very anxious indeed this Sunday morning. He had made two attempts to shave but his hand had been so unsteady that he had been obliged to desist. Three days' reddish beard fringed his jaws and every two or three minutes a mist gathered on his glasses so that he had to take them off and polish them with his pocket-handkerchief. The recollection of his confession [6] of the night before was a cause of acute pain to him; the priest had drawn out every ridiculous detail of the affair and in the end had so magnified his sin that he was almost thankful at being afforded a loophole of reparation. The harm was done. What could he do now but marry her or run away? He could not brazen it out. The affair would be sure to be talked of and his employer would be certain to hear of it. Dublin is such a small city: everyone knows everyone else's business. He felt his heart leap warmly in his throat as he heard in his excited imagination old Mr. Leonard calling out in his rasping voice: "Send Mr. Doran here, please."

All his long years of service gone for nothing! All his industry and diligence thrown away! As a young man he had sown his wild oats, of course; he had boasted of his free-thinking and denied the existence of God to his companions in public-houses[19]. But that was all passed and done with...nearly. He still bought a copy of *Reynolds's Newspaper*[20] every week but he attended to his religious duties and for nine-tenths of the year lived a regular life. He had money enough to settle down on; it was not that. But the family would look down on her. First of all there was her disreputable father and then her mother's boarding house was beginning to get a certain fame[21]. He had a notion that he was being had. He could imagine his friends talking of

---

19 public-houses: a pub where beers and other drinks are served.

20 *Reynolds's Newspaper*: a London Sunday paper known for reporting scandalous events.

21 a certain fame: a dubious reputation.

the affair and laughing. She *was* a little vulgar; some times she said *I seen* and *If I had've known*. But what would grammar matter if he really loved her? He could not make up his mind whether to like her or despise her for what she had done. Of course he had done it too. His instinct urged him to remain free, not to marry. Once you are married you are done for, it said.

While he was sitting helplessly on the side of the bed in shirt and trousers she tapped lightly at his door and entered. She told him all, that she had made a clean breast of it to her mother and that her mother would speak with him that morning. She cried and threw her arms round his neck, saying:

" O, Bob! Bob! What am I to do? What am I to do at all?"

She would put an end to herself, she said.

He comforted her feebly, telling her not to cry, that it would be all right, never fear. He felt against his shirt the agitation of her bosom.

It was not altogether his fault that it had happened. He remembered well, with the curious patient memory of the celibate, the first casual caresses her dress, her breath, her fingers had given him. Then late one night as he was undressing for bed she had tapped at his door, timidly. She wanted to relight her candle at his for hers had been blown out by a gust. It was her bath night. She wore a loose open combing jacket[22] of printed flannel. Her white instep shone in the opening of her furry slippers and the blood glowed warmly behind her perfumed skin. From her hands and wrists too as she lit and steadied her candle a faint perfume arose.

On nights when he came in very late it was she who warmed up his dinner. He scarcely knew what he was eating feeling her beside him alone, at night, in the sleeping house. And her thoughtfulness! If the night was anyway cold or wet or windy there was sure to be a

22 combing jacket: bathrobe.

little tumbler of punch ready for him. Perhaps they could be happy together…

They used to go upstairs together on tiptoe, each with a candle, and on the third landing exchange reluctant good-nights. They used to kiss. He remembered well her eyes, the touch of her hand and his delirium…

But delirium passes. He echoed her phrase, applying it to himself: *What am I to do?* The instinct of the celibate warned him to hold back. But the sin was there; even his sense of honour told him that reparation must be made for such a sin.

While he was sitting with her on the side of the bed Mary came to the door and said that the missus[23] wanted to see him in the parlour. He stood up to put on his coat and waistcoat, more helpless than ever. When he was dressed he went over to her to comfort her. It would be all right, never fear. He left her crying on the bed and moaning softly: *O my God*!

Going down the stairs his glasses became so dimmed with moisture that he had to take them off and polish them. He longed to ascend through the roof and fly away to another country where he would never hear again of his trouble, and yet a force pushed him downstairs step by step. The implacable faces of his employer and of the Madam stared upon his discomfiture. On the last flight of stairs he passed Jack Mooney who was coming up from the pantry nursing two bottles of *Bass*[24]. They saluted coldly; and the lover's eyes rested for a second or two on a thick bulldog face and a pair of thick short arms. When he reached the foot of the staircase he glanced up and saw Jack regarding him from the door of the return-room[25].

Suddenly he remembered the night when one of the music-hall

23 missus: an informal and misused variant for missis, the mistress of a household.
24 *Bass*: a strong English-brewed brown ale.
25 return-room: a little room on the first landing of the stairs.

artistes, a little blond Londoner, had made a rather free allusion to Polly. The reunion had been almost broken up on account of Jack's violence. Everyone tried to quiet him. The music-hall *artiste*, a little paler than usual, kept smiling and saying that there was no harm meant: but Jack kept shouting at him that if any fellow tried that sort of a game on with his sister he'd bloody well put his teeth down his throat, so he would.

Polly sat for a little time on the side of the bed, crying. Then she dried her eyes and went over to the looking-glass. She dipped the end of the towel in the water-jug and refreshed her eyes with the cool water. She looked at herself in profile and readjusted a hairpin above her ear. Then she went back to the bed again and sat at the foot. She regarded the pillows for a long time and the sight of them awakened in her mind secret, amiable memories. She rested the nape of her neck against the cool iron bed-rail and fell into a revery. There was no longer any perturbation visible on her face.

She waited on patiently, almost cheerfully, without alarm, her memories gradually giving place to hopes and visions of the future. Her hopes and visions were so intricate that she no longer saw the white pillows on which her gaze was fixed or remembered that she was waiting for anything.

At last she heard her mother calling. She started to her feet and ran to the banisters.

" Polly! Polly!"

"Yes, mamma?"

" Come down, dear. Mr. Doran wants to speak to you."

Then she remembered what she had been waiting for.

NOTES ON THE TEXT

[1] The detail of Mrs. Mooney's judicial separation from her husband here seems to be deliberately given. As the provisions for divorce of the marriage law in England and Wales had not been extended to the Irish people in the early twentieth century, their separation granted by the Church court did not allow either of the pair to behave like an unmarried. Therefore, rumors of Mrs. Mooney's indiscretion even in her boarding house business contribute to our overall judgment of this crucial figure of the story.

[2] When the young male residents of the boarding house spoke of Mrs. Mooney as the "madam," they may not have necessarily taken it as a respectful form of address because, owing to the dubious reputation of her business, the word "madam" might have taken its disapproving meaning: a female owner of a brothel.

[3] "Wise innocence" was the epithet people around Polly tended to depict her with, which might be a subtle hint about the similar character of the young girl to her mother, Mrs. Mooney. The reference to her as a "little perverse madonna" reminds us of the hinted indecent nature of the boarding house and the development of the story seems to validate our suspicion.

[4] Mrs. Mooney is said to be an imposing woman, extremely calculating both in running her business and in dealing with her own family affairs. Mrs. Mooney's patience and care in the manipulation of her daughter's life and in the trapping of Mr. Doran for her daughter are brilliantly depicted by the author.

[5] The almost actionless plot of the story successfully draws our attention to the rather sophisticated trains of thought of the major characters. Quite a number of long passages, for instance, are devoted to the depiction of the working of Mrs. Mooney's mind, which, as a technique of narration called stream of consciousness, is one of the most outstanding features of modernist fiction.

[6] In Roman Catholic churches, a cabinet, often called a confessional, is prepared with a priest sitting inside a compartment, hearing through a latticed opening the confessions of a penitent who sits or kneels in an adjacent compartment separated from the priest's by a partition. Mr. Doran behaved like a pious Catholic.

QUESTIONS FOR DISCUSSION

1. Even though some stories in *Dubliners* may be, to some extent, autobiographical, most of them are not taken as "true." They are more often than not invented or imaginary. In what way then do you think they are all the same appealing to us? You may want to use Joyce's "The Boarding House" as an example in your discussion.

2. Joyce is supposed to be the most definitive modernist novelist after Conrad and stream of consciousness, the most outstanding feature of Joyce's *Ulysses*, is also well employed in his short stories. Could you comment on the success of his "The Boarding House" in this particular aspect?

3. As one of the commentators observes, Joyce never fails in his *Dubliners* to identify the source of much of the human misery he so clinically diagnoses. Could you give instances from the story you have just read to show the author's attention to details that depict the actual life of the ordinary people of the city?

4. Mr. Doran is obviously a crucial figure in the short story. What impressions does this young man leave upon you? Do you believe that "he was being bad" in his affair with Polly?

5. Mrs. Mooney called Polly to get down and talk at the end of the story, but we are not told what the young girl would be facing downstairs. What do you think is the most possible denouement of the story? Give your reasons to justify your rough guess.

SUGGESTED REFERENCES

Boysen, Benjamin. "The Necropolis of Love: James Joyce's *Dubliners*." *Neohelicon* 35.1 (2008): 157-69.

Brooks, Cleanth. "James Joyce's 'The Boarding House'." *Studies in Short Fiction* 24.4 (1988): 405-08.

Ingersoll, Earl G. "The Stigma of Femininity in James Joyce's 'Eveline' and 'The Boarding House'." *Studies in Short Fiction* 30.4 (1993): 501-10.

Joseph, Kelly. "Joyce's Marriage Cycle." *Studies in Short Fiction* 30.3 (1995): 367-79.

O'Gorman, Francis. "What Is Haunting *Dubliners*?" *James Joyce Quarterly* 48.3 (2011): 445-56.

Unit 16 D. H. Lawrence

(1885—1930)

A GUIDE TO LITERARY TERMINOLOGY

"Oedipus Complex": *As one of the Greek legends goes, Oedipus unknowingly slew a king who happened to be his father and, after getting on to the throne, took the widow as his queen who happened to be his mother. According to the story of this legendary figure, Sigmund Freud explained the psychological attachment of a child to a parent of the opposite sex in his work* ***Interpretation of Dreams*** *published in 1899 and, known as Oedipus complex, the concept has been widely used in the psychoanalytical interpretation of family relationships of the same nature in such literary works as Shakespeare's* ***Hamlet*** *and D. H. Lawrence's* ***Sons and Lovers****.*

According to Freud, children of about the ages three to five tend to reveal the development of ties with their parents of different sex. The ties exist until the time when they begin to identify themselves with parents of the same sex and thus the tendency resulting from their sexual instincts is repressed. He also observes in the book that, if parental attitudes at this particular stage are excessively prohibitive or excessively stimulating, this infantile tendency may become the forerunner of similar behavioral problems when the children grow into their adult age.

Female children may also show their infantile tendency of having intimate involvement with their male parents, which is explained as the behavior of Electra complex, named after another mythological figure, who helped slay her mother.

NOTES ON THE AUTHOR

D. H. Lawrence was born in 1885 to a rather hard-up family at Eastwood, a coal-mining town in England. His father was an uneducated miner who conducted a rough lower-class Nottingham dialect whereas his mother, a lady of some refinement, was a school-teacher who exerted tremendous influence upon D. H. Lawrence right from his young days and eventually sent him to Nottingham University College for education. The rather complicated and unharmonious family atmosphere had its effect both on the author's life and on his later writings.

Being one of the most original and controversial writers of the twentieth-century England, Lawrence has long been a particular interest to scholars and critics ever since the first couple of decades of his writing career. His works once aroused fierce debates between his admirers and hostile critics. The negative criticism over his writing was so hostile that he was even accused of intending to drag England down to the level of savages. His last novel *Lady Chatterley's Lover*, for instance, was condemned as obscene and, owing to the bitter accusation and severe censorship, it had never been published in its full form in England until 1960, some thirty years after Lawrence had died of tuberculosis in France.

The major theme of Lawrence's novels is the rather Freudian relationship between parents and children and the sham morality of modern industrialized society. As he observed in 1913, he has a strong belief in flesh and blood which, in his own words, are "wiser than intellect." He does not seem to have been certain, however, about the way to solve the problems of modern society which, as many of his works indicate, is the ultimate source of evils of life.

SYNOPSIS OF THE WORK

Sons and Lovers is perhaps the most important novel written by D. H. Lawrence. As it is a story of the Morel family, Walter and Gertrude Morel and their four children, one daughter and three sons, with its focus on the growth of the spiritual attachment of the second son Paul with his mother, the novel was originally titled by the author "Paul Morel."

The sons of the family grow up, and Gertrude gradually turns her attention and love from her husband, who is sensuous but primitive and clumsy in the expression of his affection, to her sons and, after two of her sons have left her, she feels the intense passion for Paul who is a sensitive lad of remarkable refinement. The son, feeling difficult to develop a normal relationship with any other woman as a result of his complete spiritual dependence upon his mother, eventually gives up Miriam, his girlfriend, and Clara, an older married woman, from whom he has gratified his burning physical need. The strong ties Paul has felt with his mother makes him hate his father and dedicate all his heart to her even beyond her lifetime. The story comes to an end when Gertrude dies of illness, leaving Paul an extremely lonely soul, wishing only for his own death. He releases himself, as Lawrence indicates at the end of the novel, from his heartfelt agony and turns himself away from death, walking towards the town and towards a new life.

Chapter 8, subtitled by the author as "Strife in Love," describes in detail the development of the complicated relationship, both physical and spiritual, between Paul and two of the most important women in his life, namely his mother and Miriam.

SELECTED READINGS

Sons and Lovers

(An excerpt from Chapter VIII)

…

Friday night was reckoning night for the miners. Morel "reckoned" — shared up the money of the stall — either in the New Inn at Bretty or in his own house, according as his fellow-butties wished. Barker had turned a non-drinker, so now the men reckoned at Morel's house.

Annie, who had been teaching away, was at home again. She was still a tomboy[1]; and she was engaged to be married. Paul was studying design.

Morel was always in good spirits on Friday evening, unless the week's earnings were small. He bustled immediately after his dinner, prepared to get washed. It was decorum for the women to absent themselves while the men reckoned. Women were not supposed to spy into such a masculine privacy as the buttles' reckoning, nor were they to know the exact amount of the week's earnings. So, whilst her father was spluttering in the scullery, Annie went out to spend an hour with a neighbour. Mrs. Morel attended to her baking.

"Shut that doo-er!" bawled Morel furiously.

Annie banged it behind her, and was gone.

"If tha oppens it again while I'm weshin' me, I'll ma'e thy jaw rattle," he threatened from the midst of his soap-suds. Paul and the

---

1 tomboy: a young girl who enjoys activities and games that are traditionally considered to be for boys.

mother frowned to hear him.

Presently he came running out of the scullery, with the soapy water dripping from him, dithering with cold.

"Oh, my sirs!" he said. "Wheer's my towel?"

It was hung on a chair to warm before the fire, otherwise he would have bullied and blustered. He squatted on his heels before the hot baking-fire to dry himself.

"F-ff-f!" he went, pretending to shudder with cold.

"Goodness, man, don't be such a kid!" said Mrs. Morel. "It's not cold."

"Thee strip thysen stark nak'd to wesh thy flesh i' that scullery," said the miner, as he rubbed his hair; "nowt b'r a ice-'ouse!"

"And I shouldn't make that fuss," replied his wife.

"No, tha'd drop down stiff, as dead as a door-knob, wi' thy nesh sides."

"Why is a door-knob deader than anything else?" asked Paul, curious.

"Eh, I dunno; that's what they say," replied his father. "But there's that much draught i' yon scullery, as it blows through your ribs like through a five-barred gate."

"It would have some difficulty in blowing through yours," said Mrs. Morel.

Morel looked down ruefully at his sides.

"Me!" he exclaimed. "I'm nowt b'r a skinned rabbit. My bones fair juts out on me."

"I should like to know where," retorted his wife.

"Iv'ry-wheer! I'm nobbut a sack o' faggots."

Mrs. Morel laughed. He had still a wonderfully young body, muscular, without any fat. His skin was smooth and clear. It might have been the body of a man of twenty-eight, except that there were, perhaps, too many blue scars, like tattoo-marks, where the coal-dust remained under the skin, and that his chest was too hairy. But he put his hand on his side ruefully. It was his fixed belief that, because he did not get fat, he was as thin as a starved rat.

Paul looked at his father's thick, brownish hands all scarred, with broken nails, rubbing the fine smoothness of his sides, and the incongruity struck him. It seemed strange they were the same flesh.

"I suppose," he said to his father, "you had a good figure once."

"Eh!" exclaimed the miner, glancing round, startled and timid, like a child.

"He had," exclaimed Mrs. Morel, "if he didn't hurtle himself up as if he was trying to get in the smallest space he could."

"Me!" exclaimed Morel — "me a good figure! I wor niver much more n'r a skeleton."

"Man!" cried his wife, "don't be such a pulamiter!"

"'Strewth!" he said. "Tha's niver knowed me but what I looked as if I wor goin' off in a rapid decline."

She sat and laughed.

"You've had a constitution like iron," she said; "and never a man had a better start, if it was body that counted. You should have seen him as a young man," she cried suddenly to Paul, drawing herself up to imitate her husband's once handsome bearing.

Morel watched her shyly. He saw again the passion she had had for him. It blazed upon her for a moment. He was shy, rather scared, and humble. Yet again he felt his old glow. And then immediately he felt the ruin he had made during these years. He wanted to bustle about, to run away from it.

"Gi'e my back a bit of a wesh," he asked her.

His wife brought a well-soaped flannel and clapped it on his shoulders. He gave a jump.

"Eh, tha mucky little 'ussy!" he cried. "Cowd as death!"

"You ought to have been a salamander," she laughed, washing his back. It was very rarely she would do anything so personal for him. The children did those things.

"The next world won't be half hot enough for you," she added.

"No," he said; "tha'lt see as it's draughty for me."

But she had finished. She wiped him in a desultory fashion, and went upstairs, returning immediately with his shifting-trousers. When he was dried he struggled into his shirt. Then, ruddy and shiny, with hair on end, and his flannelette shirt hanging over his pit-trousers, he stood warming the garments he was going to put on. He turned them, he pulled them inside out, he scorched them.

"Goodness, man!" cried Mrs. Morel, "get dressed!"

"Should thee like to clap thysen into britches as cowd as a tub o' water?" he said.

At last he took off his pit-trousers and donned decent black. He did all this on the hearth-rug, as he would have done if Annie and her familiar friends had been present. [1]

Mrs. Morel turned the bread in the oven. Then from the red earthenware panchion of dough that stood in a corner she took another handful of paste, worked it to the proper shape, and dropped it into a tin. As she was doing so Barker knocked and entered. He was a quiet, compact little man, who looked as if he would go through a stone wall. His black hair was cropped short, his head was bony. Like most miners, he was pale, but healthy and taut.

"Evenin', missis," he nodded to Mrs. Morel, and he seated himself with a sigh.

"Good-evening," she replied cordially.

"Tha's made thy heels crack," said Morel.

"I dunno as I have," said Barker.

He sat, as the men always did in Morel's kitchen, effacing himself rather.

"How's missis?" she asked of him.

He had told her some time back:

"We're expectin' us third just now, you see."

"Well," he answered, rubbing his head, "she keeps pretty middlin', I think."

"Let's see — when?" asked Mrs. Morel.

"Well, I shouldn't be surprised any time now."

"Ah! And she's kept fairly?"

"Yes, tidy."

"Tha's a blessing, for she's none too strong."

"No. An' I've done another silly trick."

"What's that?"

Mrs. Morel knew Barker wouldn't do anything very silly.

"I'm come be-out th' market-bag."

"You can have mine."

"Nay, you'll be wantin' that yourself."

"I shan't. I take a strong bag always."

She saw the determined little collier buying in the week's groceries and meat on the Friday nights, and she admired him. "Barker's little but he's ten times the man you are," she said to her husband.

Just then Wesson entered. He was thin, rather frail-looking, with a boyish ingenuousness and a slightly foolish smile, despite his seven children. But his wife was a passionate woman.

"I see you've kested me," he said, smiling rather vapidly.

"Yes," replied Barker.

The newcomer took off his cap and his big woolen muffler. His nose was pointed and red.

"I'm afraid you're cold, Mr. Wesson," said Mrs. Morel.

"It's a bit nippy," he replied.

"Then come to the fire."

"Nay, I s'll do where I am."

Both colliers sat away back. They could not be induced to come on to the hearth. The hearth is sacred to the family.

"Go thy ways i' th' arm-chair," cried Morel cheerily.

"Nay, thank yer; I'm very nicely here."

"Yes, come, of course," insisted Mrs. Morel.

He rose and went awkwardly. He sat in Morel's arm-chair awkwardly. It was too great a familiarity. But the fire made him blissfully happy.

"And how's that chest of yours?" demanded Mrs. Morel.

He smiled again, with his blue eyes rather sunny.

"Oh, it's very middlin'[2]," he said.

"Wi' a rattle in it like a kettle-drum," said Barker shortly.

"T-t-t-t!" went Mrs. Morel rapidly with her tongue. "Did you have that flannel singlet made?"

"Not yet," he smiled.

"Then, why didn't you?" she cried.

"It'll come," he smiled.

"Ah, an' Doomsday!" exclaimed Barker.

Barker and Morel were both impatient of Wesson. But, then, they were both as hard as nails, physically.

When Morel was nearly ready he pushed the bag of money to Paul.

"Count it, boy," he asked humbly.

Paul impatiently turned from his books and pencil, tipped the bag upside down on the table. There was a five-pound bag of silver[3], sovereigns[4] and loose money. He counted quickly, referred to the cheques — the written papers giving amount of coal — put the money in order. Then Barker glanced at the cheques.

Mrs. Morel went upstairs, and the three men came to table. Morel, as master of the house, sat in his arm-chair, with his back to the

---

2 middlin': not too bad.

3 silver: coins made of metal that looks like silver.

4 sovereign: old gold coins worth one pound.

hot fire. The two butties had cooler seats. None of them counted the money.

"What did we say Simpson's was?" asked Morel; and the butties[5] cavilled for a minute over the dayman's earnings. Then the amount was put aside.

"An' Bill Naylor's?"

This money also was taken from the pack.

Then, because Wesson lived in one of the company's houses, and his rent had been deducted, Morel and Barker took four-and-six each. And because Morel's coals had come, and the leading was stopped, Barker and Wesson took four shillings each. Then it was plain sailing[6]. Morel gave each of them a sovereign till there were no more sovereigns; each half a crown[7] till there were no more half-crowns; each a shilling till there were no more shillings. If there was anything at the end that wouldn't split, Morel took it and stood drinks[8].

Then the three men rose and went. Morel scuttled out of the house before his wife came down. She heard the door close, and descended. She looked hastily at the bread in the oven. Then, glancing on the table, she saw her money lying. Paul had been working all the time. But now he felt his mother counting the week's money, and her wrath rising.

"T-t-t-t-t!" went her tongue.

He frowned. He could not work when she was cross. She counted again.

"A measly twenty-five shillings!" she exclaimed. "How much was the cheque?"

"Ten pounds eleven," said Paul irritably. He dreaded what was coming.

---

5 butties: fellow workers.
6 plain sailing: simple and free from trouble.
7 crown: an old coin worth five shillings.
8 stand drinks: stand them to drinks; treat them with drinks.

"And he gives me a scrattlin' twenty-five, an' his club this week! But I know him. He thinks because *you're* earning he needn't keep the house any longer. No, all he has to do with his money is to guttle it. But I'll show him!"

"Oh, mother, don't!" cried Paul.

"Don't what, I should like to know?" she exclaimed.

"Don't carry on again. I can't work."

She went very quiet.

"Yes, it's all very well," she said; "but how do you think I'm going to manage?"

"Well, it won't make it any better to whittle about it."

"I should like to know what you'd do if you had it to put up with."

"It won't be long. You can have my money. Let him go to hell."

He went back to his work, and she tied her bonnet-strings grimly. When she was fretted he could not bear it. But now he began to insist on her recognising him.

"The two loaves at the top," she said, "will be done in twenty minutes. Don't forget them."

"All right," he answered; and she went to market.

He remained alone working. But his usual intense concentration became unsettled. He listened for the yard-gate. At a quarter-past seven came a low knock, and Miriam entered.

"All alone?" she said.

"Yes."

As if at home, she took off her tam-o'-shanter and her long coat, hanging them up. It gave him a thrill. This might be their own house, his and hers. Then she came back and peered over his work.

"What is it?" she asked.

"Still design, for decorating stuffs, and for embroidery."

She bent short-sightedly over the drawings.

It irritated him that she peered so into everything that was his, searching him out. He went into the parlour and returned with a bundle of brownish linen. Carefully unfolding it, he spread it on the floor. It proved to be a curtain or *portiére*, beautifully stencilled with a design on roses.

"Ah, how beautiful!" she cried.

The spread cloth, with its wonderful reddish roses and dark green stems, all so simple, and somehow so wicked-looking, lay at her feet. She went on her knees before it, her dark curls dropping. He saw her crouched voluptuously before his work, and his heart beat quickly. Suddenly she looked up at him.

"Why does it seem cruel?" she asked.

"What?"

"There seems a feeling of cruelty about it," she said.

"It's jolly good, whether or not," he replied, holding up his work with a lover's hands.

She rose slowly, pondering.

"And what will you do with it?" she asked.

"Send it to Liberty's. I did it for my mother, but I think she'd rather have the money."

"Yes," said Miriam. He had spoken with a touch of bitterness, and Miriam sympathised. Money would have been nothing to her.

He took the cloth back into the parlour. When he returned he threw to Miriam a smaller piece. It was a cushion-cover with the same design.

"I did that for you," he said.

She fingered the work with trembling hands, and did not speak. He became embarrassed.

"By Jove, the bread!" he cried.

He took the top loaves out, tapped them vigorously. They were done. He put them on the hearth to cool. Then he went to the scullery, wetted his hands, scooped the last white dough out of the panchion, and dropped it in a baking-tin. Miriam was still bent over her painted cloth. He stood rubbing the bits of dough from his hands.

"You do like it?" he asked.

She looked up at him, with her dark eyes one flame of love. He laughed uncomfortably. Then he began to talk about the design. There was for him the most intense pleasure in talking about his work to Miriam. All his passion, all his wild blood, went into this intercourse with her, when he talked and conceived his work. She brought forth to him his imaginations. She did not understand, any more than a woman understands when she conceives a child in her womb. But this was life for her and for him.

While they were talking, a young woman of about twenty-two, small and pale, hollowed-eyed, yet with a relentless look about her, entered the room. She was a friend at the Morel's.

"Take your things off," said Paul.

"No, I'm not stopping."

She sat down in the arm-chair opposite Paul and Miriam, who were on the sofa. Miriam moved a little farther from him. The room was hot, with a scent of new bread. Brown, crisp loaves stood on the hearth.

"I shouldn't have expected to see you here to-night, Miriam Leivers," said Beatrice wickedly.

"Why not?" murmured Miriam huskily.

"Why, let's look at your shoes."

Miriam remained uncomfortably still.

"If tha doesna tha durs'na," laughed Beatrice.

Miriam put her feet from under her dress. Her boots had that queer, irresolute, rather pathetic look about them, which showed how self-conscious and self-mistrustful she was. And they were covered with mud.

"Glory! You're a positive muck-heap," exclaimed Beatrice. "Who cleans your boots?"

"I clean them myself."

"Then you wanted a job," said Beatrice. "It would ha' taken a lot of men to ha' brought me down here to-night. But love laughs at sludge[9], doen't it, 'Postle my duck[10]?"

"*Inter alia*[11]," he said.

"Oh, Lord! Are you going to spout foreign languages? What does it mean, Miriam?"

There was a fine sarcasm in the last question, but Miriam did not see it.

"'Among other things,' I believe," she said humbly.

Beatrice put her tongue between her teeth and laughed wickedly.

"'Among other things,' 'Postle?" she repeated. "Do you mean love laughs at mothers, and fathers, and sisters, and brothers, and men friends, and lady friends, and even at the b'loved himself?"

She affected a great innocence.

"In fact, it's one big smile," he replied.

"Up its sleeve[12], 'Postle Morel — you believe me," she said; and she went off into another burst of wicked, silent laughter.

Miriam sat silent, withdrawn into herself. Every one of Paul's friends delighted in taking sides against her, and he left her in the lurch[13] — seemed almost to have a sort of revenge upon her then.

"Are you still at school?" asked Miriam of Beatrice.

"Yes."

"You've not had your notice, then?"

"I expect it at Easter."

---

9 sludge: thick wet mud.

10 duck: dear love.

11 Inter alia: (latin) among other things.

12 up its sleeve: keep it secret.

13 failed to help her when she needed it.

"Isn't it an awful shame, to turn you off merely because you didn't pass the exam?"

"I don't know," said Beatrice coldly.

"Agatha says you're as good as any teacher anywhere. It seems to me ridiculous. I wonder why you didn't pass."

"Short of brains, eh, 'Postle?" said Beatrice briefly.

"Only brains to bite with," replied Paul, laughing.

"Nuisance!" she cried; and, springing from her seat, she rushed and boxed his ears. She had beautiful small hands. He held her wrists while she wrestled with him. At last she broke free, and seized two handfuls of his thick, dark brown hair, which she shook.

"Beat!" he said, as he pulled his hair straight with his fingers. "I hate you!"

She laughed with glee.

"Mind!" she said. "I want to sit next to you."

"I'd as lief[14] be neighbours with a vixen[15]," he said, nevertheless making place for her between him and Miriam.

"Did it ruffle his pretty hair, then!" she cried; and, with her hair-comb, she combed him straight. "And his nice little moustache!" she exclaimed. She tilted his head back and combed his young moustache, "It's a wicked moustache, 'Postle," she said. "It's a red for danger. Have you got any of those cigarettes?"

He pulled his cigarette-case from his pocket. Beatrice looked inside it.

"And fancy me having Connie's last cig.," said Beatrice, putting the thing between her teeth. He held a lit match to her, and she puffed daintily.

"Thanks so much, darling," she said mockingly.

It gave her a wicked delight.

---

14 lief: willingly.

15 vixen: a female fox; an unpleasant woman.

"Don't you think he does it nicely, Miriam?" she asked.

"Oh, very!" said Miriam.

He took a cigarette for himself.

"Light, old boy?" said Beatrice, tilting her cigarette at him.

He bent forward to her to light his cigarette at hers. She was winking at him as he did so. Miriam saw his eyes trembling with mischief, and his full, almost sensual, mouth quivering. He was not himself, and she could not bear it. As he was now, she had no connection with him; she might as well not have existed. She saw the cigarette dancing on his full red lips. She hated his thick hair for being tumbled loose on his forehead.

"Sweet boy!" said Beatrice, tipping up his chin and giving him a little kiss on the cheek.

"I s'll kiss thee back, Beat," he said.

"Tha wunna!" she giggled, jumping up and going away. "Isn't he shameless, Miriam?"

"Quite," said Miriam. "By the way, aren't you forgetting the bread?"

"By Jove!" he cried, flinging open the oven door.

Out puffed the bluish smoke and a smell of burned bread.

"Oh, golly!" cried Beatrice, coming to his side. He crouched before the oven, she peered over his shoulder. "This is what comes of the oblivion of love, my boy."

Paul was ruefully removing the loaves. One was burnt black on the hot side; another was hard as a brick.

"Poor mater[16]!" said Paul.

"You want to grate it," said Beatrice. "Fetch me the nutmeg-grater."

She arranged the bread in the oven. He brought the grater, and she grated the bread on to a newspaper on the table. He set the doors

16 mater: mother.

open to blow away the smell of burned bread. Beatrice grated away, puffing her cigarette, knocking the charcoal off the poor loaf.

"My word, Miriam! You're in for it this time," said Beatrice.

"I!" exclaimed Miriam in amazement.

"You'd better be gone when his mother comes in. I know why King Alfred[17] burned the cakes. Now I see it! 'Postle would fix up a tale about his work making him forget, if he thought it would wash. If that old woman had come in a bit sooner, she'd have boxed the brazen thing's ears who make the oblivion, instead of poor Alfred's."

She giggled as she scraped the loaf. Even Miriam laughed in spite of herself. Paul mended the fire ruefully.

The garden gate was heard to bang.

"Quick!" cried Beatrice, giving Paul the scraped loaf. "Wrap it up in a damp towel."

Paul disappeared into the scullery. Beatrice hastily blew her scrapings into the fire, and sat down innocently. Annie[18] came bursting in. She was an abrupt, quite smart young woman. She blinked in the strong light.

"Smell of burning!" she exclaimed.

"It's the cigarettes," replied Beatrice demurely.

"Where's Paul?"

Leonard had followed Annie. He had a long comic face and blue eyes, very sad.

"I suppose he's left you to settle it between you," he said. He nodded sympathetically to Miriam, and became gently sarcastic to Beatrice.

"No," said Beatrice, "he's gone off with number nine."

"I just met number five inquiring for him," said Leonard.

17 King Alfred: Alfred the Great, the ninth-century king of the West Saxons, who repelled the Danes and confined them in Danelaw, northeast of England. He helped consolidate England into a unified kingdom.

18 Annie: daughter of the Morels.

"Yes — we're going to share him up like Solomon's[19] baby," said Beatrice.

Annie laughed.

"Oh, ay," said Leonard. "And which bit should you have?"

"I don't know," said Beatrice. "I'll let all the others pick first."

"An' you'd have the leavings, like?" said Leonard, twisting up a comic face.

Annie was looking in the oven. Miriam sat ignored. Paul entered.

"This bread's a fine sight, our Paul," said Annie.

"Then you should stop an' look after it," said Paul.

"You mean *you* should do what you're reckoning to do," replied Annie.

"He should, shouldn't he!" cried Beatrice.

"I s'd think he'd got plenty on hand," said Leonard.

"You had a nasty walk, didn't you, Miriam?" said Annie.

"Yes — but I'd been in all week — "

"And you wanted a bit of a change, like," insinuated Leonard kindly.

"Well, you can't be stuck in the house for ever," Annie agreed. She was quite amiable. Beatrice pulled on her coat, and went out with Leonard and Annie. She would meet her own boy.

"Don't forget that bread, our Paul," cried Annie. "Good-night, Miriam. I don't think it will rain."

When they had all gone, Paul fetched the swathed loaf, unwrapped it, and surveyed it sadly.

"It's a mess!" he said.

"But," answered Miriam impatiently, "what is it, after all — twopence ha'penny."

"Yes, but — it's the mater's precious baking, and she'll take it to

19 Solomon: king of the ancient Israelites who ruled ca. 962-922 BCE.

heart. However, it's no good bothering."

He took the loaf back into the scullery. There was a little distance between him and Miriam. He stood balanced opposite her for some moments considering, thinking of his behaviour with Beatrice. He felt guilty inside himself, and yet glad. For some inscrutable reason it served Miriam right. He was not going to repent. She wondered what he was thinking of as he stood suspended. His thick hair was tumbled over his forehead. Why might she not push it back for him, and remove the marks of Beatrice's comb? Why might she not press his body with her two hands. It looked so firm, and every whit living. And he would let other girls, why not her?

Suddenly he started into life. It made her quiver almost with terror as he quickly pushed the hair off his forehead and came towards her.

"Half-past eight!" he said. "We'd better buck up[20]. Where's your French?"

Miriam shyly and rather bitterly produced her exercise-book. Every week she wrote for him a sort of diary of her inner life, in her own French. He had found this was the only way to get her to do compositions. And her diary was mostly a love-letter. He would read it now, she felt as if her soul's history were going to be desecrated by him in his present mood. He sat beside her. She watched his hand, firm and warm, rigorously scoring her work. He was reading only the French, ignoring her soul that was there. But gradually his hand forgot its work. He read in silence, motionless. She quivered.

"'*Ce matin les oiseaux m'ont éveillé,*'" he read. " '*Il faisait encore un crepuscule. Mais la petite fenêtre de ma chambre était blême, et puis, jaûne, et tous les oiseaux du bois éclatèrent dans un chanson vif et résonant. Toute l'aube tressaillit. J'avais revé de vous. Est-ce*

20 buck up: cheer up.

que vous voyez aussi l'aube? Les oiseaux m'éveillent presque tous les matins, et toujours il y a quelque chose de terreur dans le cri des grives. Il est si clair — '"

Miriam sat tremulous, half ashamed. He remained quite still, trying to understand. He only knew she loved him. He was afraid of her love for him. It was too good for him, and he was inadequate. His own love was at fault, not hers. Ashamed, he corrected her work, humbly writing above her words.

"Look," he said quietly, "the past participle conjugated with *avoir* agrees with the direct object when it precedes."

She bent forward, trying to see and to understand. Her free, fine curls tickled his face. He started as if they had been red hot, shuddering. He saw her peering forward at the page, her red lips parted piteously, the black hair springing in fine strands across her tawny, ruddy cheek. She was coloured like a pomegranate for richness. His breath came short as he watched her. Suddenly she looked up at him. Her dark eyes were naked with their love, afraid, and yearning. His eyes, too, were dark, and they hurt her. They seemed to master her. She lost all her self-control, was exposed in fear. And he knew, before he could kiss her, he must drive something out of himself. And a touch of hate for her crept back again into his heart. He returned to her exercise.

Suddenly he flung down the pencil, and was at the oven in a leap, turning the bread. For Miriam he was too quick. She started violently, and it hurt her with real pain. Even the way he crouched before the oven hurt her. There seemed to be something cruel in it, something cruel in the swift way he pitched the bread out of the tins, caught it up again. If only he had been gentle in his movements she would have felt so rich and warm. As it was, she was hurt.

He returned and finished the exercise.

"You've done well this week," he said.

"You really do blossom out sometimes," he said. "You ought to write poetry."

She lifted her head with joy, then she shook it mistrustfully.

"I don't trust myself," she said.

"You should try!"

Again she shook her head.

"Shall we read, or is it too late?" he asked.

"It is late — but we can read just a little," she pleaded.

She was really getting now the food for her life during the next week. He made her copy Baudelaire's "Le Balcon". Then he read it for her. His voice was soft and caressing, but growing almost brutal. He had a way of lifting his lips and showing his teeth, passionately and bitterly, when he was much moved. This he did now. It made Miriam feel as if he were trampling on her. She dared not look at him, but sat with her head bowed. She could not understand why he got into such a tumult and fury. It made her wretched. She did not like Baudelaire, on the whole — nor Verlaine.

> "Behold her singing in the field
> Yon solitary highland lass."

That nourished her heart. So did "Fair Ines". And —

> "It was a beauteous evening, calm and pure,
> And breathing holy quiet like a nun."

These were like herself. And there was he, saying in his throat bitterly,

> "*Tu te rappelleras la beaute des caresses*."

The poem was finished; he took the bread out of the oven, arranging the burnt loaves at the bottom of the panchion, the good ones at the top. The desiccated loaf remained swathed up in the scullery.

"Mater needn't know till morning," He said. "It won't upset her so much then as at night."

Miriam looked in the bookcase, saw what postcards and letters he had received, saw what books were there. She took one that had interested him. Then he turned down the gas and they set off. He did not trouble to lock the door.

He was not home again until a quarter to eleven. His mother was seated in the rocking-chair. Annie, with a rope of hair hanging down her back, remained sitting on a low stool before the fire, her elbows on her knees, gloomily. On the table stood the offending loaf unswathed. Paul entered rather breathless. No one spoke. His mother was reading the little local newspaper. He took off his coat, and went to sit down on the sofa. His mother moved curtly aside to let him pass. No one spoke. He was very uncomfortable. For some minutes he sat pretending to read a piece of paper he found on the table. Then —

"I forgot that bread, mother," he said.

There was no answer from either woman.

"Well," he said. "it's only twopence h'penny. I can pay you for that."

Being angry, he put three pennies on the table and slid them towards his mother. She turned away her head. Her mouth was shut tightly.

"Yes," said Annie, "you don't know how badly my mother is!"

The girl sat staring glumly into the fire.

"Why is she badly?" asked Paul, in his overbearing way.

"Well!" said Annie. "She could scarcely get home."

He looked closely at his mother. She looked ill.

"*Why* could you scarcely get home?" he asked her, still sharply. She would not answer.

"I found her as white as a sheet sitting here," said Annie, with a suggestion of tears in her voice.

"Well, *why*?" insisted Paul. His brows were knitting, his eyes dilating passionately.

"It was enough to upset anybody," said Mrs. Morel, "hugging those parcels — meat, and green-groceries, and a pair of curtains — "

"Well, why *did* you hug them; you needn't have done."

"Then who would?"

"Let Annie fetch the meat."

"Yes, and I *would* fetch the meat, but how was I to know. You were off with Miriam, instead of being in when my mother came."

"And what was the matter with you?" asked Paul of his mother.

"I suppose it's my heart," she replied. Certainly she looked bluish round the mouth.

"And have you felt it before?"

"Yes — often enough."

"Then why haven't you told me? — and why haven't you seen a doctor?"

Mrs. Morel shifted in her chair, angry with him for his hectoring.

"You'd never notice anything," said Annie. "You're too eager to be off with Miriam."

"Oh, am I — and any worse than you with Leonard?"

"I was in at a quarter to ten."

There was silence in the room for a time.

"I should have thought," said Mrs. Morel bitterly, "that she wouldn't have occupied you so entirely as to burn a whole ovenful of bread."

"Beatrice was here as well as she."

"Very likely. But we know why the bread is spoilt."

"Why?" he flashed.

"Because you were engrossed with Miriam," replied Mrs. Morel hotly.

"Oh, very well — then it was not!" he replied angrily.

He was distressed and wretched. Seizing a paper, he began to read. Annie, her blouse unfastened, her long ropes of hair twisted into a plait, went up to bed, bidding him a very curt good-night.

Paul sat pretending to read. He knew his mother wanted to upbraid him. He also wanted to know what had made her ill, for he was troubled. So, instead of running away to bed, as he would have liked to do, he sat and waited. There was a tense silence. The clock ticked loudly.

"You'd better go to bed before your father comes in," said the mother harshly. "And if you're going to have anything to eat, you'd better get it."

"I don't want anything."

It was his mother's custom to bring him some trifle for supper on Friday night, the night of luxury for the colliers. He was too angry to go and find it in the pantry this night. This insulted her.

"If I *wanted* you to go to Selby on Friday night, I can imagine the scene," said Mrs. Morel. "But you're never too tired to go if *she* will come for you. Nay, you neither want to eat nor drink then."

"I can't let her go alone."

"Can't you? And why does she come?"

"Not because I ask her."

"She doesn't come without you want her — "

"Well, what if I *do* want her — " he replied.

"Why, nothing, if it was sensible or reasonable. But to go trapseing up there miles and miles in the mud, coming home at midnight, and got to go to Nottingham in the morning — "

"If I hadn't, you'd be just the same."

"Yes, I should, because there's no sense in it. Is she so fascinating that you must follow her all that way?" Mrs. Morel was bitterly sarcastic. She sat still, with averted face, stroking with a rhythmic, jerked movement, the black sateen of her apron. It was a movement that hurt Paul to see.

"I do like her," he said, "but — "

"*Like* her!" said Mrs. Morel, in the same biting tones. "It seems to me you like nothing and nobody else. There's neither Annie, nor me, nor anyone now for you."

"What nonsense, mother — you know I don't love her — I — I tell you I *don't* love her — she doesn't even walk with my arm, because I don't want her to."

"Then why do you fly to her so often?"

"I *do* like to talk to her — I never said I didn't. But I *don't* love her."

"Is there nobody else to talk to?"

"Not about the things we talk of. There's a lot of things that you're not interested in, that — "

"What things?"

Mrs. Morel was so intense that Paul began to pant.

"Why — painting — and books. *You* don't care about Herbert Spencer[21]."

"No," was the sad reply. "And *you* won't at my age."

"Well, but I do now — and Miriam does — "

"And how do you know," Mrs. Morel flashed defiantly, "that *I* shouldn't. Do you ever try me!"

"But you don't, mother, you know you don't care whether a picture's decorative or not; you don't care what *manner* it is in."

"How do you know I don't care? Do you ever try me? Do you ever talk to me about these things, to try?"

---

21 Herbert Spencer: nineteenth-century British philosopher who attempted to apply the theory of evolution to philosophy and ethics in his series *Synthetic Philosophy*.

"But it's not that that matters to you, mother, you know it's not."

"What is it, then — what is it, then, that matters to me?" she flashed. He knitted his brows with pain.

"You're old, mother, and we're young."

He only meant that the interests of *her* age were not the interests of his. But he realised the moment he had spoken that he had said the wrong thing.

"Yes, I know it well — I am old. And therefore I may stand aside; I have nothing more to do with you. You only want me to wait on you — the rest is for Miriam."

He could not bear it. Instinctively he realised that he was life to her. And, after all, she was the chief thing to him, the only supreme thing.

"You know it isn't, mother, you know it isn't!"

She was moved to pity by his cry.

"It looks a great deal like it," she said, half putting aside her despair.

"No, mother — I really *don't* love her. I talk to her, but I want to come home to you."

He had taken off his collar and tie, and rose, bare-throated, to go to bed. As he stooped to kiss his mother, she threw her arms round his neck, hid her face on his shoulder, and cried, in a whimpering voice, so unlike her own that he writhed in agony:

"I can't bear it. I could let another woman — but not her. She'd leave me no room, not a bit of room — "

And immediately he hated Miriam bitterly.

"And I've never — you know, Paul — I've never had a husband — not really — " [2]

He stroked his mother's hair, and his mouth was on her throat.

"And she exults so in taking you from me — she's not like ordinary girls."

"Well, I don't love her, mother," he murmured, bowing his head and hiding his eyes on her shoulder in misery. His mother kissed him a long, fervent kiss.

"My boy!" she said, in a voice trembling with passionate love.

Without knowing, he gently stroked her face.

"There," said his mother, "now go to bed. You'll be so tired in the morning." As she was speaking she heard her husband coming. "There's your father — now go." Suddenly she looked at him almost as if in fear. "Perhaps I'm selfish. If you want her, take her, my boy."

His mother looked so strange, Paul kissed her, trembling.

"Ha — mother!" he said softly.

Morel came in, walking unevenly. His hat was over one corner of his eye. He balanced in the doorway.

"At your mischief again?" he said venomously.

Mrs. Morel's emotion turned into sudden hate of the drunkard who had come in thus upon her.

"At any rate, it is sober," she said.

"H'm — h'm! h'm — h'm!" he sneered. He went into the passage, hung up his hat and coat. Then they heard him go down three steps to the pantry. He returned with a piece of pork-pie in his fist. It was what Mrs. Morel had bought for her son.

"Nor was that bought for you. If you can give me no more than twenty-five shillings, I'm sure I'm not going to buy you pork-pie to stuff, after you've swilled a bellyful of beer."

"Wha-at — wha-at — " snarled Morel, toppling in his balance. "Wha-at — not for me?" He looked at the piece of meat and crust, and suddenly, in a vicious spurt of temper, flung it into the fire.

Paul started to his feet.

"Waste your own stuff!" he cried.

"What — what!" suddenly shouted Morel, jumping up and

clenching his fist. "I'll show yer, yer young jockey[22]!"

"All right!" said Paul viciously, putting his head on one side. "Show me!"

He would at that moment dearly have loved to have a smack at something. Morel was half crouching, fists up, ready to spring. The young man stood, smiling with his lips.

"Ussha!" hissed the father, swiping round with a great stroke just past his son's face. He dared not, even though so close, really touch the young man, but swerved an inch away.

"Right!" said Paul, his eyes upon the side of his father's mouth, where in another instant his fist would have hit. He ached for that stroke. But he heard a faint moan from behind. His mother was deadly pale and dark at the mouth. Morel was dancing up to deliver another blow.

"Father!" said Paul, so that the word rang.

Morel started, and stood at attention.

"Mother!" moaned the boy. "Mother!"

She began to struggle with herself. Her open eyes watched him, although she could not move. Gradually she was coming to herself. He laid her down on the sofa, and ran upstairs for a little whisky, which at last she could sip. The tears were hopping down his face. As he kneeled in front of her he did not cry, but the tears ran down his face quickly. Morel, on the opposite side of the room, sat with his elbows on his knees glaring across.

"What's a-matter with 'er?" he asked.

"Faint!" replied Paul.

"H'm!"

The elderly man began to unlace his boots. He stumbled off to bed. His last fight was fought in that home.

---

22 jockey: a kid who can only ride a bike.

Paul kneeled there, stroking his mother's hand.

"Don't be poorly, mother — don't be poorly!" he said time after time.

"It's nothing, my boy," she murmured.

At last he rose, fetched in a large piece of coal, and raked the fire. Then he cleared the room, put everything straight, laid the things for breakfast, and brought his mother's candle.

"Can you go to bed, mother?"

"Yes, I'll come."

"Sleep with Annie, mother, not with him."

"No. I'll sleep in my own bed."

"Don't sleep with him, mother."

"I'll sleep in my own bed."

She rose, and he turned out the gas, then followed her closely upstairs, carrying her candle. On the landing he kissed her close.

"Good-night, mother."

"Good-night!" she said.

He pressed his face upon the pillow in a fury of misery. And yet, somewhere in his soul, he was at peace because he still loved his mother best. It was the bitter peace of resignation.

The efforts of his father to conciliate him next day were a great humiliation to him.

Everybody tried to forget the scene.

NOTES ON THE TEXT

[1] We have here a warm scene of family life when Walter and Gertrude Morel and even Paul talk to each other with warmth and tenderness, which seldom occurs in the latter part of the novel.

[2] This is the episode when Mrs. Morel makes one of the most significant statements of the novel to his son "I have never had a husband" in a voice of love and Paul responds to it with a long and passionate kiss.

QUESTIONS FOR DISCUSSION

1. As one commentator observes, Lawrence's underlying idea throughout the novel is that sex is the mysterious life force that must be brought into the consciousness. Is this argument supported by the details from Chapter 8 in the novel?

2. Freudian interpretations of *Sons and Lovers* often relate the theme of the work to Oedipus Complex. Show your opinion concerning this and support yourself with details from your reading.

3. Complicated relationships between Paul and his mother, and between Paul and Miriam are contrastive and at the same time interconnected. Analyze them in detail.

4. Lawrence shows remarkable skill at using color to signify the mood of scenes. Could you illustrate the power of the author in this particular aspect with instances from the chapter you have read?

5. Miriam is to blame for her unsuccessful relationship with Paul because, according to some critics, her behavior, especially her humility, unusual and abnormal, is not acceptable to any male. How are you going to respond to this judgment?

SUGGESTED REFERENCES

Bergquist, Carolyn. "Lawrence's *Sons and Lovers*." *The Explicator* 53.3 (1995):167-69.

Coates, Kimberly. "Eros in the Sick Room: Phosphorescent Form and Aesthetic Ecstasy in D. H. Lawrence's *Sons and Lovers*." *Journal of Narrative Theory* 38.2 (2008): 135-76.

Fox, Elizabeth M. "Psychodynamics, Seeing, and Being in D. H. Lawrence." *Modern Fiction Studies* 46.4 (2000): 971-78.

Granofsky, Ronald. "His Father's Dirty Digging: Recuperating the Masculine in D. H. Lawrence's *Sons and Lovers*." *Modern Fiction Studies* 55.2 (2009): 242-64.

Marsh, Nicholas. *D. H. Lawrence: The Novels*. New York: St. Martin's Press, 2000.

Unit 17 George Bernard Shaw

(1856–1950)

A GUIDE TO LITERARY TERMINOLOGY

"Soliloquy": *Perhaps all the English majors are familiar with the famous line "To be or not to be" and the subsequent heart-stirring lines, which effectively lead us into the inner world of the deeply troubled prince. The term for this passage in drama is "soliloquy" or "monolog" in which the character directly addresses the audience by speaking his thought aloud and alone upon the stage. This scene in Shakespeare's tragedy* ***Hamlet*** *is typical on the stage before the eighteenth century where characters do this either alone or with others keeping silent. The handy examples are those from the works of the Elizabethan playwrights such as Thomas Kyd and Christopher Marlowe. They are all artfully designed outpourings of the characters' thoughts and emotions and they all serve in the plays as crucial indicators of the minds of those powerful and memorable characters.*

The twentieth century saw experiments in the field of English drama to substitute the set speeches of the soliloquy. In the plays by Eugene O'Neill and Samuel Beckett, for example, other ways of expression were explored so as to reveal to the audience or readers the innermost secrets of the characters. Masks and interior monologs are used in the works of the two dramatists as a device of disclosing what may not be shown via speeches at a certain point of time on the stage. Their contribution to the expressiveness of drama is of course significant.

There are playwrights in our modern times, however, who have shown the power of their art in drama by using conventional soliloquys. Set speeches like the one delivered by the protagonist at the court in George Bernard Shaw's ***Saint Joan****, are by no means outdated. The passages are key to our understanding of the characters and, therefore, are worth our time to read and read closely.*

NOTES ON THE AUTHOR

George Bernard Shaw was born in 1856 and did not seem to have a very happy childhood because of the unsuccessful marriage of his parents. His effort to make a living by writing started early in his life even though his early writing effort was not particularly encouraged by his readers. It is said that he made no more than ten pounds during the first eight years of his writing career.

He tried his hand in various areas including music but, as he found his writings on drama were better received, soon turned his attention to drama criticism. As his impatience with artificiality of the London theater and his pleading for the performance of plays on social and moral problems made his periodical articles stand out among those by his contemporaries, he became one of the most noteworthy critics in the campaign for a theater of ideas in Britain, resulting from the influence of the works by Ibsen and Strindberg.

Shaw's major achievements, needless to say, are his plays, which eventually made him a success because of the uniqueness of the serious conflict his works depict of thought and belief, rather than that of neurosis or physical passion. His plays attracted the attention both the audience and their critics because of his emphasis upon the "Life Force" that had been frustrated by such modern problems as war, disease, as well as the brevity of the lifespan of human beings. According to the playwright, a current of creative evolution activated by the power of human will was crucial to the survival and the progress of human society.

He was awarded the Nobel Prize in 1925 and died another 25 years later at the age of 94.

NOTES ON THE WORK

Based on the fifteenth-century legendary story of Joan of Arc, the play is one of the most well-known plays written by George Bernard Shaw who titled it *Saint Joan*: *A Chronicle Play in Six Scenes and an Epilogue*.

As the story goes, Joan, a French illiterate farmer girl, was inspired by the voices of Sts. Michael, Catherine, and Margaret, and answered the call of the nation. She became soon the key military leader in the national effort to liberate France from the English and put Charles VII upon his throne. Her unbelievable accomplishments made her a legend and also the target of bitter enmity of both kingdoms. She was eventually taken prisoner by the Burgundians and handed over by them to the hostile English. The scene of the play that follows describes the trial-at-law she was brought to by both parties with the help of the Inquisition. Joan was sentenced as a heretic at the trial and was burned by the English at the market-place of Rouen.

Shaw's plays are always known for their serious conflicts of thought and belief, and *Saint Joan* is powerful and dramatic too in this aspect. In the preface he wrote to the play, Shaw claimed that there were no villains particularly in the work. What made the scene tragic is not only that Joan never understood what her persecutors, political and religious, were accusing her of, but also that the murder was not committed by murderers. To the playwright, the persecution itself was not interesting as a historical event. Just like the lies the fifteenth-century people told about Joan, lies of the same nature would not cease so long as their political and social circumstances were not obsolete.

SELECTED READINGS

Saint Joan

(An excerpt from Scene VI)

Rouen, 30th May 1431. A great stone hall in the castle, arranged for a trial-at-law, but not a trial-by-jury, the court being the Bishop's court with the Inquisition[1] *participating: hence there are two raised chairs side by side for the Bishop and the Inquisitor as judges. Rows of chairs radiating from them at an obtuse angle are for the canons, the doctors of law and theology, and the Dominican monks*[2]*, who act as assessors. In the angle is a table for the scribes, with stools. There is also a heavy rough wooden stool for the prisoner. All these are at the inner end of the hall. The further end is open to the courtyard through a row of arches. The court is shielded from the weather by screens and curtains.*

Looking down the great hall from the middle of the inner end, the judicial chairs and scribes' table are to the right. The prisoner's stool is to the left. There are arched doors right and left. It is a fine sunshiny May morning.

...

1 Inquisition: a tribunal formerly held by the Roman Catholic Church and directed at the suppression of heresy.

2 Dominican monk: members of an order of friars founded by St. Dominic, a thirteenth-century Spanish-born priest.

...

THE INQUISITOR. Let the accused be brought in.

LADVENU [*calling*] The accused. Let her be brought in.

Joan, chained by the ankles, is brought in through the arched door behind the prisoner's stool by a guard of English soldiers. With them is the Executioner[3] *and his assistants. They lead her to the prisoner's stool, and place themselves behind it after taking off her chain. She wears a page's black suit. Her long imprisonment and the strain of the examinations which have preceded the trial have left their mark on her; but her vitality still holds: she confronts the court unabashed, without a trace of the awe which their formal solemnity seems to require for the complete success of its impressiveness.*

THE INQUISITOR [*kindly*] Sit down, Joan. [*She sits on the prisoner's stool*]. You look very pale today. Are you not well?

JOAN. Thank you kindly: I am well enough. But the Bishop sent me some carp; and it made me ill.

CAUCHON. I am sorry. I told them to see that it was fresh.

JOAN. You meant to be good to me, I know; but it is a fish that does not agree with me. The English thought you were trying to poison me —

CAUCHON [*together with Chaplain*] What!

THE CHAPLAIN [*together with Cauchon*] No, my lord.

JOAN [*continuing*] They are determined that I shall be burnt as a witch; and they sent their doctor to cure me; but he was forbidden to bleed me[4] because the silly people believe that a witch's witchery leaves her if she is bled; so he only called me filthy names. Why do you leave me in the hands of the English? I should be in the hands of The Church. And why must I be chained by the feet to a log of wood?

---

3 Executioner: an official who is to execute the condemned criminal.

4 According to medieval physiology, blood letting may cure diseases because it could help keep the balance of four bodily fluids, namely blood, phlegm, black bile and yellow bile, in the body of a sick person.

Are you afraid I will fly away?

D'ESTIVET [*harshly*] Woman: it is not for you to question the court: it is for us to question you.

COURCELLES. When you were left unchained, did you not try to escape by jumping from a tower sixty feet high? If you cannot fly like a witch, how is it that you are still alive?

JOAN. I suppose because the tower was not so high then. It has grown higher every day since you began asking me questions about it.

D'ESTIVET. Why did you jump from the tower?

JOAN. How do you know that I jumped?

D'ESTIVET. You were found lying in the moat. Why did you leave the tower?

JOAN. Why would anybody leave a prison if they could get out?

D'ESTIVET. You tried to escape?

JOAN. Of course I did; and not for the first time either. If you leave the door of the cage open the bird will fly out.

D'ESTIVET [*rising*] That is a confession of heresy. I call the attention of the court to it.

JOAN. Heresy, he calls it! Am I a heretic because I try to escape from prison?

D'ESTIVET. Assuredly, if you are in the hands of The Church, and you willfully take yourself out of its hands, you are deserting The Church; and that is heresy.

JOAN. It is great nonsense. Nobody could be such a fool as to think that.

D'ESTIVET. You hear, my lord, how I am reviled in the execution of my duty by this woman. [*He sits down indignantly*].

CAUCHON. I have warned you before, Joan, that you are doing yourself no good by these pert answers.

JOAN. But you will not talk sense to me. I am reasonable if you will be reasonable.

THE INQUISITOR [*interposing*] This is not yet in order. You forget, Master Promoter, that the proceedings have not been formally opened. The time for questions is after she has sworn on the Gospels[5] to tell us the whole truth.

JOAN. You say this to me every time. I have said again and again that I will tell you all that concerns this trial. But I cannot tell you the whole truth: God does not allow the whole truth to be told. You do not understand it when I tell it. It is an old saying that he who tells too much truth is sure to be hanged. I am weary of this argument: we have been over it nine times already. I have sworn as much as I will swear; and I will swear no more.

COURCELLES. My lord: she should be put to the torture.

THE INQUISITOR. You hear, Joan? That is what happens to the obdurate. Think before you answer. Has she been shewn[6] the instruments?

THE EXECUTIONER. They are ready, my lord. She has seen them.

JOAN. If you tear me limb from limb until you separate my soul from my body you will get nothing out of me beyond what I have told you. What more is there to tell that you could understand? Besides, I cannot bear to be hurt; and if you hurt me I will say anything you like to stop the pain. But I will take it all back afterwards; so what is the use of it?

LADVENU. There is much in that. We should proceed mercifully.

COURCELLES. But the torture is customary.

THE INQUISITOR. It must not be applied wantonly. If the accused will confess voluntarily, then its use cannot be justified.

COURCELLES. But this is unusual and irregular. She refuses to

5 Gospels: the first four books of the New Testament.
6 shewn: shown.

take the oath.

LADVENU [*disgusted*] Do you want to torture the girl for the mere pleasure of it?

COURCELLES [*bewildered*] But it is not a pleasure. It is the law. It is customary. It is always done.

THE INQUISITOR. That is not so, Master, except when the inquiries are carried on by people who do not know their legal business.

COURCELLES. But the woman is a heretic[7]. I assure you it is always done.

CAUCHON [*decisively*] It will not be done today if it is not necessary. Let there be an end of this. I will not have it said that we proceeded on forced confessions. We have sent our best preachers and doctors to this woman to exhort and implore her to save her soul and body from the fire: we shall not now send the executioner to thrust her into it.

COURCELLES. Your lordship is merciful, of course. But it is a great responsibility to depart from the usual practice.

JOAN. Thou art a rare noodle[8], Master. Do what was done last time is thy rule, eh? [1]

COURCELLES [*rising*] Thou wanton: dost thou dare call me noodle?

THE INQUISITOR. Patience, Master, patience: I fear you will soon be only too terribly avenged.

COURCELLES [*mutters*] Noodle indeed! [*He sits down, much discontented*].

THE INQUISITOR. Meanwhile, let us not be moved by the rough side of a shepherd lass's tongue.

JOAN. Nay: I am no shepherd lass, though I have helped with the

---

7 heretic: one who is supposed to be guilty of holding a belief that goes against traditional religious doctrines.
8 noodle: a silly person.

sheep like anyone else. I will do a lady's work in the house — spin or weave — against any woman in Rouen.

THE INQUISITOR. This is not a time for vanity, Joan. You stand in great peril.

JOAN. I know it: have I not been punished for my vanity? If I had not worn my cloth of gold surcoat[9] in battle like a fool, that Burgundian soldier[10] would never have pulled me backwards off my horse; and I should not have been here.

THE CHAPLAIN. If you are so clever at woman's work why do you not stay at home and do it?

JOAN. There are plenty of other women to do it; but there is nobody to do my work.

CAUCHON. Come! We are wasting time on trifles. Joan: I am going to put a most solemn question to you. Take care how you answer; for your life and salvation are at stake on it. Will you for all you have said and done, be it good or bad, accept the judgment of God's Church on earth? More especially as to the acts and words that are imputed to you in this trial by the Promoter here, will you submit your case to the inspired interpretation of the Church Militant?

JOAN. I am a faithful child of The Church. I will obey The Church —

CAUCHON [*hopefully leaning forwad*] You will?

JOAN. — provided it does not command anything impossible.

Cauchon sinks back in his chair with a heavy sigh. The Inquisitor purses his lips and frowns. Ladvenu shakes his head pitifully.

D'ESTIVET. She imputes to The Church the error and folly of commanding the impossible.

JOAN. If you command me to declare that all that I have done and said, and all the visions and revelations I have had, were not from

---

9 surcoat: a tunic worn over the armor.

10 Burgundian soldier: a soldier from Burgundy, a historical region of eastern France.

God, then that is impossible: I will not declare it for anything in the world. What God made me do I will never go back on; and what He has commanded or shall command I will not fail to do in spite of any man alive. That is what I mean by impossible. And in case The Church should bid me do anything contrary to the command I have from God, I will not consent to it, no matter what it may be.

THE ASSESSORS [*shocked and indignant*] Oh! The Church contrary to God! What do you say now? Flat heresy. This is beyond everything, etc., etc.

D'ESTIVET [*throwing down his brief*[11]] My lord: do you need anything more than this?

CAUCHON. Woman: you have said enough to burn ten heretics. Will you not be warned? Will you not understand?

THE INQUISITOR. If the Church Militant tells you that your revelations and visions are sent by the devil to tempt you to your damnation, will you not believe that The Church is wiser than you?

JOAN. I believe that God is wiser than I; and it is His commands that I will do. All the things that you call my crimes have come to me by the command of God. I say that I have done them by the order of God: it is impossible for me to say anything else. If any Churchman says the contrary I shall not mind him: I shall mind God alone, whose command I always follow.

LADVENU [*pleading with her urgently*] You do not know what you are saying, child. Do you want to kill yourself? Listen. Do you not believe that you are subject to the Church of God on earth?

JOAN. Yes. When have I ever denied it?

LADVENU. Good. That means, does it not, that you are subject to our Lord the Pope, to the cardinals, the archbishops, and the bishops for whom his lordship stands here today?

---

11 brief: document containing points of law pertinent to the case.

JOAN. God must be served first.

D'ESTIVET. Then your voices command you not to submit yourself to the Church Militant?

JOAN. My voices do not tell me to disobey The Church; but God must be served first.

CAUCHON. And you, and not The Church are to be the judge?

JOAN. What other judgment can I judge by but my own?

THE ASSESSORS [*scandalised*] Oh! [*They cannot find words*].

CAUCHON. Out of your own mouth you have condemned yourself. We have striven for your salvation to the verge of sinning ourselves: we have opened the door to you again and again; and you have shut it in our faces and in the face of God. Dare you pretend, after what you have said, that you are in a state of grace[12]?

JOAN. If I am not, may God bring me to it: if I am, may God keep me in it!

LADVENU. That is a very good reply, my lord.

COURCELLES. Were you in a state of grace when you stole the Bishop's horse?

CAUCHON [*rising in a fury*] Oh, devil take the Bishop's horse and you too! We are here to try a case of heresy; and no sooner do we come to the root of the matter than we are thrown back by idiots who understand nothing but horses. [*Trembling with rage, he forces himself to sit down*].

THE INQUISITOR. Gentlemen, gentlemen: in clinging to these small issues you are The Maid's best advocates. I am not surprised that his lordship has lost patience with you. What does the Promoter say? Does he press these trumpery matters?

D'ESTIVET. I am bound by my office to press everything; but when the woman confesses a heresy that must bring upon her the

---

12 state of grace: state of enjoying the favor of God.

doom of excommunication, of what consequence is it that she has been guilty also of offences which expose her to minor penances? I share the impatience of his lordship as to these minor charges. Only, with great respect, I must emphasise the gravity of two very horrible and blasphemous crimes which she does not deny. First, she has intercourse[13] with evil spirits, and is therefore a sorceress. Second, she wears men's clothes, which is indecent, unnatural, and abominable; and in spite of our most earnest remonstrances and entreaties, she will not change them even to receive the sacrament.

JOAN. Is the blessed St. Catherine an evil spirit? Is St. Margaret? Is Michael the Archangel?

COURCELLES. How do you know that the spirit which appears to you is an archangel? Does he not appear to you as a naked man?

JOAN. Do you think God cannot afford clothes for him?

The assessors cannot help smiling, especially as the joke is against Courcelles.

LADVENU. Well answered, Joan.

THE INQUISITOR. It is, in effect, well answered. But no evil spirit would be so simple as to appear to a young girl in a guise that would scandalise her when he meant her to take him for a messenger from the Most High. Joan: The Church instructs you that these apparitions are demons seeking your soul's perdition. Do you accept the instruction of The Church?

JOAN. I accept the messenger of God. How could any faithful believer in The Church refuse him?

CAUCHON. Wretched woman: again I ask you, do you know what you are saying?

THE INQUISITOR. You wrestle in vain with the devil for her soul, my lord: she will not be saved. Now as to this matter of the

13 intercourse: dealings.

man's dress. For the last time, will you put off that impudent attire, and dress as becomes your sex?

JOAN. I will not.

D'ESTIVET [*pouncing*] The sin of disobedience, my lord.

JOAN [*distressed*] But my voices tell me I must dress as a soldier.

LADVENU. Joan, Joan: does not that prove to you that the voices are the voices of evil spirits? Can you suggest to us one good reason why an angel of God should give you such shameless advice?

JOAN. Why, yes: what can be plainer commonsense? I was a soldier living among soldiers. I am a prisoner guarded by soldiers. If I were to dress as a woman they would think of me as a woman; and then what would become of me? If I dress as a soldier they think of me as a soldier, and I can live with them as I do at home with my brothers. That is why St. Catherine tells me I must not dress as a woman until she gives me leave.

COURCELLES. When will she give you leave?

JOAN. When you take me out of the hands of the English soldiers. I have told you that I should be in the hands of The Church, and not left night and day with four soldiers of the Earl of Warwick [2]. Do you want me to live with them in petticoats[14]?

LADVENU. My lord: what she says is, God knows, very wrong and shocking; but there is a grain of worldly sense in it such as might impose on a simple village maiden.

JOAN. If we were as simple in the village as you are in your courts and palaces, there would soon be no wheat to make bread for you.

CAUCHON. That is the thanks you get for trying to save her, Brother Martin.

---

14 petticoats: women's light under-garments.

LADVENU. Joan: we are all trying to save you. His lordship is trying to save you. The Inquisitor could not be more just to you if you were his own daughter. But you are blinded by a terrible pride and self-sufficiency.

JOAN. Why do you say that? I have said nothing wrong. I cannot understand.

THE INQUISITOR. The blessed St. Athanasius [3] has laid it down in his creed that those who cannot understand are damned. It is not enough to be simple. It is not enough even to be what simple people call good. The simplicity of a darkened mind is no better than the simplicity of a beast.

JOAN. There is great wisdom in the simplicity of a beast, let me tell you; and sometimes great foolishness in the wisdom of scholars.

LADVENU. We know that, Joan: we are not so foolish as you think us. Try to resist the temptation to make pert replies to us. Do you see that man who stands behind you [*he indicates the Executioner*]?

JOAN [*turning and looking at the man*] Your torturer? But the Bishop said I was not to be tortured.

LADVENU. You are not to be tortured because you have confessed everything that is necessary to your condemnation. That man is not only the torturer: he is also the Executioner. Executioner: let The Maid hear your answers to my questions. Are you prepared for the burning of a heretic this day?

THE EXECUTIONER. Yes, Master.

LADVENU. Is the stake ready?

THE EXECUTIONER. It is. In the market-place. The English have built it too high for me to get near her and make the death easier. It will be a cruel death.

JOAN [*horrified*] But you are not going to burn me now?

THE INQUISITOR. You realise it at last.

LADVENU. There are eight hundred English soldiers waiting to take you to the market-place the moment the sentence of excommunication has passed the lips of your judges. You are within a few short moments of that doom.

JOAN [*looking round desperately for rescue*] Oh God!

LADVENU. Do not despair, Joan. The Church is merciful. You can save yourself.

JOAN [*hopefully*] Yes: my voices promised me I should not be burnt. St. Catherine bade me be bold.

CAUCHON. Woman: are you quite mad? Do you not yet see that your voices[15] have deceived you?

JOAN. Oh no: that is impossible.

CAUCHON. Impossible! They have led you straight to your excommunication, and to the stake which is there waiting for you.

LADVENU [*pressing the point hard*] Have they kept a single promise to you since you were taken at Compiégne [4]? The devil has betrayed you. The Church holds out its arms to you.

JOAN [*despairing*] Oh, it is true: it is true: my voices have deceived me. I have been mocked by devils: my faith is broken. I have dared and dared; but only a fool will walk into a fire; God, who gave me my commonsense, cannot will me to do that.

LADVENU. Now God be praised that He has saved you at the eleventh hour[16]! [*He hurries to the vacant seat at the scribes' table, and snatches a sheet of paper, on which he sets to work writing eagerly*].

CAUCHON. Amen!

JOAN. What must I do?

CAUCHON. You must sign a solemn recantation[17] of your heresy.

JOAN. Sign? That means to write my name. I cannot write.

CAUCHON. You have signed many letters before.

---

15 your voices: the voices of saints Joan claimed to have heard.

16 at the eleventh hour: at the last minute.

17 recantation: withdrawal.

JOAN. Yes; but someone held my hand and guided the pen. I can make my mark.

THE CHAPLAIN [*who has been listening with growing alarm and indignation*] My lord: do you mean that you are going to allow this woman to escape us?

THE INQUISITOR. The law must take its course, Master de Stogumber. And you know the law.

THE CHAPLAIN [*rising, purple with fury*] I know that there is no faith in a Frenchman. [*Tumult, which he shouts down*]. I know what my lord the Cardinal of Winchester [5] will say when he hears of this. I know what the Earl of Warwick will do when he learns that you intend to betray him. There are eight hundred men at the gate who will see that this abominable witch is burnt in spite of your teeth.

THE ASSESSORS [*meanwhile*] What is this? What did he say? He accuses us of treachery! This is past bearing. No faith in a Frenchman! Did you hear that? This is an intolerable fellow. Who is he? Is this what English Churchmen are like? He must be mad or drunk, etc., etc.

THE INQUISITOR [*rising*] Silence, pray[18]! Gentlemen: pray silence! Master Chaplain: bethink you[19] a moment of your holy office: of what you are, and where you are. I direct you to sit down.

THE CHAPLAIN [*folding his arms doggedly, his face working convulsively*] I will NOT sit down.

CAUCHON. Master Inquisitor: this man has called me a traitor to my face before now.

THE CHAPLAIN. So you are a traitor. You are all traitors. You have been doing nothing but begging this damnable witch on your knees to recant all through this trial.

THE INQUISITOR [*placidly resuming his seat*] If you will not

18 pray: please.
19 bethink you: remind yourself.

sit, you must stand: that is all.

THE CHAPLAIN. I will NOT stand [*he flings himself back into his chair*].

LADVENU [*rising with the paper in his hand*] My lord: here is the form of recantation for The Maid to sign.

CAUCHON. Read it to her.

JOAN. Do not trouble. I will sign it.

THE INQUISITOR. Woman: you must know what you are putting your hand to. Read it to her, Brother Martin. And let all be silent.

LADVENU [*reading quietly*] "I, Joan, commonly called The Maid, a miserable sinner, do confess that I have most grievously sinned in the following articles[20]. I have pretended to have revelations from God and the angels and the blessed saints, and perversely rejected The Church's warnings that these were temptations by demons. I have blasphemed abominably by wearing an immodest dress, contrary to the Holy Scripture[21] and the canons of The Church. Also I have clipped my hair in the style of a man, and, against all the duties which have made my sex specially acceptable in heaven, have taken up the sword, even to the shedding of human blood, inciting men to slay each other, invoking evil spirits to delude them, and stubbornly and most blasphemously imputing these sins to Almighty God. I confess to the sin of sedition, to the sin of idolatry, to the sin of disobedience, to the sin of pride, and to the sin of heresy. All of which sins I now renounce and abjure and depart from, humbly thanking you Doctors and Masters who have brought me back to the truth and into the grace of our Lord. And I will never return to my errors, but will remain in communion with our Holy Church and in obedience to our Holy Father the Pope of Rome. All this I swear by God Almighty and the Holy Gospels, in witness whereto I sign my name to this recantation."

---

20 articles: points of a legal document.
21 the Holy Scripture: the Bible.

THE INQUISITOR. You understand this, Joan?

JOAN [*listless*] It is plain enough, sir.

THE INQUISITOR. And it is true?

JOAN. It may be true. If it were not true, the fire would not be ready for me in the market-place.

LADVENU [*taking up his pen and a book, and going to her quickly lest she should compromise herself again*] Come, child: let me guide your hand. Take the pen. [*She does so; and they begin to write, using the book as a desk*] J.E.H.A.N.E.[22] So. Now make your mark by yourself.

JOAN [*makes her mark, and gives him back the pen, tormented by the rebellion of her soul against her mind and body*] There!

LADVENU [*replacing the pen on the table, and handing the recantation to Cauchon with a reverence*] Praise be to God, my brothers, the lamb has returned to the flock [6]; and the shepherd rejoices in her more than in ninety and nine just persons. [*He returns to his seat*].

THE INQUISITOR [*taking the paper from Cauchon*] We declare thee by this act set free from the danger of excommunication in which thou stoodest. [*He throws the paper down to the table.*]

JOAN. I thank you.

THE INQUISITOR. But because thou hast sinned most presumptuously against God and the Holy Church, and that thou mayst repent thy errors in solitary contemplation, and be shielded from all temptation to return to them, we, for the good of thy soul, and for a penance that may wipe out thy sins and bring thee finally unspotted to the throne of grace, do condemn thee to eat the bread of sorrow and drink the water of affliction to the end of thy earthly days in perpetual imprisonment.

JOAN [*rising in consternation and terrible anger*] Perpetual im-

22 J.E.H.A.N.E.: formal spelling of Joan's name.

prisonment! Am I not then to be set free?

LADVENU [*mildly shocked*] Set free, child, after such wickedness as yours! What are you dreaming of?

JOAN. Give me that writing. [*She rushes to the table; snatches up the paper; and tears it into fragments*] Light your fire: do you think I dread it as much as the life of a rat in a hole? My voices were right.

LADVENU. Joan! Joan!

JOAN. Yes: they told me you were fools [*the word gives great offence*], and that I was not to listen to your fine words nor trust to your charity. You promised me my life; but you lied [*indignant exclamations*]. You think that life is nothing but not being stone dead. It is not the bread and water I fear: I can live on bread: when have I asked for more? It is no hardship to drink water if the water be clean. Bread has no sorrow for me, and water no affliction. But to shut me from the light of the sky and the sight of the fields and flowers; to chain my feet so that I can never again ride with the soldiers nor climb the hills; to make me breathe foul damp darkness, and keep from me everything that brings me back to the love of God when your wickedness and foolishness tempt me to hate Him: all this is worse than the furnace in the Bible [7] that was heated seven times. I could do without my warhorse; I could drag about in a skirt; I could let the banners and the trumpets and the knights and soldiers pass me and leave me behind as they leave the other women, if only I could still hear the wind in the trees, the larks in the sunshine, the young lambs crying through the healthy frost, and the blessed blessed church bells that send my angel voices floating to me on the wind. But without these things I cannot live; and by your wanting to take them away from me, or from any human creature, I know that your counsel is of the devil, and that mine is of God.

THE ASSESSORS [*in great commotion*] Blasphemy! Blasphemy! She is possessed. She said our counsel was of the devil. And hers of God. Monstrous! The devil is in our midst, etc., etc.

D'ESTIVET [*shouting above the din*] She is a relapsed heretic, obstinate, incorrigible, and altogether unworthy of the mercy we have shewn her. I call for her excommunication.

THE CHAPLAIN [*to the Executioner*] Light your fire, man. To the stake with her.

The Executioner and his assistants hurry out through the courtyard.

LADVENU. You wicked girl: if your counsel were of God would He not deliver you?

JOAN. His ways are not your ways. He wills that I go through the fire to His bosom; for I am His child, and you are not fit that I should live among you. That is my last word to you.

The soldiers seize her.

CAUCHON [*rising*] Not yet.

They wait. There is a dead silence. Cauchon turns to the Inquisitor with an inquiring look. The Inquisitor nods affirmatively. They rise solemnly, and intone the sentence antiphonally.

CAUCHON. We decree that thou art a relapsed heretic.

THE INQUISITOR. Cast out from the unity of The Church.

CAUCHON. Sundered from her body.

THE INQUISITOR. Infected with the leprosy of heresy.

CAUCHON. A member of Satan.

THE INQUISITOR. We declare that thou must be excommunicate.

CAUCHON. And now we do cast thee out, segregate thee, and abandon thee to the secular power.

THE INQUISITOR. Admonishing the same secular power that it moderate its judgment of thee in respect of death and division of the limbs. [*He resumes his seat*].

CAUCHON. And if any true sign of penitence appear in thee,

to permit out Brother Martin to administer to thee the sacrament of penance.

THE CHAPLAIN. Into the fire with the witch [*he rushes at her, and helps the soldiers to push her out*].

Joan is taken away through the courtyard. The assessors rise in disorder and follow the soldiers, except Ladvenu, who has hidden his face in his hand.

...

NOTES ON THE TEXT

[1] Joan is here accusing Courcelles of being foolish even though he spoke in a manner of stateliness. Notice that Joan is trying to be sarcastic by imitating his tone.

[2] Warwick was a mighty statesman in the history of England who was responsible to put Edward IV on the throne in 1461. The dates given here, however, may not be historically accurate. Joan was burned in 1431 when she was nineteen years of age and Richard Neville, the first Earl of Warwick, was born in 1428, some three years before her death. It does not seem likely, therefore, the Earl of Warwick was the leader of those English soldiers at the time.

[3] Athanasius, also known as St. Athanasius or Athanasius the Great, was a fourth-century Greek patriarch of Alexandria and an outstanding champion of Christian orthodoxy against Arianis. The Athanasius creed of the early fifth century used to be attributed to Athanasius but people tend to consider it now as the work of unknown origin.

[4] Compiégne is believed to be the place where Joan was captured. She was imprisoned then and condemned as a heretic by an English-dominated church court in 1431, and burned at the stake.

[5] Cardinals are members of the Sacred College of the Roman Catholic Church whose major duties, according to *Britannica*, include electing the pope, acting as his principal counselors and aiding in the government of the Roman Catholic Church throughout the world. They have also been cardinal bishops of major dioceses. The chaplain is here referring to the Cardinal of Winchester, one of the most powerful leaders of the Church of England.

[6] Lamb is taken in Christianity as the title of Jesus Christ as is referred in Luke 10:3 of the New Testament and Christians are often referred to as lambs of the Church.

[7] Matthew 13:42 relates that Jesus shall gather all the children of the wicked one and cast them into a furnace of fire and there shall be wailing and gnashing of teeth from those tortured in the furnace.

QUESTIONS FOR DISCUSSION

1. There seems to be a contrast in the scene you have read between a rather formal language and relatively trivial topics. Could you give examples from the dialogs in the scene and try to explain what effect they have produced?

2. Joan is obviously a very interesting figure, simple-minded and sophisticated at the same time. In terms of her personality, what do you think is the most outstanding feature the playwright stresses throughout the scene?

3. Shaw has made the theater into an effective medium for expressing his ideas, ideas of a polemicist and of a prophet in particular. What message do you think the artist wants to deliver in his retelling of this old story in such a dramatic manner?

4. Shaw calls *Saint Joan* a tragedy. According to what you have learned about tragedy as a genre, do you think his claim makes sense? If your answer is positive, support yourself with details.

5. As Shaw once observed in his discussion of the significance of Joan as a legendary figure, the easiest way to make the Roman Catholic Church and the Inquisition the villains of a melodrama is to make Joan its heroine. Could you explain what Shaw means and how he treats Joan as the most important character of the play?

SUGGESTED REFERENCES

Bentley, Eric. *Bernard Shaw, 1856-1950.* New York: New Directions, 1957.

Henderson, Archibald. *George Bernard Shaw: Man of the Century.* New York: Appleton-Century-Crofts, 1956.

Meisel, Martin. *Shaw and the Nineteenth-Century Theater.* Princeton: Princeton UP, 1963.

Shaw, George Bernard. *Shaw's Dramatic Criticism (1895-1898).* Selected by John F. Matthew. New York: Hill and Wang, 1959.

SELECTED READINGS IN ENGLISH AND AMERICAN LITERATURE

PART II

American Literature

Unit 1 Washington Irving

(1783 – 1859)

A GUIDE TO LITERARY TERMINOLOGY

"Romanticism in American Literature": *Romanticism refers to an artistic and intellectual movement originated in the late eighteenth century in Germany and England, followed by America and other European countries. Revolting against neoclassicism, romantic artists and writers valued emotions and expressed their ideas in everyday language and their own individual styles. They rejected the artistic forms and conventions associated with classicism and neoclassicism by emphasizing emotion over intellect; the individual over society; inspiration, imagination, and intuition over logic, discipline, and order; the wild and natural over the tamed. Romantics believed that humans, as well as their emotions, are good by nature, but civilization corrupts this essential goodness. As a matter of fact, they took emotions to be more reliable than reason which they tended to view as a negative product of civilization. They highly valued nature — which was often seen as the antithesis of the materialism and artifice created by civilized society — and gave it a prominent place in their works. They also eulogized individualism, exploring the inner self, bringing it into the realms of literature, and opposing the bourgeois established order.*

The Romantic period in American literature stretched roughly from the beginning of the nineteenth century to the end of the American Civil War in 1865. It was a time of rapid expansion and growth that fueled intuition, imagination, and individualism in literature. Famous American romantic writers included Washington Irving, Nathaniel Hawthorne, Herman Melville, Edgar Allan Poe, Ralph Waldo Emerson, Henry David Thoreau, Walt Whitman, and Emily Dickinson. Although they were heavily influenced by English romanticism, they had produced the first truly distinctive American works.

NOTES ON THE AUTHOR

Washington Irving was born in 1783 to a prosperous New York merchant's family. He was the first great writer of American romanticism and the first American writer to gain international fame. At the age of 16, he began the study of law, but he showed little interest in it. He preferred to spend his time reading literature and in the company of the literary wits of New York City. He made his literary debut at the age of 19 with a series of sketches, or "letters," on society and theater to the *Morning Chronicle*, a New York newspaper. When he was 21, he went to Europe and stayed there for two years before he returned to New York and was admitted to the New York bar, beginning his leisurely life as a gentleman lawyer. In 1809, he published *A History of New York*, which satirized the early complacent Dutch settlers and derided the political follies of the American society then. In 1815, he moved to England to supervise a family firm, where he achieved international fame with the publication of *The Sketch Book of Geoffrey Crayon, Gent.* (1820), which contains two small masterpieces that initiated the great tradition of the American short story, "The Legend of Sleepy Hollow" and "Rip Van Winkle." He finished a five-volume biography of George Washington just eight months before his death, at age 76, in Tarrytown, New York.

SYNOPSIS OF THE WORK

"Rip Van Winkle" is a beautiful fairy tale with a distinctively American flavor. The plot of the tale is inspired by the old idea of long sleep as found in "The Sleeping Beauty" where the heroine slept for 100 years, "The Seven Sleepers of Ephesus" whose sleep in a cave lasted for 250 years, and Endymion, a character in Greek mythology who retained his eternal youth by sleeping forever. Irving gave his story an American setting and interwove in it the legend of Hendrick Hudson, the discoverer of the Hudson River, who was supposed to return, together with the ghosts of his crew, to the Hundson River Valley, the scene of his achievement, every twenty years. The story is set in the Catskill mountain region along the Hudson River in New York. It begins before the American Revolution, when King George is ruling the colonies. Rip Van Winkle, the protagonist of the story, is a henpecked husband and an amiable man who is very popular with his fellow villagers, especially children with whom he plays and to whom he tells stories and gives toys. However, he hates doing any work that is profitable to his family, and is therefore often chastised by his nagging wife Dame Van Winkle. One day, Rip, trying to break free from his nagging wife, wanders up the mountains with his dog, Wolf. On his way, Rip helps a man to carry a keg up the mountain. They hike up to a hollow where they join a group of men (who turn out to be the ghosts of Hendrick Hudson and his crew) playing nine-pins. Rip drinks some of their liquor and falls asleep. We are now in the scene in which Rip has just awakened from a slumber which has lasted twenty years.

SELECTED READINGS

Rip Van Winkle [1]

[...]

It was with some difficulty he found the way to his own house, which he approached with silent awe, expecting every moment to hear the shrill voice of Dame Van Winkle. He found the house gone to decay — the roof fallen in, the windows shattered, and the doors off the hinges. A half-starved dog, that looked like Wolf, was skulking about it. Rip called him by name, but the cur snarled, showed his teeth, and passed on. This was an unkind cut[1] indeed — "My very dog," sighed poor Rip, "has forgotten me!"

He entered the house, which, to tell the truth, Dame Van Winkle had always kept in neat order. It was empty, forlorn[2], and apparently abandoned. This desolateness overcame all his connubial fears[3] — he called loudly for his wife and children — the lonely chambers rung for a moment with his voice, and then all again was silence.

He now hurried forth, and hastened to his old resort, the little village inn — but it too was gone. A large rickety wooden building stood in its place, with great gaping windows, some of them broken, and mended with old hats and petticoats, and over the door was painted, "The Union Hotel, by Jonathan Doolittle." Instead of the great tree which used to shelter the quiet little Dutch inn of yore[4], there now was reared a tall naked pole, with something on the top that looked like a red night-cap [2], and from it was fluttering a flag, on which was a singular assemblage of stars and stripes [3] — all this was strange and incomprehensible. He recognized on the sign, however, the ruby face

---

1 cut: an act of refusing to recognize an acquaintance.

2 forlorn: alone and unhappy.

3 connubial fear: fear of marriage.

4 of yore: of a period of time in the past.

of King George [4], under which he had smoked so many a peaceful pipe, but even this was singularly metamorphosed. The red coat was changed for one of blue and buff [5], a sword was stuck in the hand instead of a scepter, the head was decorated with a cocked hat, and underneath was painted in large characters, GENERAL WASHINGTON.

There was, as usual, a crowd of folk about the door, but none whom Rip recollected. The very character of the people seemed changed. There was a busy, bustling, disputatious tone about it, instead of the accustomed phlegm and drowsy tranquility. He looked in vain for the sage Nicholas Vedder, with his broad face, double chin, and fair long pipe, uttering clouds of tobacco-smoke instead of idle speeches; or Van Bummel, the schoolmaster, doling forth the contents of an ancient newspaper. In place of these, a lean, bilious-looking fellow, with his pockets full of handbills, was haranguing vehemently about rights of citizens — election — members of Congress — liberty — Bunker's Hill[5] — heroes of '76[6] — and other words, that were a perfect Babylonish jargon [6] to the bewildered Van Winkle.

The appearance of Rip, with his long grizzled beard, his rusty fowling-piece[7], his uncouth dress, and the army of women and children that had gathered at his heels, soon attracted the attention of the tavern politicians. They crowded around him, eying him from head to foot, with great curiosity. The orator bustled up to him, and drawing him partly aside, inquired "on which side he voted?" Rip stared in vacant stupidity. Another short but busy little fellow pulled him by the arm, and raising on tiptoe, inquired in his ear, "whether he was Federal or Democrat [7]." Rip was equally at a loss to comprehend the question; when a knowing, self-important old gentleman, in a sharp

---

5 Bunker's Hill: a hill near Boston, the site of the first major battle of the American Revolution fought on June 17, 1775.

6 Heroes of '76: heroes of 1776 — that is, heroes of American Revolution.

7 fowling piece: a light shotgun for shooting birds and small animals.

cocked hat, made his way through the crowd, putting them to the right and left with his elbows as he passed, and planting himself before Van Winkle, with one arm akimbo[8], the other resting on his cane, his keen eyes and sharp hat penetrating, as it were, into his very soul, demanded, in an austere tone, "what brought him to the election with a gun on his shoulder, and a mob at his heels, and whether he meant to breed a riot in the village?" "Alas! gentlemen," cried Rip, somewhat dismayed, "I am a poor quiet man, a native of the place, and a loyal subject of the king, God bless him!"

Here a general shout burst from the by-standers — "A Tory[9]! a Tory! a spy! a refugee! hustle him! away with him!" It was with great difficulty that the self-important man in the cocked hat restored order; and having assumed a tenfold austerity of brow, demanded again of the unknown culprit, what he came there for, and whom he was seeking. The poor man humbly assured him that he meant no harm; but merely came there in search of some of his neighbors, who used to keep about the tavern.

"Well — who are they? — name them."

Rip bethought himself a moment, and then inquired, "Where's Nicholas Vedder?"

There was silence for a little while, when an old man replied in a thin, piping voice, "Nicholas Vedder? Why, he is dead and gone these eighteen years! There was a wooden tombstone in the churchyard that used to tell all about him, but that's rotted and gone, too."

"Where's Brom Dutcher?"

"Oh, he went off to the army in the beginning of the war; some say he was killed at the battle of Stony Point[10] — others say he was drowned in a squall, at the foot of Antony's Nose[11]. I don't know — he

---

8 with one arm akimbo: with one hand on his hip.

9 Tory: a member of the British Conservative Party.

10 Stony Point: a place on the Hudson River, south of the West Point.

11 Antony's Nose: the name of a mountain near West Point.

never came back again."

"Where's Van Bummel, the schoolmaster?"

"He went off to the wars, too, was a great militia general, and is now in Congress."

Rip's heart died away, at hearing of these sad changes in his home and friends, and finding himself thus alone in the world. Every answer puzzled him, too, by treating of such enormous lapses of time, and of matters which he could not understand: war — Congress — Stony Point! — he had no courage to ask after any more friends, but cried out in despair, "Does nobody here know Rip Van Winkle?"

"Oh, Rip Van Winkle!" exclaimed two or three, "Oh, to be sure! that's Rip Van Winkle yonder[12], leaning against the tree."

Rip looked, and beheld a precise counterpart of himself, as he went up the mountain: apparently as lazy, and certainly as ragged. The poor fellow was now completely confounded. He doubted his own identity, and whether he was himself or another man. In the midst of his bewilderment, the man in the cocked hat demanded who he was, and what was his name?

"God knows," exclaimed he, at his wit's end; "I'm not myself — I'm somebody else — that's me yonder — no — that's somebody else, got into my shoes — I was myself last night, but I fell asleep on the mountain, and they've changed my gun, and everything's changed, and I'm changed, and I can't tell what's my name, or who I am!"

The by-standers began now to look at each other, nod, wink significantly, and tap their fingers against their foreheads. There was a whisper, also, about securing the gun, and keeping the old fellow from doing mischief; at the very suggestion of which, the self-important man in the cocked hat retired with some precipitation. At this critical moment a fresh, comely woman pressed through the throng to get a peep at the gray-bearded man. She had a chubby child in her arms,

12 yonder: over there.

which, frightened at his looks, began to cry. "Hush, Rip," cried she, "hush, you little fool, the old man won't hurt you." The name of the child, the air of the mother, the tone of her voice, all awakened a train of recollections in his mind. "What is your name, my good woman?" asked he.

"Judith Gardenier."

"And your father's name?"

"Ah, poor man, his name was Rip Van Winkle; it's twenty years since he went away from home with his gun, and never has been heard of since — his dog came home without him; but whether he shot himself, or was carried away by the Indians, nobody can tell. I was then but a little girl."

Rip had but one question more to ask; but he put it with a faltering voice: — "Where's your mother?"

"Oh, she too had died but a short time since; she broke a blood-vessel in a fit of passion at a New-England peddler."

There was a drop of comfort, at least, in this intelligence. The honest man could contain himself no longer. — He caught his daughter and her child in his arms. — "I am your father!" cried he — "Young Rip Van Winkle once — old Rip Van Winkle now! — Does nobody know poor Rip Van Winkle!"

All stood amazed, until an old woman, tottering out from among the crowd, put her hand to her brow, and peering under it in his face for a moment, exclaimed, "Sure enough! it is Rip Van Winkle — it is himself. Welcome home again, old neighbor. — Why, where have you been these twenty long years?"

Rip's story was soon told, for the whole twenty years had been to him but as one night. The neighbors stared when they heard it; some were seen to wink at each other, and put their tongues in their cheeks[13];

13 put their tongues in their cheeks: a facial expression indicating that one is suppressing mirth — biting one's tongue to prevent an outburst of laughter.

and the self-important man in the cocked hat, who, when the alarm was over, had returned to the field, screwed down the corners of his mouth, and shook his head — upon which there was a general shaking of the head throughout the assemblage.

It was determined, however, to take the opinion of old Peter Vanderdonk, who was seen slowly advancing up the road. He was a descendant of the historian of that name, who wrote one of the earliest accounts of the province. Peter was the most ancient inhabitant of the village, and well versed in[14] all the wonderful events and traditions of the neighborhood. He recollected Rip at once, and corroborated his story in the most satisfactory manner. He assured the company that it was a fact, handed down from his ancestor the historian, that the Catskill Mountains had always been haunted by strange beings. That it was affirmed that the great Hendrick Hudson, the first discoverer of the river and country, kept a kind of vigil there every twenty years, with his crew of the *Half-Moon*[15], being permitted in this way to revisit the scenes of his enterprise, and keep a guardian eye upon the river, and the great city called by his name. That his father had once seen them in their old Dutch dresses playing at nine-pins[16] in a hollow of the mountain; and that he himself had heard, one summer afternoon, the sound of their balls, like long peals of thunder.

To make a long story short, the company broke up, and returned to the more important concerns of the election. Rip's daughter took him home to live with her; she had a snug, well-furnished house, and a stout cheery farmer for a husband, whom Rip recollected for one of the urchins that used to climb upon his back. As to Rip's son and heir, who was the ditto of himself, seen leaning against the tree, he was

14 well versed in: familiar with.

15 *Half-Moon*: a Dutch East India Company ship with which Henry Hudson (Henrick Hudson) explored parts of North America.

16 nine-pins: a game in which nine wooden pins are the target, which is similar to the modern sport of bowling

employed to work on the farm; but evinced an hereditary disposition to attend to anything else but his business.

Rip now resumed his old walks and habits; he soon found many of his former cronies, though all rather the worse for the wear and tear[17] of time; and preferred making friends among the rising generation, with whom he soon grew into great favor.

Having nothing to do at home, and being arrived at that happy age when a man can do nothing with impunity, he took his place once more on the bench, at the inn door, and was reverenced as one of the patriarchs of the village, and a chronicle of the old times "before the war." It was some time before he could get into the regular track of gossip, or could be made to comprehend the strange events that had taken place during his torpor. How that there had been a revolutionary war — that the country had thrown off the yoke of old England — and that, instead of being a subject of his Majesty, George III, he was now a free citizen of the United States. Rip, in fact, was no politician; the changes of states and empires made but little impression on him; but there was one species of despotism under which he had long groaned, and that was — petticoat government [8]; happily, that was at an end; he had got his neck out of the yoke of matrimony, and could go in and out whenever he pleased, without dreading the tyranny of Dame Van Winkle. Whenever her name was mentioned, however, he shook his head, shrugged his shoulders, and cast up his eyes; which might pass either for an expression of resignation to his fate, or joy at his deliverance.

NOTES ON THE TEXT

[1] Irving took the plot for "Rip Van Winkle" from a German folk-legend. The story shows the influence of German romantic literature on him. It also owes a debt, in terms of stylistic influence, to Sir Walter Scotts. Nevertheless, it exploits a specifically American setting and

17 wear and tear: damage resulting from normal use and exposure

explores the social and cultural transformations occurring in America. This famous tale is regarded as the first American short story.

[2] The cap was adopted as a symbol of liberty during the French Revolution, and the pole was a "liberty pole."

[3] Stars and stripes were symbols on the national flag of the United States; the stars represented the number of states, and the stripes represented the number of colonies.

[4] King George III (June 4, 1738 – January 29, 1820) was King of Great Britain and King of Ireland from October 25, 1760 until the union of these two countries on January 1, 1801, after which he was King of the United Kingdom of Great Britain and Ireland until his death.

[5] Red coat was the uniform of the British Army; blue and buff were colors of the uniform of the Revolutionary Army.

[6] Here the author mistook Babel, which, according to the Bible (Genesis 11:1-9), marks the beginning of linguistic confusion, for Babylon.

[7] The Federalists were then led by Alexander Hamilton and the Democrats by Thomas Jefferson. They were the earliest American political parties.

[8] Petticoat government here refers to government by women, whether in politics or domestic affairs. Notice that Rip Van Winkle's trip to the mountains is itself an attempt to escape from his wife's harassments.

QUESTIONS FOR DISCUSSION

1. Rip Van Winkle's sleep has lasted 20 years. How did he learn of the lapse of time? What changes in the village has Rip Van Winkle discovered after he returns home? Do these changes excite him or puzzle him? Why?

2. How does Rip Van Winkle respond to the social and political transformations in the town since his absence?

3. What makes Rip Van Winkle happy and what makes him sad? How do you understand Rip Van Winkle's escapism (from both "matrimony" and politics)?

4. It is the Romantic elements, such as supernatural qualities, the woods as a mysterious and magical place as opposed to the city, that drive the plot of the story. Discuss the elements of romanticism in the story with respect to its setting, thematic expression, and plot.

SUGGESTED REFERENCES

Aderman, R. ed. *Critical Essays on Washington Irving.* Boston: G. K. Hall, 1990.

Martin, Terence. "Rip, Ichabod, and the American Imagination." *American Literature* 31(1959): 137-49.

Myers, Andrew B. ed. *A Century of Commentary on the Works of Washington Irving: 1860–1974.* Tarrytown: Sleepy Hollow Press, 1976.

Oates, Joyce Carol. *American Gothic Tales.* New York: Penguin, 1996.

Ringe, Donald A. "New York and New England: Irving's Criticism of American Society." *American Literature* 21(1967): 455-67.

Robin-Dorsky, Jeffrey. *Adrift in the Old World: The Psychological Pilgrimage of Washington Irving.* Chicago: U of Chicago P: 1988.

Roth Martin. *Comedy and America: The Lost World of Washington Irving.* NY: Kennikat Press, 1976.

Seelye, John. "Root and Branch: Washington Irving and American Humor." *Nineteenth-Century Fiction* 38(1984): 415-25.

Young, Philip. "Fallen from Time: The Mythic Rip Van Winkle." *Kenyon Review* 22 (1960): 547-73.

Unit 2 David Henry Thoreau

(1817 — 1862)

A GUIDE TO LITERARY TERMINOLOGY

"Transcendentalism": *Transcendentalism was a literary and philosophical movement that flourished in New England in the middle of the nineteenth century. It represented the height of American Romanticism. Led by Ralph Waldo Emerson and Henry David Thoreau, American transcendentalists reacted against eighteenth-century empiricism and asserted the supremacy of mind over matter, defending intuition as a guide to truth. They firmly believed that each human being is innately divine, that God's essence lies within every individual and within nature itself. They also contended that individuals have the ability to discover higher truths intuitively or mystically, without relying on the senses or logic. Indeed, reliance on sensory experience and rational thought — transcendentalists suggested — may actually impede the acquisition of transcendental truths. They valued consciousness over experience (or history) and encouraged people to discover truths in nature with the guidance of their own conscience rather than dogmatic religious doctrine.*

However, American Transcendentalism was not a rigorously systematic philosophy. It stood for self-expression, individualism, self-reliance, the worth of common humanity, the equality of races and sexes, and the interdependence of nature and humans. The ideas of Transcendentalism were most eloquently expressed by Ralph Waldo Emerson in ***Nature*** *(1836), and by Henry David Thoreau in* ***Walden*** *(1854).*

NOTES ON THE AUTHOR

David Henry Thoreau (1817 — 1862), best known for his book *Walden*, or *Life in the Woods* (1854) and his essay "Resistance to Civil Government," was an American writer, dissenter, and an outstanding transcendentalist. He was born on July 12, 1817 in Concord, Massachusetts. After graduating from Harvard College in 1837, he taught school intermittently until 1841. Then he began his career as a writer. He led a simple life, writing poems and essays while trying to make an independent living. Influenced by Ralph Waldo Emerson (1803 — 1882), he published many pieces in the transcendentalist magazine *The Dial*. In the years 1845 — 1847, to demonstrate self-reliance and the significance of a simple life, he lived alone in the woods beside Walden Pond near Concord. In 1854, he published his masterpiece *Walden* which recorded his experiences and thoughts there. His *A Week on the*

Concord and Merrimack Rivers (1849) was the only other book he published in his lifetime. His advocacy of civil disobedience against an unjust government, though it caused hardly a ripple in his time, later influenced Mohandas Gandhi's campaign for Indian independence and Martin Luther King.

Thoreau was a member of the Transcendental Club which included such scholars as Ralph Waldo Emerson, Theodore Parker (1810—1860), Bronson Alcott (1799—1888), and Margaret Fuller (1810—1850). What was unusual was Thoreau not only advocated but also tried to live according to the dictates of Transcendentalism. He suggests, "to be a philosopher is not merely to have subtle thoughts, nor even to found a school, but so to love wisdom as to live according to its dictates, a life of simplicity, independence, magnanimity, and trust." Far more than his friend and mentor Ralph Waldo Emerson, Thoreau wanted to know how it felt to live in nature and to experience in person the benefits nature brought to people.

NOTES ON THE WORK

Thoreau began his experiment of simple living at Walden Pond four years after Emerson published his essay "Self-Reliance." Thoreau's experiment was meant to put into practice Emerson's principle of "self-reliance." In Walden, which details Thoreau's experiences over the course of two years, two months, and two days in a cabin he built near Walden Pond amidst woodland owned by Emerson, Thoreau outlines his philosophy of life, politics, and nature. The book shortens the time to one year and uses passages of four seasons to symbolize human development. Although *Walden* enjoyed only moderate success in Thoreau's lifetime, his experiment at the pond had sparked considerable interest in the decades to come. Thoreau's words express the concerns not only of his contemporaries, but of later generations who had experienced the disturbances brought about by industrialization and wars. They struck a chord in a generation of young people in the 1960s and 1970s who opposed the modern military-industrial complex and sought peace and simplicity in life. John Updike wrote of *Walden*, "A century and a half after its publication, *Walden* has become such a totem of the back-to-nature, preservationist, anti-business, civil-disobedience mindset, and Thoreau so vivid a protester, so perfect a crank and hermit saint, that the book risks being as revered and unread as the Bible."[1]

1 John Updike, "A Sage for all seasons," *The Daily Mail*, June 25, 2004.

The selection here is from chapter five of *Walden*. In this chapter, Thoreau seeks first to explain why he is not lonely while living "alone" in the woods. The reason he gives is: he has become a part of nature and many natural objects have befriended him. He shows his distaste at village life, where people see too much of each other, so that human interaction becomes trivial. He then argues for more meaningful connections between human beings. Instead of simply practicing artificial etiquette in our relations with others, we ought to abandon this pretence and only engage with others for "all important and hearty communications." This chapter is actually not about "solitude." Rather, it is about Thoreau's townsmen's misapprehensions regarding his solitude. Thoreau has shunned their company for what he calls a "more normal and natural society." He takes care to emphasize that all parts of nature are companionship for him and that he is not lonesome. Thoreau praises the benefits of nature and of his deep communion with it. He maintains that the only medicine he needs in life is "a draught of undiluted morning air."

SELECTED READINGS

Solitude

[...]

There is commonly sufficient space about us. Our horizon is never quite at our elbows.[2] The thick wood is not just at our door, nor the pond, but somewhat is always clearing, familiar and worn by us, appropriated and fenced in some way, and reclaimed from Nature. For what reason have I this vast range and circuit, some square miles of unfrequented forest, for my privacy, abandoned to me by men? My nearest neighbor is a mile distant, and no house is visible from any place but the hill-tops within half a mile of my own. I have my horizon bounded by woods all to myself; a distant view of the railroad where it touches the pond on the one hand, and of the fence which skirts[3] the woodland road on the other. But for the most part it is as solitary where I live as on the prairies. It is as much Asia or Africa as

2 not quite at our elbows: quite a distance away; the living space is not narrow.
3 skirt: run around.

New England. I have, as it were, my own sun and moon and stars, and a little world all to myself. At night there was never a traveller passed my house, or knocked at my door, more than if I were the first or last man;[4] unless it were in the spring, when at long intervals some came from the village to fish for pouts — they plainly fished much more in the Walden Pond of their own natures, and baited their hooks with darkness — but they soon retreated, usually with light baskets, and left "the world to darkness and to me," and the black kernel of the night was never profaned by any human neighborhood. I believe that men are generally still a little afraid of the dark, though the witches are all hung, and Christianity and candles have been introduced.

Yet I experienced sometimes that the most sweet and tender, the most innocent and encouraging society [1] may be found in any natural object, even for the poor misanthrope and most melancholy man. There can be no very black melancholy to him who lives in the midst of Nature and has his senses still.[5] There was never yet such a storm but it was Æolian music [2] to a healthy and innocent ear. Nothing can rightly compel a simple and brave man to a vulgar sadness. While I enjoy the friendship of the seasons I trust that nothing can make life a burden to me. The gentle rain which waters my beans and keeps me in the house today is not drear and melancholy, but good for me too. Though it prevents my hoeing them, it is of far more worth than my hoeing. If it should continue so long as to cause the seeds to rot in the ground and destroy the potatoes in the low lands, it would still be good for the grass on the uplands, and, being good for the grass, it would be good for me. Sometimes, when I compare myself with other men, it seems as if I were more favored by the gods than they, beyond

---

4 There was never a traveller passed my house, or knocked at my door, more than if I were the first or last man: There was never a traveller who passed my house or knocked at my door, as if I were the first or last man living there.

5 There can be no very black melancholy to him who lives in the midst of Nature and has his senses still: For anyone who lives in the midst of Nature and who still has his senses, it is impossible for him or her to feel very black melancholy.

any deserts that I am conscious of; as if I had a warrant and surety at their hands which my fellows have not, and were especially guided and guarded. I do not flatter myself, but if it be possible they flatter me. I have never felt lonesome, or in the least oppressed by a sense of solitude, but once, and that was a few weeks after I came to the woods, when, for an hour, I doubted if the near neighborhood of man was not essential to a serene and healthy life. To be alone was something unpleasant. But I was at the same time conscious of a slight insanity in my mood, and seemed to foresee my recovery. In the midst of a gentle rain while these thoughts prevailed, I was suddenly sensible of such sweet and beneficent society in Nature, in the very pattering of the drops[6], and in every sound and sight around my house, an infinite and unaccountable friendliness all at once like an atmosphere sustaining me, as made the fancied advantages of human neighborhood insignificant, and I have never thought of them since. Every little pine needle expanded and swelled with sympathy and befriended me. I was so distinctly made aware of the presence of something kindred to me, even in scenes which we are accustomed to call wild and dreary, and also that the nearest of blood to me and humanest was not a person nor a villager, that I thought no place could ever be strange to me again.

[...]

I find it wholesome to be alone the greater part of the time. To be in company, even with the best, is soon wearisome and dissipating. I love to be alone. I never found the companion that was so companionable as solitude. We are for the most part more lonely when we go abroad among men than when we stay in our chambers. A man thinking or working is always alone, let him be where he will. Solitude is not measured by the miles of space that intervene between a man and his fellows. The really diligent student in one of the crowded hives of

6 drops: rain drops.

Cambridge College is as solitary as a dervish in the desert. The farmer can work alone in the field or the woods all day, hoeing or chopping, and not feel lonesome, because he is employed; but when he comes home at night he cannot sit down in a room alone, at the mercy of his thoughts, but must be where he can "see the folks," and recreate, and as he thinks remunerate himself for his day's solitude; and hence he wonders how the student can sit alone in the house all night and most of the day without ennui and "the blues"[7]; but he does not realize that the student, though in the house, is still at work in his field, and chopping in his woods, as the farmer in his, and in turn seeks the same recreation and society that the latter does, though it may be a more condensed form of it.

Society is commonly too cheap. We meet at very short intervals, not having had time to acquire any new value for each other. We meet at meals three times a day, and give each other a new taste of that old musty cheese that we are. We have had to agree on a certain set of rules, called etiquette and politeness, to make this frequent meeting tolerable and that we need not come to open war. We meet at the post-office, and at the sociable, and about the fireside every night; we live thick and are in each other's way, and stumble over one another, and I think that we thus lose some respect for one another. Certainly less frequency would suffice for all important and hearty communications. Consider the girls in a factory — never alone, hardly in their dreams. It would be better if there were but one inhabitant to a square mile, as where I live. The value of a man is not in his skin, that we should touch him.

[...]

I have a great deal of company in my house; especially in the morning, when nobody calls. Let me suggest a few comparisons, that

---

7 the blues: feeling of sadness.

some one may convey an idea of my situation. I am no more lonely than the loon in the pond that laughs so loud, or than Walden Pond itself. What company has that lonely lake, I pray? And yet it has not the blue devils[8], but the blue angels in it, in the azure tint of its waters. The sun is alone, except in thick weather[9], when there sometimes appear to be two, but one is a mock sun. God is alone — but the devil, he is far from being alone; he sees a great deal of company; he is legion. I am no more lonely than a single mullein or dandelion in a pasture, or a bean leaf, or sorrel, or a horse-fly, or a bumblebee. I am no more lonely than the Mill Brook, or a weathercock, or the north star, or the south wind, or an April shower, or a January thaw, or the first spider in a new house.

[…]

The indescribable innocence and beneficence of Nature — of sun and wind and rain, of summer and winter — such health, such cheer, they afford forever! and such sympathy have they ever with our race, that all Nature would be affected, and the sun's brightness fade, and the winds would sigh humanely, and the clouds rain tears, and the woods shed their leaves and put on mourning in midsummer, if any man should ever for a just cause grieve. Shall I not have intelligence with the earth? Am I not partly leaves and vegetable mould myself?

What is the pill which will keep us well, serene, contented? Not my or thy great-grandfather's, but our great-grandmother Nature's universal, vegetable, botanic medicines, by which she has kept herself young always, outlived so many old Parrs [3] in her day, and fed her health with their decaying fatness. For my panacea, instead of one of those quack vials of a mixture dipped from Acheron[10] and the Dead Sea, which come out of those long shallow black-schooner looking

8 blue devils: a state of depression; hypochondriac melancholy.

9 in thick weather: when it is overcast.

10 Acheron: in Greek mythology, a river in Hades, a place under the earth where people went when they died.

wagons which we sometimes see made to carry bottles, let me have a draught of undiluted morning air. Morning air! If men will not drink of this at the fountainhead of the day, why, then, we must even bottle up some and sell it in the shops, for the benefit of those who have lost their subscription ticket to morning time in this world. But remember, it will not keep quite till noon-day even in the coolest cellar, but drive out the stopples long ere that and follow westward the steps of Aurora.[4] I am no worshipper of Hygeia[11], who was the daughter of that old herb-doctor Æsculapius[12], and who is represented on monuments holding a serpent in one hand, and in the other a cup out of which the serpent sometimes drinks; but rather of Hebe[13], cup-bearer to Jupiter[14], who was the daughter of Juno and wild lettuce[15], and who had the power of restoring gods and men to the vigor of youth. [5] She was probably the only thoroughly sound-conditioned, healthy, and robust young lady that ever walked the globe, and wherever she came it was spring.

NOTES ON THE TEXT

[1] Notice "society" here does not refer to human society, but to the companionship of animals and natural objects. Thoreau regards man as a part of nature. No one who lives in the midst of nature can be unhappy because there is companionship to be found in any natural object.

[2] In Greek mythology, the Aeolian harp was the instrument of Æolus or Aeolus, the ancient Greek god of wind. Aeolian harps were played by wind. So Æolian music is the music of the wind. Thoreau uses many mythological allusions in this piece, which reveals the extent to which he was influenced by a classical education. Notice also that Thoreau, through this allusion, associates what is natural (wind) with what is human (music). The idea he wants to convey is that nature's companionship is the source of happiness for man. Since man is a part of nature, nature is always beneficial to man and nothing nature does can make life a burden.

---

11 Hygeia: in Greek mythology, goddess of health.

12 Æsculapius: in Greek mythology, god of medicine, father of Hygeia.

13 Hebe: in Greek mythology, goddess of youth.

14 Jupiter: in Roman mythology, chief of the gods.

15 the daughter of Juno and wild lettuce: in Roman mythology, Juno is the queen of heaven who conceived Hebe after eating lettuce.

[3] "Old Parrs" refers to people who enjoy longevity. This name derives from Thomas Parr who was an Englishman said to have lived 152 years. Here Thoreau contrasts Nature, which enjoys eternal youth, with Old Parrs, whose "decaying fatness" can only serve to feed nature's health.

[4] In Roman mythology, Aurora is the goddess of the dawn. Thoreau's eulogy of fresh morning air prefigures the modern mania for clean, unpolluted air which has become so scarce and precious. Here Thoreau flirts with the idea of bottling the morning air for those who get up late; however, even bottled air will follow the westward steps of Aurora. In other words, an intimate contact with nature is not something you can possibly buy from a store.

[5] Notice Thoreau's use of mythological figures is more creative than most because of his juxtaposition of them not with intellectual matters but with everyday, nineteenth-century life. Thoreau's choice of Hebe, goddess of youth, over Hygeia, goddess of health, provides a way for Thoreau to reformulate notions of youth and nature with symbols familiar to a nineteenth-century educated audience. Thoreau makes references to mythology in other chapters as well. In "Economy" he mentions the Greek myth of Deucalion and Pyrrha who created men by throwing stones over their shoulders; in "The Pond in Winter" he compares a pile of ice to Valhalla, palace of the Scandinavian gods. In "Sounds" he describes the Fitchburg Railway train as a great mythical beast invading the calm of Walden. Despite his pursuit of simplicity in life, Thoreau's literary style, while concise, is far from simple. It contains witticisms, double meanings, puns. *Walden* is an elevated text that is much more accessible to educated city-dwellers than to the uneducated country-dwellers.

QUESTIONS FOR DISCUSSION

1. What is Thoreau's definition of society? Why didn't Thoreau feel lonely living all by himself in the woods? Why did he believe that compared with other men, he was living a happier life out there in the woods?

2. What does Thoreau imply when he talks about rains which ruined his potatoes but helped the grass grow? What does he suggests when he states "I was so distinctly made aware of the presence of something kindred to me, even in scenes which we are accustomed to call wild and dreary, and also that the nearest of blood to me and humanest was not a person nor a villager, that I thought no place could ever be strange to me again"?

3. Thoreau writes, "The really diligent student in one of the crowded hives of Cambridge College is as solitary as a dervish in the desert." What can you infer, from this statement, about Thoreau's idea of solitude?

4. In what ways is Thoreau's idea about nature still meaningful to the maintenance

of ecological balance in the present world? In *Wolf Totem*, Chinese writer Jiang Rong warns about the consequences of the disappearance of wolves in the Inner Mongolian grasslands due to human activities. Discuss the role of wolves in the grasslands in light of Thoreau's conception of nature.

5. Thoreau uses nature metaphors in his depiction of society and social metaphors in his depiction of nature. Find out examples of these from the text and discuss their significance.

SUGGESTED REFERENCES

Bickman, Martin. *Walden: Volatile Truths.* New York: Twayne, 1992.

Bridgman, Richard. *Dark Thoreau.* Lincoln: U of Nebraska P, 1982.

Cavell, Stanley. *The Senses of Walden: An Expanded Edition.* San Francisco: North Point Press, 1981.

Hansen, Olaf. *Aesthetic Individualism and Practical Intellect: American Allegory in Emerson, Thoreau, Adams, and James.* Princeton: Princeton UP, 1990.

Johnson, William C. *What Thoreau Said: Walden and the Unsayable.* Moscow, Idaho: U of Idaho P, 1991.

Myerson, Joel ed. *Critical Essays on Henry David Thoreau's* ***Walden****.* Boston: G. K. Hall, 1988.

Myerson, Joel ed. *The Cambridge Companion to Henry David Thoreau.* New York: Cambridge UP, 1995.

Porte, Joel. *Emerson and Thoreau: The Contemporary Reviews.* New York: Cambridge UP, 1992.

Sayre, Robert F. ed. *New Essays on* ***Walden****.* Cambridge: Cambridge UP, 1992.

Unit 3 Edgar Allan Poe

(1809–1849)

A GUIDE TO LITERARY TERMINOLOGY

"Trochaic Octameter": *Trochaic octameter is a poetic meter that has eight trochaic metrical feet per line. A trochee is a foot composed of a long (stressed) syllable followed by a short (unstressed) syllable, as in the word "running." It is known as a "falling foot," as opposed to the iamb which is a rising foot because it ends on a stressed syllable. Octameter is an eight-foot line of verse. So, a line of trochaic octameter has in it eight trochees, or sixteen syllables. The best known work in trochaic octameter is Edgar Allan Poe's "The Raven," which has five lines of trochaic octameter followed by a "short" half line by the end of the poem. But if we look really closely, we can see that the second, fourth, and fifth lines only have fifteen syllables. The trick is that in each of the lines ending in an "or" sound, Poe leaves off a syllable. In this way, the crucial "or" sound receives special emphasis.*

We can scan a line of trochaic octameter with an 'x' mark representing an unstressed syllable and a '/' mark representing a stressed syllable. It looks like this:

/ x / x / x / x / x / x / x / x
Once upon a midnight dreary, while I pondered, weak and weary

NOTES ON THE AUTHOR

Edgar Allan Poe, viewed as an important poet and writer of the American Romantic Movement and known for his tales of mystery and the macabre, was born in Boston in 1809 to David and Elizabeth Poe, both being itinerant theater players. His father left the family when Edgar was eighteen months old. His mother died in 1811. He was adopted by a tobacco merchant named John Allan. In youth he enjoyed the genteel and thorough education. As he turned into a mature young man, he became estranged from his foster father who wanted him to be in business. Poe wanted, instead, to be a poet and a writer. So he was forced to make his own way in the world. From 1831 until his death in 1849, Poe made his living by contributing verses, essays and short stories to various magazines and by occasional editorial jobs in Philadelphia, Baltimore, and New York City. He began his literary career with a volume of poetry, *Tamerlane and Other Poems* (1827). In 1845 he reached the apex of his literary career by publishing "The Raven" in the *Evening Mirror* and *The Raven and Other Poems*. On October 7, 1849, he died in delirium at the age of 40. Poe had lived a short life of poverty, anxiety, and fantastic tragedy. Yet his literary achievements are tremendous: he established a new symbolic poetry within the small compass of 48 poems; he invented and formalized a new form of short story, the detective story; he founded a new form of fiction, fiction of psychological analysis and symbolism.

In his seminal essays "The Philosophy of Composition" and "The Poetic Principle," Poe suggests that the poet should be concerned with the "circumscribed Eden" of his own dreams. The poet's task is to weave a tapestry talismanic signs and sounds in order to draw, or rather subdue, the reader into sharing the world beyond phenomenal experience. Poems make nothing happen in any practical, immediate sense, Poe suggests. Poe occupies an important position in American literature as a great lyric poet. No other American poet ever surpassed him in representing musical and rhythmical beauty. His poems are "word music." As he himself puts it, "I would define, in brief, the Poetry of words as The Rhythmical Creation of Beauty." Love, among other things, is a recurring theme of his poetry, but his tone is often sad and melancholy. In his view, "Love, the purest and truest of all poetical themes, is the highest variety of beauty, and beauty is the province of the poem." "The Raven" is among his best-known poems.

SYNOPSIS OF THE WORK

"The Raven" was first published in 1845. It is about a mourning young man's encounter with a raven on a December night. The poem opens with his attempt to ease his sorrow from the loss of his love Lenore by distracting his mind with some old books of "forgotten lore." He is interrupted, while he is dozing off, by a tapping on his chamber door. As he opens the door, he finds "darkness there and nothing more." He whispers into the darkness the name of his beloved lady "Lenore," hoping his lost love had come back, but all that could be heard was an echo that murmured back the word "Lenore!" and "merely this and nothing more." With a burning soul, the narrator returns to his chamber, and this time he can hear a tapping at the window lattice. He opens the window, only to find "a stately Raven" perching itself on the bust of Pallas over his chamber door. When he asks the bird for his name, it croaks "Nevermore." The lonely and melancholy fellow knows that the bird does not speak from wisdom, but has been taught by "some unhappy master," and that the word "nevermore" is its only "stock and store." Still, he delights in its company, and fears it will be gone in the morning, as his hopes have flown away before. But the raven croaks again, "Nevermore," to which the young man smiles and pulls up a chair, interested in what the raven "meant in croaking, 'Nevermore.'" The chair, where Lenore once sat, provokes his painful memories. Although he knows that the raven can only respond with one and the same word, he cannot help but ask it questions. "Is there balm in Gilead?' — "Nevermore." "Can I find Lenore in the paradise?" — "Nevermore." "Take thy form from off my door!" — "Nevermore." Eventually the heart-broken narrator realizes it is meaningless to continue the dialogue. And he comes to the conclusion that his "soul from out that shadow" that the raven throws on the floor "shall be lifted — Nevermore!"

SELECTED READINGS

The Raven

Once upon a midnight dreary, while I pondered, weak and weary,
Over many a quaint and curious volume of forgotten lore[1],
While I nodded, nearly napping, suddenly there came a tapping,
As of some one gently rapping, rapping [1] at my chamber door.
"'Tis some visitor," I muttered, "tapping at my chamber door —
    Only this, and nothing more." [2]

Ah, distinctly I remember it was in the bleak December, [3]
And each separate dying ember wrought its ghost upon the floor.[2]
Eagerly I wished the morrow[3]; — vainly I had sought to borrow
From my books surcease[4] of sorrow — sorrow for the lost Lenore —
For the rare and radiant maiden whom the angels named Lenore —
    Nameless here[5] for evermore. [4]

1 lore: the traditional stories of a people.
2 wrought its ghost upon the floor: (the dying embers) cast their shadows on the floor.
3 the morrow: tomorrow, the next day.
4 surcease: (arch.) cessation, stop.
5 here: in the earthly world, as opposed to heaven

And the silken, sad, uncertain rustling of each purple curtain
Thrilled me[6] — filled me with fantastic terrors never felt before;
So that now, to still the beating of my heart, I stood repeating
"'Tis some visitor entreating entrance at my chamber door —
Some late visitor entreating entrance at my chamber door; —
    This it is, and nothing more,"

Presently my soul grew stronger; hesitating then no longer,
"Sir," said I, "or Madam, truly your forgiveness I implore;
But the fact is I was napping, and so gently you came rapping,
And so faintly you came tapping, tapping at my chamber door,
That I scarce was sure I heard you" — here I opened wide the door; —
    Darkness there, and nothing more.

Deep into that darkness peering, long I stood there wondering, fearing,
Doubting, dreaming dreams no mortal ever dared to dream before;
But the silence was unbroken, and the stillness gave no token,
And the only word there spoken was the whispered word, "Lenore!"
This I whispered, and an echo murmured back the word, "Lenore!"
    Merely this, and nothing more.

Back into the chamber turning, all my soul within me burning,
Soon I heard again a tapping somewhat louder than before.
"Surely," said I, "surely that is something at my window lattice;
Let me see then, what thereat is,[7] and this mystery explore —
Let my heart be still a moment and this mystery explore; —
    'Tis the wind, and nothing more!"

Open here I flung the shutter, when, with many a flirt and flutter,[8]

---

6 Thrilled me: made me quiver.
7 what thereat is: what is there at the place; thereat: at the place.
8 flirt: quick short flight; flutter: quick, light movements of a bird's wings.

In there stepped a stately Raven [5] of the saintly days of yore[9].
Not the least obeisance made he; not a minute stopped or stayed he;
But, with mien[10] of lord or lady, perched above my chamber door —
Perched upon a bust of Pallas [6] just above my chamber door —
    Perched, and sat, and nothing more.

Then this ebony[11] bird beguiling my sad fancy into smiling,
By the grave and stern decorum of the countenance it wore,
"Though thy crest be shorn[12] and shaven, thou," I said, "art sure no craven[13].
Ghastly grim and ancient Raven wandering from the Nightly shore —
Tell me what thy lordly name is on the Night's Plutonian [7] shore!"
    Quoth[14] the Raven, "Nevermore."

Much I marvelled this ungainly fowl to hear discourse so plainly,
Though its answer little meaning — little relevancy bore;
For we cannot help agreeing that no sublunary being[15]
Ever yet was blessed with seeing bird above his chamber door —
Bird or beast above the sculptured bust above his chamber door,
    With such name as "Nevermore."

But the Raven, sitting lonely on the placid bust, spoke only,
That one word, as if his soul in that one word he did outpour.
Nothing farther then he uttered — not a feather then he fluttered —
Till I scarcely more than muttered, "Other friends have flown before —

---

9 yore: time long past.
10 mien: the air, bearing, carriage or manner of a person, as expressive of character or mood.
11 ebony: black.
12 shorn: cut short.
13 craven: a coward.
14 Quoth: (arch.) past tense of "quethe," to say; it is used to indicate that the words of a speaker are being repeated.
15 sublunary being: earthly being; sublunary, situated beneath the moon, of this world.

On the morrow *he* will leave me, as my Hopes have flown before."
Then the bird said, "Nevermore."

Startled at the stillness broken by reply so aptly spoken,
"Doubtless," said I, "what it utters is its only stock and store[16],
Caught from some unhappy master whom unmerciful Disaster
Followed fast and followed faster — till his song one burden bore —
Till the dirges of His Hope that melancholy burden bore
Of 'Never — nevermore.'"

But the Raven still beguiling all my sad soul into smiling,
Straight I wheeled a cushioned seat in front of bird, and bust, and door;
Then upon the velvet sinking, I betook myself to linking
Fancy unto fancy, thinking what this ominous bird of yore —
What this grim, ungainly, ghastly, gaunt, and ominous bird of yore [8]
Meant in croaking "Nevermore."

This I sat engaged in guessing, but no syllable expressing
To the fowl whose fiery eyes now burned into my bosom's core;
This and more I sat divining[17], with my head at ease reclining
On the cushion's velvet lining that the lamp-light gloated o'er,
But whose velvet-violet lining with the lamp-light gloating o'er,
She shall press, ah, nevermore![18]

Then, methought[19], the air grew denser, perfumed from an unseen censer

16 its only stock and store: the only word it can speak.
17 divine: to find out something by guessing.
18 Lenore shall never again press her back against (the cushion's velvet violet lining).
19 methought: past tense of "methinks" which means: it seems to me.

Swung by Sera phim whose foot-falls[20] tinkled on the tufted floor.
"Wretch," I cried, "thy God hath lent thee — by these angels he has sent thee
Respite — respite and Nepenthe[21] from thy memories of Lenore!
Quaff, oh quaff[22] this kind Nepenthe, and forget this lost Lenore!"
Quoth the Raven, "Nevermore."

"Prophet!" said I, "thing of evil! — prophet still, if bird or devil! —
Whether Tempter sent, or whether tempest tossed thee here ashore,
Desolate yet all undaunted, on this desert land enchanted —
On this home by Horror haunted — tell me truly, I implore —
Is there — is there balm in Gilead? [9] — tell me — tell me, I implore!'"
Quoth the Raven, "Nevermore."

"Prophet!" said I, "thing of evil! — prophet still, if bird or devil!
By that Heaven that bends above us — by that God we both adore —
Tell this soul with sorrow laden if, within the distant Aidenn[23],
It shall clasp a sainted maiden whom the angels named Lenore —
Clasp a rare and radiant maiden, whom the angels named Lenore."
Quoth the Raven, "Nevermore."

"Be that word our sign of parting, bird or fiend!" I shrieked, upstarting —
"Get thee back into the tempest and the Night's Plutonian shore!
Leave no black plume as a token of that lie thy soul hath spoken!
Leave my loneliness unbroken! — quit the bust above my door!
Take thy beak from out my heart, and take thy form from off my door!"

---

20 foot-fall: arrival (of angels).

21 respite: a short period of rest from something unpleasant; Nepenthe: a drink or drug supposed to bring forgetfulness of trouble or grief.

22 quaff: drink copiously or in a large draught.

23 Aidenn: a place name used by Poe to suggest Eden, or paradise.

Quoth the Raven, "Nevermore."

And the Raven, never flitting, still is sitting, still is sitting
On the pallid bust of Pallas just above my chamber door;
And his eyes have all the seeming of a demon's that is dreaming,
And the lamp-light o'er him streaming throws his shadow on the floor;
And my soul from out that shadow that lies floating on the floor
Shall be lifted — nevermore!

NOTES ON THE TEXT

[1] The word "rapping," which rhymes with "napping" and "tapping" in the previous line, is repeated here, creating an onomatopoeic effect of the knock on the door which startles the nodding narrator. This pattern of repetition is found also in several other stanzas, e.g. "sorrow" in line 4, stanza 2, "tapping" in line 4, stanza 4, and "is there" in line 5, stanza 15. Notice also the use of internal rhyme, that is, patterns of rhyming that occur in the middle of lines. In lines 3 – 4, for example, there is "napping" and "rapping." Another example of internal rhyme is found in lines 9 – 10 with "morrow" and "sorrow."

[2] "The Raven," first published in 1845, is known for its musicality. The 108-line poem consists of 18 stanzas, in each of which the first five lines are in trochaic octameter (eight trochaic feet per line, each foot having one stressed syllable followed by an unstressed one 扬抑格八音步), and the last line in trochaic tetrameter (four trochaic feet, each foot having one stressed syllable followed by an unstressed one 扬抑格四音步), with a rhyme scheme of abcbbb.

[3] The "bleak December" here echoes "midnight" in the first stanza. Both add to the sorrows of the mourning narrator who grieves over the death of his love, Lenore. Notice also that Poe's mother died in December. The sad melancholy mood of the narrator is reinforced by the darkness of the December midnight and the occurrence of a raven in the seventh stanza.

[4] The most important elements to recognize in this poem are the use of repetition and rhyme. Notice that the use of end rhymes "door," "Lenore," "nothing more" and "nevermore" in the poem creates a feeling of gloom and despair.

[5] Traditionally ravens are emblematic of evil and death. The ill-omened raven in this poem symbolizes intuitive truth and "mournful and never-ending remembrance" (Poe). In "The Philosophy of Composition," Poe implies that he chose the raven because it is a bird of ill omen. In the following stanzas, the deranged narrator asks the raven many times about the possibility of meeting his love after death, but the monadic bird repeatedly replies "Nevermore." As all his questions are given negative answers, which intensifies the narrator's suf-

ferance and despair, the hopeless young man is forced to realize that there will be no reunion, after death, with his deceased love Lenore. It is also worth our notice that since the answers to his questions are already known, the narrator actually inflicts tortures on himself when he compulsively raises questions to the raven.

[6] Pallas is the goddess of wisdom in Greek mythology. The marble bust of Pallas on which the raven perches stands for intellectual wisdom. A raven perching on the bust of Pallas forms a contrast between intuition and reason. As the unreasoning bird represents the narrator's lamentation, the contrast here is intended to reveal the presence of grief and sorrow and the absence of wisdom and rationality.

[7] Plutonian: of Pluto, the god of the underworld (the dead) in Roman mythology, brother of Jupiter and Neptune.

[8] "This grim, ungainly, ghastly, gaunt, and ominous bird of yore"— the repletion of the initial consonant sound g in the words "grim," "ghastly," and "gaunt"— is a poetic device called alliteration (头韵). It is used here to create onomatopoeia which makes the raven sound scary, hence intensifying the mood of terror. Another example can be found in the first line of the seventh stanza, "Open here I flung the shutter, when, with many a flirt and flutter," in which the f sound is repeated in "flung," "flirt," and "flutter."

[9] Balm is a cream that has a pleasant smell and is used to make wounds less painful. Gilead: a mountainous area east of Jordan River. "Is there balm in Gilead?" is an echo of the ironic words of Jeremiah (a Hebrew prophet in the Bible), who asks: "Is there no balm in Gilead? Is there no physician there? Why then has the health of the daughter of my people not been restored?" See Jeremiah 8:22.

QUESTIONS FOR DISCUSSION

1. Poe's symbolic raven — which follows the Romantic tradition of Coleridge's albatross, Shelley's skylark, and Keats's nightingale — was influenced not only by Elizabeth Barrett's "Lady Geraldine's Courtship" but also by Grip, the raven, "the embodied spirit of evil," in Dickens's *Barnaby Rudge* (1841). Discuss why Poe chose a raven to appear at the narrator's door and how the raven as a symbol has contributed to the creation of a melancholy and gloomy atmosphere in the poem.

2. In "The Philosophy of Composition" Poe expressed a crucial aesthetic principle by stating, "The death of a beautiful woman is, unquestionably, the most poetical topic in the world." Discuss how in the poem Poe portrays the monomaniacal obsession of a lonely and sad soul who is hovering on the edge of madness because of the decease of "a rare and radiant maiden, whom the angels named Lenore."

3. The poem is known for its musicality. Read the poem aloud several times to discover Poe's use of repetition, of rhymes (both internal and end rhymes) and

alliteration. Discuss how the musical effects created in the poem help express the theme and the narrator's moods.

参考译文

乌鸦

曹明伦译

从前一个阴郁的子夜，我独自沉思，慵懒疲竭，
沉思许多古怪而离奇、早已被人遗忘的传闻——
当我开始打盹，几乎入睡，突然传来一阵轻擂，
仿佛有人在轻轻叩击，轻轻叩击我的房门。
"有人来了，"我轻声嘟喃，"正在叩击我的房门——
　　唯此而已，别无他般。"

哦，我清楚地记得那是在萧瑟的十二月；
每一团奄奄一息的余烬都形成阴影伏在地板。
我当时真盼望翌日；——因为我已经枉费心机
想用书来消除悲哀——消除因失去丽诺尔的悲叹——
因那被天使叫作丽诺尔的少女，她美丽娇艳——
　　在这儿却默默无闻，直至永远。

那柔软、暗淡、飒飒飘动的每一块紫色窗布
使我心中充满前所未有的恐怖——我毛骨悚然；
为平息我心儿悸跳，我站起身反复叨念
"这是有人想进屋，在叩我的房门——
更深夜半有人想进屋，在叩我的房门；——
　　唯此而已，别无他般。"

很快我的心变得坚强；不再犹疑，不再彷徨，
"先生，"我说，"或夫人，我求你多多包涵；
刚才我正睡意昏昏，而你来敲门又那么轻，
你来敲门又那么轻，轻轻叩击我的房门，
我差点以为没听见你"—— 说着我拉开门扇；——
　　唯有黑夜，别无他般。

凝视着夜色幽幽，我站在门边惊惧良久，
疑惑中似乎梦见从前没人敢梦见的梦幻；
可那未被打破的寂静，没显示任何迹象，
“丽诺尔？”便是我嗫嚅念叨的唯一字眼，
我念叨“丽诺尔！”回声把这名字轻轻送还，
　　唯此而已，别无他般。

我转身回到房中，我的整个心烧灼般疼痛，
很快我又听到叩击声，比刚才听起来明显。
“肯定，”我说，“肯定有什么在我的窗棂；
让我瞧瞧是什么在那里，去把那秘密发现——
让我的心先镇静一会儿，去把那秘密发现；——
　　那不过是风，别无他般！”

我猛然推开窗户，心儿扑扑直跳就像打鼓，
一只神圣往昔的健壮乌鸦慢慢走进我房间；
它既没向我致意问候；也没有片刻的停留；
而以绅士淑女的风度，栖在我房门的上面——
栖在我房门上方一尊帕拉斯半身雕像上面——
　　栖坐在那儿，仅如此这般。

于是这只黑鸟把我悲伤的幻觉哄骗成微笑，
以它那老成持重一本正经温文尔雅的容颜，
“虽然冠毛被剪除，”我说，“但你肯定不是懦夫，
你这幽灵般可怕的古鸦，漂泊来自夜的彼岸——
请告诉我你尊姓大名，在黑沉沉的冥府阴间！”
　　乌鸦答曰“永不复还。”

听见如此直率的回答，我惊叹这丑陋的乌鸦，
虽说它的回答不着边际——与提问几乎无关；
因为我们不得不承认，从来没有活着的世人
曾如此有幸地看见一只鸟栖在他房门的上面——
鸟或兽栖在他房间门上方的半身雕像上面，
　　有这种名字“永不复还。”

但那只独栖于肃穆的半身雕像上的乌鸦只说了

这一句话，仿佛它倾泻灵魂就用那一个字眼。
然后它便一声不吭——也不把它的羽毛拍动——
直到我几乎是喃喃自语“其他朋友早已消散——
明晨它也将离我而去——如同我的希望已消散。”
　　这时那鸟说“永不复还。”

惊异于那死寂漠漠被如此恰当的回话打破，
“肯定，”我说，“这句话是它唯一的本钱，
从它不幸的主人那儿学来，一连串无情飞灾
曾接踵而至，直到它主人的歌中有了这字眼——
直到他希望的挽歌中有了这个忧伤的字眼
　　‘永不复还，永不复还。’”

但那只乌鸦仍然把我悲伤的幻觉哄骗成微笑，
我即刻拖了张软椅到门旁雕像下那只鸟跟前；
然后坐在天鹅绒椅垫上，我开始冥思苦想，
浮想连着浮想，猜度这不祥的古鸟何出此言——
这只狰狞丑陋可怕不吉不祥的古鸟何出此言，
　　为何聒噪“永不复还。”

我坐着猜想那意思，但没对那鸟说片语只言，
此时，它炯炯发光的眼睛已燃烧进我的心坎；
我依然坐在那儿猜度，把我的心靠得很舒服，
舒舒服服地靠在那被灯光凝视的天鹅绒衬垫，
但被灯光爱慕地凝视着的紫色的天鹅绒衬垫，
　　她将显出，啊，永不复还！

接着我想，空气变得稠密，被无形香炉熏香，
提香炉的撒拉弗的脚步声响在有簇饰的地板。
“可怜的人，”我呼道，“是上帝派天使为你送药，
这忘忧药能中止你对失去的丽诺尔的思念；
喝吧，喝吧，忘掉对失去的丽诺尔的思念！”
　　乌鸦说“永不复还。”

“先知！”我说，“凶兆！——仍是先知，不管是鸟是魔！
是不是魔鬼送你，或是暴风雨抛你来到此岸，

孤独但毫不气馁，在这片妖惑鬼祟的荒原——
在这恐怖萦绕之家——告诉我真话，求你可怜——
基列有香膏吗？——告诉我——告诉我，求你可怜！”
　　乌鸦说“永不复还。”

“先知！”我说，“凶兆！——仍是先知，不管是鸟是魔！
凭我们头顶的苍天起誓——凭我们都崇拜的上帝起誓——
告诉这充满悲伤的灵魂，它能否在遥远的仙境
拥抱被天使叫作丽诺尔的少女，她纤尘不染——
拥抱被天使叫作丽诺尔的少女，她美丽娇艳。”
　　乌鸦说“永不复还。”

“让这话做我们的道别之辞，鸟或魔！”我突然叫道——
“回你的暴风雨中去吧，回你黑沉沉的冥府阴间！
别留下黑色羽毛作为你的灵魂谎言的象征！
留给我完整的孤独！——快从我门上的雕像滚蛋！
从我心中带走你的嘴，从我房门带走你的外观！”
　　乌鸦说“永不复还。”

那乌鸦并没飞去，它仍然栖息，仍然栖息
在房门上方那苍白的帕拉斯半身雕像上面；
而它的眼光与正在做梦的魔鬼眼光一模一样，
照在它身上的灯光把它的阴影投射在地板；
而我的灵魂，会从那团在地板上漂浮的阴暗
　　被擢升么——永不复还！

SUGGESTED REFERENCES

Davidson, Edward. *Poe: A Critical Study.* Cambridge: Harvard UP, 1957.

Hoffman, Daniel. *Poe Poe Poe Poe Poe Poe Poe.* Garden City: Doubleday, 1972.

Meyers, Jeffrey. "Edgar Allan Poe." *The Columbia History of American Poetry.* Ed. Jay Parini and Brett C. Millier. Beijing: Foreign Language Teaching and Research Press, 2005. 172-202.

Meyers, Jeffrey. *Edgar Allan Poe: His Life and Legacy.* New York: Scribner's, 1992.

Stovall, Floyd. *Edgar Allan Poe the Poet.* Charlottesville: U of Virginia P, 1969.

Wilbur, Richard. "Poe." *Major Writers of America.* Ed. Perry Miller. New York: Harcourt Brace, 1962. 369-98.

Unit 4 Nathaniel Hawthorne

(1804—1864)

A GUIDE TO LITERARY TERMINOLOGY

"Dark Romance": *Nathaniel Hawthorne's story "Young Goodman Brown" fits into a subgenre of American Romanticism, i.e. the dark romance. Novels and stories of this type feature depictions of morbid or gloomy events, and emotional or psychological torment. The dark Romantics shared the Romantic movement's emphasis on emotion and extremity with a gothic sensibility. They tended to create stories that would move readers to fear and question their surroundings. Edgar Allan Poe, who wrote "The Fall of the House of Usher" (1839) and "The Tell-Tale Heart" (1843), was probably the most famous of the dark romance writers. Goodman Brown's encounter with the devil and battle with the evil within himself are both classic elements of a dark romance.*

Herman Melville, one of Hawthorne's close friends, thus comments on the underlying depth of the story: "you would of course suppose that it was a simple little tale, intended as a supplement to 'Goody Two Shoes.' Whereas it is as deep as Dante."

NOTES ON THE AUTHOR

Nathaniel Hawthorne was born on July 4, 1804, in Salem, Massachusetts. He was the descendant of his Puritan ancestors including William Hathorne, one of the first Puritan settlers who arrived in New England in 1630, and John Hathorne, a presiding magistrate in the Salem Witch Trials. Hawthorne's sea captain father died when he was 4. As an adolescent, he was interested in hiking and reading eighteenth century writers, such as Henry Fielding, Horace Walpole, William Godwin and Walter Scott. Hawthorne began his career as a writer in Salem after he graduated from Bowdoin College (where he was a classmate of Longfellow and of Franklin Pierce who later became the fourteenth President of the U. S.) in 1825. In Salem, he lived a life of isolation and seclusion that lasted for twelve years. Between 1825—1837, he wrote several works, including the historical novel *Fanshawe and Seven Tales of My Native Land*. A collection of his stories *Twice-Told Tales*, which brought him critical acclaim, was published in 1837. In the preface, Hawthorne referred to his tales as having "the pale tint of flowers blossomed in too retired a shade." These tales, collectively, explore these issues that obsessed Hawthorne: guilt and secrecy, intellectual and moral pride, the impact of the Puritan past on the New England present.

For the next five years, Hawthorne worked as an editor for Goodrich, then became involved in the experiment in communal living at Brook Farm. Used to solitude, he found communal living unpleasant. Hawthorne married Sophia Peabody in 1842. The couple moved to Concord where they lived for three years in the Old Manse, the former home of Ralph Waldo Emerson. The family had close contacts with their neighbors and friends: Emerson, Henry David Thoreau, Amos Bronson Alcott, and Margaret Fuller. Three children — one son and two daughters — were born between 1844 – 1851. During this period, he turned to writing sketches and tales he called "allegories of the heart." To support the family, Hawthorne began to work as surveyor of the Port of Salem in 1846, a position he held for only three years due to the change of administration in Washington after the presidential election of 1848. In 1849, he began writing the novel that was to become his masterpiece *The Scarlet Letter* which was published in 1850 and brought him wide recognition. With the sales of the novel easing his poverty, Hawthorne left Salem and moved his family to Lenox, Massachusetts, where he developed a friendship with Herman Melville, who was writing *Moby Dick* then. In Lenox, he completed *The House of the Seven Gables* (1851), *The Blithedale Romance* (1852) and *The Tanglewood Tales* (1853). He was appointed American consul from 1853 – 1857. After five years as consul and travel in Italy, the setting of *The Marble Faun* (1860), Hawthorne returned to the U. S. in 1860, published a series of sketches of *England Our Old Home* (1863), and began several literary projects which were broken off at his death in 1864. Hawthorne is noted for his mingled critique and embodiment of the preoccupations of New England puritanism — guilt, sin, concealment, isolation, introspection, ambiguity and ambivalence. But his greatest achievement came from what Melville called his "great power of blackness," his portrayal of the dark landscape of the human mind. His repeated portrayal of hidden sin and the individual's confrontation with evil led Melville to see in Hawthorne "that Calvinistic sense of Innate Depravity and Original Sin, from whose visitations, in some shape or other, no deeply thinking mind is always and wholly free."

SYNOPSIS OF THE WORK

"Young Goodman Brown" first appeared in the April issue of *New England Magazine* in 1835 and was later included in Hawthorne's popular short story collection *Mosses from an Old Manse* published in 1846. It is known for its gripping portrayals of seventeenth-century Puritan society.

The story begins at dusk in seventeenth century Salem, Massachusetts, with the protagonist young Goodman Brown leaving Faith, his wife of three months, to meet with a mysterious man in the woods. As they meet and travel further into the dark forest, it becomes clear that Goodman Brown's companion is no other than the devil and that the purpose of their journey is to join in a Black Mass. Brown is reluctant to continue, but the devil urges him to go on. In the woods, they encounter Goody Cloyse, Brown's moral and spiritual adviser, who accepts the devil's staff and flies away to her destination. Brown sees many other townspeople, whom he had considered good Christians including his minister and deacon, traveling in the same direction. This saddens his heart and he decides to turn back. But now he hears his wife's voice and realizes that she is one of those to be initiated at the meeting. Recognizing that he has lost his Faith, he becomes disillusioned about the goodness of his society and resolves to take part in the meeting. At the ceremony, which is carried out in a clearing deep in the forest, as Brown and Faith, who are the only two of the townspeople not yet initiated to the forest rite, approach the altar to be anointed in blood to seal their alliance with wickedness, he cries out to Faith to "look up to heaven, and resist the wicked one." Instantly the scene vanishes and he finds himself standing in solitude in the calm forest, next to the cold, wet rock. After he returns to Salem the next day, Goodman Brown is uncertain whether the previous night's events were a dream or reality, but he is deeply shaken. He is unable to forgive the possibility of evil in those he loves and admires, and therefore spends the rest of his life in desperate loneliness and gloom.

SELECTED READINGS

Young Goodman Brown [1]

Young Goodman Brown came forth at sunset into the street at Salem village; but put his head back, after crossing the threshold, to exchange a parting kiss with his young wife. And Faith, as the wife was aptly named, thrust her own pretty head into the street, letting the wind play with the pink ribbons of her cap while she called to Goodman Brown.

"Dearest heart," whispered she, softly and rather sadly, when her lips were close to his ear, "prithee[1] put off your journey until sunrise and sleep in your own bed to-night. A lone woman is troubled with such dreams and such thoughts that she's afeard of[2] herself sometimes. Pray tarry with me[3] this night, dear husband, of all nights in the year."

"My love and my Faith," replied young Goodman Brown, "of all nights in the year, this one night must I tarry away from thee. My journey, as thou callest it, forth and back again, must needs be done 'twixt [4] now and sunrise. What, my sweet, pretty wife, dost thou doubt me already, and we but three months married?"

"Then God bless you!" said Faith, with the pink ribbons; "and may you find all well when you come back."

"Amen!" cried Goodman Brown. "Say thy prayers, dear Faith, and go to bed at dusk, and no harm will come to thee."

So they parted; and the young man pursued his way until, being about to turn the corner by the meeting-house, he looked back and saw the head of Faith still peeping after him with a melancholy air, in spite of her pink ribbons.

"Poor little Faith!" thought he, for his heart smote him. "What a wretch am I to leave her on such an errand! She talks of dreams, too. Methought as she spoke there was trouble in her face, as if a dream had warned her what work is to be done tonight. But no, no; 't would kill her to think it. Well, she's a blessed angel on earth; and after this one night I'll cling to her skirts and follow her to heaven."

With this excellent resolve for the future, Goodman Brown felt himself justified in making more haste on his present evil purpose.

---

1 prithee: (archaic) pray thee, used when asking somebody politely to do something.

2 afeard of: (archaic) afraid of.

3 Pray tarry with me: please stay with me.

4 'twixt: (archaic) between.

He had taken a dreary road, darkened by all the gloomiest trees of the forest, which barely stood aside to let the narrow path creep through, and closed immediately behind. It was all as lonely as could be; and there is this peculiarity in such a solitude, that the traveller knows not who may be concealed by the innumerable trunks and the thick boughs overhead; so that with lonely footsteps he may yet be passing through an unseen multitude.

"There may be a devilish Indian behind every tree," said Goodman Brown to himself; and he glanced fearfully behind him as he added, "What if the devil himself should be at my very elbow!"

His head being turned back, he passed a crook of the road, and, looking forward again, beheld the figure of a man, in grave and decent attire, seated at the foot of an old tree. He arose at Goodman Brown's approach and walked onward side by side with him.

"You are late, Goodman Brown," said he. "The clock of the Old South[5] was striking as I came through Boston, and that is full fifteen minutes agone[6]."

"Faith kept me back a while," replied the young man, with a tremor in his voice, caused by the sudden appearance of his companion, though not wholly unexpected.

It was now deep dusk in the forest, and deepest in that part of it where these two were journeying. As nearly as could be discerned, the second traveller was about fifty years old, apparently in the same rank of life as Goodman Brown, and bearing a considerable resemblance to him, though perhaps more in expression than features. Still they might have been taken for father and son. And yet, though the elder person was as simply clad as the younger, and as simple in manner too, he had an indescribable air of one who knew the world, and who would

5 the Old South: the Old South Church in Boston, first built in 1669.
6 agone: (archaic) ago.

not have felt abashed at the governor's dinner table or in King William's[7] court, were it possible that his affairs should call him thither. But the only thing about him that could be fixed upon as remarkable was his staff, which bore the likeness of a great black snake, [2] so curiously wrought that it might almost be seen to twist and wriggle itself like a living serpent. This, of course, must have been an ocular deception, assisted by the uncertain light.

"Come, Goodman Brown," cried his fellow-traveller, "this is a dull pace for the beginning of a journey. Take my staff, if you are so soon weary."

"Friend," said the other, exchanging his slow pace for a full stop, "having kept covenant by meeting thee here, it is my purpose now to return whence I came. I have scruples touching the matter thou wot'st of[8]."

"Sayest thou so?" replied he of the serpent, smiling apart. "Let us walk on, nevertheless, reasoning as we go; and if I convince thee not thou shalt turn back. We are but a little way in the forest yet."

"Too far! too far!" exclaimed the goodman, unconsciously resuming his walk. "My father never went into the woods on such an errand, nor his father before him. We have been a race of honest men and good Christians since the days of the martyrs;[3] and shall I be the first of the name of Brown that ever took this path and kept — "

"Such company, thou wouldst say," observed the elder person, interpreting his pause. "Well said, Goodman Brown! I have been as well acquainted with your family as with ever a one among the Puritans; and that's no trifle to say. I helped your grandfather, the constable, when he lashed the Quaker woman so smartly through the streets

7 King William: first cousin and husband of Queen Mary II, with whom he jointly ruled England (1689 – 1702).

8 wot'st of: (archaic) know.

of Salem;[4] and it was I that brought your father a pitch-pine knot, kindled at my own hearth, to set fire to an Indian village, in King Philip's war[9]. They were my good friends, both; and many a pleasant walk have we had along this path, and returned merrily after midnight. I would fain[10] be friends with you for their sake."

"If it be as thou sayest," replied Goodman Brown, "I marvel they never spoke of these matters; or, verily[11], I marvel not, seeing that the least rumor of the sort would have driven them from New England. We are a people of prayer, and good works, to boot[12], and abide no such wickedness."

"Wickedness or not," said the traveller with the twisted staff, "I have a very general acquaintance here in New England. The deacons of many a church have drunk the communion wine with me; the selectmen[13] of divers towns make me their chairman; and a majority of the Great and General Court[14] are firm supporters of my interest. The governor and I, too — But these are state secrets."

"Can this be so?" cried Goodman Brown, with a stare of amazement at his undisturbed companion. "Howbeit[15], I have nothing to do with the governor and council; they have their own ways, and are no rule for a simple husbandman like me. But, were I to go on with thee, how should I meet the eye of that good old man, our minister, at Salem village? Oh, his voice would make me tremble both Sabbath day and lecture day[16]."

---

9 King Philip's war: sometimes called the First Indian War, or Metacomet's War, was an armed conflict between Native American inhabitants of present-day New England and English colonists and their Native American allies in 1675–78. The war is named after the main leader of the Native American side, Metacomet, known to the English as "King Philip."

10 fain: (archaic) willingly or with pleasure.

11 verily: truly.

12 to boot: as well, in addition.

13 The selectmen: town officers.

14 the Great and General Court: the ruling body or the legislature of the Puritan Colony.

15 Howbeit: (archaic) however, be that as it may.

16 lecture day: midweek sermon day.

Thus far the elder traveller had listened with due gravity; but now burst into a fit of irrepressible mirth, shaking himself so violently that his snake-like staff actually seemed to wriggle in sympathy.

"Ha! ha! ha!" shouted he again and again; then composing himself, "Well, go on, Goodman Brown, go on; but, prithee, don't kill me with laughing."

"Well, then, to end the matter at once," said Goodman Brown, considerably nettled, "there is my wife, Faith. It would break her dear little heart; and I'd rather break my own."

"Nay, if that be the case," answered the other, "e'en go thy ways, Goodman Brown. I would not for twenty old women like the one hobbling before us that Faith should come to any harm."

As he spoke he pointed his staff at a female figure on the path, in whom Goodman Brown recognized a very pious and exemplary dame, who had taught him his catechism in youth, and was still his moral and spiritual adviser, jointly with the minister and Deacon Gookin. [5]

"A marvel, truly, that Goody Cloyse [6] should be so far in the wilderness at nightfall," said he. "But with your leave, friend, I shall take a cut through the woods until we have left this Christian woman behind. Being a stranger to you, she might ask whom I was consorting with and whither I was going."

"Be it so," said his fellow-traveller. "Betake you to the woods, and let me keep the path."

Accordingly the young man turned aside, but took care to watch his companion, who advanced softly along the road until he had come within a staff's length of the old dame. She, meanwhile, was making the best of her way, with singular speed for so aged a woman, and mumbling some indistinct words — a prayer, doubtless — as she went. The traveller put forth his staff and touched her withered neck with what seemed the serpent's tail.

"The devil!" screamed the pious old lady.

"Then Goody Cloyse knows her old friend?" observed the traveller, confronting her and leaning on his writhing stick.

"Ah, forsooth[17], and is it your worship indeed?" cried the good dame. "Yea, truly is it, and in the very image of my old gossip, Goodman Brown, the grandfather of the silly fellow that now is. But — would your worship believe it? — my broomstick hath strangely disappeared, stolen, as I suspect, by that unhanged witch, Goody Cory, and that, too, when I was all anointed with the juice of smallage, and cinquefoil, and wolf's bane — [18]"

"Mingled with fine wheat and the fat of a new-born babe," said the shape of old Goodman Brown.

"Ah, your worship knows the recipe," cried the old lady, cackling aloud. "So, as I was saying, being all ready for the meeting, and no horse to ride on, I made up my mind to foot it; for they tell me there is a nice young man to be taken into communion to-night. But now your good worship will lend me your arm, and we shall be there in a twinkling."

"That can hardly be," answered her friend. "I may not spare you my arm, Goody Cloyse; but here is my staff, if you will."

So saying, he threw it down at her feet, where, perhaps, it assumed life, being one of the rods which its owner had formerly lent to the Egyptian magi.[19] Of this fact, however, Goodman Brown could not take cognizance. He had cast up his eyes in astonishment, and, looking down again, beheld neither Goody Cloyse nor the serpentine staff, but his fellow-traveller alone, who waited for him as calmly as if nothing had happened.

---

17 forsooth: in truth, indeed.

18 smallage, and cinquefoil, and wolf's bane: these are plants thought to have magic powers and used for witchcraft.

19 It is described in Exodus 7 that the Egyptian magicians turned their rods into serpents.

"That old woman taught me my catechism," said the young man; and there was a world of meaning in this simple comment.

They continued to walk onward, while the elder traveller exhorted his companion to make good speed and persevere in the path, discoursing so aptly that his arguments seemed rather to spring up in the bosom of his auditor than to be suggested by himself. As they went, he plucked a branch of maple to serve for a walking stick, and began to strip it of the twigs and little boughs, which were wet with evening dew. The moment his fingers touched them they became strangely withered and dried up as with a week's sunshine. Thus the pair proceeded, at a good free pace, until suddenly, in a gloomy hollow of the road, Goodman Brown sat himself down on the stump of a tree and refused to go any farther.

"Friend," said he, stubbornly, "my mind is made up. Not another step will I budge on this errand. What if a wretched old woman do choose to go to the devil when I thought she was going to heaven: is that any reason why I should quit my dear Faith [7] and go after her?"

"You will think better of this by and by," said his acquaintance, composedly. "Sit here and rest yourself a while; and when you feel like moving again, there is my staff to help you along."

Without more words, he threw his companion the maple stick, and was as speedily out of sight as if he had vanished into the deepening gloom. The young man sat a few moments by the roadside, applauding himself greatly, and thinking with how clear a conscience he should meet the minister in his morning walk, nor shrink from the eye of good old Deacon Gookin. And what calm sleep would be his that very night, which was to have been spent so wickedly, but so purely and sweetly now, in the arms of Faith! Amidst these pleasant and praiseworthy meditations, Goodman Brown heard the tramp of horses along the road, and deemed it advisable to conceal himself within the verge of the forest, conscious of the guilty purpose that had brought him thither, though now so happily turned from it.

On came the hoof tramps and the voices of the riders, two grave old voices, conversing soberly as they drew near. These mingled sounds appeared to pass along the road, within a few yards of the young man's hiding-place; but, owing doubtless to the depth of the gloom at that particular spot, neither the travellers nor their steeds were visible. Though their figures brushed the small boughs by the wayside, it could not be seen that they intercepted, even for a moment, the faint gleam from the strip of bright sky, athwart[20] which they must have passed. Goodman Brown alternately crouched and stood on tip-toe, pulling aside the branches and thrusting forth his head as far as he durst[21] without discerning so much as a shadow. It vexed him the more, because he could have sworn, were such a thing possible, that he recognized the voices of the minister and Deacon Gookin, jogging along quietly, as they were wont to do, when bound to some ordination or ecclesiastical council. While yet within hearing, one of the riders stopped to pluck a switch.

"Of the two, reverend sir," said the voice like the deacon's, "I had rather miss an ordination dinner[22] than to-night's meeting. They tell me that some of our community are to be here from Falmouth and beyond, and others from Connecticut and Rhode Island, besides several of the Indian powwows, who, after their fashion, know almost as much deviltry as the best of us. Moreover, there is a goodly young woman to be taken into communion."

"Mighty well, Deacon Gookin!" replied the solemn old tones of the minister. "Spur up, or we shall be late. Nothing can be done, you

---

20 athwart: across.

21 durst: (archaic) past tense and past participle of "dare."

22 A celebration held when someone was made a Puritan minister.

know, until I get on the ground."

The hoofs clattered again; and the voices, talking so strangely in the empty air, passed on through the forest, where no church had ever been gathered or solitary Christian prayed. Whither[23], then, could these holy men be journeying so deep into the heathen wilderness? Young Goodman Brown caught hold of a tree for support, being ready to sink down on the ground, faint and overburdened with the heavy sickness of his heart. He looked up to the sky, doubting whether there really was a heaven above him. Yet there was the blue arch, and the stars brightening in it.

"With heaven above and Faith below, I will yet stand firm against the devil!" cried Goodman Brown.

While he still gazed upward into the deep arch of the firmament and had lifted his hands to pray, a cloud, though no wind was stirring, hurried across the zenith and hid the brightening stars. The blue sky was still visible, except directly overhead, where this black mass of cloud was sweeping swiftly northward. Aloft in the air, as if from the depths of the cloud, came a confused and doubtful sound of voices. Once the listener fancied that he could distinguish the accents of towns-people of his own, men and women, both pious and ungodly, many of whom he had met at the communion table, and had seen others rioting at the tavern. The next moment, so indistinct were the sounds, he doubted whether he had heard aught but[24] the murmur of the old forest, whispering without a wind. Then came a stronger swell of those familiar tones, heard daily in the sunshine at Salem village, but never until now from a cloud of night. There was one voice of a young woman, uttering lamentations, yet with an uncertain sorrow, and entreating for some favor, which, perhaps, it would grieve her to

---

23 Whither: (archaic) where.

24 aught but: anything but.

obtain; and all the unseen multitude, both saints and sinners, seemed to encourage her onward.

"Faith!" shouted Goodman Brown, in a voice of agony and desperation; and the echoes of the forest mocked him, crying, "Faith! Faith!" as if bewildered wretches were seeking her all through the wilderness.

The cry of grief, rage, and terror was yet piercing the night, when the unhappy husband held his breath for a response. There was a scream, drowned immediately in a louder murmur of voices, fading into far-off laughter, as the dark cloud swept away, leaving the clear and silent sky above Goodman Brown. But something fluttered lightly down through the air and caught on the branch of a tree. The young man seized it, and beheld a pink ribbon.

"My Faith is gone!" cried he, after one stupefied moment. "There is no good on earth; and sin is but a name. Come, devil; for to thee is this world given."

And, maddened with despair, so that he laughed loud and long, did Goodman Brown grasp his staff and set forth again, at such a rate that he seemed to fly along the forest path rather than to walk or run. The road grew wilder and drearier and more faintly traced, and vanished at length, leaving him in the heart of the dark wilderness, still rushing onward with the instinct that guides mortal man to evil. The whole forest was peopled with frightful sounds — the creaking of the trees, the howling of wild beasts, and the yell of Indians; while sometimes the wind tolled like a distant church bell, and sometimes gave a broad roar around the traveller, as if all Nature were laughing him to scorn. But he was himself the chief horror of the scene, and shrank not from its other horrors.

"Ha! ha! ha!" roared Goodman Brown when the wind laughed at him.

"Let us hear which will laugh loudest. Think not to frighten me with your deviltry. Come witch, come wizard, come Indian powwow, come devil himself, and here comes Goodman Brown. You may as well fear him as he fear you."

In truth, all through the haunted forest there could be nothing more frightful than the figure of Goodman Brown. On he flew among the black pines, brandishing his staff with frenzied gestures, now giving vent to an inspiration of horrid blasphemy, and now shouting forth such laughter as set all the echoes of the forest laughing like demons around him. The fiend in his own shape is less hideous than when he rages in the breast of man. Thus sped the demoniac on his course, until, quivering among the trees, he saw a red light before him, as when the felled trunks and branches of a clearing have been set on fire, and throw up their lurid blaze against the sky, at the hour of midnight. He paused, in a lull of the tempest that had driven him onward, and heard the swell of what seemed a hymn, rolling solemnly from a distance with the weight of many voices. He knew the tune; it was a familiar one in the choir of the village meeting-house. The verse died heavily away, and was lengthened by a chorus, not of human voices, but of all the sounds of the benighted wilderness pealing in awful harmony together. Goodman Brown cried out, and his cry was lost to his own ear by its unison with the cry of the desert.

In the interval of silence he stole forward until the light glared full upon his eyes. At one extremity of an open space, hemmed in by the dark wall of the forest, arose a rock, bearing some rude, natural resemblance either to an altar or a pulpit, and surrounded by four blazing pines, their tops aflame, their stems untouched, like candles at an evening meeting. The mass of foliage that had overgrown the summit of the rock was all on fire, blazing high into the night and fitfully illuminating the whole field. Each pendent twig and leafy festoon was in a blaze. As the red light arose and fell, a numerous congregation alternately shone forth, then disappeared in shadow, and again grew, as it were, out of the darkness, peopling the heart of the solitary woods at once.

"A grave and dark-clad company," quoth Goodman Brown.

In truth they were such. Among them, quivering to and fro between gloom and splendor, appeared faces that would be seen next day at the council board of the province, and others which, Sabbath after Sabbath, looked devoutly heavenward, and benignantly over the crowded pews, from the holiest pulpits in the land. Some affirm that the lady of the governor [8] was there. At least there were high dames well known to her, and wives of honored husbands, and widows, a great multitude, and ancient maidens, all of excellent repute, and fair young girls, who trembled lest their mothers should espy them. Either the sudden gleams of light flashing over the obscure field bedazzled Goodman Brown, or he recognized a score of the church members of Salem village famous for their especial sanctity. Good old Deacon Gookin had arrived, and waited at the skirts of that venerable saint, his revered pastor. But, irreverently consorting with these grave, reputable, and pious people, these elders of the church, these chaste dames and dewy virgins, there were men of dissolute lives and women of spotted fame, wretches given over to all mean and filthy vice, and suspected even of horrid crimes. It was strange to see that the good shrank not from the wicked, nor were the sinners abashed by the saints. Scattered also among their pale-faced enemies were the Indian priests, or powwows, who had often scared their native forest with more hideous incantations than any known to English witchcraft.

"But where is Faith?" thought Goodman Brown; and, as hope came into his heart, he trembled.

Another verse of the hymn arose, a slow and mournful strain, such as the pious love, but joined to words which expressed all that our nature can conceive of sin, and darkly hinted at far more. Unfathomable to mere mortals is the lore of fiends. Verse after verse was sung; and still the chorus of the desert swelled between like the deepest tone of a mighty organ; and with the final peal of that dreadful anthem there came a sound, as if the roaring wind, the rushing streams, the howling beasts, and every other voice of the unconcerted wilderness were mingling and according with the voice of guilty man in homage to the prince of all. The four blazing pines threw up a loftier flame, and obscurely discovered shapes and visages of horror on the smoke wreaths above the impious assembly. At the same moment the fire on the rock shot redly forth and formed a glowing arch above its base, where now appeared a figure. With reverence be it spoken, the figure bore no slight similitude, both in garb and manner, to some grave divine of the New England churches.

"Bring forth the converts!" cried a voice that echoed through the field and rolled into the forest.

At the word, Goodman Brown stepped forth from the shadow of the trees and approached the congregation, with whom he felt a loathful brotherhood by the sympathy of all that was wicked in his heart. He could have well-nigh sworn that the shape of his own dead father beckoned him to advance, looking downward from a smoke wreath, while a woman, with dim features of despair, threw out her hand to warn him back. Was it his mother? But he had no power to retreat one step, nor to resist, even in thought, when the minister and good old Deacon Gookin seized his arms and led him to the blazing rock. Thither came also the slender form of a veiled female, led between Goody Cloyse, that pious teacher of the catechism, and Martha Carrier, [9] who had received the devil's promise to be queen of hell.

A rampant hag was she. And there stood the proselytes beneath the canopy of fire.

"Welcome, my children," said the dark figure, "to the communion of your race. Ye have found thus young your nature and your destiny. My children, look behind you!"

They turned; and flashing forth, as it were, in a sheet of flame, the fiend worshippers were seen; the smile of welcome gleamed darkly on every visage.

"There," resumed the sable form[25], "are all whom ye have reverenced from youth. Ye deemed them holier than yourselves, and shrank from your own sin, contrasting it with their lives of righteousness and prayerful aspirations heavenward. Yet here are they all in my worshipping assembly. This night it shall be granted you to know their secret deeds: how hoary-bearded elders of the church have whispered wanton words to the young maids of their households; how many a woman, eager for widows' weeds, has given her husband a drink at bedtime and let him sleep his last sleep in her bosom; how beardless youths have made haste to inherit their fathers' wealth; and how fair damsels — blush not, sweet ones — have dug little graves in the garden, and bidden me, the sole guest to an infant's funeral. By the sympathy of your human hearts for sin ye shall scent out all the places — whether in church, bedchamber, street, field, or forest — where crime has been committed, and shall exult to behold the whole earth one stain of guilt, one mighty blood spot. Far more than this. It shall be yours to penetrate, in every bosom, the deep mystery of sin, the fountain of all wicked arts, and which inexhaustibly supplies more evil impulses than human power — than my power at its utmost — can make manifest in deeds. And now, my children, look upon each other."

25 the sable form: the dark figure.

They did so; and, by the blaze of the hell-kindled torches, the wretched man beheld his Faith, and the wife her husband, trembling before that unhallowed altar.

"Lo, there ye stand, my children," said the figure, in a deep and solemn tone, almost sad with its despairing awfulness, as if his once angelic nature could yet mourn for our miserable race. "Depending upon one another's hearts, ye had still hoped that virtue were not all a dream. Now are ye undeceived. Evil is the nature of mankind. Evil must be your only happiness. Welcome again, my children, to the communion of your race."

"Welcome," repeated the fiend worshippers, in one cry of despair and triumph.

And there they stood, the only pair, as it seemed, who were yet hesitating on the verge of wickedness in this dark world. A basin was hollowed, naturally, in the rock. Did it contain water, reddened by the lurid light? or was it blood? or, perchance, a liquid flame? Herein did the shape of evil dip his hand and prepare to lay the mark of baptism upon their foreheads, that they might be partakers of the mystery of sin, more conscious of the secret guilt of others, both in deed and thought, than they could now be of their own. The husband cast one look at his pale wife, and Faith at him. What polluted wretches would the next glance show them to each other, shuddering alike at what they disclosed and what they saw!

"Faith! Faith!" cried the husband, "look up to heaven, and resist the wicked one."

Whether Faith obeyed he knew not. Hardly had he spoken when he found himself amid calm night and solitude, listening to a roar of the wind which died heavily away through the forest. He staggered against the rock, and felt it chill and damp; while a hanging twig, that had been all on fire, besprinkled his cheek with the coldest dew.

The next morning young Goodman Brown came slowly into the street of Salem village, staring around him like a bewildered man. The good old minister was taking a walk along the graveyard to get an appetite for breakfast and meditate his sermon, and bestowed a blessing, as he passed, on Goodman Brown. He shrank from the venerable saint as if to avoid an anathema. Old Deacon Gookin was at domestic worship, and the holy words of his prayer were heard through the open window. "What God doth the wizard pray to?" quoth Goodman Brown. Goody Cloyse, that excellent old Christian, stood in the early sunshine at her own lattice, catechizing a little girl who had brought her a pint of morning's milk. Goodman Brown snatched away the child as from the grasp of the fiend himself. Turning the corner by the meeting-house, he spied the head of Faith, with the pink ribbons, gazing anxiously forth, and bursting into such joy at sight of him that she skipped along the street and almost kissed her husband before the whole village. But Goodman Brown looked sternly and sadly into her face, and passed on without a greeting.

Had Goodman Brown fallen asleep in the forest and only dreamed a wild dream of a witch-meeting?

Be it so if you will; but, alas! it was a dream of evil omen for young Goodman Brown. A stern, a sad, a darkly meditative, a distrustful, if not a desperate man did he become from the night of that fearful dream. On the Sabbath day, when the congregation were singing a holy psalm, he could not listen because an anthem of sin rushed loudly upon his ear and drowned all the blessed strain. When the minister spoke from the pulpit with power and fervid eloquence, and, with his hand on the open Bible, of the sacred truths of our religion, and of saint-like lives and triumphant deaths, and of future bliss or misery unutterable, then did Goodman Brown turn pale, dreading lest the roof should thunder down upon the gray blasphemer and his hearers.

Often, awaking suddenly at midnight, he shrank from the bosom of Faith; and at morning or eventide, when the family knelt down at prayer, he scowled and muttered to himself, and gazed sternly at his wife, and turned away. And when he had lived long, and was borne to his grave a hoary corpse, followed by Faith, an aged woman, and children and grandchildren, a goodly procession, besides neighbors not a few, they carved no hopeful verse upon his tombstone, for his dying hour was gloom.

NOTES ON THE TEXT

[1] Hawthorne wrote this story in 1835. It addresses the Puritan belief that all people exist in a state of depravity, except those who are born in a state of grace. As in his other literary works, Hawthorne attempts to expose the hypocrisy of Puritan society. The story begins with young Goodman Brown's journey into the forest, which symbolizes the Christian self-exploration. Goodman's journey or self-exploration, however, ends up with the loss of his faith in human goodness and in salvation. "Young Goodman Brown," as many of Hawthorne's other literary works, such as *The Scarlet Letter*, is set in seventeenth-century colonial America, in particular Salem, Massachusetts. In order to enhance the setting, Hawthorne deliberately uses the diction typical of the historical time of the story.

[2] The resemblance of the staff to a snake hints at the nature of its owner, while the phrase "he of the serpent" a few lines below confirms that Goodman Brown's companion is the devil in a disguised form. Notice the magical power this serpent-like staff has acquired as the story goes on. It has become clear at this point that Goodman Brown is honoring, though unwillingly, a covenant with the devil.

[3] The days of the martyrs refers to the reign of Mary Tudor, Queen of England (1553—1558), who was known as "Bloody Mary" for her persecution of Protestants. Notice Hawthorne uses many historical references, including the Salem Witch Trials of 1692, the Puritan intolerance of the Quakers, and King Philip's War, to make what he calls a "romance" more real and to link the past with the present. Hawthorne also wants his readers to know the dubious history of Salem Village, the legacy of the Puritans and the historical roots of Goodman Brown's fascination with the devil and the dark side of human nature.

[4] According to a law of 1661, Quaker rogues and vagabonds who disobeyed the laws should "be stripped naked from the middle upwards, and tied to a cart's tail, and whipped through the town." It's interesting to note that Hawthorne's great-great-great grandfather William Hathorne, who was the first family member to emigrate from England, once ordered the

public whipping of a Quaker woman who refused to renounce her religious belief. William Hathorne's son John Hathorne was one of the Puritan interrogators of those accused of witchcraft in Salem in 1692. He was the only judge who never repented of his actions.

[5] Deacon Gookin was probably Daniel Gookin (1612—1687), colonial Puritan magistrate and missionary to the Indians. He was never a Deacon at Salem. Here Hawthorne borrows his name to evoke memories of a pious good man.

[6] In the story, Goody Cloyse is a Christian woman who helps young people to study the Bible, but in secret she performs magic ceremonies and attends witch meetings in the forest. Both Goody Cloyse and Goody Cory mentioned below were historical figures; they were among those who were tried, convicted of witchcraft and sentenced to death during the Salem Witch Trials of 1692. Hawthorne borrows their names in this story. "Goody" is the feminine equivalent of "Goodman," a form of address applied to persons of yeoman status, below the rank of gentleman.

[7] Notice the double meanings of "Faith" here. It refers both to his young wife and his faith in God. The same is true when Goodman Brown, upon discovering his wife's joining the witch-meeting in the forest, cries out, "My Faith is gone!" Goodman Brown is both literally and metaphorically married to Faith. His Faith is what he most treasures and what he is most afraid of losing. Yet, as it turns out, he has eventually lost his faith as well as his affection for Faith after he has witnessed the Black Mass in the forest.

[8] Here Hawthorne alludes to the wife of the royal Governor of Massachusetts (1692—1694) Sir William Phips (1651—1695). She was charged but not tried for witchcraft at Salem in 1692.

[9] Martha Carrier was an authentic historical personage who was hanged as a witch at Salem in 1692. She had confessed that the devil had promised her that she would be "queen of hell."

QUESTIONS FOR DISCUSSION

1. How does the devil persuade Goodman Brown to journey to the forest to attend the witch-meeting? Whom does he encounter on his way to the meeting? What do these secret sinners have in common?

2. Discuss Brown's disillusionment about the godliness of humanity. What has led to his gradual disillusionment?

3. Hawthorne had inherited from his Puritan ancestors what he termed his "inveterate love of allegory." But his allegory often passes into symbolism: an object or event assumes multiple possible significances, rather than correspondence with one divinely ordained idea. "Young Goodman Brown" is often interpreted as an allegory. As such, what is the story's allegorical significances? Which aspects of the story are relevant to seventeenth-century New England, and which are applicable

to Hawthorne's contemporary society and even to our age?

4. Hawthorne has used many symbols in his romance. Try to find some from the text and discuss their implications and their roles in expressing themes.

5. Compare Hawthorne's story with Irving's "Rip Van Winkle." Are there aspects of this story which resemble "Rip Van Winkle"? Are there differences in their responses to nature, their portrayal of women, their moral concerns, and their approach to history? What values might Irving and Hawthorne have shared?

6. What aspects of Puritanism does Hawthorne's story attempt to criticize? What aspects does it attempt to replicate or embody?

SUGGESTED REFERENCES

Bloom, Harold, ed. *Nathaniel Hawthorne's "Young Goodman Brown"*. Philadelphia: Chelsea House, 2005.

McFarland, Philip. *Hawthorne in Concord.* New York: Grove Press, 2004.

Miller, Edwin Haviland. *Salem Is My Dwelling Place: A Life of Nathaniel Hawthorne.* Iowa City: U of Iowa P, 1991.

Porte, Joel. *The Romance in America: Studies in Cooper, Poe, Hawthorne, Melville, and James.* Middletown: Wesleyan UP, 1969.

Wineapple, Brenda. *Hawthorne: A Life.* New York: Random House, 2003.

Unit 5 Herman Melville

(1819 – 1891)

A GUIDE TO LITERARY TERMINOLOGY

"Allegory": *Allegory is an old form related to the fable or parable which presents an abstract idea through concrete means. The typical allegory is a narrative — whether in prose, verse, or drama — that has at least two levels of meaning. The first level is literal, in which some kind of literal story is told. At the second level, most the characters, places and events in the story are symbolic of larger concepts, and the whole story can be read as a parable for another, more universal story or lesson. Although allegories have coherent subplots, their authors expect readers to recognize the existence of a second and deeper level of meaning, which may be moral, political, philosophical, or religious.*

In Nathaniel Hawthorne's "Young Goodman Brown," for example, Faith is not only the name of the protagonist's wife, but also a symbol of the protagonist's religious faith. Herman Melville's novel ***Moby-Dick*** *is not merely a whaling tale or sea adventure. It can be read as a symbolic voyage of the mind in quest of the truth and knowledge of the universe, an exploration of man's longings, spirit, and psychology. In this sense, the White Whale symbolizes the destructive principle at the core of existence, the inevitability of human annihilation.*

NOTES ON THE AUTHOR

Herman Melville was born into a middle-class gentry of New York State, but when he was 12, his father died and he was forced to leave school at 15, working on a farm, as a messenger in a bank, and as a clerk in his brother's store. In 1839 he signed on as a cabin boy on a ship bound for Liverpool, an experience recorded in *Redburn* (1849). In 1841 – 1842, he spent 18 months on a whaling ship named *Acushnet*. Boredom and hardship aboard a whaling ship made him desert it at the Marquesas Islands. He was taken captive by the Typees, a tribe of savages known for their cannibalism. After being rescued by an Australian whaler, Melville spent more than two years in Tahiti and Honolulu before he returned to Boston in 1844.

In the following years, he published *Typee: A Peep at Polynesian Life* (1846), an autobiographical novel of his adventures among the Marquesas cannibals, and *Omoo: A Narrative of Adventures in the South Seas* (1847) about his experiences in Tahiti. In 1849, he published a political allegory, *Mardi: And a Voyage*

Thither, but its lack of financial success forced him to write sea adventures again. He published *Redburn* in 1849 and *White-Jacket* in 1850, but these were works he disdainfully referred to as "jobs" which he was forced to do "for money."

In 1847, Melville married Elizabeth Shaw, the daughter of Lemuel Shaw, chief justice of Massachusetts. In 1850 he bought a farm near Pittsfield, Massachusetts, and developed a friendship with his neighbor Hawthorne whose home was only six miles away. The allegorical implications in *Mardi* and *White-Jacket* were fully developed in Melville's masterpiece, *Moby-Dick; or, The Whale* (1851) which he dedicated to Hawthorne in "admiration for his genius." In 1852, Melville published *Pierre;* or, *The Ambiguities,* a melodramatic novel of a search for absolute morality. It was a commercial failure and was poorly received by the public. But he continued to produce important works, *The Piazza Tales* (1856) and *The Confidence Man: His Masquerade* (1857), a pessimistic satire on materialism. Melville was forced to sell his farm and in 1866 he secured a low-pay job in New York City as a district inspector of customs, a position he held for 19 years. His late works include collections of poems *Battle-Pieces and Aspects of the War* (1866), *John Marr and Other Sailors* (1888), and a long poem *Clarel* (1876). When Melville died in poverty in 1891, he was almost completely forgotten. It was not until the "Melville Revival" in the 1920s and 1930s that his works won wide recognition, especially *Moby-Dick*, which was regarded as one of the greatest works in American literature and a world classic. Although Melville's stories of the South Seas had captured the popular imagination of his contemporaries, his recurrent theme of the conflicts between innocence and evil, reason and lunacy, clearing and wilderness, land and sea, his depictions of the morbidity and demonism of the world, and his doubts about the nineteenth century idea of progress were less appealing to his own age than to the twentieth century.

NOTES ON THE WORK

Moby-Dick is a novel about a deranged whaling captain's obsessive voyage to hunt down and destroy a great white sperm whale that had ripped off his leg years earlier. Ahab, the captain of a whaler named *Pequod*, is determined to sacrifice everything to revenge on his nemesis Moby Dick. He asks his crew to yell if they spot the white whale and offers a gold doubloon to whoever first spots a "white-headed whale with a wrinkled brow and a crooked jaw." Over the course of the story, the reader is presented with numerous digressions providing details about whales, the whaling industry and everyday whaling life. Toward the end of the story, the *Pequod* gets close to Moby Dick's territory and sights him. Then comes the voyage's tragic end: the ship and the white whale battle against each other for three long days, with the latter shattering the ship's whale boats and finally, before he dies, sinking the ship itself. Ahab and all his crew drown except for Ishmael who survives to tell the story.

In Ahab, Melville creates a tragic hero comparable to King Lear or Don Quixote. His stubborn pursuit of Moby Dick is both terrifying and awe-inspiring. He turns his commercial venture into a vengeance on a seemingly invincible enemy. The racially, ethnically, and nationally diverse crew of the *Pequod* become the victims of a madman's quest. Though the novel has only a simple plot, it takes in the wider themes of nature, religion, society, war, history and civilization. The novel is at once an exciting seafaring tale, a social commentary, an encyclopedia of whaling lore and legend, an exploration of the uncharted regions of the soul, and an inquiry into the essence of the human and natural worlds. The novel is rich in symbols. The monstrous whale represents the uncontrollable natural force. In the poetry of Whitman and the prose writings of Emerson and Thoreau, a ship is sometimes a metaphor for the soul. In the novel, the ship is the borderline between the land and the sea and symbolizes the human society.

Melville, in a letter to Nathaniel Hawthorne, exuberantly described *Moby-Dick* as "a wicked book" that yet made him "feel spotless as the lamb." Although Melville's contemporaries found the novel frustratingly opaque, the tale of the tormented Captain Ahab has been valued by modern readers for its stylistic innovativeness and for the range of metaphysical, political, and cultural issues it addresses. D. H. Lawrence called it "the greatest book of the sea ever written." It is doubtless a leading work of American Romanticism, and possibly the greatest American novel to date.

The selection presented here, "The Mast-Head," is from Chapter 35 of the novel in which Ishmael tells of his first experience as a lookout for whales, or for anything else, on the mast-head on a sunny day.

SELECTED READINGS

The Mast-Head

It was during the more pleasant weather, that in due rotation with the other seamen my first mast-head came round. [1]

In most American whalemen the mast-heads are manned almost simultaneously with the vessel's leaving her port; even though she may have fifteen thousand miles, and more, to sail ere reaching her proper cruising ground. And if, after a three, four, or five years' voyage she is drawing nigh home[1] with anything empty in her — say, an empty vial even — then, her mast-heads are manned to the last; and not till her skysail-poles sail in among the spires of the port, does she altogether relinquish the hope of capturing one whale more.

Now, as the business of standing mast-heads, ashore or afloat, is a very ancient and interesting one, let us in some measure expatiate[2] here. I take it, that the earliest standers of mast-heads were the old Egyptians; because, in all my researches, I find none prior to them. For though their progenitors, the builders of Babel[3], must doubtless, by their tower, have intended to rear the loftiest mast-head in all Asia, or Africa either; yet (ere the final truck was put to it) as that great stone mast of theirs may be said to have gone by the board[4], in the dread gale of God's wrath; therefore, we cannot give these Babel builders priority over the Egyptians. And that the Egyptians were a nation of mast-head standers, is an assertion based upon the general belief among archaeologists, that the first pyramids were founded for astronomical purposes: a theory singularly supported by the peculiar stair-like formation of all four sides of those edifices; whereby, with prodigious long upliftings of their legs, those old astronomers were wont to mount to the apex, and sing out for new stars; even as the look-outs of a modern ship sing out for a sail, or a whale just bearing in sight. In Saint Stylites, the famous Christian hermit of old times, who built him a lofty stone pillar in the desert and spent the whole latter portion of

1 drawing nigh home: drawing near home; nigh: (old use or literary) near.
2 expatiate: to speak and write at some length; to be copious in description or discussion.
3 Babel: the tower and city of Babylon. The attempted construction of the Tower of Babel is described in Genesis xi. The confusion of languages is said to have taken place since then.
4 gone by the board: fail, cease to exist.

his life on its summit, hoisting his food from the ground with a tackle; in him we have a remarkable instance of a dauntless stander-of-mast-heads; who was not to be driven from his place by fogs or frosts, rain, hail, or sleet; but valiantly facing everything out to the last, literally died at his post. Of modern standers-of-mast-heads we have but a lifeless set; mere stone, iron, and bronze men; who, though well capable of facing out a stiff gale, are still entirely incompetent to the business of singing out upon discovering any strange sight. There is Napoleon; who, upon the top of the column of Vendome[5], stands with arms folded, some one hundred and fifty feet in the air; careless, now, who rules the decks below; whether Louis Philippe[6], Louis Blanc[7], or Louis the Devil. Great Washington, too, stands high aloft on his towering main-mast in Baltimore, and like one of Hercules' pillars[8], his column marks that point of human grandeur beyond which few mortals will go. Admiral Nelson,[9] also, on a capstan of gun-metal, stands his mast-head in Trafalgar Square; and ever when most obscured by that London smoke, token is yet given that a hidden hero is there; for where there is smoke, must be fire. But neither great Washington, nor Napoleon, nor Nelson, will answer a single hail from below, however madly invoked to befriend by their counsels the distracted decks upon which they gaze; however it may be surmised, that their spirits penetrate through the thick haze of the future, and descry what shoals and what rocks must be shunned.

It may seem unwarrantable to couple in any respect the mast-

---

5 column of Vendome: Vendome column with statue of Napoleon Bonaparte, on the Place Vendome in Paris, France. Vendome column has 425 spiraling bas-relief bronze plates made out of cannon.

6 Louis Philippe (1773—1850) was King of the French from 1830 to 1848 in what was known as the July Monarchy.

7 Louis Jean Joseph Charles Blanc (1811—1882) was a French politician and historian.

8 Hercules' pillars: a phrase used in the past to refer to the promontories that flank the entrance to the Strait of Gibraltar.

9 Admiral Nelson (1758—1805): a British naval commander and national hero, famous for his naval victories against the French during the Napoleonic Wars. Nelson, in his most famous engagement at Cape Trafalgar, saved Britain from threat of invasion by Napoleon.

head standers of the land with those of the sea; but that in truth it is not so, is plainly evinced by an item for which Obed Macy, [2] the sole historian of Nantucket,[10] stands accountable. The worthy Obed tells us, that in the early times of the whale fishery, ere ships were regularly launched in pursuit of the game[11], the people of that island erected lofty spars[12] along the sea-coast, to which the look-outs ascended by means of nailed cleats, something as fowls go upstairs in a hen-house. A few years ago this same plan was adopted by the Bay whalemen of New Zealand, who, upon descrying the game, gave notice to the ready-manned boats nigh the beach. But this custom has now become obsolete; turn we then to the one proper mast-head, that of a whale-ship at sea. The three mast-heads are kept manned from sun-rise to sun-set; the seamen taking their regular turns (as at the helm), and relieving each other every two hours. In the serene weather of the tropics it is exceedingly pleasant the mast-head; nay, to a dreamy meditative man it is delightful. There you stand, a hundred feet above the silent decks, striding along the deep, as if the masts were gigantic stilts, while beneath you and between your legs, as it were, swim the hugest monsters of the sea, even as ships once sailed between the boots of the famous Colossus at old Rhodes[13]. There you stand, lost in the infinite series of the sea, with nothing ruffled but the waves. The tranced ship indolently rolls; the drowsy trade winds blow; everything resolves you into languor. For the most part, in this tropic whaling life, a sublime uneventfulness invests[14] you; you hear no news; read no gazettes; extras with startling accounts of commonplaces never delude you into unnecessary excitements; you hear of

10 Nantucket: an island resort off Cape Cod, formerly a center of the whaling industry.
11 the game: wild animals that people hunt for sport or for food; here, it refers to the whale.
12 spar: a strong pole to which a sail is attached on a sailing ship.
13 Colossus at old Rhodes: a gigantic statue that stood with one foot on either side of the harbor on the island of Rhodes, Greece. It was about 30.5 meters tall. When it broke down, there was one remaining piece of the body, the thumb.
14 invest: envelope, besiege.

no domestic afflictions; bankrupt securities; fall of stocks; are never troubled with the thought of what you shall have for dinner — for all your meals for three years and more are snugly stowed in casks, and your bill of fare is immutable.

In one of those southern whalesmen, on a long three or four years' voyage, as often happens, the sum of the various hours you spend at the mast-head would amount to several entire months. And it is much to be deplored that the place to which you devote so considerable a portion of the whole term of your natural life, should be so sadly destitute of [15] anything approaching to a cosy inhabitiveness, or adapted to breed a comfortable localness of feeling, such as pertains to a bed, a hammock, a hearse, a sentry box, a pulpit, a coach, or any other of those small and snug contrivances in which men temporarily isolate themselves. Your most usual point of perch is the head of the t'-gallant-mast[16], where you stand upon two thin parallel sticks (almost peculiar to whalemen) called the t'-gallant cross-trees. Here, tossed about by the sea, the beginner feels about as cosy as he would standing on a bull's horns. To be sure, in cold weather you may carry your house aloft with you, in the shape of a watch-coat; but properly speaking the thickest watch-coat is no more of a house than the unclad body; for as the soul is glued inside of its fleshy tabernacle, and cannot freely move about in it, nor even move out of it, without running great risk of perishing (like an ignorant pilgrim crossing the snowy Alps in winter); so a watch-coat is not so much of a house as it is a mere envelope, or additional skin encasing you. You cannot put a shelf or chest of drawers in your body, and no more can you make a convenient closet of your watch-coat.

Concerning all this, it is much to be deplored that the mast-heads of a southern whale ship are unprovided with those enviable little tents

---

15 destitute of: utterly lacking, devoid of.

16 t'-gallant-mast is a mast fixed to the head of a topmast on a square-rigged vessel.

or pulpits, called *crow's-nests*[17], in which the look-outs of a Greenland whaler are protected from the inclement weather of the frozen seas. In the fireside narrative of Captain Sleet[18], entitled "A Voyage among the Icebergs, in quest of the Greenland Whale, and incidentally for the re-discovery of the Lost Icelandic Colonies of Old Greenland"; in this admirable volume, all standers of mast-heads are furnished with a charmingly circumstantial account of the then recently invented *crow's-nest* of the Glacier, which was the name of Captain Sleet's good craft. He called it the *Sleet's crow's-nest*, in honor of himself; he being the original inventor and patentee, and free from all ridiculous false delicacy, and holding that if we call our own children after our own names (we fathers being the original inventors and patentees), so likewise should we denominate after ourselves any other apparatus we may beget. In shape, the Sleet's crow's-nest is something like a large tierce or pipe; it is open above, however, where it is furnished with a movable side-screen to keep to windward of your head in a hard gale. Being fixed on the summit of the mast, you ascend into it through a little trap-hatch in the bottom. On the after side, or side next the stern of the ship, is a comfortable seat, with a locker underneath for umbrellas, comforters, and coats. In front is a leather rack, in which to keep your speaking trumpet, pipe, telescope, and other nautical conveniences. When Captain Sleet in person stood his mast-head in this crow's-nest of his, he tells us that he always had a rifle with him (also fixed in the rack), together with a powder flask and shot, for the purpose of popping off the stray narwhales, or vagrant sea unicorns infesting those waters; for you cannot successfully shoot at them from the deck owing to the resistance of the water, but to

17 crow's-nests: a barrel or cylindrical box fixed to the mast-head of a whaling ship, as a shelter for the look-out man.

18 Captain Sleet: Melville's name for William Scoresby Sr., the father of Captain William Scoresby (1789—1857), an English Arctic explorer, scientist and clergyman.

shoot down upon them is a very different thing. Now, it was plainly a labor of love for Captain Sleet to describe, as he does, all the little detailed conveniences of his crow's-nest; but though he so enlarges upon many of these, and though he treats us to a very scientific account of his experiments in this crow's-nest, with a small compass he kept there for the purpose of counteracting the errors resulting from what is called the "local attraction" of all binnacle[19] magnets; an error ascribable to the horizontal vicinity of the iron in the ship's planks, and in the Glacier's case, perhaps, to there having been so many broken-down blacksmiths among her crew; I say, that though the Captain is very discreet and scientific here, yet, for all his learned "binnacle deviations," "azimuth compass observations," and "approximate errors," he knows very well, Captain Sleet, that he was not so much immersed in those profound magnetic meditations, as to fail being attracted occasionally towards that well replenished little case-bottle, so nicely tucked in on one side of his crow's nest, within easy reach of his hand. Though, upon the whole, I greatly admire and even love the brave, the honest, and learned Captain; yet I take it very ill of him that he should so utterly ignore that case-bottle, seeing what a faithful friend and comforter it must have been, while with mittened fingers and hooded head he was studying the mathematics aloft there in that bird's nest within three or four perches[20] of the pole.

But if we Southern whale-fishers are not so snugly housed aloft as Captain Sleet and his Greenlandmen were; yet that disadvantage is greatly counter-balanced by the widely contrasting serenity of those seductive seas in which we South fishers mostly float. For one, I used to lounge up the rigging very leisurely, resting in the top to have a chat with Queequeg, [3] or any one else off duty whom I might find there;

---

19 A binnacle is a nonmagnetic housing for a ship's compass (usually in front of the helm).
20 a perch: a linear measure of 16.5 feet.

then ascending a little way further, and throwing a lazy leg over the top-sail yard, take a preliminary view of the watery pastures, and so at last mount to my ultimate destination.

Let me make a clean breast of it[21] here, and frankly admit that I kept but sorry[22] guard. With the problem of the universe revolving in me, how could I — being left completely to myself at such a thought-engendering altitude — how could I but lightly hold my obligations to observe all whale-ships' standing orders, "Keep your weather eye open, and sing out every time."

And let me in this place movingly admonish you, ye ship-owners of Nantucket! Beware of enlisting in your vigilant fisheries any lad with lean brow and hollow eye; given to unseasonable meditativeness; and who offers to ship with the Phaedon [4] instead of Bowditch [5] in his head. Beware of such an one, I say; your whales must be seen before they can be killed; and this sunken-eyed young Platonist will tow you ten wakes round the world, and never make you one pint of sperm the richer. [6] Nor are these monitions at all unneeded. For nowadays, the whale-fishery furnishes an asylum for many romantic, melancholy, and absent-minded young men, disgusted with the carking cares of earth, and seeking sentiment in tar and blubber. Childe Harold not unfrequently perches himself upon the mast-head of some luckless disappointed whale-ship, and in moody phrase ejaculates: —

"Roll on, thou deep and dark blue ocean, roll!

Ten thousand blubber-hunters sweep over thee in vain." [7]

Very often do the captains of such ships take those absent-minded young philosophers to task,[23] upbraiding them with not feeling sufficient "interest" in the voyage; half-hinting that they are so hopelessly lost to all honorable ambition, as that in their secret souls they

---

21 make a clean breast of it: to make a full disclosure; to confess.

22 sorry: (only before noun) very sad or bad.

23 take…to task: blame or scold severely.

would rather not see whales than otherwise. But all in vain; those young Platonists have a notion that their vision is imperfect; they are short-sighted; what use, then, to strain the visual nerve? They have left their opera-glasses at home.

"Why, thou monkey," said a harpooneer to one of these lads, "we've been cruising now hard upon three years, and thou hast not raised a whale yet. Whales are scarce as hen's teeth whenever thou art up here." Perhaps they were; or perhaps there might have been shoals of them in the far horizon; but lulled into such an opium-like listlessness of vacant, unconscious reverie is this absent-minded youth by the blending cadence of waves with thoughts, that at last he loses his identity; takes the mystic ocean at his feet for the visible image of that deep, blue, bottomless soul, pervading mankind and nature; and every strange, half-seen, gliding, beautiful thing that eludes him; every dimly-discovered, uprising fin of some undiscernible form, seems to him the embodiment of those elusive thoughts that only people the soul by continually flitting through it. In this enchanted mood, thy spirit ebbs away to whence it came; becomes diffused through time and space; like Crammer's sprinkled Pantheistic ashes, forming at last a part of every shore the round globe over.

There is no life in thee, now, except that rocking life imparted by a gently rolling ship; by her, borrowed from the sea; by the sea, from the inscrutable tides of God. But while this sleep, this dream is on ye, move your foot or hand an inch; slip your hold at all; and your identity comes back in horror. Over Descartian vortices [8] you hover. And perhaps, at mid-day, in the fairest weather, with one half-throttled shriek you drop through that transparent air into the summer sea, no more to rise for ever. Heed it well, ye Pantheists![24]

---

24 Pantheist: one who believes that God is all forces and powers of the universe; God in Nature, or God is Nature.

NOTES ON THE TEXT

[1] *Moby-Dick* begins with "Call me Ishmael," which is one of the most memorable first sentences in novels. The narrator of story, Ishmael, has established a direct relationship with the reader. So the story we're hearing has been filtered through him. He tells us that whenever he finds himself in a bad mood, he feels drawn to the ocean where he will go to lift his spirits and cheer himself up. He is well-educated, but does not have money. He reminds us of the biblical Ishmael. According to the *Book of Genesis*, Ishmael and Isaac are half-brothers and sons of Abraham. Abraham's wife Sarah, unable to bear children herself, lets her maidservant, Hagar, to bear Abraham a child named Ishmael. Sarah later miraculously gets pregnant in her old age and gives birth to Isaac. At Sarah's request, Abraham banishes Hagar and Ishmael to the wilderness so that his younger son Isaac can become the next patriarch. Ishmael and Hagar are protected by God. Ishmael later becomes a patriarch and the forefather of the Arab peoples, and Isaac becomes the forefather of the Jewish tribes. The literary Ishmael and the biblical Ishmael are both outcasts and creators. The latter creates the Arab peoples, while the former creates the story we have here.

[2] Obed Macy (1801 – 1857) was a pioneer in Los Angeles County, California, arriving there together with his son by wagon train shortly after California became a part of the United States following the Mexican-American War.

[3] Queequeg, the son of the king in a South Seas island and a harpooner onboard the ill-fated Pequod, is Ishmael's best friend. When Ishmael first sees Queequeg, the man's tattooed body and racial difference terrify him. But after just one night spent sharing a bed, Ishmael has fallen head-over-heels for Queequeg. He even willingly worships Queequeg's god, Yojo, though he claims himself to be a faithful Christian.

[4] Phaedon was Plato's fourth and last dialogue to detail Socrates's last days, following Euthyphro, Apology, and Crito. In the dialogue, Socrates discusses the nature of the afterlife on his last day before executed. The dialogue is told from the perspective of one of Socrates's students, Phaedon of Elis. Having been present at Socrates's death bed, Phaedon relates the dialogue to Echecrates, a philosopher. One of the main themes in the Phaedon is the idea that the soul is immortal.

[5] Nathaniel Bowditch (1773 – 1838) was an early American mathematician remembered for his work on ocean navigation. He is remembered arguably as the most influential person in the development of American navigation.

[6] He won't even find a single sperm whale in ten whaling voyages. "Sperm" here refers to sperm oil, a white waxy substance from oil of the sperm whale. Also, a sperm whale has a large cavity in the head containing spermaceti and oil.

[7] From the second canto, CLXXIX of "Childe Harold's Pilgrimage," a long poem written by Lord Byron and published between 1812 and 1818 which describes the travels and

reflections of a world-weary young man who, disillusioned with a life of pleasure, looks for distraction in foreign lands. Notice here the resemblance of Ishmael, who has turned to the sea out of a feeling of alienation from the society, to the Childe Harold, the Byronic hero.

[8] Descartes believed that everything had to be proved rationally; he based his proof of identity on the theory, "I think; therefore, I am." Vortice is a situation drawing into its center all that surrounds it — that is, the whirlpool effect.

QUESTIONS FOR DISCUSSION

1. Why does Ishmael regard himself as an unqualified lookout? How does he feel on top of the mast-head? Why can't he concentrate on his job?

2.The Nature as represented by Ishmael in this chapter seems to have a power and will of its own rather than a passive collection animals and elements. Is Nature important because human beings can make use of it? Does it have any value outside of its uses for mankind? Does Nature have a personality, or is it impersonal and chaotic?

3.In this chapter, Ishmael meditates on pantheism and the possibility of dissolving into the natural world. He describes a type of young men, including himself, on the mast-head who are more likely to feel their identities dissolve into the natural world than to spot the whales they are hired to do. Comment on Ishmael's meditations. Is he transcendent or delusional?

SUGGESTED REFERENCES

Bercaw, Mary. *Melville's Sources.* Evanston: Northwestern UP, 1987.

Bezanson, Walter E. "*Moby-Dick*: Document, Drama, Dream." *A Companion to Melville Studies.* Ed. John Bryant. New York: Greenwood Press, 1986. 176-80.

Faiella, Gramham. ***Moby Dick** and the Whaling Industry of the 19th Century.* New York: The Rosen Publishing Group, 2004.

Kelley, Wyn. *Herman Melville: An Introduction.* Oxford: Wiley-Blackwell, 2008.

Lee, A. Robert, ed. *Herman Melville: Critical Assessments.* Volume IV. Mountfield: Helm Information, 2001.

Sten, Christopher. "Threading the Labyrinth: *Moby-Dick* as Hybrid Epic." *The Blackwell Companion to Herman Melville.* Ed. Wyn Kelley. Oxford: Blackwell, 2006. 408-22.

Unit 6 Walt Whitman

(1819 – 1891)

A GUIDE TO LITERARY TERMINOLOGY

"Free Verse": *Free verse is a term used to describe the poems of Walt Whitman and other poets whose verse is based not on the recurrence of stress accent in a regular, strictly measurable pattern, but rather on the irregular rhythmic cadence of the recurrence, with variations, of significant phrases, image patterns, and the like. Free verse treats the device of rhyme with a similar freedom and irregularity. Whenever a persistent irregularity of the metrical pattern is established in a poem, it can justly be called free verse. During the twentieth century free verse has become so common as to have some claim to being the characteristic verse form of the age. Among the typical practitioners may be mentioned T. S. Eliot, Ezra Pound, and William Carlos Williams. It may be noted that the most important English and American free verse poets of the first half of the century were either involved in or influenced by the imagist program formulated by T. E. Hulme and Ezra Pound between roughly 1905 and 1915.*

NOTES ON THE AUTHOR

Walt Whitman was born in West Hills, Long Island, New York on May 31, 1819. When Whitman was five, his family moved to Brooklyn, New York where he attended public school for five years. He left school in 1830, at the age of 11, to work as an office boy first in a law firm and later for a doctor. In 1931, he began to work in printing offices. He became an apprentice on the *Long Island Patriot* in 1832. Whitman rejoined his family, now in Hempstead, Long Island, in 1835 and taught for the next five years in various small town schools on Long Island while writing for local newspapers. Around 1842, he came back to New York City to work, over the next few years, as a newspaperman and editor of the New York *Aurora*, *The Evening Tatler*, and the New York *Democrat*. In March 1842, Whitman attended a lecture on poetry delivered by Ralph Waldo Emerson, who said, "The poets are thus liberating gods. The ancient British bards had for the title of their order, 'Those who are free throughout the world.' They are free, and they make free." After hearing the lecture, Whitman wanted to remake himself in Emerson's image of the poet. He wrote poems, theater columns, book reviews, and political editorials for a number of newspapers, including the *Brooklyn Daily Eagle*. In 1848, he went to New Orleans for an editorial position for the *New Orleans Daily Crescent*, which lasted for less than three months. He then returned to New York to edit a *Free Soil* paper, the Freeman. The most important period in Whitman's life was the year between 1850 and 1855, during which he gave up his newspaper work and devoted himself to writing experimental poems, while working as a part-time carpenter. On July 11, 1855, the first edition of his *Leaves of Grass*, which contained only 12 poems, came out and created a new epoch not only in American but also in world literature. Emerson wrote to Whitman, "I find it the most extraordinary piece of wit and wisdom that American has yet contributed…I greet you at the beginning of a great career, which yet must have had a long foreground somewhere, for such a start." In the lecture he gave in 1842, Emerson called for an American bard. Whitman, in his poem "Song of Myself," had announced himself to be such a poet.

From 1855 to 1859, while Whitman edited the *Brooklyn Times*, he continued to work on *Leaves of Grass,* publishing an extended second edition in 1856, which contained 32 poems, and a third edition in 1860. During the Civil War, Whitman went to Washington, D. C. to work as a volunteer nurse in military hospitals. He published *Drum-Taps* (1865) and had added his Civil War poems to the fourth edition of *Leaves of Grass* (1867). The fifth edition was published 1871. In 1873, he left Washington, D. C., due to poor health, to move in with his brother, George Whitman, in Camden, New Jersey. And there, he spent most of the remaining 19 years of life preparing other editions of *Leaves of Grass* until his death in 1892. The ninth edition contained more than 400 poems, which was unprecedented in the history of American literature.

NOTES ON HIS WORK

Probably as early as 1847, Walt Whitman had begun to write what was to become his masterpiece, *Leaves of Grass*, a collection of poetry which he published in 1855 and continued to edit, revise and expand until his death in 1892. In a period of 37 years, Whitman had published nine editions of the work. Whitman wrote in the preface to the 1855 edition, "The proof of a poet is that his country absorbs him as affectionately as he has absorbed it." Indeed, Whitman's poetry has made him the representative, or even the creator, of the American spirit. Whitman also states in the preface: "The United States themselves are essentially the greatest poem," which echoes Emerson's idea that "America is a poem in our eyes." Whitman intended to write a distinctly American epic, which differs enormously from the traditional epic.

Instead of telling the story of the traditional third-person epic hero, the American epic is more concerned with the spiritual possibility and the growth of the mind of the first-person "I." In his poems, he sings of democracy and freedom, of the greatness of the working class, praising greatness of their occupations and skills.

Also, Whitman wrote in free verse, abandoning the conventional poetic meter, rhyme scheme, and hackneyed poetic figures and delighted in using colloquial expressions and the rhythms of speech, which better suits his extolment of the free spirit and American democracy. In his poem "Song of Myself," Whitman proclaims himself as a symbolic representative of the common people. The poetic "I" is presented as being able to identify sympathetically with people from all walks of life. This, however, doesn't mean the poet, or any individual, has totally lost his self by merging with the other. It is, as Whitman presents it, a discovery of the self in the other. He also praises the commonplace and the equality of people despite racial, religious, cultural differences. He writes, "I believe a leaf of grass is no less than the journeywork of the stars, /And the pismire is equally perfect, and a grain of sand, and the egg of a wren."

The title of Whitman's book is symbolic. The grass is seen as the commonest, plainest and the most vigorous life. Whitman himself called his *Leaves of Grass* "the Bible of Democracy."

SELECTED READINGS

One's-Self I Sing [1]

One's-Self I sing, a simple separate person,
Yet utter the word Democratic, the word En-Masse[1]. [2]

Of physiology from top to toe I sing,
Not physiognomy[2] alone nor brain alone is worthy for the Muse, I say
the Form complete is worthier far,
The Female equally with the Male I sing.

1 En-Masse: all together, and usually in large numbers.
2 physiognomy: facial features, especially when regarded as revealing character.

Of Life immense in passion, pulse, and power,
Cheerful, for freest action form'd under the laws divine,
The Modern Man I sing.

NOTES ON THE TEXT

[1] "One's-Self I sing" was published in 1867. It is the first poem in the last edition of *Leaves of Grass*.

[2] The combination of the "one" and the "self" in the first line can be interpreted as "everyman's self." What Whitman sings of is then not himself, but the "self" of everybody. In fact, the poet identifies his "self," or his ego, with the world, and, more specifically, with the democratic "en-masse" of America. What Whitman sings of is therefore brotherhood, universality, and equality as well as individuality, democracy, and freedom.

QUESTIONS FOR DISCUSSION

1. Whitman's poetic form is free verse. What do you think are the strengths and weaknesses of the free verse? How do you like Whitman's poetry?

2. In line 4, the poet states, "Not physiognomy alone nor brain alone is worthy for the Muse, I say the Form complete is worthier far." Why is "the Form complete" better than "physiognomy alone" or "brain alone"? What does the poet suggest here?

3. Several relationships are touched upon in this short poem: the relationships between the "Self" and the "En-Masse," between "Physiognomy" and "Brain," between the "Male" and the "Female," between "free action" and "law." How does Whitman perceive such relationships? How are his ideas of democracy and equality conveyed in the poem?

4. Study the cohesion of the poem and discuss how the poet weaves into a pattern of unity what appear to be diverse entities.

参考译文

我歌唱“自己”

赵萝蕤译

我歌唱“自己”，一个单一的、脱离的人，

然而也说出“民主”这个词，“全体”这个词。

我从头到脚歌唱生理学，
值得献给诗神的不只是相貌或头脑，我是说整个结构的价值要大得多，
女性和男性我同样歌唱。

歌唱饱含热情、脉搏和力量的广阔“生活”，
心情愉快，支持那些神圣法则指导下形成的、最自由的行动，
我歌唱“现代人”。

SELECTED READINGS

O Captain! My Captain! [1]

O Captain! My Captain! [2] Our fearful trip [3] is done,
The ship has weather'd every rack[3], the prize[4] we sought is won,
The port is near, the bells I hear, the people all exulting[5],
While follow eyes the steady keel[6], the vessel grim and daring;
　But O heart! Heart! Heart!
　　O the bleeding drops of red!
　　　Where on the deck my Captain lies,
　　　　Fallen cold and dead. [4]

O Captain! My Captain! Rise up and hear the bells;
Rise up - for you the flag is flung — for you the bugle trills[7],
For you bouquets and ribbon'd wreaths — for you the shores a-crowding[8],
For you they call, the swaying mass[9], their eager faces turning;

3 weather'd every rack: went through all the hardships.
4 the prize: the victory of Civil War and the abolition of slavery.
5 exulting: rejoicing; leaping for joy.
6 keel: the long piece of wood or steel along the bottom of a ship. Here it stands for the ship.
7 bugle: trumpet used in the army to announce activities; trill: to sound with tremulous vibration.
8 the shores a-crowding: the shores are crowded with gathering people.
9 swaying mass: people moving to and fro.

Here, Captain! Dear father!
This arm beneath your head; [5]
It is some dream that on the deck,
You 've fallen cold and dead.

My Captain does not answer, his lips are pale and still,
My father does not feel my arm, he has no pulse nor will;
The ship is anchor'd safe and sound, its voyage closed and done;
From fearful trip the victor ship comes in with object won;
Exult, O shores! And ring, O bells!
But I, with mournful tread[10],
Walk the deck my Captain lies,
Fallen cold and dead.

NOTES ON THE TEXT

[1] "O Captain! My Captain!" is an elegy written in 1865, to mourn the death of Abraham Lincoln, the 16th president of the United States, who was assassinated on April 14, 1865, five days after the termination of the Civil War. The poem was first published in the pamphlet *Sequel to Drum-Taps* which assembled 18 poems regarding the American Civil War, including another Lincoln elegy, "When Lilacs Last in the Dooryard Bloom'd," Which was included in Whitman's *Leaves of Grass* beginning with its fourth edition published in 1867.

[2] "Captain" here refers to Abraham Lincoln, who is the captain of the ship representing the United States of America. Also, the page layout of the poem resembles the shape of a ship.

[3] "Our fearful trip" refers to the American Civil War (1861 — 1865) which, though a hard-won battle, had now come to an end.

[4] The repetition of "heart" in line five calls attention to the poet's vast grief and heartache caused by the Captain's bleeding and imminent death.

[5] Here the poet imagines that the wounded captain is lying in his arms, dying. In this stanza, the poet presents a staggering contrast between scenes of admiring people eager to welcome their hero (flags flinging, bouquets and ribbon'd wreaths, shores crowding, mass swaying) and his collapse.

10 tread: the sound you make when you are walking.

QUESTIONS FOR DISCUSSION

1. Most of Whitman's poems were written in the form of free verse, but "O Captain! My Captain!" follows a distinct rhyme scheme, which is quite unusual for Whitman. Analyze the rhyme scheme and other poetic devices in the poem. Do you think Whitman is justified in giving up free verse in this particular poem? Why?

2. Find some examples of repetition in the poem and discuss their functions in the poem.

3. How does the poet show his sense of history in this poem? How does the poet show his profound affection and respect for Abraham Lincoln? What did Whitman have in common with Lincoln?

4. Is there any difference in tone between the first two stanzas and the last? Explain the difference.

参考译文

啊，船长，我的船长哟！

楚图南 译

啊！船长，我的船长哟！我们可怕的航程已经终了，
我们的船渡过了每一个难关，我们追求的锦标已经得到，
港口就在前面，我已经听见钟声，听见人们的欢呼，
千万只眼睛在望着我们的船，它坚定、威严而且勇敢；
　　只是，啊，心哟！心哟！心哟！
　　　　啊，鲜红的血滴，
　　　　　　就在那甲板上，我的船长躺下了，
　　　　　　　　他已浑身冰凉，停止了呼吸。

啊，船长，我的船长哟！起来听听这钟声，
起来吧，——旗旗正为你招展，——号角为你长鸣，
为你，人们准备了无数的花束和花环——为你，人群挤满了海岸，
为你，这晃动着的群众在欢呼，转动着他们殷切的面孔；
　　这里，船长，亲爱的父亲哟！
　　　　让你的头枕着我的手臂吧！
　　　　　　在甲板上，这真是一场梦——

你已经浑身冰凉，停止了呼吸。

我的船长不回答我的话，他的嘴唇惨白而僵硬，
我的父亲，感觉不到我的手臂，他已经没有脉搏，也没有了生命，
我们的船已经安全地下锚了，它的航程已经终了，
从可怕的旅程归来，这胜利的船，目的已经达到；
啊，欢呼吧，海岸，鸣响吧，钟声！
只是我以悲痛的步履，
漫步在甲板上，那里，我的船长躺着，
他已浑身冰凉，停止了呼吸。

SELECTED READINGS

Song of Myself [1]

1

I celebrate myself, and sing myself,
And what I assume[11] you shall assume,
For every atom belonging to me as good belongs to you. [2]

I loafe[12] and invite my soul,
I lean and loafe at my ease observing a spear of[13] summer grass.

My tongue, every atom of my blood, form'd from[14] this soil, this air,
Born here of parents born here from parents the same, and their parents the same,
I, now thirty-seven years old in perfect health begin,
Hoping to cease not till death.

11 assume: take upon oneself; undertake.
12 loafe: (=loaf) wander.
13 A spear of: a narrow piece of.
14 form'd from: created by.

Creeds and schools[15] in abeyance[16],
Retiring back a while sufficed at what they are, but never forgotten,
I harbor for[17] good or bad, I permit to speak at every hazard[18],
Nature without check[19] with original energy.

6

A child said *What is the grass*? fetching it to me with full hands;
How could I answer the child? I do not know what it is any more than he.

I guess it must be the flag of my disposition, out of hopeful green stuff woven.

Or I guess it is the handkerchief of the Lord,
A scented gift and remembrancer[20] designedly dropt[21],
Bearing the owner's name someway in the corners, that we may see and remark, and say *Whose*?

Or I guess the grass is itself a child, the produced babe of the vegetation.

Or I guess it is a uniform hieroglyphic[22],
And it means, Sprouting alike in broad zones and narrow zones,
Growing among black folks as among white,
Kanuck, Tuckahoe, Congressman, Cuff, I give them the same, I receive them the same. [3]

And now it seems to me the beautiful uncut hair of graves.

---

15 schools: schools of thought.
16 in abeyance: the condition of being temporarily suspended.
17 harbor for: entertain or nourish (a specific thought or feeling).
18 at every hazard: at all risks; in spite of every peril.
19 check: control; restraint.
20 remembrancer: souvenir; one who reminds another.
21 designedly dropt: intentionally dropped for someone to pick up.
22 hieroglyphic: characters or mode of writing used by the ancient Egyptians.古埃及的象形文字

Tenderly will I use you curling grass,
It may be you transpire from[23] the breasts of young men,
It may be if I had known them I would have loved them,
It may be you are from old people, or from offspring taken soon out of their mothers' laps,
And here you are the mothers' laps.

This grass is very dark to be from the white heads of old mothers,
Darker than the colorless beards of old men,
Dark to come from under the faint red roofs of mouths.

O I perceive after all so many uttering tongues,
And I perceive they do not come from the roofs of mouths for nothing.

I wish I could translate the hints about the dead young men and women,
And the hints about old men and mothers, and the offspring taken soon out of their laps.
What do you think has become of the young and old men?
And what do you think has become of the women and children?

They are alive and well somewhere,
The smallest sprout shows there is really no death,
And if ever there was it led forward life,[24] and does not wait at the end to arrest it[25],
And ceas'd the moment life appear'd.

All goes onward and outward, nothing collapses,
And to die is different from what any one supposed, and luckier.

---

23 transpire from: emanate from; come from.
24 And if ever there was it led forward life: And if there ever was death at all, it led forward to life.
25 arrest it: bring life to an end.

NOTES ON THE TEXT

[1] "The Song of Myself" is the longest, consisting of 1345 lines, and the best-known piece in *Leaves of Grass*. When it first appeared in the 1855 edition, it had no title and was not divided into sections. In the second edition (1856), Whitman used the title "Poem of Walt Whitman, an American," which was shortened to "Walt Whitman" for the third edition (1860). In the 1867 edition, it was divided into fifty-two sections. Whitman gave it its present title in the 1881 edition. The title, however, is misleading, for the poem is neither an autobiography nor a memoire. The pronoun "I" or "myself" in the poem is more generic and cosmic than personal.

[2] In the first stanza, the poet identifies "myself" with "you," the readers or all others. Whitman intends to show that people can form a community while remaining individuals. They can achieve a kind of dynamic equilibrium between the needs of the self and the needs of the world, between what T. S. termed "tradition" and "individual talent." Literary critic Alice L. Cook believes that the key to understanding Whitman's poem lies in the "concept of self" as "both individual and universal." John. B. Mason also discusses "the reader's involvement in the poet's movement from the singular to the cosmic." The "self" serves as an ideal, yet, in contrast to traditional epic poetry, this identity is one of the common people rather than a hero.

[3] In these three stanzas beginning with "Or," the poet depicts the qualities and nature of grass. "Kanuck" denotes a French Canadian; "Tuckahoe," a Virginian who lived on poor lands in the tidewater region and ate Tuckahoe, a fungus; and "Cuff," a black. Apparently the poet has demonstrated his support of the equality of these people, native or foreign, rich or poor, black or white.

QUESTIONS FOR DISCUSSION

1. The poet opens the poem with a direct address to his audience, "you," thus inviting the reader to share his experiences and consciousness, and the things and beings he presents. Whitman and his song become a source of inspiration and contact for the reader to be led to a journey in the imaginary world Whitman creates. Find more examples from the text which illustrate the connection between the poet and the reader, between the poet and the world, the grass. What effects has the poet achieved with respect to the expression of his two major themes, i.e. universality and equality?

2. "Grass" has been compared to various things in the poem. Make a list of them and discuss the question, "what does 'grass' stand for?"

3. How does the poet reason out, in section 6, that "there is really no death"? How do you understand the last line, "to die is different from what any one supposed, and luckier"?

参考译文

我自己的歌

赵萝蕤 译

一

我赞美我自己，歌唱我自己，
我承担的你也将承担，
因为属于我的每一个原子也同样属于你。

我闲步，还邀请了我的灵魂，
我俯身悠然观察着一片夏日的草叶。

我的舌，我血液的每个原子，是在这片土壤、这个空气里形成的，
我是生在这里的父母生下的，父母的父母也是在这里生下的，他们的父母也一样，
我，现在三十七岁，一开始身体就十分健康，
希望永不终止，直到死去。

信条和学派暂时不论，
且后退一步，明了它们当前的情况已足，但也决不是忘记，
不论我从善从恶，我允许随意发表意见，
顺乎自然，保持原始的活力。

六

一个孩子说"这草是什么？"两手满满捧着它递给我看；
我哪能回答孩子呢？我和他一样，并不知道。

我猜它定是我性格的旗帜，是充满希望的绿色物质织成的。

我猜他或者是上帝的手帕，

是有意抛下的一件带有香味的礼物和纪念品，
四角附有物主的名字，是为了让我们看见又注意到，并且说，“是谁的？”

我猜想这草本身就是个孩子，是植物界生下的婴儿。

我猜它或者是一种统一的象形文字，
其含义是，在宽广或狭窄的地带都能长出新叶，
在黑人中间和白人中一样能成长，
凯纳克人，特卡荷人，国会议员，柯甫人，我给他们同样的东西，同样对待。

它现在又似乎是墓地里未曾修剪过的秀发。

我要温柔地对待你，弯弯的青草，
你也许是青年人胸中吐出的，
也许我如果认识他们的话会热爱他们，
也许你是从老人那里来的，或来自即将离开母怀的后代，
在这里你就是母亲们的怀抱。

这枝草乌黑又乌黑，不可能来自老母亲们的白头，
它比老年人的无色胡须还要乌黑，
乌黑得不像来自口腔的浅红上颚。

啊，我终于看到了那么许多说着话的舌头，
并看到它们不是无故从口腔的上颚出现的。

我深愿能翻译出那些有关已死青年男女们隐晦的提示，
和那些有关老人、母亲，和即将离开母怀的后代们的提示。
你想这些青年和老人们后来怎么样了？
你想这些妇女和孩子们后来怎么样了？

他们还在某个地方活着并且生活得很好，
那最小的幼芽说明世上其实并无死亡，
即使有，也会导致生命，不会等着在最后把它扼死，

而且生命一出现，死亡就终止。

一起都向前向外发展，无所谓溃灭，
死亡不像人们所想象的那样，不是那么不幸。

SUGGESTED REFERENCES

Allen, Gay Wilson. *The Solitary Singer: A Critical Biography of Walt Whitman.* New York: Macmillan, 1955.

Bloom, Harold. *Agon: Towards a Theory of Revisionism.* New York: Oxford UP, 1982.

Donald, Pease. "Walt Whitman's Revolutionary Democracy." *The Columbia History of American Poetry.* Jay Parini and Brett C. Miller eds. Beijing: Foreign Language Teaching and Research Press, 2005. 148-71.

Donoghue, Denis. "Leaves of Grass." *The American Classics.* New Haven: Yale UP, 2005. 177-216.

Mason, John B. "Walt Whitman's Catalogues: Rhetorical Means for Two Journeys in 'Song of Myself'." *American Literature* 45.1 (1973): 34-49.

Miller, James E., Jr. *"Leaves of Grass": America's Lyric-Epic of Self and Democracy.* New York: Twayne Publishers, 1992.

Miller, James E. *Walt Whitman.* New York: Twayne Publishers, 1962.

Mirsky, D.S. *Walt Whitman and the World.* Iowa City: U of Iowa P, 1995.

Moon, Michael. *Disseminating Whitman: Revision and Corporealty in "Leaves of Grass."* Cambridge: Harvard UP, 1992.

Roper, Robert. *Now the Drum of War: Walt Whitman and His Brothers in the Civil War.* New York: Walker Publishing, 2008.

Rubin, Joseph Jay. *The Historic Whitman.* University Park: Pennsylvania State UP, 1973.

Williams, C. K. *On Whitman.* Princeton: Princeton UP, 2010.

Unit 7 Emily Dickinson

(1830 – 1886)

A GUIDE TO LITERARY TERMINOLOGY

"Aphorism": *An aphorism is a short statement that expresses a true or wise idea. The meaning of an aphorism should be so broad that it comes across as folklore or established wisdom rather than personal observation. The expression should be compressed beyond the point of immediate accessibility, for an aphorism requires figuring out and thus promotes reflection. Whatever its form, an aphorism should have three qualities (evident in many Dickinson poems): generalization, compression, and memorability.*

Brevity is perhaps the most prominent feature of Emily Dickinson's poems. Her work approaches poetry's irreducible minimum, which is poetry's immortal part. Her bent for condensed and oracular statement partly accounts for this. Indeed, her readers have no difficulty observing the existence aphoristic spirit in her poetry. It is no exaggeration at all to say that it is because Emily Dickinson is a surpassingly great aphorist that she is a great poet. Many of Dickinson's poems — such as "Hope is the thing with feather" (Poem 254), and "Success is counted sweetest / By those who ne'er succeed" (Poem 67) — begin with aphorisms and then reflect on and unfold them.

NOTES ON THE AUTHOR

Emily Dickinson was born on December 10, 1830 in Amherst, Massachusetts, a small New England town. She had an older brother, Austin, and a younger sister, Lavinia. Her father, Edward Dickinson, was a successful lawyer and politician. Though she did not receive much formal education, she had read widely at home. While she was young, she had been socially active, but became increasingly secluded from society since the 1860s, largely due to her visual disability. She suffered periods of blindness and made two long visits, in 1864 and 1865 respectively, to Boston to receive treatments from an eye surgeon. Emily Dickinson spent almost her entire life within her family home, writing poetry and helping to run the household.

Dickinson began writing poems seriously in 1848. Her poems were read by family and friends. She never married, but had befriended several men during her lifetime, whom she regarded as her "preceptors": Benjamin F. Newton, a young attorney who studied under her father, Edward Dickinson; Reverend Charles Wadsworth of Philadelphia, whom she got to know while traveling with her father to

Philadelphia; Samuel Bowles, owner and editor of the *Springfield Republican* and close friend of Austin and his wife Susan; Thomas W. Higginson, a fervent advocate of women's rights and abolition and an editor of the *Atlantic Monthly*. Except for her correspondence with Higginson, whose encouragement and guidance were a strong emotional and intellectual support for her, she wrote in secret and guarded her poems even from her family.

Emily Dickinson wrote nearly 1,800 poems, but only seven were published during her lifetime, six of which without her consent. In one of her poems (no. 709), she wrote, "Publication — is the Auction/Of the Mind of Man." When she died in May1886, her sister Lavinia discovered 814 poems bound into 40 packets hidden in her bedroom bureau, together with 333 poems ready for binding and many worksheet drafts. It was not until the appearance of *Poems by Emily Dickinson* (edited by Mabel Loomis Todd, Austin's friend, and Thomas W. Higginson) in 1890, four years after her death, that her poetry became known to the public. In 1955, the first reliable complete collection, *The Poems of Emily Dickinson*, which contains all Dickinson's 1,775 known poems, came out. Only then did Emily Dickinson really make her entrance into the world as an American lyric poet.

NOTES ON HER WORK

Today, Emily Dickinson, the shy, reclusive poet, has come to be regarded as one of America's best. She expressed her thoughts, her feelings and poignancy in an aphoristic style. Her poems are short, fresh and original. She habitually uses the standard hymn stanza form with some innovations, reversing rhythms, omitting rhymes, lengthening or shortening lines. She prefers a more straightforward declarative style, placing phrases and clauses paratactically. Her usual poetic form, which receives both praises and criticism from early critics, has a sort of fragmented, multiple, and imagistic qualities in it that are comparable to the modernist poetic strategies. Some of her poems even assume multiple voices contradicting each other. And such contradiction lies at the very center of her poems. Long before the Modernist and feminist movements, Dickinson's poems had embodied the principle of fragmentation, isolation, independence, and self-reliance. In a narrow, provincial town where anyone who did not follow the conventions was vilified,

Dickinson dared to live by her own rules rather than follow conventional values and social codes. Despite the rigid instruction from teachers, society, religion, and her own father, Dickinson had shown in her poetry an ironic and playful stance toward social constraints and traditional values, and had expressed her love of individualism through her female voice. She was a fervent supporter of the rights of the individual versus the goals of society or tradition.

Emily Dickinson was closely aligned with the Transcendentalist Movement, which believed in an individual's ability to transcend the mortal world through reflection, intuition, and an affinity with Nature. The transcendentalist writers, including Ralph Waldo Emerson, Henry David Thoreau, and Walt Whitman, advocated individualism, self-reliance, racial and sexual equality. They believed that the individual could attain enlightenments and grace by studying nature and becoming the moral embodiment of God. Emily Dickinson read and quoted from Emerson, who stayed with Austin and Sue Dickinson shortly in 1857 and 1865. Her poetry also shows her tacit agreement with Emerson about the traditions of poetry and religion. She changed the standard meter and rhyme, abandoned conventional grammar so as to urge her readers to explore the meanings of her poems. Like the Transcendentalists, Dickinson's rejection of religious doctrines did not mean an abandonment of spiritual discovery, but rather an embrace of personal revelation. Dickinson's assertion that the self shall "Suffice... for a Crowd" sounds remarkably similar to Emerson's claim in "Self-Reliance" that "every true man is a cause, a country, and an age."

SELECTED READINGS

I'm Nobody (288) [1]

I'm nobody! Who are you?
Are you nobody, too?
Then there's a pair of us [2] — don't tell!

They'd banish us, you know.

How dreary to be somebody!
How public like a frog [3]
To tell your name the livelong day
To an admiring bog! [4]

NOTES ON THE TEXT

[1] Few of Emily Dickinson's poems were given titles. The titles in the selected poems are added for convenience sake. The numbers used are from *The Poems of Emily Dickinson*, 3 vols. Ed. T. Johnson, 1955. This poem, one of Dickinson's best known, was written in 1861.

[2] Although the speaker is considered a "Nobody," she is not completely alone; she, together with "you," forms a pair.

[3] Dickinson compares "Sombody" to a frog who is very noisy and boastful. Dickinson playfully expresses her delight in being a "Nobody" and her desire to avoid being made "public" like a frog.

[4] The "Somebody," whose name is known, whose work is published, receives admiration. But what good is admiration, Dickinson asks, if it comes from a bog? Bog: a swamp; an area of land very wet and muddy.

QUESTIONS FOR DISCUSSION

1. What's the tone of the first stanza? Is it different from the second stanza? What does the change of tone in the second stanza show?

2. In the third and fourth lines of the first stanza, "Then there's a pair of us — don't tell!/They'd banish us, you know," the poet attempts to build a rapport with the reader, or "you," who she believes is the same type of people. Why should we be "banished" if we "tell" that we are nobody? Who are "they"?

3. What are some of the possible benefits of anonymity? And the drawbacks of celebrity?

参考译文

我是无名之辈

我是无名之辈！你是谁？
你也是无名之辈？
那咱俩就成了一对——别出声！
他们会把咱们驱除——要小心！

多无聊——身为赫赫显要！
多招摇——不过像只青蛙
向一片仰慕的泥沼
整日炫耀自己的名号！

SELECTED READINGS

"Hope" Is the Thing with Feathers (254)

"Hope" is the thing with feathers — [1]
That perches in the soul —
And sings the tune without the words —
And never stops — at all —

And sweetest — in the Gale — is heard —
And sore must be the storm —
That could abash the little Bird
That kept so many warm — [2]

I've heard it in the chillest land — [3]
And on the strangest sea — [4]
Yet, never, in extremity,
It asked a crumb — of Me. [5]

NOTES ON THE TEXT

[1] "The thing with feathers" here refers to a songbird. In this stanza, the poet imagines "hope," something abstract and intangible, as a songbird, a living creature, "that perches in the soul." The bird of "hope" keeps singing, without a stop, which implies its eternity.

[2] The song of hope is the sweetest in a gale (an extremely strong wind). And if at all possible, it must be an enormously ferocious storm that could shake the bird of hope which keeps so many hearts warm.

[3] I can hear the song of hope even in the most depressingly cold land, which shows the resilience of hope.

[4] I can hear the song of hope in the strangest sea, which indicates the adaptability and fearlessness of hope.

[5] Hope only gives; it never takes, not even a small breadcrumb, not even under extreme difficulty, which signals the self-sacrifice and the power of hope.

QUESTIONS FOR DISCUSSION

1. What is the theme of this poem? What are the qualities that the poet has attributed to "Hope"?

2. What effects has the poet achieved by comparing Hope to a songbird? Cite other metaphors used by the poet in this poem and discuss their roles.

参考译文

希望是一只飞鸟

长风 译

希望是一只飞鸟，
栖息在心灵的树梢，
它不停
吟唱的曲调，

在狂风中越发美妙；
风暴因此懊恼，
本以为可以击败
给人温暖的小鸟。

严寒的大地，陌生的狂涛，
我仍能听到它的鸣叫；
即便在极端的周遭，
它也从未向我索要。

SELECTED READINGS

Success (67)

Success is counted sweetest
By those who ne'er succeed. [1]
To comprehend a nectar [2]
Requires sorest need.

Not one of all the purple host [3]
Who took the flag today [4]
Can tell the definition,
So clear, of victory, [5]

As he, defeated, dying,
On whose forbidden ear
The distant strains of triumph [6]
Break, agonized and clear. [7]

NOTES ON THE TEXT

[1] To lose is to show weakness, failure, and despair, but to win is to exhibit strength, success, and great satisfaction. Dickinson, however, perceives an essential paradox within the dichotomies of winning and losing in this poem. Dickinson holds that no one understands what victory means more than those who have lost. Dickinson wrote this poem in 1859.

[2] Nectar: sweet liquid produced by flowers, which bees and other insect collect. In Greek mythology, nectar is the food for gods and goddesses in the Olympian mountains. In this line, success is compared to nectar, which can be obtained only by those who need it most badly.

[3] The purple host — people of high ranks. Purple is the color of robes worn by Roman emperors and Catholic cardinals.

[4] Took the flag — won the victory.

[5] Notice the poet ends this stanza with a comma. This stanza consists of only a half of a comparative sentence. The next stanza will complete it.

[6] Distant strains of triumph: the music heard in the distance, celebrating a victory.

[7] The last two stanzas can be paraphrased as: No one among those who are of high ranks and who win one victory after another can understand the meaning of victory better than a defeated soldier who, while dying, hears the enemy celebrating their victory.

QUESTIONS FOR DISCUSSION

1. Do you agree with Dickinson's notion that a loser can understand the meaning of success better than a winner?

2. Within the dichotomy of winning and losing, which side has the poet shown more sympathy on? What is the paradox perceived by the poet in terms of the definition of success?

参考译文

成功

罗鑫 译

在未成功者眼里
成功最甜蜜
欲尝神酒之美味
苦涩必经历

紫袍金甲骏马骑
虎视执战旗
竟也无人能知晓
胜利真含义

唯有垂死战败者
失聪耳朵里
惊闻遥远凯旋声
痛极而清晰

SELECTED READINGS

I Died for Beauty (449) [1]

I died for beauty, but was scarce
Adjusted in the tomb, [2]
When one who died for truth was lain
In an adjoining room. [3]

He questioned softly why I failed?
"For beauty," I replied.
"And I for truth — the two are one;
We brethren are," [4] he said.

And so, as kinsmen met a-night, [5]
We talked between the rooms,
Until the moss had reached our lips,
And covered up our names.

NOTES ON THE TEXT

[1] This poem recalls John Keats's oft-quoted lines from "Ode on a Grecian Urn": "Beauty is truth, truth beauty — that is all ye know on earth and all ye need to know." Dickinson wrote this poem in 1862. Her idea that beauty and truth are closely related to each other clearly shows Keats's influence.

[2] was scarce/Adjusted in the tomb: was scarcely accustomed to the tomb.

[3] Stanza 1 can be paraphrased as: I died pursuing artistic beauty. Hardly have I got used to the tomb when another, who died pursuing truth, has arrived in a room next to mine.

[4] We brethren are: We are brothers.

[5] a-night: at night.

QUESTIONS FOR DISCUSSION

1. How do you understand the idea that beauty and truth are one? In what sense are they the same? In what sense are they different?

2. What is the implication of the last two lines of the poem, "Until the moss had reached our lips,/And covered up our names"?

参考译文

殉美

余光中 译

我为美死去，但是还不曾
安息在我的墓里，
又有个为真理而死去的人
来躺在我的隔壁。

他悄悄地问我为何以身殉?
“为了美。”我说。
“而我为真理，两者不分家;
我们是兄弟两个。”

于是像亲戚在夜间相遇，
我们便隔墙谈天，
直到青苔爬到了唇际，
将我们的名字遮掩。

SUGGESTED REFERENCES

Bloom, Harold, ed. *Modern Critical Views: Emily Dickinson.* New York: Chelsea House Publishers, 1985.

Cameron, Sharon. "Naming as History: Dickinson's Poems of Definition," *Critical Inquiry* 5. 2 (1978): 223-51.

Habegger, Alfred. *My Wars Are Laid Away in Books: The Life of Emily Dickinson.* New York: Modern Library, 2002.

Johnson, Thomas H., ed. *Emily Dickinson: Selected Letters.* Cambridge: Belknap Press of Harvard University, 1986.

Johnson, Thomas, ed. *The Poems of Emily Dickinson.* 3 vols. Cambridge: Harvard UP, 1951.

Loeffelholz, Mary. *Dickinson and the Boundaries of Feminist Theory.* Urbana: U of Illinois P, 1991.

Martin, Wendy, ed. *The Cambridge Companion to Emily Dickinson.* Cambridge: Cambridge UP, 2002.

Wolf, Cynthia Griffin. *Emily Dickinson.* New York: Knopf, 1986.

Unit 8 Jack London

(1876–1916)

A GUIDE TO LITERARY TERMINOLOGY

"Naturalism": *The term describes a type of literature that attempts to apply scientific principles of objectivity and detachment to its study of human beings. Naturalism was a literary movement or tendency from the 1880s to 1930s in Europe and America that emphasizes the influence of social conditions, heredity, and environment on the shaping of human character. Naturalism found its greatest number of practitioners in America. Naturalistic writers there include Jack London, Stephen Crane, Frank Norris, Theodore Dreiser, Eugene O'Neill, John Steinbeck, and Richard Wright.*

Naturalistic writers studied human beings governed by their instincts and passions as well as the ways in which the characters' lives were governed by forces of heredity and environment. This is a logical extension of realism. In fact, many authors of the period are identified as both Naturalists and Realists. However, naturalism is not synonymous with realism. In realism, characters have at least some degree of free will, which they are able to exercise to affect their situations. Naturalism almost entirely dispensed with the idea of free will, assuming humans as passive victims of natural forces and social environment. Naturalistic writers adopted a more documentary-like approach to their subjects, without making comments on the morality or the fairness of the situations in which characters find themselves. Their works are written in accordance with Charles Darwin's theory of evolution. Natural selection and "survival of the fittest" help to depict the struggle against nature as a hopeless fight. Moreover, since naturalists believe that everything that is real is found in nature and is subject to scientific investigation and verification, they reject supernatural explanations of situations and events.

NOTES ON THE AUTHOR

Born in San Francisco to Flora Wellman, a young unmarried woman who had run away from her Ohio family, Jack London was adopted and raised in Oakland by John London, a partially disabled Civil War veteran, whom his mother soon after married. Jack London never saw his father and took the name of his stepfather. During his adolescence, London supported himself with menial and dangerous jobs, experiencing the struggle of survival. By the time he was 18, he had dropped out of school, held a variety of manual jobs (an oyster pirate, seaman, jute-mill worker, coal shoveler, electrician), and became a tramp. He was jailed in the Erie Country Penitentiary for vagrancy. The "unspeakable" brutalities he witnessed in his 30 days in prison awakened him to the reality of his downward class mobility. At this point, he determined to educate himself to improve his own condition and that of others. London spent the winter of 1897–1898 in the Klondike with the gold prospectors in search of gold, but without success. He then determined to turn to writing as a way of living. By the time he published his first collection of stories, *The Son of the Wolf* (1900), he was on his way to becoming a successful writer. *The Call of the Wild* (1903) brought him national fame at the age of 26.

London embraced socialism of Marx on the one hand and the rather darker views of Nietzsche and Darwinism on the other. He believed at once in the inevitable triumph of the working class and in the evolutionary necessity of the survival of the strongest individuals. His socialist views are revealed in his literary and polemical works such as *The People of the Abyss* (1903), *The Iron Heel* (1908), *War of the Classes* (1905), and *Revolution* (1910); his commitment to the fundamental reality of the law of survival and the will to power is portrayed in his most popular novels, *The Call of the Wild* (1903) and *The Sea Wolf* (1904). The contradiction between these competing beliefs is most vividly projected in his autobiographical novel *Martin Eden* (1909) which chronicles his own struggle to become a writer and his disillusionment with success. London wrote on an astonishing array of topics in his brief but productive life. His works present diverse subjects and styles, including characters drawn from cavemen, lepers, the desperate poor, the homeless, prisoners, the mentally retarded, Solomon Islanders, Native Americans, and so on, focusing for the most part on characters who suffer some form of oppression, including colonization by whites. His popular stories often involve the primitive struggle of individuals in face of irresistible natural forces. Like his contemporaries Stephen Crane and Frank Norris, London was fascinated by the way violence tested and defined human nature. His style is often called "naturalistic," that is, focused on physical survival and struggle against natural forces, while his style is also described as "romantic," as any reader of *The Call of the Wild* can attest. His devotion to realism, to opening readers' eyes to things they fail to see every day (the plight of the poor at the hands of the era's robber baron capitalists) or things they had never imagined (cannibalism in Fiji). At the time of his death he was in poor health, his body marked by the strenuous life he had sometimes glorified in his fiction. He died of a self-administered overdose of morphine, which he was taking to counter the pain of nephritis, a side effect of his alcoholism.

SYNOPSIS OF THE WORK

"Love of Life," one of London's most memorable Klondike stories, is a gripping narrative of desperate survival. Having sprained his ankle and abandoned by his partner Bill, the anonymous protagonist endures a terrible journey, first limping, then crawling, then merely pulling himself ahead with his arms for mile upon mile. His destination is the Coronation Bay far away, which he has seen on Hudson Bay Company chart. Despite adverse circumstances, he does not want to give up, creeping his way along, chewing berries and milk grass, which sicken him, occasionally catching a bird, and a few minnows, but slowly starving. Enduring snow and rain, he crawls along feeling the life slowly dying within him: "He, as a man, no longer strove. It was the life in him, unwilling to die, that drove him on. He did not suffer. His nerves had become blunted, numb, while his mind was filled with weird visions and delicious dreams." Soon a wolf is on his trail. The wolf is sick, but it is as persistent and patient as the protagonist. The man is the wolf's last hope of survival, while the man understands he has to get rid of the wolf if he doesn't want to become its meat. Playing dead, the man allows the wolf to approach and even sink its teeth into his hand. However, with his last strength, he strangles the wolf and then, fastening his teeth onto the wolf's neck, drinks its blood. He is saved and falls asleep at last. When he awakes, he finds himself at Coronation Bay, where a whaling ship sits in the harbor. He is rescued, but it is months before he recovers from this terrible experience.

SELECTED READINGS

LOVE OF LIFE

(First printed in *McClure's Magazine*, Vol. 26, Dec., 1905)

"This out of all will remain —
They have lived and have tossed:
So much of the game will be gain,
Though the gold of the dice has been lost."

They limped painfully down the bank, and once the foremost of the two men staggered among the rough-strewn rocks. They were tired and weak, and their faces had the drawn expression of patience which comes of[1] hardship long endured. They were heavily burdened with blanket packs which were strapped to their shoulders. Head-straps, passing across the forehead, helped support these packs. Each man carried a rifle. They walked in a stooped posture, the shoulders well forward, the head still farther forward, the eyes bent upon the ground.

"I wish we had just about two of them cartridges that's layin' in that cache of ourn,"[2] said the second man.

His voice was utterly and drearily expressionless. He spoke without enthusiasm; and the first man, limping into the milky stream that foamed over the rocks, vouchsafed[3] no reply.

The other man followed at his heels. They did not remove their foot-gear, though the water was icy cold — so cold that their ankles ached and their feet went numb. In places the water dashed against their knees, and both men staggered for footing.

The man who followed slipped on a smooth boulder, nearly fell, but recovered himself with a violent effort, at the same time uttering a sharp exclamation of pain. He seemed faint and dizzy and put out his free hand while he reeled, as though seeking support against the air. When he had steadied himself he stepped forward, but reeled again and nearly fell. Then he stood still and looked at the other man, who had never turned his head.

The man stood still for fully a minute, as though debating with himself. Then he called out:

"I say, Bill, I've sprained my ankle."

Bill staggered on through the milky water. He did not look around. The man watched him go, and though his face was expressionless as

---

1 come of: come from; is a result of.

2 I wish we had just about two of them cartridges that's layin' in that cache of ourn: I wish we had two of the cartridges laying in our cache. Ourn: ours.

3 vouchsafe: (archaic, formal) to give.

ever, his eyes were like the eyes of a wounded deer.

The other man limped up the farther bank and continued straight on without looking back. The man in the stream watched him. His lips trembled a little, so that the rough thatch of brown hair which covered them was visibly agitated. His tongue even strayed out to moisten them.

"Bill!" he cried out. It was the pleading cry of a strong man in distress, but Bill's head did not turn. [1] The man watched him go, limping grotesquely and lurching forward with stammering gait up the slow slope toward the soft sky-line of the low-lying hill. He watched him go till he passed over the crest and disappeared. Then he turned his gaze and slowly took in[4] the circle of the world that remained to him now that Bill was gone.

Near the horizon the sun was smouldering dimly, almost obscured by formless mists and vapors, which gave an impression of mass and density without outline or tangibility. [2] The man pulled out his watch, the while resting his weight on one leg. It was four o'clock, and as the season was near the last of July or first of August, — he did not know the precise date within a week or two, — he knew that the sun roughly marked the northwest. He looked to the south and knew that somewhere beyond those bleak hills lay the Great Bear Lake; [3] also, he knew that in that direction the Arctic Circle cut its forbidding way across the Canadian Barrens[5]. This stream in which he stood was a feeder to the Coppermine River[6], which in turn flowed north and emptied into Coronation Gulf [4] and the Arctic Ocean. He had never been there, but he had seen it, once, on a Hudson Bay Company[7] chart.

Again his gaze completed the circle of the world about him. It was not a heartening spectacle. Everywhere was soft sky-line. The

---

4 take in something: inspect it; see all of it with just one look.

5 the Canadian Barrens: Canadian tundra, within the Arctic Circle.

6 Coppermine River: a river in the North Slave and Kitikmeot regions of the Northwest Territories and Nunavut in Canada. It is 845 kilometers long.

7 Hudson Bay Company: a Canadian company dealing in fur business.

hills were all low-lying. There were no trees, no shrubs, no grasses — naught but a tremendous and terrible desolation that sent fear swiftly dawning into his eyes.

"Bill!" he whispered, once and twice; "Bill!"

He cowered in the midst of the milky water, as though the vastness were pressing in upon him with overwhelming force, brutally crushing him with its complacent awfulness. He began to shake as with an ague fit[8], till the gun fell from his hand with a splash. This served to rouse him. He fought with his fear and pulled himself together, groping in the water and recovering the weapon. He hitched his pack farther over on his left shoulder, so as to take a portion of its weight from off the injured ankle. Then he proceeded, slowly and carefully, wincing with pain, to the bank.

He did not stop. With a desperation that was madness, unmindful of the pain, he hurried up the slope to the crest of the hill over which his comrade had disappeared — more grotesque and comical by far than that limping, jerking comrade. But at the crest he saw a shallow valley, empty of life. He fought with his fear again, overcame it, hitched the pack still farther over on his left shoulder, and lurched on down the slope.

The bottom of the valley was soggy with water, which the thick moss held, spongelike, close to the surface. This water squirted out from under his feet at every step, and each time he lifted a foot the action culminated in a sucking sound as the wet moss reluctantly released its grip. He picked his way from muskeg to muskeg, and followed the other man's footsteps along and across the rocky ledges which thrust like islets through the sea of moss.

Though alone, he was not lost. Farther on he knew he would come to where dead spruce and fir, very small and weazened[9], bordered the shore of a little lake, the titchin-nichilie, in the tongue of

8 ague fit: a fit of acute fever.

9 weazened: wizened, dried up.

the country, the "land of little sticks."[10] And into that lake flowed a small stream, the water of which was not milky. There was rush-grass on that stream — this he remembered well — but no timber, and he would follow it till its first trickle ceased at a divide. He would cross this divide to the first trickle of another stream, flowing to the west, which he would follow until it emptied into the river Dease[11], and here he would find a cache under an upturned canoe and piled over with many rocks. And in this cache would be ammunition for his empty gun, fish-hooks and lines, a small net — all the utilities for the killing and snaring of food. Also, he would find flour, — not much, — a piece of bacon, and some beans.

Bill would be waiting for him there, and they would paddle away south down the Dease to the Great Bear Lake. And south across the lake they would go, ever south, till they gained the Mackenzie[12]. And south, still south, they would go, while the winter raced vainly after them, and the ice formed in the eddies, and the days grew chill and crisp, south to some warm Hudson Bay Company post, where timber grew tall and generous and there was grub without end.

These were the thoughts of the man as he strove onward. But hard as he strove with his body, he strove equally hard with his mind, trying to think that Bill had not deserted him, that Bill would surely wait for him at the cache. He was compelled to think this thought, or else there would not be any use to strive, and he would have lain down and died. And as the dim ball of the sun sank slowly into the northwest he covered every inch — and many times — of his and Bill's flight south before the down-coming winter. And he conned the grub[13] of the cache and the grub of the Hudson Bay Company post over and

10 the titchin-nichilie, in the tongue of the country, the "land of little sticks": "titchin-nichilie" means "land of little sticks" in the language of the natives living there.

11 The Dease River flows through northwestern British Columbia, Canada and is a tributary of the Liard River. The river descends from Dease Lake and flows 265 km generally north-eastward, draining into the Liard River near Lower Post, British Columbia.

12 Mackenzie: a District Municipality near Williston Lake in east central British Columbia, Canada.

13 conned the grub: thought of again and again the food.

over again. He had not eaten for two days; for a far longer time he had not had all he wanted to eat. Often he stooped and picked pale muskeg berries, put them into his mouth, and chewed and swallowed them. A muskeg berry is a bit of seed enclosed in a bit of water. In the mouth the water melts away and the seed chews sharp and bitter. The man knew there was no nourishment in the berries, but he chewed them patiently with a hope greater than knowledge and defying experience.

At nine o'clock he stubbed his toe on a rocky ledge, and from sheer weariness and weakness staggered and fell. He lay for some time, without movement, on his side. Then he slipped out of the pack-straps and clumsily dragged himself into a sitting posture. It was not yet dark, and in the lingering twilight he groped about among the rocks for shreds of dry moss. When he had gathered a heap he built a fire, — a smouldering, smudgy fire, — and put a tin pot of water on to boil.

He unwrapped his pack and the first thing he did was to count his matches. There were sixty-seven. He counted them three times to make sure. He divided them into several portions, wrapping them in oil paper, disposing of one bunch in his empty tobacco pouch, of another bunch in the inside band of his battered hat, of a third bunch under his shirt on the chest. This accomplished, a panic came upon him, and he unwrapped them all and counted them again. There were still sixty-seven.

He dried his wet foot-gear by the fire. The moccasins were in soggy shreds. The blanket socks were worn through in places, and his feet were raw and bleeding. His ankle was throbbing, and he gave it an examination. It had swollen to the size of his knee. He tore a long strip from one of his two blankets and bound the ankle tightly. He tore other strips and bound them about his feet to serve for both moccasins and socks. Then he drank the pot of water, steaming hot, wound his watch, and crawled between his blankets.

He slept like a dead man. The brief darkness around midnight came and went. The sun arose in the northeast — at least the day dawned in that quarter, for the sun was hidden by gray clouds.

At six o'clock he awoke, quietly lying on his back. He gazed straight up into the gray sky and knew that he was hungry. As he rolled over on his elbow he was startled by a loud snort, and saw a bull caribou regarding him with alert curiosity. The animal was not more than fifty feet away, and instantly into the man's mind leaped the vision and the savor of a caribou steak sizzling and frying over a fire. Mechanically he reached for the empty gun, drew a bead, and pulled the trigger. The bull snorted and leaped away, his hoofs rattling and clattering as he fled across the ledges.

The man cursed and flung the empty gun from him. He groaned aloud as he started to drag himself to his feet. It was a slow and arduous task. His joints were like rusty hinges. They worked harshly in their sockets, with much friction, and each bending or unbending was accomplished only through a sheer exertion of will. When he finally gained his feet, another minute or so was consumed in straightening up, so that he could stand erect as a man should stand.

He crawled up a small knoll and surveyed the prospect. There were no trees, no bushes, nothing but a gray sea of moss scarcely diversified by gray rocks, gray lakelets, and gray streamlets. The sky was gray. There was no sun nor hint of sun. He had no idea of north, and he had forgotten the way he had come to this spot the night before. But he was not lost. He knew that. Soon he would come to the land of the little sticks. He felt that it lay off to the left somewhere, not far — possibly just over the next low hill.

He went back to put his pack into shape for travelling. He assured himself of the existence of his three separate parcels of matches, though he did not stop to count them. But he did linger, debating, over a squat moose-hide sack. It was not large. He could hide it under his two hands. He knew that it weighed fifteen pounds, — as much as all the rest of the pack, — and it worried him. He finally set it to one side and proceeded to roll the pack. He paused to gaze at the squat moose-hide sack. He picked it up hastily with a defiant glance about him, as though the desolation were trying to rob him of it; and when he rose to his feet to stagger on into the day, it was included in the pack on his back.

He bore away to the left, stopping now and again to eat muskeg berries. His ankle had stiffened, his limp was more pronounced, but the pain of it was as nothing compared with the pain of his stomach. The hunger pangs were sharp. They gnawed and gnawed until he could not keep his mind steady on the course he must pursue to gain the land of little sticks. The muskeg berries did not allay this gnawing, while they made his tongue and the roof of his mouth sore with their irritating bite.

He came upon a valley where rock ptarmigan rose on whirring wings from the ledges and muskegs. Ker — ker — ker was the cry they made. He threw stones at them, but could not hit them. He placed his pack on the ground and stalked them as a cat stalks a sparrow. The sharp rocks cut through his pants' legs till his knees left a trail of blood; but the hurt was lost in the hurt of his hunger. He squirmed over the wet moss, saturating his clothes and chilling his body; but he was not aware of it, so great was his fever for food. And always the ptarmigan rose, whirring, before him, till their ker — ker — ker became a mock to him, and he cursed them and cried aloud at them with their own cry.

Once he crawled upon one that must have been asleep. He did not see it till it shot up in his face from its rocky nook. He made a clutch as startled as was the rise of the ptarmigan, and there remained in his hand three tail-feathers. As he watched its flight he hated it, as though it had done him some terrible wrong. Then he returned and shouldered his pack.

As the day wore along he came into valleys or swales where

game was more plentiful. A band of caribou passed by, twenty and odd animals, tantalizingly within rifle range. He felt a wild desire to run after them, a certitude that he could run them down. A black fox came toward him, carrying a ptarmigan in his mouth. The man shouted. It was a fearful cry, but the fox, leaping away in fright, did not drop the ptarmigan.

Late in the afternoon he followed a stream, milky with lime, which ran through sparse patches of rush-grass. Grasping these rushes firmly near the root, he pulled up what resembled a young onion-sprout no larger than a shingle-nail. It was tender, and his teeth sank into it with a crunch that promised deliciously of food. But its fibers were tough. It was composed of stringy filaments saturated with water, like the berries, and devoid of nourishment. He threw off his pack and went into the rush-grass on hands and knees, crunching and munching, like some bovine creature.

He was very weary and often wished to rest — to lie down and sleep; but he was continually driven on — not so much by his desire to gain the land of little sticks as by his hunger. He searched little ponds for frogs and dug up the earth with his nails for worms, though he knew in spite that neither frogs nor worms existed so far north.

He looked into every pool of water vainly, until, as the long twilight came on, he discovered a solitary fish, the size of a minnow, in such a pool. He plunged his arm in up to the shoulder, but it eluded him. He reached for it with both hands and stirred up the milky mud at the bottom. In his excitement he fell in, wetting himself to the waist. Then the water was too muddy to admit of his seeing the fish, and he was compelled to wait until the sediment had settled.

The pursuit was renewed, till the water was again muddied. But he could not wait. He unstrapped the tin bucket and began to bale the pool. He baled wildly at first, splashing himself and flinging the water so short a distance that it ran back into the pool. He worked more carefully, striving to be cool, though his heart was pounding against his chest and his hands were trembling. At the end of half an hour the pool was nearly dry. Not a cupful of water remained. And there was no fish. He found a hidden crevice among the stones through which it had escaped to the adjoining and larger pool — a pool which he could not empty in a night and a day. Had he known of the crevice, he could have closed it with a rock at the beginning and the fish would have been his.

Thus he thought, and crumpled up and sank down upon the wet earth. At first he cried softly to himself, then he cried loudly to the pitiless desolation that ringed him around; and for a long time after he was shaken by great dry sobs.

He built a fire and warmed himself by drinking quarts of hot water, and made camp on a rocky ledge in the same fashion he had the night before. The last thing he did was to see that his matches were dry and to wind his watch. The blankets were wet and clammy. His ankle pulsed with pain. But he knew only that he was hungry, and through his restless sleep he dreamed of feasts and banquets and of food served and spread in all imaginable ways.

He awoke chilled and sick. There was no sun. The gray of earth and sky had become deeper, more profound. A raw wind was blowing, and the first flurries of snow were whitening the hilltops. The air about him thickened and grew white while he made a fire and boiled more water. It was wet snow, half rain, and the flakes were large and soggy. At first they melted as soon as they came in contact with the earth, but ever more fell, covering the ground, putting out the fire, spoiling his supply of moss-fuel.

This was a signal for him to strap on his pack and stumble onward, he knew not where. He was not concerned with the land of little sticks, nor with Bill and the cache under the upturned canoe by the river Dease. He was mastered by the verb "to eat." He was hunger-mad. He took no heed of the course he pursued, so long as that course led him through the swale bottoms. He felt his way through the wet snow to the watery muskeg berries, and went by feel as he pulled up the rush-grass by the roots. But it was tasteless stuff and did not satisfy. He found a weed that tasted sour and he ate all he could find of it, which was not much, for it was a creeping growth, easily hidden under the several inches of snow.

He had no fire that night, nor hot water, and crawled under his blanket to sleep the broken hunger-sleep. The snow turned into a cold rain. He awakened many times to feel it falling on his upturned face. Day came — a gray day and no sun. It had ceased raining. The keenness of his hunger had departed. Sensibility, as far as concerned the yearning for food, had been exhausted. There was a dull, heavy ache in his stomach, but it did not bother him so much. He was more rational, and once more he was chiefly interested in the land of little sticks and the cache by the river Dease.

He ripped the remnant of one of his blankets into strips and bound his bleeding feet. Also, he recinched[14] the injured ankle and prepared himself for a day of travel. When he came to his pack, he paused long over the squat moose-hide sack, but in the end it went with him.

The snow had melted under the rain, and only the hilltops showed white. The sun came out, and he succeeded in locating the points of the compass, though he knew now that he was lost. Perhaps, in his previous days' wanderings, he had edged away too far to the left. He now bore off to the right to counteract the possible deviation from his true course.

Though the hunger pangs were no longer so exquisite, he realized that he was weak. He was compelled to pause for frequent rests, when he attacked the muskeg berries and rush-grass patches. His tongue felt

---

14 recinch: to fasten again.

dry and large, as though covered with a fine hairy growth, and it tasted bitter in his mouth. His heart gave him a great deal of trouble. When he had travelled a few minutes it would begin a remorseless thump, thump, thump, and then leap up and away in a painful flutter of beats that choked him and made him go faint and dizzy.

In the middle of the day he found two minnows in a large pool. It was impossible to bale it, but he was calmer now and managed to catch them in his tin bucket. They were no longer than his little finger, but he was not particularly hungry. The dull ache in his stomach had been growing duller and fainter. It seemed almost that his stomach was dozing. He ate the fish raw, masticating with painstaking care, for the eating was an act of pure reason. While he had no desire to eat, he knew that he must eat to live.

In the evening he caught three more minnows, eating two and saving the third for breakfast. The sun had dried stray shreds of moss, and he was able to warm himself with hot water. He had not covered more than ten miles that day; and the next day, travelling whenever his heart permitted him, he covered no more than five miles. But his stomach did not give him the slightest uneasiness. It had gone to sleep. He was in a strange country, too, and the caribou were growing more plentiful, also the wolves. Often their yelps drifted across the desolation, and once he saw three of them slinking away before his path.

Another night; and in the morning, being more rational, he untied the leather string that fastened the squat moose-hide sack. From its open mouth poured a yellow stream of coarse gold-dust and nuggets. He roughly divided the gold in halves, caching one half on a prominent ledge, wrapped in a piece of blanket, and returning the other half to the sack. He also began to use strips of the one remaining blanket for his feet. He still clung to his gun, for there were cartridges in that cache by the river Dease. This was a day of fog, and this day hunger awoke in him again. He was very weak and was afflicted with a giddiness which at times blinded him. It was no uncommon thing now for him to stumble and fall; and stumbling once, he fell squarely into a ptarmigan nest. There were four newly hatched chicks, a day old — little specks of pulsating life no more than a mouthful; and he ate them ravenously, thrusting them alive into his mouth and crunching them like egg-shells between his teeth. The mother ptarmigan beat about him with great outcry. He used his gun as a club with which to knock her over, but she dodged out of reach. He threw stones at her and with one chance shot broke a wing. Then she fluttered away, running, trailing the broken wing, with him in pursuit.

The little chicks had no more than whetted his appetite. He hopped and bobbed clumsily along on his injured ankle, throwing stones and screaming hoarsely at times; at other times hopping and bobbing silently along, picking himself up grimly and patiently when he fell, or rubbing his eyes with his hand when the giddiness threatened to overpower him.

The chase led him across swampy ground in the bottom of the valley, and he came upon footprints in the soggy moss. They were not his own — he could see that. They must be Bill's. But he could not stop, for the mother ptarmigan was running on. He would catch her first, then he would return and investigate.

He exhausted the mother ptarmigan; but he exhausted himself. She lay panting on her side. He lay panting on his side, a dozen feet away, unable to crawl to her. And as he recovered she recovered, fluttering out of reach as his hungry hand went out to her. The chase was resumed. Night settled down and she escaped. He stumbled from weakness and pitched head foremost on his face, cutting his cheek, his pack upon his back. He did not move for a long while; then he rolled over on his side, wound his watch, and lay there until morning.

Another day of fog. Half of his last blanket had gone into

foot-wrappings. He failed to pick up Bill's trail. It did not matter. His hunger was driving him too compellingly — only — only he wondered if Bill, too, were lost. By midday the irk of his pack became too oppressive. Again he divided the gold, this time merely spilling half of it on the ground. In the afternoon he threw the rest of it away, there remaining to him only the half-blanket, the tin bucket, and the rifle.

An hallucination began to trouble him. He felt confident that one cartridge remained to him. It was in the chamber of the rifle and he had overlooked it. On the other hand, he knew all the time that the chamber was empty. But the hallucination persisted. He fought it off for hours, then threw his rifle open and was confronted with emptiness. The disappointment was as bitter as though he had really expected to find the cartridge.

He plodded on for half an hour, when the hallucination arose again. Again he fought it, and still it persisted, till for very relief he opened his rifle to unconvince himself. At times his mind wandered farther afield, and he plodded on, a mere automaton, strange conceits and whimsicalities gnawing at his brain like worms. But these excursions out of the real were of brief duration, for ever the pangs of the hunger-bite called him back. He was jerked back abruptly once from such an excursion by a sight that caused him nearly to faint. He reeled and swayed, doddering like a drunken man to keep from falling. Before him stood a horse. A horse! He could not believe his eyes. A thick mist was in them, intershot with sparkling points of light. He rubbed his eyes savagely to clear his vision, and beheld, not a horse, but a great brown bear. The animal was studying him with bellicose curiosity.

The man had brought his gun halfway to his shoulder before he realized. He lowered it and drew his hunting-knife from its beaded sheath at his hip. Before him was meat and life. He ran his thumb along the edge of his knife. It was sharp. The point was sharp. He would fling himself upon the bear and kill it. But his heart began its warning thump, thump, thump. Then followed the wild upward leap and tattoo of flutters, the pressing as of an iron band about his forehead, the creeping of the dizziness into his brain.

His desperate courage was evicted by a great surge of fear. In his weakness, what if the animal attacked him? He drew himself up to his most imposing stature, gripping the knife and staring hard at the bear. The bear advanced clumsily a couple of steps, reared up, and gave vent to a tentative growl. If the man ran, he would run after him; but the man did not run. He was animated now with the courage of fear. He, too, growled, savagely, terribly, voicing the fear that is to life germane and that lies twisted about life's deepest roots.

The bear edged away to one side, growling menacingly, himself appalled by this mysterious creature that appeared upright and unafraid. But the man did not move. He stood like a statue till the danger was past, when he yielded to a fit of trembling and sank down into the wet moss.

He pulled himself together and went on, afraid now in a new way. It was not the fear that he should die passively from lack of food, but that he should be destroyed violently before starvation had exhausted the last particle of the endeavor in him that made toward surviving. There were the wolves. Back and forth across the desolation drifted their howls, weaving the very air into a fabric of menace that was so tangible that he found himself, arms in the air, pressing it back from him as it might be the walls of a wind-blown tent.

Now and again the wolves, in packs of two and three, crossed his path. But they sheered clear of him. They were not in sufficient numbers, and besides they were hunting the caribou, which did not battle, while this strange creature that walked erect might scratch and bite.

In the late afternoon he came upon scattered bones where the wolves had made a kill. The debris had been a caribou calf an hour before, squawking and running and very much alive. He contemplated the bones, clean-picked and polished, pink with the cell-life in them which had not yet died. Could it possibly be that he might be that ere the day was done! Such was life, eh? A vain and fleeting thing. It was only life that pained. There was no hurt in death. To die was to sleep. It meant cessation, rest. Then why was he not content to die?

But he did not moralize long. He was squatting in the moss, a bone in his mouth, sucking at the shreds of life that still dyed it faintly pink. The sweet meaty taste, thin and elusive almost as a memory, maddened him. He closed his jaws on the bones and crunched. Sometimes it was the bone that broke, sometimes his teeth. Then he crushed the bones between rocks, pounded them to a pulp, and swallowed them. He pounded his fingers, too, in his haste, and yet found a moment in which to feel surprise at the fact that his fingers did not hurt much when caught under the descending rock.

Came frightful days of snow and rain. He did not know when he made camp, when he broke camp. He travelled in the night as much as in the day. He rested wherever he fell, crawled on whenever the dying life in him flickered up and burned less dimly. He, as a man, no longer strove. It was the life in him, unwilling to die, that drove him on. He did not suffer. His nerves had become blunted, numb, while his mind was filled with weird visions and delicious dreams.

But ever he sucked and chewed on the crushed bones of the caribou calf, the least remnants of which he had gathered up and carried with him. He crossed no more hills or divides, but automatically followed a large stream which flowed through a wide and shallow valley. He did not see this stream nor this valley. He saw nothing save[15] visions. Soul and body walked or crawled side by side, yet apart, so slender was the thread that bound them.

He awoke in his right mind, lying on his back on a rocky ledge.

15 save: except.

The sun was shining bright and warm. Afar off he heard the squawking of caribou calves. He was aware of vague memories of rain and wind and snow, but whether he had been beaten by the storm for two days or two weeks he did not know.

For some time he lay without movement, the genial sunshine pouring upon him and saturating his miserable body with its warmth. A fine day, he thought. Perhaps he could manage to locate himself. By a painful effort he rolled over on his side. Below him flowed a wide and sluggish river. Its unfamiliarity puzzled him. Slowly he followed it with his eyes, winding in wide sweeps among the bleak, bare hills, bleaker and barer and lower-lying than any hills he had yet encountered. Slowly, deliberately, without excitement or more than the most casual interest, he followed the course of the strange stream toward the sky-line and saw it emptying into a bright and shining sea. He was still unexcited. Most unusual, he thought, a vision or a mirage — more likely a vision, a trick of his disordered mind. He was confirmed in this by sight of a ship lying at anchor in the midst of the shining sea. He closed his eyes for a while, then opened them. Strange how the vision persisted! Yet not strange. He knew there were no seas or ships in the heart of the barren lands, just as he had known there was no cartridge in the empty rifle.

He heard a snuffle behind him — a half-choking gasp or cough. Very slowly, because of his exceeding weakness and stiffness, he rolled over on his other side. He could see nothing near at hand, but he waited patiently. Again came the snuffle and cough, and outlined between two jagged rocks not a score of feet away he made out the gray head of a wolf. The sharp ears were not pricked so sharply as he had seen them on other wolves; the eyes were bleared and bloodshot, the head seemed to droop limply and forlornly. The animal blinked continually in the sunshine. It seemed sick. As he looked it snuffled and coughed again.

This, at least, was real, he thought, and turned on the other side so that he might see the reality of the world which had been veiled from him before by the vision. But the sea still shone in the distance and the ship was plainly discernible. Was it reality, after all? He closed his eyes for a long while and thought, and then it came to him. He had been making north by east, away from the Dease Divide and into the Coppermine Valley. This wide and sluggish river was the Coppermine. That shining sea was the Arctic Ocean. That ship was a whaler, strayed east, far east, from the mouth of the Mackenzie, and it was lying at anchor in Coronation Gulf. He remembered the Hudson Bay Company chart he had seen long ago, and it was all clear and reasonable to him.

He sat up and turned his attention to immediate affairs. He had worn through the blanket-wrappings, and his feet were shapeless lumps of raw meat. His last blanket was gone. Rifle and knife were both missing. He had lost his hat somewhere, with the bunch of matches in the band, but the matches against his chest were safe and dry inside the tobacco pouch and oil paper. He looked at his watch. It marked eleven o'clock and was still running. Evidently he had kept it wound.

He was calm and collected. Though extremely weak, he had no sensation of pain. He was not hungry. The thought of food was not even pleasant to him, and whatever he did was done by his reason alone. He ripped off his pants' legs to the knees and bound them about his feet. Somehow he had succeeded in retaining the tin bucket. He would have some hot water before he began what he foresaw was to be a terrible journey to the ship.

His movements were slow. He shook as with a palsy. When he started to collect dry moss, he found he could not rise to his feet. He tried again and again, then contented himself with crawling about on hands and knees. Once he crawled near to the sick wolf. The animal dragged itself reluctantly out of his way, licking its chops with a tongue which seemed hardly to have the strength to curl. The man noticed that the tongue was not the customary healthy red. It was a yellowish brown and seemed coated with a rough and half-dry mucus.

After he had drunk a quart of hot water the man found he was able to stand, and even to walk as well as a dying man might be supposed to walk. Every minute or so he was compelled to rest. His steps were feeble and uncertain, just as the wolf's that trailed him were feeble and uncertain; and that night, when the shining sea was blotted out by blackness, he knew he was nearer to it by no more than four miles.

Throughout the night he heard the cough of the sick wolf, and now and then the squawking of the caribou calves. There was life all around him, but it was strong life, very much alive and well, and he knew the sick wolf clung to the sick man's trail in the hope that the man would die first. In the morning, on opening his eyes, he beheld it regarding him with a wistful and hungry stare. It stood crouched, with tail between its legs, like a miserable and woe-begone dog. It shivered in the chill morning wind, and grinned dispiritedly when the man spoke to it in a voice that achieved no more than a hoarse whisper.

The sun rose brightly, and all morning the man tottered and fell toward the ship on the shining sea. The weather was perfect. It was the brief Indian Summer [5] of the high latitudes. It might last a week. To-morrow or next day it might be gone.

In the afternoon the man came upon a trail. It was of another man, who did not walk, but who dragged himself on all fours[16]. The man thought it might be Bill, but he thought in a dull, uninterested way. He had no curiosity. In fact, sensation and emotion had left him. He was no longer susceptible to pain. Stomach and nerves had gone to sleep. Yet the life that was in him drove him on. He was very weary,

16 on all fours: on hands and knees.

but it refused to die. It was because it refused to die that he still ate muskeg berries and minnows, drank his hot water, and kept a wary eye on the sick wolf.

He followed the trail of the other man who dragged himself along, and soon came to the end of it — a few fresh-picked bones where the soggy moss was marked by the foot-pads of many wolves. He saw a squat moose-hide sack, mate to his own, which had been torn by sharp teeth. He picked it up, though its weight was almost too much for his feeble fingers. Bill had carried it to the last. Ha! ha! He would have the laugh on Bill. He would survive and carry it to the ship in the shining sea. His mirth was hoarse and ghastly, like a raven's croak, and the sick wolf joined him, howling lugubriously. The man ceased suddenly. How could he have the laugh on Bill if that were Bill; if those bones, so pinky-white and clean, were Bill? [6]

He turned away. Well, Bill had deserted him; but he would not take the gold, nor would he suck Bill's bones. Bill would have, though, had it been the other way around, he mused as he staggered on. He came to a pool of water. Stooping over in quest of minnows, he jerked his head back as though he had been stung. He had caught sight of his reflected face. So horrible was it that sensibility awoke long enough to be shocked. There were three minnows in the pool, which was too large to drain; and after several ineffectual attempts to catch them in the tin bucket he forbore. He was afraid, because of his great weakness, that he might fall in and drown. It was for this reason that he did not trust himself to the river astride one of the many drift-logs which lined its sand-spits.

That day he decreased the distance between him and the ship by three miles; the next day by two — for he was crawling now as Bill had crawled; and the end of the fifth day found the ship still seven miles away and him unable to make even a mile a day. Still the Indian Summer held on, and he continued to crawl and faint, turn and turn about; and ever the sick wolf coughed and wheezed at his heels. His knees had become raw meat like his feet, and though he padded them with the shirt from his back it was a red track he left behind him on the moss and stones. Once, glancing back, he saw the wolf licking hungrily his bleeding trail, and he saw sharply what his own end might be — unless — unless he could get the wolf. Then began as grim a tragedy of existence as was ever played — a sick man that crawled, a sick wolf that limped, two creatures dragging their dying carcasses across the desolation and hunting each other's lives.

Had it been a well wolf, it would not have mattered so much to the man; but the thought of going to feed the maw of that loathsome and all but dead thing was repugnant to him. He was finicky. His mind had begun to wander again, and to be perplexed by hallucinations, while his lucid intervals grew rarer and shorter.

He was awakened once from a faint by a wheeze close in his ear. The wolf leaped lamely back, losing its footing and falling in its weakness. It was ludicrous, but he was not amused. Nor was he even afraid. He was too far gone for that. But his mind was for the moment clear, and he lay and considered. The ship was no more than four miles away. He could see it quite distinctly when he rubbed the mists out of his eyes, and he could see the white sail of a small boat cutting the water of the shining sea. But he could never crawl those four miles. He knew that, and was very calm in the knowledge. He knew that he could not crawl half a mile. And yet he wanted to live. It was unreasonable that he should die after all he had undergone. Fate asked too much of him. And, dying, he declined to die. It was stark madness, perhaps, but in the very grip of Death he defied Death and refused to die.

He closed his eyes and composed himself with infinite precaution. He steeled himself to keep above the suffocating languor that lapped like a rising tide through all the wells of his being. It was very like a sea, this deadly languor, that rose and rose and drowned his consciousness bit by bit. Sometimes he was all but submerged, swimming through oblivion with a faltering stroke; and again, by some strange alchemy of soul, he would find another shred of will and strike out more strongly.

Without movement he lay on his back, and he could hear, slowly drawing near and nearer, the wheezing intake and output of the sick wolf's breath. It drew closer, ever closer, through an infinitude of time, and he did not move. It was at his ear. The harsh dry tongue grated like sandpaper against his cheek. His hands shot out — or at least he willed them to shoot out. The fingers were curved like talons, but they closed on empty air. Swiftness and certitude require strength, and the man had not this strength.

The patience of the wolf was terrible. The man's patience was no less terrible. For half a day he lay motionless, fighting off unconsciousness and waiting for the thing that was to feed upon him and upon which he wished to feed. Sometimes the languid sea rose over him and he dreamed long dreams; but ever through it all, waking and dreaming, he waited for the wheezing breath and the harsh caress of the tongue.

He did not hear the breath, and he slipped slowly from some dream to the feel of the tongue along his hand. He waited. The fangs pressed softly; the pressure increased; the wolf was exerting its last strength in an effort to sink teeth in the food for which it had waited so long. But the man had waited long, and the lacerated hand closed on the jaw. Slowly, while the wolf struggled feebly and the hand clutched feebly, the other hand crept across to a grip. Five minutes later the whole weight of the man's body was on top of the wolf. The hands had not sufficient strength to choke the wolf, but the face of the man was pressed close to the throat of the wolf and the mouth of the man was full of hair. At the end of half an hour the man was aware of a warm trickle in his throat. It was not pleasant. It was like molten lead being forced into his stomach, and it was forced by his will alone. Later the man rolled over on his back and slept. [7]

There were some members of a scientific expedition on the whale-ship *Bedford*. From the deck they remarked a strange object on the shore. It was moving down the beach toward the water. They were unable to classify it, and, being scientific men, they climbed into the whale-boat alongside and went ashore to see. And they saw something that was alive but which could hardly be called a man. It was blind, unconscious. It squirmed along the ground like some monstrous worm. Most of its efforts were ineffectual, but it was persistent, and it writhed and twisted and went ahead perhaps a score of feet an hour.

Three weeks afterward the man lay in a bunk on the whale-ship *Bedford*, and with tears streaming down his wasted cheeks told who he was and what he had undergone. He also babbled incoherently of his mother, of sunny Southern California, and a home among the orange groves and flowers.

The days were not many after that when he sat at table with the scientific men and ship's officers. He gloated over the spectacle of so much food, watching it anxiously as it went into the mouths of others. With the disappearance of each mouthful an expression of deep regret came into his eyes. He was quite sane, yet he hated those men at meal-time. He was haunted by a fear that the food would not last. He inquired of the cook, the cabin-boy, the captain, concerning the food stores. They reassured him countless times; but he could not believe them, and pried cunningly about the lazarette[17] to see with his own eyes.

It was noticed that the man was getting fat. He grew stouter with each day. The scientific men shook their heads and theorized.

17 lazaratte: = lazaretto, a storage space between the decks of a ship.

They limited the man at his meals, but still his girth increased and he swelled prodigiously under his shirt.

The sailors grinned. They knew. And when the scientific men set a watch on the man, they knew too. They saw him slouch for'ard after breakfast, and, like a mendicant, with outstretched palm, accost a sailor. The sailor grinned and passed him a fragment of sea biscuit. He clutched it avariciously, looked at it as a miser looks at gold, and thrust it into his shirt bosom. Similar were the donations from other grinning sailors. The scientific men were discreet. They let him alone. But they privily[18] examined his bunk. It was lined with hardtack; the mattress was stuffed with hardtack; every nook and cranny was filled with hardtack. Yet he was sane. He was taking precautions against another possible famine — that was all. He would recover from it, the scientific men said; and he did, ere the *Bedford*'s anchor rumbled down in San Francisco Bay.

NOTES ON THE TEXT

[1] It should be noted that in the Northland Code of Brotherhood on the Trail a person is not supposed to travel alone. But this maxim is broken by Bill. The protagonist's misguided faith that Bill is waiting for him up ahead fuels his desperate fight for life, ironically illustrating the great importance of brotherhood to decent men like him. And, of course, there is a sense of justice in Bill's death at the end of the story.

[2] As in London's other Klondike stories, the SUN is depicted as a witness to the false deeds of men. Hence in London's stories, the natural forces are capable of both merciless brutalities and impartial observation. Bill's abandonment of his partner, an act that eventually brings him bad luck, cannot escape the eye of the SUN, and the protagonist's extraneous struggle, which is to be rewarded, is not completely out of sight (of the god of sun, so to speak), though in the deserted Canadian tundra within the Arctic Circle.

[3] Great Bear Lake is the largest lake entirely within Canada, the fourth largest in North America. The lake is in the Northwest Territories and is situated on the Arctic Circle between 65 and 67 degrees of northern latitude and between 118 and 123 degrees western longitude, 186 m (610 ft) above sea level.

18 privily: in a private manner, secretly.

[4] Coronation Gulf lies between Victoria Island and mainland Nunavut in Canada. To the northwest it connects with Dolphin and Union Strait and thence the Beaufort Sea and Arctic Ocean; to the northeast it connects with Dease Strait and thence Queen Maud Gulf.

[5] An Indian summer is a period of unseasonably warm, dry weather, occurring after the end of summer proper. The US National Weather Service defines this as weather conditions that are sunny and clear with temperatures above 21°C, following a sharp frost. It is normally associated with late-September to mid-November. There are multiple explanations for the name. The North American Indians — native Americans — depended upon periods of fine, quiet, sunny weather at this time of the year to complete their harvest to see them through the winter.

[6] Please notice that Jack London was never comfortable with the amoral aspects of Evolution. Huxley was troubled by Spencer's "survival of the fittest" as the only possible conclusion as evolution applied to human society. London agreed; he upheld the individual, championed the underdog, and was an avowed socialist. London repeatedly shows in his fiction that merely surviving isn't everything and that what might make one fittest in one environment would not in another, and most of all, that there is a crucial moral dimension to understanding evolution and its impact on humanity. In this story, the protagonist obviously differs, in personality and morality, from his partner Bill, who breaks the code of brotherhood. The protagonist has not only shown his courage and moral sense, he has also proved himself to be the more rational of the two, giving up his gold nuggets to increase his chance of survival, whereas Bill takes the gold with him till his death, a mark of his avarice and lack of common sense.

[7] Notice the brutal competition between man and beast here, which testifies London's sense of the primacy of the will to live and the Darwinian imperative of survival and adaptation to a threatening environment. The protagonist becomes like the wolf that pursues him, learning to wait as patiently as it does for a chance. He eventually kills and drinks blood from the wolf. The story upholds his indomitable spirit of survival.

QUESTIONS FOR DISCUSSION

1. Jack London's writing was influenced by both romanticism and naturalism. In what ways has he shown his naturalistic tendency in his portrayal of characters and depiction of natural environment? To what extent does London's work support or challenge the idea of the "survival of the fittest"?

2. London offers many minute details in his depiction of the man's trek across the Canadian tundra. How do these details contribute to London's represent of the protagonist's indomitable spirit of survival?

3. What does the author want to show by describing the different ways in which the protagonist and Bill handle their respective squat moose-hide sack, which contains gold-dust and nuggets?
4. In this story, Jack London has put a civilized man in confrontation with the brute force of animals. "Then began as grim a tragedy of existence as was ever played — a sick man that crawled, a sick wolf that limped, two creatures dragging their dying carcasses across the desolation and hunting each other's lives." Cite some other examples from the text to illustrate how the protagonist has, in a desperate attempt to survive, been reduced to a beast. Do you think he is any better than a beast under such circumstances? What do you think is the most admirable feature in the protagonist character?

5. In the epigram at the beginning of the story, London writes, "This out of all will remain." What exactly do you think remains for the protagonist after this terrible experience, and for the reader after reading about it? What does Jack London want to show in the story?

SUGGESTED REFERENCES

Auerbach, Jonathan. *Male Call: Becoming Jack London.* Durham: Duke UP, 1996.

Barltrop, Robert. *Jack London: The Man, the Writer, the Rebel.* London: Pluto Press, 1976.

Hedrick, Joan D. *Solitary Comrade, Jack London and His Work.* Chapel Hill: U of North Carolina P, 1982.

London, Joan. *Jack London and His Times.* Seatle: U of Washington P, 1968.

Sheriman, Joan R. *Jack London: A Reference Guide.* Boston: G. K. Hall, 1977.

Sinclair, Andrew. *Jack: A Biography of Jack London.* London: Weidenfeld and Nicolson, 1978.

Stasz, Clarice. *American Dreamers: Charmian and Jack London.* New York: Paragon House, 1991.

Tennant, Roy and Clarice Stasz. *The Jack London Online Collection.* Sonoma State University <http://london.sonoma.edu>.

Unit 9 Mark Twain

(1835 – 1910)

A GUIDE TO LITERARY TERMINOLOGY

"Realism": *Realism was a literary movement that developed in the latter half of the nineteenth century in reaction to the excesses of romanticism. Realism differs from romanticism particularly in its emphasis on an objective presentation of details and events rather than a subjective concentration on personal feelings, perceptions, and imaginings of various characters. Realists often rely heavily on local color, deliberately attempting to portray faithfully the customs, speech, dress, and living and working conditions of their chosen locale. In the decade before the turning of the century, realism had largely given way to naturalism.*

Realism in American literature spanned the years 1865 through 1900. The advent of realism in the U. S. was marked by a shift away from the imaginative sensibility and Emersonian optimism characteristic of the writing of the earlier nineteenth century. The prevailing tenets of the romanticism gave way to the spirit of the new industrialism and to commonplace middle-class life and manners. William Dean Howells, Henry James, and Mark Twain had established the realistic standards for American fiction. Howells outlined the tenets of realism in a book entitled ***Criticism and Fiction*** *(1891). James crafted intricate novels that featured completely realized characters. He was remarkable for his ability to dispense with commentary or subjectivity within his narratives. The reader sees the events through the eyes of the characters. Twain was noteworthy for his faithful reproduction of vernacular speech patterns and vocabulary. He gave birth to "local color," a sub-genre of the novel that still enjoys wide appeal today.*

NOTES ON THE AUTHOR

Mark Twain was a prominent figure in the American Realist movement. He was born Samuel Langhorne Clemens in Florida, Missouri on November 30, 1835 to a Tennessee country merchant, John Marshall Clemens, and Jane Lampton Clemens. When Twain was four, his family relocated to Hannibal, a port town on the Mississippi River which later gave Twain the inspirations for the fictional town of St. Petersburg in *The Adventures of Tom Sawyer* (1876) and *The Adventures of Huckleberry Finn* (1885). When he was 11, his father died of pneumonia. He became a printer's apprentice in 1848 and began to work in 1851 at the *Hannibal Journal*, a newspaper owned by his brother, Orion. He began his career as a writer by writing short sketches while he was still a typesetter for the newspaper. In June 1835, he left Hannibal and travelled, as a journalist, back and forth between New York, Philadelphia, Washington, and Iowa. At the age of 24, he realized his boyhood dream by becoming a steamboat pilot on the Mississippi, which brought him both entertainment and good payment. However, the American Civil War, which broke out in 1861, brought his career as a pilot to an end. He later became a reporter for the Virginia *Territorial Enterprise* and adopted the pen name Mark Twain in 1863. But he left newspaper work after the publication of his first book, *The Innocents Abroad* (1869) and devoted the rest of his life to writing. During his most productive years (1870—1897), he published 18 books, including *Roughing It* (1876), *A Tramp Abroad* (1880), *Life on Mississippi* (1883), *A Connecticut Yankee in King Arthur's Court* (1889), *The Gilded Age* (1873), *The Tragedy of Pudd'nhead Wilson* (1894), *Personal Recollections of Joan of Arc by the Sieur Louis de Conte* (1896), and *Following the Equator* (1897).

Mark Twain wrote his masterpiece, *Huckleberry Finn*, at a time when the lighthearted qualities of his earlier days were in balance with his later skepticism. The book is not only about the historical injustice of racism and slavery, but also about the fundamental conflict that confronts Huck: he has to choose between the law and liberty, the sanctions of the community and the perception of the individual, civil and natural justice. Obviously he has chosen the latter. Mark Twain's novel is characterized by his implicit ironies expressed through the voice of Huck, his use of vernacular English, his local color regionalism, and his portrayal of innocence and evil. His portraits of common, lowly characters as vernacular spokesman were intended to ridicule the values of official culture of his day and the folly of American politics. He has influenced numerous American writers. Ernest Hemingway acknowledges his debt by writing, "All modern American literature comes from one book by Mark Twain called *Huckleberry Finn*."

SYNOPSIS OF THE WORK

Mark Twain wrote *The Adventures of Huckleberry Finn* from 1876 through 1884, as a sequel to *The Adventures of Tom Sawyer*. However, the new tale is told by Huck from a first-person point of view, which differs from the third- person omniscient perspective in *Tom Sawyer*. The novel is essentially the tale of a runaway, Huck, who teams with a runaway slave, Jim, in an ultimately failed attempt to find freedom. The opening of the new novel picks up where the earlier novel has left off: Huck and Tom, who are from opposite ends of the social spectrum, have acquired, at the end of a series of adventures, a pile of loot hidden by some robbers. Huck, a motherless boy raised by an abusive, drunken father, is now placed under the guardianship of the Widow Douglas who, together with her sister, Miss Watson, attempts to "civilize" him by teaching him religion. Constrained by the social order, the false piety of St. Petersburg, and the Widow Douglas and Miss Watson, Huck decides to escape from their house to join Tom's gang of self-proclaimed "robbers." But Huck's shiftless father, Pap Finn, reappears to claim Huck's part of the treasure discovered at the end of *Tom Sawyer*. Pap abducts Huck and imprisons him in an isolated cabin in the woods along the Illinois shoreline. Fortunately, however, Huck succeeds in fleeing his vicious father by faking his own death. His journey changes radically when he meets a runaway slave, Jim who, like Huck, wants to escape to freedom. The two befriend each other and travel together down the Mississippi River on a raft. Yet, they drift past their destination — the free state of Ohio — and make their way farther and farther into the depth of the slaveholding South.

Along the way, Huck and Jim face a series of external threats from a corrupt and parsimonious society, including the Grangerford and Shepherdson feud, the scams of the fake Duke and King (who have in the end secretly sold Jim to Sila Phelps), the Sherburn episode, and a failed attempt to save Jim from bondage after he is imprisoned at the Phelps farm. Finally, Tom Sawyer delivers the news that Jim has already been set free months ago in the will of his now-deceased owner, Miss Watson. And Huck once again faces the possibility of social constraints from Aunt Sally Phelps, who wants to adopt him. However, at the very end of the novel, Huck announces his plan to flee west to the Indian Territory.

SELECTED READINGS

The Adventures of Huckleberry Finn

(Chapter XXXI)

WE dasn't[1] stop again at any town for days and days; kept right along down the river. We was down south in the warm weather now, and a mighty long ways from home. We begun to come to trees with Spanish moss[2] on them, hanging down from the limbs like long, gray

1 dasn't: didn't dare to.

2 Spanish moss: dense festoons of greenish-grey hair-like flexuous strands anchored to tree trunks and branches by sparse wiry roots.

beards. It was the first I ever see it growing, and it made the woods look solemn and dismal. So now the frauds [1] reckoned they was out of danger, and they begun to work the villages again.

First they done a lecture on temperance; but they didn't make enough for them both to get drunk on. Then in another village they started a dancing school; but they didn't know no more how to dance than a kangaroo does; so the first prance they made, the general public jumped in and pranced them out of town. Another time they tried to go at yellocution;[2] but they didn't yellocute long till the audience got up and give them a solid good cussing, and made them skip out. They tackled missionarying, and mesmerizing, and doctoring, and telling fortunes, and a little of everything; but they couldn't seem to have no luck.[3] So at last they got just about dead broke[4], and laid around the raft as she floated along, thinking and thinking, and never saying nothing, by the half a day at a time, and dreadful blue and desperate.

And at last they took a change and begun to lay their heads together in the wigwam and talk low and confidential two or three hours at a time. Jim and me got uneasy. We didn't like the look of it. We judged they was studying up some kind of worse deviltry than ever. We turned it over and over, and at last we made up our minds they was going to break into somebody's house or store, or was going into the counterfeit-money business, or something. So then we was pretty scared, and made up an agreement that we wouldn't have nothing in the world to do with such actions, and if we ever got the least show we would give them the cold shake and clear out and leave them behind. Well, early one morning we hid the raft in a good, safe place about two mile below a little bit of a shabby village named Pikesville, and the king he went ashore and told us all to stay hid whilst he went up to town and smelt around to see if anybody had got any wind of the Royal Nonesuch there yet. ("House to rob, you MEAN," says I to

3 They didn't have any good luck.

4 dead broke: penniless.

myself; "and when you get through robbing it you'll come back here and wonder what has become of me and Jim and the raft — and you'll have to take it out in wondering.") And he said if he warn't[5] back by midday the duke and me would know it was all right, and we was to come along.

So we stayed where we was. The duke he fretted and sweated around, and was in a mighty[6] sour way. He scolded us for everything, and we couldn't seem to do nothing right; he found fault with every little thing. Something was a-brewing, sure. I was good and glad when midday come and no king; we could have a change, anyway — and maybe a chance for the change, on top of it. So me and the duke went up to the village, and hunted around there for the king, and by and by we found him in the back room of a little low doggery, very tight[7], and a lot of loafers bullyragging[8] him for sport, and he a-cussing and a-threatening with all his might, and so tight he couldn't walk, and couldn't do nothing to them. The duke he begun to abuse him for an old fool, and the king begun to sass[9] back,and the minute they was fairly at it, I lit out and shook the reefs out[10] of my hind legs, and spun down the river road like a deer, for I see our chance; and I made up my mind that it would be a long day before they ever see me and Jim again. I got down there all out of breath but loaded up with joy, and sung out —

"Set her loose, Jim! we're all right now!"

But there warn't no answer, and nobody come out of the wigwam. Jim was gone! I set up a shout — and then another — and then another one; and run this way and that in the woods, whooping and screeching; but it warn't no use — old Jim was gone. Then I set down and cried; I couldn't help it. But I couldn't set still long. Pretty soon I

5 warn't: wasn't.
6 mighty: very.
7 tight: (slang) drunk; intoxicated.
8 bullyragging: bullying, teasing.
9 sass: to speak to sb in a rude way, without respect.
10 shook the reefs out: let out the sail on a boat so as to make it go faster. In this sentence, "shook the reefs out of my hind legs" means: get ready to run.

went out on the road, trying to think what I better do, and I run across a boy walking, and asked him if he'd seen a strange nigger dressed so and so, and he says:

"Yes."

"Whereabouts?" says I.

"Down to Silas Phelps'[11] place, two mile below here. He's a runaway nigger, and they've got him. Was you looking for him?"

"You bet I ain't! I run across him in the woods about an hour or two ago, and he said if I hollered he'd cut my livers out — and told me to lay down and stay where I was; and I done it. Been there ever since; afeard[12] to come out."

"Well," he says, "you needn't be afeard no more, becuz they've got him. He run off f'm down South, som'ers."[13]

"It's a good job they got him."

"Well, I *reckon*! There's two hundred dollars reward on him. It's like picking up money out'n the road."

"Yes, it is — and *I* could 'a' had it if I'd been big enough; I see him *first*. Who nailed him?"

"It was an old fellow — a stranger — and he sold out his chance in him for forty dollars, becuz he's got to go up the river and can't wait. Think o' that, now! You bet *I'd* wait, if it was seven year."

"That's me, every time," says I. "But maybe his chance ain't worth no more than that, if he'll sell it so cheap. Maybe there's something ain't straight about it."

"But it *is*, though — straight as a string. I see the handbill myself. It tells all about him, to a dot — paints him like a picture, and tells the plantation he's frum, below NewrLEANS. No-sirree-BOB,[14] they ain't no trouble 'bout *that* speculation, you bet you. Say, gimme a

11 Sila Phelps: Tom's uncle to whom the frauds have sold Jim.

12 afeared: (archaic) afraid.

13 He run off f'm down South, som'ers: he ran off from down south, somewhere.

14 No-sirree-BOB: No, sir.

chaw tobacker, won't ye?"[15]

I didn't have none, so he left. I went to the raft, and set down in the wigwam to think. But I couldn't come to nothing. I thought till I wore my head sore, but I couldn't see no way out of the trouble. After all this long journey, and after all we'd done for them scoundrels, here it was all come to nothing, everything all busted up and ruined, because they could have the heart to serve Jim such a trick as that, and make him a slave again all his life, and amongst strangers, too, for forty dirty dollars.

Once I said to myself it would be a thousand times better for Jim to be a slave at home where his family was, as long as he'd *got* to be a slave, and so I'd better write a letter to Tom Sawyer and tell him to tell Miss Watson [3] where he was. But I soon give up that notion for two things: she'd be mad and disgusted at his rascality and ungratefulness for leaving her, and so she'd sell him straight down the river again; and if she didn't, everybody naturally despises an ungrateful nigger, and they'd make Jim feel it all the time, and so he'd feel ornery and disgraced. And then think of *me*! It would get all around that Huck Finn helped a nigger to get his freedom; and if I was ever to see anybody from that town again, I'd be ready to get down and lick his boots for shame. That's just the way: a person does a low-down thing, and then he don't want to take no consequences of it. Thinks as long as he can hide, it ain't no disgrace. That was my fix[16] exactly. The more I studied about this the more my conscience went to grinding me, and the more wicked and low-down and ornery I got to feeling. And at last, when it hit me all of a sudden that here was the plain hand of Providence[17] slapping me in the face and letting me know my wickedness was being watched all the time from up there in heaven, whilst I was

15 gimme a chaw tobacker, won't ye: Give me a chew of tobacco, won't you?

16 fix: idea, understanding.

17 Providence: God.

stealing a poor old woman's nigger that hadn't ever done me no harm, and now was showing me there's One[18] that's always on the lookout, and ain't agoing to allow no such miserable doings to go only just so fur and no further. I most dropped in my tracks I was so scared. Well, I tried the best I could to kinder soften it up somehow for myself by saying I was brung up wicked, and so I warn't so much to blame; but something inside of me kept saying, "There was the Sunday school, you could 'a' gone to it; and if you'd 'a' done it they'd 'a' learnt you, there, that people that acts as I'd been acting about that nigger goes to everlasting fire[19]."

It made me shiver. And I about made up my mind to pray, and see if I couldn't try to quit being the kind of a boy I was and be better. So I kneeled down. But the words wouldn't come. Why wouldn't they? It warn't no use to try and hide it from Him[20]. Nor from *me*, neither. I knowed very well why they wouldn't come. It was because my heart warn't right; it was because I warn't square; it was because I was playing double. I was letting *on* to give up sin, but away inside of me I was holding on to the biggest one of all. I was trying to make my mouth *say* I would do the right thing and the clean thing, and go and write to that nigger's owner and tell where he was; but deep down in me I knowed it was a lie, [4] and He[21] knowed it. You can't pray a lie — I found that out.

So I was full of trouble, full as I could be; and didn't know what to do. At last I had an idea; and I says, I'll go and write the letter — and *then* see if I can pray. Why, it was astonishing, the way I felt as light as a feather right straight off, and my troubles all gone. So I got a piece of paper and a pencil, all glad and excited, and set down and wrote:

Miss Watson, your runaway nigger Jim is down here two mile

---

18 One: God.
19 everlasting fire: In Christianity, the hell is a place of everlasting fire.
20 Him: God.
21 He: God.

below Pikesville, and Mr. Phelps has got him and he will give him up for the reward if you send.

Huck Finn

I felt good and all washed clean of sin for the first time I had ever felt so in my life, and I knowed I could pray now. But I didn't do it straight off, but laid the paper down and set there thinking — thinking how good it was all this happened so, and how near I come to being lost and going to hell. And went on thinking. And got to thinking over our trip down the river; and I see Jim before me all the time: in the day and in the night-time, sometimes moonlight, sometimes storms, and we a-floating along, talking and singing and laughing. But somehow I couldn't seem to strike no places to harden me against him, but only the other kind. I'd see him standing my watch on top of his'n, 'stead of calling me,[22] so I could go on sleeping; and see him how glad he was when I come back out of the fog; and when I come to him again in the swamp, up there where the feud was; and such-like times; and would always call me honey, and pet me and do everything he could think of for me, and how good he always was; and at last I struck the time I saved him by telling the men we had small-pox aboard, and he was so grateful, and said I was the best friend old Jim ever had in the world, and the *only* one he's got now; and then I happened to look around and see that paper.

It was a close place. I took it up, and held it in my hand. I was a-trembling, because I'd got to decide, forever, betwixt[23] two things, and I knowed it. I studied a minute, sort of holding my breath, and then says to myself:

"All right, then, I'll *go* to hell" — and tore it up. [5]

It was awful thoughts and awful words, but they was said. And

22 He continued to stand watch after finishing his turn, because he didn't want to wake me up. "on top of his'n": in addition to his turn.

23 betwixt: between.

I let them stay said; and never thought no more about reforming.[24] I shoved the whole thing out of my head, and said I would take up wickedness again, which was in my line, being brung up to it, and the other warn't. [6] And for a starter I would go to work and steal Jim out of slavery again; and if I could think up anything worse, I would do that, too; because as long as I was in, and in for good, I might as well go the whole hog[25].

Then I set to thinking over how to get at it, and turned over some considerable many ways in my mind; and at last fixed up a plan that suited me. So then I took the bearings of a woody island[26] that was down the river a piece, and as soon as it was fairly dark I crept out with my raft and went for it, and hid it there, and then turned in. I slept the night through, and got up before it was light, and had my breakfast, and put on my store clothes, and tied up some others and one thing or another in a bundle, and took the canoe and cleared for shore. I landed below where I judged was Phelps's place, and hid my bundle in the woods, and then filled up the canoe with water, and loaded rocks into her and sunk her where I could find her again when I wanted her, about a quarter of a mile below a little steam sawmill that was on the bank.

Then I struck up the road, and when I passed the mill I see a sign on it, "Phelps's Sawmill," and when I come to the farm-houses, two or three hundred yards further along, I kept my eyes peeled,[27] but didn't see nobody around, though it was good daylight now. But I didn't mind, because I didn't want to see nobody just yet — I only wanted to get the lay of the land[28]. According to my plan, I was going to turn up there from the village, not from below. So I just took a look, and

---

24 I've made up my mind. I won't change my decision.
25 go the whole hog: spare no effort and get it done completely.
26 took the bearings of a woody island: found out the direction of the woody island.
27 kept my eyes peeled: kept my eyes open.
28 get the lay of the land: become familiar with the area.

shoved along, straight for town. Well, the very first man I see when I got there was the duke. He was sticking up a bill for the Royal Nonesuch — three-night performance — like that other time. *They* had the cheek[29], them frauds! I was right on him before I could shirk. He looked astonished, and says:

"Hel-lo! Where'd *you* come from?" Then he says, kind of glad and eager, "Where's the raft? — got her in a good place?"

I says:

"Why, that's just what I was going to ask your grace."

Then he didn't look so joyful, and says:

"What was your idea for asking *me*?" he says.

"Well," I says, "when I see the king in that doggery yesterday, I says to myself, we can't get him home for hours, till he's soberer; so I went a-loafing around town to put in the time, and wait. A man up and offered me ten cents to help him pull a skiff over the river and back to fetch a sheep, and so I went along; but when we was dragging him to the boat, and the man left me a-holt of[30] the rope and went behind him to shove him along, he was too strong for me and jerked loose and run, and we after him. We didn't have no dog, and so we had to chase him all over the country till we tired him out. We never got him till dark; then we fetched him over, and I started down for the raft. When I got there and see it was gone, I says to myself, 'They've got into trouble and had to leave; and they've took my nigger, which is the only nigger I've got in the world, and now I'm in a strange country, and ain't got no property no more, nor nothing, and no way to make my living;' so I set down and cried. I slept in the woods all night. But what *did* become of the raft, then? — and Jim — poor Jim!"

"Blamed if I know — that is, what's become of the raft. That old fool had made a trade and got forty dollars, and when we found him in

---

29 had the cheek: were shameless, had the nerve.

30 left me a-holt of: let me hold.

the doggery the loafers had matched half dollars with him and got every cent but what he'd spent for whisky; [31] and when I got him home late last night and found the raft gone, we said, 'That little rascal has stole our raft and shook us, and run off down the river.'"

"I wouldn't shake my *nigger*, would I? — the only nigger I had in the world, and the only property."

"We never thought of that. Fact is, I reckon we'd come to consider him *our* nigger; yes, we did consider him so — goodness knows we had trouble enough for him. So when we see the raft was gone and we flat broke[32], there warn't anything for it but to try the Royal Nonesuch another shake[33]. And I've pegged along[34] ever since, dry as a powder-horn. Where's that ten cents? Give it here."

I had considerable money, so I give him ten cents, but begged him to spend it for something to eat, and give me some, because it was all the money I had, and I hadn't had nothing to eat since yesterday. He never said nothing. The next minute he whirls on me and says:

"Do you reckon that nigger would blow on us[35] ? We'd skin him if he done that!"

"How can he blow? Hain't he run off?"

"No! That old fool sold him, and never divided with me, and the money's gone."

"*Sold* him?" I says, and begun to cry; "why, he was *my* nigger, and that was my money. Where is he? — I want my nigger."

"Well, you can't *get* your nigger, that's all — so dry up your blubbering. Looky here — do you think *you'd* venture to blow on us? Blamed if I think I'd trust you. Why, if you *was* to blow on us — "

He stopped, but I never see the duke look so ugly out of his eyes

31 The loafers gambled with him and won all his money except his whisky fee.
32 we flat broke: we were left with nothing, we were completely broke.
33 shake: a bargain or deal.
34 I've pegged along: I've worked very hard.
35 blow on us: report on us.

before. I went on a-whimpering, and says:

"I don't want to blow on nobody; and I ain't got no time to blow, nohow. I got to turn out and find my nigger."

He looked kinder bothered, and stood there with his bills fluttering on his arm, thinking, and wrinkling up his forehead. At last he says:

"I'll tell you something. We got to be here three days. If you'll promise you won't blow, and won't let the nigger blow, I'll tell you where to find him."

So I promised, and he says:

"A farmer by the name of Silas Ph — " and then he stopped. You see, he started to tell me the truth; but when he stopped that way, and begun to study and think again, I reckoned he was changing his mind. And so he was. He wouldn't trust me; he wanted to make sure of having me out of the way the whole three days. So pretty soon he says:

"The man that bought him is named Abram Foster — Abram G. Foster — and he lives forty mile back here in the country, on the road to Lafayette."

"All right," I says, "I can walk it in three days. And I'll start this very afternoon."

"No you won't, you'll start *now*; and don't you lose any time about it, neither, nor do any gabbling by the way. Just keep a tight tongue in your head and move right along, and then you won't get into trouble with *us*, d'ye hear?"

That was the order I wanted, and that was the one I played for. I wanted to be left free to work my plans.

"So clear out," he says; "and you can tell Mr. Foster whatever you want to. Maybe you can get him to believe that Jim *is* your nigger — some idiots don't require documents — leastways I've heard there's such down South here. And when you tell him the handbill and the reward's bogus, maybe he'll believe you when you explain to him what the idea was for getting 'em out. Go 'long now, and tell him anything you want to; but mind you don't work your jaw any *between* here and there."[36]

So I left, and struck for the back country. I didn't look around, but I kinder felt like he was watching me. But I knowed I could tire him out at that. I went straight out in the country as much as a mile before I stopped; then I doubled back through the woods towards Phelps'. I reckoned I better start in on my plan straight off without fooling around, because I wanted to stop Jim's mouth till these fellows could get away. I didn't want no trouble with their kind. I'd seen all I wanted to of them, and wanted to get entirely shut of them.

NOTES ON THE TEXT

[1] The "frauds" here refers to the two swindlers who claim themselves to be the Duke (of Bridgewater) and the King (the son of Louis XVI). Earlier, Jim and Huck, thinking that they were escaping from persecution, took them aboard their raft. But soon the "duke" and "king" become permanent passengers on Jim and Huck's raft, committing all along their journey a series of confidence schemes. In this part of the story, they have advertised a three-night engagement of a play called the "Royal Nonesuch," which turns out to be a money-making scam.

[2] "Yellocution" is a word coined by Huck, which means "elocution" — or the art of public speaking; notice the use of "yell" in the word. Huck also uses "yellocute" as the verb. "Missionarying" (which means "giving sermons") and "doctoring" (which means "treating patients) are two other examples of the improper use of words. It is worthy of our notice that Huck is a motherless child brought up by an irresponsible and shiftless father (who is in fact a town drunk) and a semiliterate adolescent. Mark Twain makes him the narrator of the story. So the book, in a sense, is Huck's autobiography. The language in which Huck uses in telling his story is colloquial and ungrammatical, which reflects the reality of his education as well as the characteristics of the dialect Huck speaks.

[3] Miss Watson is Jim's owner. She is the sister of Huck's guardian, Widow Douglas, who is kind to Huck and tries to train Huck into a "civilized" man, believing this to be her Christian duty.

[4] Here Huck is caught in the dilemma of being true to himself and being true to the religion

36 Don't work your jaw any between here and there: Don't tell lies.

he is taught and the law. What he regards as "right" (in this case, telling Miss Watson Jim's whereabouts is a law-abiding act) is perceived to be wrong (in this case, telling Miss Watson Jim's whereabouts is an act of betraying a close friend) in the bottom of his heart. Mark Twain, by putting Huck in such a complex and difficult situation, would elicit Huck's reasoning intellect as well as the reader's.

[5] Huck's final decision to tear up the letter indicates both his courage and his sense of morality. Huck's capacity to make his own choice in accordance to his judgment, a trait of his maturity, makes him a kind of existential hero. By saying "All right, then, I'll go to hell," he has clearly accepted his personal moral responsibility as well as his personal moral freedom. By making Huck feel condemned to the everlasting hellish fire, Mark Twain has, artistically and with a touch of humor, condemned the value system both he and Huck rejects.

[6] "I shoved the whole thing out of my head, and said I would take up wickedness again, which was in my line, being brung up to it, and the other warn't." It is sad to note here that Huck regards himself as being born wicked. He sounds as if wickedness were in his nature. He is brought up to it, so to speak. The implicit irony that Mark Twain intends is that Huck considers his ultimate decision — an act of morality — to be an immoral act under the terms of conventional morality of his day. This contradiction reveals the evil effect of socio-cultural indoctrination to which Huck has been subjected.

QUESTIONS FOR DISCUSSION

1. Discuss some of the ironies contained in this chapter. What, for instance, is ironic about Huck's view of religion and of God? What is ironic about the scams of the Duke and the King? What is the author's intention in bringing them to the story?

2. Discuss Huck's equivocation about what to do when he is faced with a vital ethical dilemma. What has finally made him decide to free Jim from imprisonment on the Phelps Farm? In what ways has this chapter captured the most important traits of the character of Huck and Jim? How do both characters reveal both strength and vulnerability? How does this mixed trait in their character make them depend more on each other?

3. The novel's concern with race has become more prominent during the past fifty years. The novel is sometimes criticized for its use of racist language for instance, the word "nigger" appears over two hundred times in the novel. Is there any difference in the way Huck treats Jim and the way he thinks about blacks and fugitive slaves in general? If yes, then how do you interpret the difference? How do Huck and Jim struggle with how they are defined by the society? Does contact with characters and communities along the river affect Huck's awareness of Jim's humanity? To what extent has Huck found emotional comfort in Jim?

4. Why does Huck lie to a boy, to whom he inquires about the whereabouts of a "strange nigger," about his relationship with the "nigger," and to the Duke about his activities of the previous day? How do you view Huck's dishonesty?

SUGGESTED REFERENCES

Camfield, Gregg. *The Oxford Companion to Mark Twain.* New York: Oxford UP, 2003.

Chadwick-Joshua, Jocelyn. *The Jim Dilemma: Reading Race in **Huckleberry Finn**.* Jackson: UP of Mississippi, 1998.

Doyno, Victor A. *Writing **Huck Finn**: Mark Twain's Creative Process.* Philadelphia: U of Pennsylvania P , 1991.

Emerson, Everett. *Mark Twain: A Literary Life.* Philadelphia: University of Pennsylvania Press, 2000.

Graff, Gerald and James Phelan. ***Adventures of Huckleberry Finn**: A Case Study in Critical Controversy.* Boston: Bedford Books of St. Martin's Press, 1995.

Leonard, James S., Thomas A. Tenney, and Thadious M. Davis, eds. *Satire or Evasion? Black Perspectives of **Huckleberry Finn**.* Durham: Duke UP, 1992.

Power, Ron. *Mark Twain: A Life.* New York: Free Press, 2005.

Quirk, Tom. *Coming to Grips with **Huckleberry Finn**: Essays on a Book, a Boy, and a Man.* Columbia: U of Missouri P, 1993.

Stattelmeyer, Robert and J. Donald Crowley, eds. *One Hundred Years of **Huckleberry Finn**.* Columbia: U of Missouri P, 1985.

Unit 10 Theodore Dreiser

(1871 – 1945)

A GUIDE TO LITERARY TERMINOLOGY

"Naturalism and Biological Determinism": *Naturalism was a movement in literature that sought to portray events and characters in a detailed, detached, and realistic way. Another important element of naturalism is the idea that a story's characters are conditioned or controlled by environment, heredity, instinct or chance. In his novels* ***Sister Carrie*** *and* ***An American Tragedy****, Dreiser departs from traditional plots in which hard work and perseverance inevitably yield success and happiness. Instead, he depicts the world as an animal kingdom in which the "human beasts" are controlled and conditioned by random occurrences and their biological instincts. For example,* ***Sister Carrie*** *shows a marked difference from the gentility and timidity that characterized the nineteenth-century realistic fiction. Dreiser portrays, in uncompromising detail, the events that led his protagonist first into prostitution and then to the attainment of success and financial security as an actress. He seemed to have deliberately avoided the question of morality. The novel illustrates Dreiser's interpretation of complex human relationships as purely biological functions: Carrie exhibits what has been called "neo-Darwinian adaptability," surviving and prospering because she is able to adjust to whatever advantageous situations develop.*

NOTES ON THE AUTHOR

Theodore Dreiser, one of the greatest American literary Naturalists (including Stephen Crane, Frank Norris, and Jack London), was brought up in Terre Haute, Indiana, by his German immigrant father John Dreiser, a fiercely pious Catholic, and his mother Sarah Dreiser, who was converted to Roman Catholicism in order to marry John. Theodore was one of the 13 children in the family who were reared as Catholics. At 15, Theodore fled to Chicago where he picked up some sporadic menial jobs to make a living. Finally, he got a job at a newspaper, working in various cities: St. Louis, Cleveland, Pittsburgh, and eventually New York City, where he became a freelance journalist and a magazine editor. He began to write his first novel *Sister Carrie* in 1899 and published it in 1900. Although the novel did not sell well (fewer than 500 copies) in the beginning, the novel remains a great work of naturalism and realism for its exploration of the gritty details of human nature as well as how the process of industrialization affected the American people.

Continuing to work as a journalist, Dreiser took ten years to publish his next novel *Jennie Gerhardt* (1911), which was followed by his "Trilogy of Desire" consisting of *The Financier* (1912), *The Titan* (1914), and *The Stoic*, which was published posthumously in 1947. Dreiser was influenced by Thomas Huxley and Herbert Spencer's idea of the "survival of the fittest." In this trilogy, he not only sympathizes with the weak and the victimized but also empathizes with the Nietzschean business superman, Frank Cowperwood, the hero of all three novels, who resolves to be like an animal that can "adapt itself to conditions." He rises to power, but he, too, is eventually defeated. Dreiser would like his reader to understand that there is no moral to Cowperwood's failure any more than there is to his success. *An American Tragedy*, his greatest work and a critical and commercial success, was published in 1925. The book tells the story of how Clyde falls in love with a rich girl, Sondra. In order to marry her, he murders, or at least intends to murder, his pregnant girlfriend, Roberta. He spends the rest of his time facing indictment, trial, conviction, and execution. Like *Sister Carrie*, the novel captures the real condition of life — the restless heart of man. It depicts a protagonist who is the victim of both circumstance and of his own dream.

Politically, Dreiser was a socialist and was involved in several political campaigns including the lynching of Frank Little, the Sacco and Vanzetti case, the deportation of Emma Goldman, and the conviction of Tom Mooney. Dreiser had written some non-fiction books on political issues, including *Dreiser Looks at Russia* (1928), a result of his trip to the Soviet Union in 1927, *Tragic America* (1931) and *America Is Worth Saving* (1941). He joined the Communist Party shortly before he died in Hollywood in 1945, at the age of 74.

SYNOPSIS OF THE WORK

Sister Carrie was Dreiser's first novel (1900), which has come to be regarded as an American classic. It depicts the inevitable condition of human beings as the naturalistic victims of circumstance. Dreiser reproduces the standard sentimental plot in which a young girl journeys from the rural hinterland to the sinful city. But Dreiser reverts and distort this tradition: the girl's seduction results in her fortune rising rather than falling.

Money, success, sex seem to be the only aims for Dreiser's characters, including Carrie Meeber and George Hurstwood, but none of these can ultimately satisfy them. Dreiser thus commented on man: "His feet are in the trap of circumstance;

his eyes are on an illusion."

In August 1889, the protagonist of the novel, Carrie, an 18 years old Midwestern country girl, heads off for the metropolis of Chicago where her older sister Minnie and her husband agree to take her in while she looks for a job. On the train, she gets acquainted with a travelling salesman, Charles Drouet, who is attracted to her pretty looks and unspoiled manner. In Chicago, Carrie finds a job in a shoe factory, but she soon loses it after an illness. One day, Carrie encounters Charles Drouet, who promises to buy her good clothes and persuades her to move in with him. Tempted by a vista of comfortable life, Carrie agrees. Before too long, Drouet introduces to Carrie a friend of his, George Hurstwood, the manager of a respectable bar called Fitzgerald and Moy's. Hurstwood is swept off his feet by Carrie's youth and beauty. Carrie is also attracted by Hurstwood's fine manners and the qualities of his clothes. They soon start an affair secretly. By now, Carrie becomes a small-time actress for a local theater. Later, Drouet discovers he has been cuckolded, Carrie learns that Hurstwood is married with chidren, and Hurstwood's wife Julia is informed of her husband's affair with another woman. Julia threatens to divorce him. In a fit of frenzy, Hurstwood absconds with a large sum of money stolen from the bar he works for and manages to convince Carrie to board a train with him headed for Canada. In Montreal, Hurstwood's guilty conscience induces him to return most of the stolen money and marries Carrie under an assumed name. They move to New York City, where Hurstwood gradually sinks into depression and despair. He gambles away all his money, becomes a drunken beggar, joins the homeless of New York, and finally takes his own life in a Bowery flophouse. Carrie, on the other hand, prospers as a showgirl on the Broadway stage. She deserts Hurstwood when he falls on hard times, establishes a friendship with a colleague named Lola Osborne and moves in with her.

Carrie is, like so many of Dreiser's outcasts, given to moral expediency. When her conscience questions her about what she is doing, the reply is simple: "The voice of want made answer for her." This stance has provoked many controversies over Dreiser's moral position and has made his novel a departure from the conventional literature of his times. At the end of the novel, Carrie is unhappy and lonely. She is destined to know "neither surfeit nor content" as she sits dreamily in her rocking chair. That, Dreiser believes, is the human condition, not a punishment for the errant protagonist.

The following selection of reading is from chapter 47 of *Sister Carrie*, the last of the novel.

SELECTED READINGS

Sister Carrie

(Excerpts from Chapter XLVII "The Way of the Beaten: A Harp in the Wind")

...

By January he had about concluded that the game was up with him. Life had always seemed a precious thing, but now constant want and weakened vitality had made the charms of earth rather dull and inconspicuous. Several times, when fortune pressed most harshly, he thought he would end his troubles; but with a change of weather, or the arrival of a quarter or a dime, his mood would change, and he would wait. Each day he would find some old paper lying about and look into it, to see if there was any trace of Carrie, but all summer and fall he had looked in vain. Then he noticed that his eyes were beginning to hurt him, and this ailment rapidly increased until, in the dark chambers of the lodgings he frequented, he did not attempt to read. Bad and irregular eating was weakening every function of his body. The one recourse left him was to doze when a place offered and he could get the money to occupy it.

He was beginning to find, in his wretched clothing and meager state of body, that people took him for a chronic type of bum and beggar. Police hustled him along, restaurant and lodging-house keepers turned him out promptly the moment he had his due; pedestrians waved him off. He found it more and more difficult to get anything from anybody.

At last he admitted to himself that the game was up. It was after a long series of appeals to pedestrians, in which he had been refused and refused — every one hastening from contact.

"Give me a little something, will you, mister?" he said to the last one. "For God's sake, do; I'm starving."

"Aw, get out," said the man, who happened to be a common type himself. "You're no good. I'll give you nawthin[1]'."

Hurstwood put his hands, red from cold, down in his pockets. Tears came into his eyes.

"That's right," he said; "I'm no good now. I was all right. I had money. I'm going to quit this," and, with death in his heart, he started down toward the Bowery. [1] People had turned on the gas before and died; why shouldn't he? He remembered a lodging-house where there were little, close rooms, with gas-jets in them, almost pre-arranged, he thought, for what he wanted to do, which rented for fifteen cents. Then he remembered that he had no fifteen cents.

On the way he met a comfortable-looking gentleman, coming, clean-shaven, out of a fine barber shop. "Would you mind giving me a little something?" he asked this man boldly.

The gentleman looked him over and fished for a dime. Nothing but quarters were in his pocket.

"Here," he said, handing him one, to be rid of him. "Be off, now."

Hurstwood moved on, wondering. The sight of the large, bright coin pleased him a little. He remembered that he was hungry and that he could get a bed for ten cents. With this, the idea of death passed, for the time being, out of his mind. It was only when he could get nothing but insults that death seemed worth while.

One day, in the middle of the winter, the sharpest spell of the season set in. It broke gray and cold in the first day, and on the second snowed. Poor luck pursuing him, he had secured but ten cents by nightfall, and this he had spent for food. At evening he found himself at the Boulevard and Sixty-seventh Street, where he finally turned his face Bowery-ward. Especially fatigued because of the wandering propensity which had seized him in the morning, he now half dragged his wet feet, shuffling the soles upon the sidewalk. An old, thin coat was

1 nawthin': nothing.

turned up about his red ears — his cracked derby hat was pulled down until it turned them outward. His hands were in his pockets.

"I'll just go down Broadway," he said to himself.

When he reached Forty-second Street, the fire signs were already blazing brightly. Crowds were hastening to dine. Through bright windows, at every corner, might be seen gay companies in luxuriant restaurants. There were coaches and crowded cable cars.

In his weary and hungry state, he should never have come here. The contrast was too sharp. Even he was recalled keenly to better things.

"What's the use?" he thought. "It's all up with me. I'll quit this."

People turned to look after him, so uncouth was his shambling figure. Several officers followed him with their eyes, to see that he did not beg of anybody.

Once he paused in an aimless, incoherent sort of way and looked through the windows of an imposing restaurant, before which blazed a fire sign, and through the large, plate windows of which could be seen the red and gold decorations, the palms, the white napery, and shining glassware, and, above all, the comfortable crowd. Weak as his mind had become, his hunger was sharp enough to show the importance of this. He stopped stock still, his frayed trousers soaking in the slush, and peered foolishly in.

"Eat," he mumbled. "That's right, eat. Nobody else wants any." [2]

Then his voice dropped even lower, and his mind half lost the fancy it had.

"It's mighty cold," he said. "Awful cold."

At Broadway and Thirty-ninth Street was blazing, in incandescent fire, Carrie's name. "Carrie Madenda," it read, "and the Casino Company." All the wet, snowy sidewalk was bright with this radiated fire. It was so bright that it attracted Hurstwood's gaze. He looked up, and then at a large, gilt-framed posterboard, on which was a fine lithograph of Carrie, life-size.

Hurstwood gazed at it a moment, snuffling and hunching one shoulder, as if something were scratching him. He was so run down, however, that his mind was not exactly clear.

He approached that entrance and went in.

"Well?" said the attendant, staring at him. Seeing him pause, he went over and shoved him. "Get out of here," he said.

"I want to see Miss Madenda," he said.

" You do, eh?" the other said, almost tickled at the spectacle. "Get out of here," and he shoved him again.

Hurstwood had no strength to resist. "I want to see Miss Madenda," he tried to explain, even as he was being hustled away. "I'm all right. I —"

The man gave him a last push and closed the door. As he did so, Hurstwood slipped and fell in the snow. It hurt him, and some vague sense of shame returned. He began to cry and swear foolishly.

"God damned dog!" he said. "Damned old cur," wiping the slush from his worthless coat. "I — I hired such people as you once."

Now a fierce feeling against Carrie welled up — just one fierce, angry thought before the whole thing slipped out of his mind.

"She owes me something to eat," he said. "She owes it to me."

Hopelessly he turned back into Broadway again and slopped onward and away, begging, crying, losing track of his thoughts, one after another, as a mind decayed and disjointed is wont to do.

It was truly a wintry evening, a few days later, when his one distinct mental decision was reached. Already, at four o'clock, the somber hue of night was thickening the air. A heavy snow was falling — a fine picking, whipping snow, borne forward by a swift wind in long, thin lines. The streets were bedded with it — six inches of cold, soft carpet, churned to a dirty brown by the crush of teams and the feet of men. Along Broadway men picked their way in ulsters[2] and umbrellas. Along the Bowery, men slouched through it with collars and hats pulled over their ears. In the former thoroughfare businessmen and travelers were making for comfortable hotels.

In the latter, crowds on cold errands[3] shifted past dingy stores, in the deep recesses of which lights were already gleaming. There were early lights in the cable cars, whose usual clatter was reduced by the mantle about the wheels. The whole city was muffled by this fast-thickening mantle[4].

In her comfortable chambers at the Waldorf[5], Carrie was reading at this time "Pere Goriot," [3] which Ames had recommended to her. It was so strong, and Ames's mere recommendation had so aroused her interest, that she caught nearly the full sympathetic significance of it. For the first time, it was being borne in upon her how silly and worthless had been her earlier reading, as a whole. Becoming wearied, however, she yawned and came to the window, looking out upon the old winding procession of carriages rolling up Fifth Avenue.

"Isn't it bad?" she observed to Lola.

"Terrible!" said that little lady, joining her. "I hope it snows enough to go sleigh riding."

"Oh, dear," said Carrie, with whom the sufferings of Father Goriot were still keen.

"That's all you think of. Aren't you sorry for the people who haven't anything to-night?"

"Of course I am," said Lola; "but what can I do? I haven't anything."

Carrie smiled.

---

2 ulster: a long, loose overcoat of frieze or other rough cloth, frequently with a waist-belt.
3 crowds on cold errands: people who were in the streets running their business in cold weather.
4 this fast-thickening mantle: this snow that quickly accumulated and thickened.
5 the Waldorf: a luxury hotel in New York City then.

"You wouldn't care, if you had," she returned.

"I would, too," said Lola. "But people never gave me anything when I was hard up."

"Isn't it just awful?" said Carrie, studying the winter's storm.

"Look at that man over there," laughed Lola, who had caught sight of some one falling down. "How sheepish men look when they fall, don't they?"

"We'll have to take a coach to-night," answered Carrie absently.

In the lobby of the Imperial[6], Mr. Charles Drouet was just arriving, shaking the snow from a very handsome ulster. Bad weather had driven him home early and stirred his desire for those pleasures which shut out the snow and gloom of life. A good dinner, the company of a young woman, and an evening at the theater were the chief things for him.

"Why, hello, Harry!" he said, addressing a lounger in one of the comfortable lobby chairs. "How are you?"

"Oh, about six and six,"[7] said the other.

"Rotten weather, isn't it?"

"Well, I should say," said the other. "I've been just sitting here thinking where I'd go to-night."

"Come along with me," said Drouet. "I can introduce you to something dead swell[8]."

"Who is it?" said the other.

"Oh, a couple of girls over here in Fortieth Street. We could have a dandy time. I was just looking for you."

"Supposing you get 'em and take 'em out to dinner?"

"Sure," said Drouet. "Wait'll I go upstairs and change my clothes."

"Well, I'll be in the barber shop," said the other. "I want to get a

---

6 the Imperial: an expensive hotel in New York City.

7 about six and six: just so so.

8 something dead swell: something really nice.

shave."

"All right," said Drouet, creaking off in his good shoes toward the elevator. The old butterfly was as light on the wing as ever.

On an incoming vestibuled Pullman[9], speeding at forty miles an hour through the snow of the evening, were three others, all related.

"First call for dinner in the dining-car," a Pullman servitor was announcing, as he hastened through the aisle in snow-white apron and jacket.

"I don't believe I want to play any more," said the youngest, a black-haired beauty, turned supercilious by fortune, as she pushed a euchre hand [4] away from her.

"Shall we go into dinner?" inquired her husband, who was all that fine raiment can make.[10]

"Oh, not yet," she answered. "I don't want to play any more, though."

"Jessica," said her mother, who was also a study in what good clothing can do for age, "push that pin down in your tie — it's coming up."

Jessica obeyed, incidentally touching at her lovely hair and looking at a little jewel-faced watch. Her husband studied her, for beauty, even cold, is fascinating from one point of view.

"Well, we won't have much more of this weather," he said. "It only takes two weeks to get to Rome."

Mrs. Hurstwood nestled comfortably in her corner and smiled. It was so nice to be the mother-in-law of a rich young man — one whose financial state had borne her personal inspection. [5]

"Do you suppose the boat will sail promptly?" asked Jessica, "if it keeps up like this?"

---

9 Pullman: a type of railway carriage which is extremely comfortable and luxurious.
10 who was all that fine raiment can make: who was extremely well-dressed.

"Oh, yes," answered her husband. "This won't make any difference."

Passing down the aisle came a very fair-haired banker's son, also of Chicago, who had long eyed this supercilious beauty. Even now he did not hesitate to glance at her, and she was conscious of it. With a specially conjured show of indifference, she turned her pretty face wholly away. It was not wifely modesty at all. By so much was her pride satisfied.

At this moment Hurstwood stood before a dirty four-story building in a side street quite near the Bowery, whose one-time coat of buff had been changed by soot and rain. He mingled with a crowd of men — a crowd which had been, and was still, gathering by degrees.

It began with the approach of two or three, who hung about the closed wooden doors and beat their feet to keep them warm. They had on faded derby hats with dents in them. Their misfit coats were heavy with melted snow and turned up at the collars. Their trousers were mere bags, frayed at the bottom and wobbling over big, soppy shoes, torn at the sides and worn almost to shreds. They made no effort to go in, but shifted ruefully about, digging their hands deep in their pockets and leering at the crowd and the increasing lamps. With the minutes, increased the number. There were old men with grizzled beards and sunken eyes, men who were comparatively young but shrunken by diseases, men who were middle-aged. None were fat. There was a face in the thick of the collection which was as white as drained veal. There was another red as brick. Some came with thin, rounded shoulders, others with wooden legs, still others with frames so lean that clothes only flapped about them. There were great ears, swollen noses, thick lips, and, above all, red, blood-shot eyes. Not a normal, healthy face in the whole mass; not a straight figure; not a straightforward, steady glance. [6]

In the drive of the wind and sleet they pushed in on one another.

There were wrists, unprotected by coat or pocket, which were red with cold. There were ears, half covered by every conceivable semblance of a hat, which still looked stiff and bitten. In the snow they shifted, now one foot, now another, almost rocking in unison.

With the growth of the crowd about the door came a murmur. It was not conversation, but a running comment directed at any one in general. It contained oaths and slang phrases.

"By damn, I wish they'd hurry up."

"Look at the copper watchin'[11]."

"Maybe it ain't winter, nuther!"

"I wisht I was in Sing Sing[12]."

Now a sharper lash of wind cut down and they huddled closer. It was an edging, shifting, pushing throng. There was no anger, no pleading, no threatening words. It was all sullen endurance, unlightened by either wit or good fellowship.

A carriage went jingling by with some reclining figure in it. One of the men nearest the door saw it.

"Look at the bloke ridin'."

"He ain't so cold."

"Eh, eh, eh!" yelled another, the carriage having long since passed out of hearing.

Little by little the night crept on. Along the walk a crowd turned out on its way home. Men and shop-girls went by with quick steps. The cross-town cars began to be crowded. The gas lamps were blazing, and every window bloomed ruddy with a steady flame. Still the crowd hung about the door, unwavering.

"Ain't they ever goin' to open up?" queried a hoarse voice, suggestively.

This seemed to renew the general interest in the closed door, and

---

11 copper watchin': (slang) a cop watching.

12 Sing Sing: a prison in New York state.

many gazed in that direction. They looked at it as dumb brutes look, as dogs paw and whine and study the knob. They shifted and blinked and muttered, now a curse, now a comment. Still they waited and still the snow whirled and cut them with biting flakes. On the old hats and peaked shoulders it was piling. It gathered in little heaps and curves and no one brushed it off. In the center of the crowd the warmth and steam melted it, and water trickled off hat rims and down noses, which the owners could not reach to scratch. On the outer rim the piles remained unmelted. Hurstwood, who could not get in the center, stood with head lowered to the weather and bent his form.

A light appeared through the transom overhead. It sent a thrill of possibility through the watchers. There was a murmur of recognition. At last the bars grated inside and the crowd pricked up its ears. Footsteps shuffled within and it murmured again. Some one called: "Slow up there, now," and then the door opened. It was push and jam for a minute, with grim, beast silence to prove its quality, and then it melted inward, like logs floating, and disappeared. There were wet hats and wet shoulders, a cold, shrunken, disgruntled mass, pouring in between bleak walls. It was just six o'clock and there was supper in every hurrying pedestrian's face. And yet no supper was provided here — nothing but beds.

Hurstwood laid down his fifteen cents and crept off with weary steps to his allotted room. It was a dingy affair — wooden, dusty, hard. A small gas-jet furnished sufficient light for so rueful a corner.

"Hm!" he said, clearing his throat and locking the door.

Now he began leisurely to take off his clothes, but stopped first with his coat, and tucked it along the crack under the door. His vest he arranged in the same place. His old wet, cracked hat he laid softly upon the table. Then he pulled off his shoes and lay down.

It seemed as if he thought a while, for now he arose and turned the gas out, standing calmly in the blackness, hidden from view. After a few moments, in which he reviewed nothing, but merely hesitated, he turned the gas on again, but applied no match. Even then he stood there, hidden wholly in that kindness which is night, while the uprising fumes filled the room. When the odor reached his nostrils, he quit his attitude and fumbled for the bed.

"What's the use?" he said weakly, as he stretched himself to rest.

And now Carrie had attained that which in the beginning seemed life's object, or at least, such fraction of it as human beings ever attain of their original desires. She could look about on her gowns and carriage, her furniture and bank account. Friends there were, as the world takes it — those who would bow and smile in acknowledgment of her success. For these she had once craved. Applause there was, and publicity — once far off, essential things, but now grown trivial and indifferent. Beauty also — her type of loveliness — and yet she was lonely. In her rocking-chair she sat, when not otherwise engaged — singing and dreaming.

Thus in life there is ever the intellectual and the emotional nature — the mind that reasons, and the mind that feels. Of one come the men of action — generals and statesmen; of the other, the poets and dreamers — artists all.

As harps in the wind, the latter respond to every breath of fancy, voicing in their moods all the ebb and flow of the ideal.

Man has not yet comprehended the dreamer any more than he has the ideal. For him the laws and morals of the world are unduly severe. Ever hearkening[13] to the sound of beauty, straining for the flash of its distant wings, he watches to follow, wearying his feet in travelling. So watched Carrie, so followed, rocking and singing.

And it must be remembered that reason had little part in this. Chicago dawning, she saw the city offering more of loveliness than she had ever known, and instinctively, by force of her moods alone, clung

13 hearkening: listening to.

to it. In fine raiment and elegant surroundings, men seemed to be contented. Hence, she drew near these things. Chicago, New York; Drouet, Hurstwood; the world of fashion and the world of stage — these were but incidents. Not them, but that which they represented, she longed for. Time proved the representation false.

Oh, the tangle of human life! How dimly as yet we see. Here was Carrie, in the beginning poor, unsophisticated, emotional; responding with desire to everything most lovely in life, yet finding herself turned as by a wall. Laws to say: "Be allured, if you will, by everything lovely, but draw not nigh unless by righteousness." Convention to say: "You shall not better your situation save by honest labor." If honest labor be unremunerative and difficult to endure; if it be the long, long road which never reaches beauty, but wearies the feet and the heart; if the drag to follow beauty be such that one abandons the admired way, taking rather the despised path leading to her dreams quickly, who shall cast the first stone? [7] Not evil, but longing for that which is better, more often directs the steps of the erring. Not evil, but goodness more often allures the feeling mind unused to reason.

Amid the tinsel and shine of her state walked Carrie, unhappy. As when Drouet took her, she had thought: "Now am I lifted into that which is best"; as when Hurstwood seemingly offered her the better way: "Now am I happy." But since the world goes its way past all who will not partake of its folly, she now found herself alone. Her purse was open to him whose need was greatest. In her walks on Broadway, she no longer thought of the elegance of the creatures who passed her. Had they more of that peace and beauty which glimmered afar off, then were they to be envied.

Drouet abandoned his claim and was seen no more. Of Hurstwood's death she was not even aware. A slow, black boat setting out from the pier at Twenty-seventh Street upon its weekly errand bore, with many others, his nameless body to the Potter's Field[14].

Thus passed all that was of interest concerning these twain in their relation to her. Their influence upon her life is explicable alone by the nature of her longings. Time was when both represented for her all that was most potent in earthly success. They were the personal representatives of a state most blessed to attain — the titled ambassadors of comfort and peace, aglow with their credentials. It is but natural that when the world which they represented no longer allured her, its ambassadors should be discredited. Even had Hurstwood returned in his original beauty and glory, he could not now have allured her. She had learned that in his world, as in her own present state, was not happiness.

Sitting alone, she was now an illustration of the devious ways by which one who feels, rather than reasons, may be led in the pursuit of beauty. Though often disillusioned, she was still waiting for that halcyon day when she should be led forth among dreams become real. Ames had pointed out a farther step, but on and on beyond that, if accomplished, would lie others for her. It was forever to be the pursuit of that radiance of delight which tints the distant hilltops of the world.

Oh, Carrie, Carrie! Oh, blind strivings of the human heart! Onward, onward, it saith, and where beauty leads, there it follows. Whether it be the tinkle of a lone sheep bell o'er some quiet landscape, or the glimmer of beauty in sylvan places, or the show of soul in some passing eye, the heart knows and makes answer, following. It is when the feet weary and hope seems vain that the heartaches and the longings arise. Know, then, that for you is neither surfeit nor content. In your rocking-chair, by your window dreaming, shall you long, alone. In your rocking-chair, by your window, shall you dream such happiness as you may never feel. [8]

14 the Potter's Field: a cemetery in the suburbs of New York City.

NOTES ON THE TEXT

[1] The Bowery is a place in New York City where the homeless live. Constantly tortured by hunger, humiliation, and shame, Hurstwood vacillates between survival and suicide. He knows of a way to commit suicide — that is, rent a room in the Bowery for 15 cents, turn on the gas and lie on bed, which is exactly what he does at the very end of the story.

[2] Hurstwood is now reduced to his animal instincts, struggling hard to get enough food to eat by begging. This drastic change in fate seems to confirm Dreiser's idea that man is under the control of circumstance instead of his free will.

[3] *Le Père Goriot* is an 1835 novel by French novelist Honoré de Balzac (1799—1850) — translated into *Father Goriot* in English. In the novel, Balzac transposes Shakespeare's King Lear to the 1820s Paris in order to critique the lack of love, except the love of money, in the French society at a time of booming capitalism.

[4] A euchre hand here refers to a hand with poker cards. Euchre is a card game played usually with the highest 32 cards, in which each player is dealt 5 cards and the player making the trump is required to take at least 3 tricks to win. 尤克牌：32张牌，每人发5张，定主牌的一方须至少赢三墩牌才算赢。

[5] It is worth noting that Dreiser, in this part of the story, deliberately juxtaposes several quickly succeeding scenes on a wintry evening, which shows in quick succession all the major characters of the novel in their respective condition of life, in order to bring out an ironic contrast: Carrie in an expensive hotel room with Lola; Charles Drouet in the lobby of the Imperial and planning with Harris for dining out with some girls; Mrs. Hurstwood sitting cozily in a luxurious train carriage with her daughter and her wealthy son-in-law, who is a banker; Hurstwood shivering with cold and begging on the street.

[6] In line with the Naturalists' emphasis on factual details and avoidance of sentimentality, Dreiser's portrayal of the beggars here is objective, specific and realistic, paying attention to minute details of their outer appearances, their movements and expressions. Notice the kind of "journalistic objectivity" such depictions have arrived at.

[7] This is a biblical allusion to John 8:7. The narrator asks who "will cast the first stone" at a person such as Carrie for pursuing a shortcut to happiness. The woman mentioned in the Bible was, like Carrie, guilty of adultery. The Pharisees wanted to stone her according to Moses's commandments. Jesus, however, undercut their self-righteousness by saying: "Let anyone among you who is without sin be the first to throw a stone at her." Jesus wanted to force the Pharisees to search for their own conscience. Through this allusion, Dreiser wants to strive the same effect on his reader, and to convey the idea that Carrie's moral expediency, like Hurstwood's degradation, is accidental and has no moral value in it, since it is caused by random circumstance rather than virtue or vice.

[8] In this chapter, Carrie is found sitting in the rocking chair more than once. The rocking chair moves, but it does not go anywhere. It is a symbol of Carrie's fate. She keeps moving from

one man to another, but she never truly achieves anything. In New York, when she finally has got what she wants, Ames reveals to her the existence of an entirely different world beyond the material — an aesthetic or philosophical world. This seems to be a new hope for Carrie, and may also be a new illusion for her. "Oh, Carrie, Carrie! Oh, blind strivings of the human heart!" As the novel approaches its conclusion, Dreiser adopts a self-consciously lofty tone. Dreiser seems to suggest that life can never truly live up to our ideals, and that life is a process of disillusionment.

QUESTIONS FOR DISCUSSION

1. The Naturalists gleaned from Zola a scientific model for diagnosing social ills; from Darwin the metaphor of the jungle; from Spencer the notion of "struggle for existence"; from Marx a sense of economic determinism. Like the earlier Realists, the Naturalists focused on factual details and avoid sentimentality. They wrote more frankly about previously taboo subjects such as sexuality, alcoholism, disease and depravity, often describing aberrant, irrational, or cruel behavior. Discuss how Dreiser implements Naturalism in *Sister Carrie*. What is Dreiser's style? As a form of extreme realism, how is naturalism manifested in the story?

2. Compare and contrast the protagonist in Jack London's "Love of Life" and Hurstwood. What are the differences and resemblances between the two characters in terms of their attitudes to death? In what ways are the environments of the two stories different and similar?

3. Consider the role economic forces play in determining the value of the major characters, Carrie and Hurstwood. Do you think human relationships are seen as a kind of commodity exchange in the story? Is there true love demonstrated in the story?

4. What responsibility do environmental and social forces have for the characters' behaviors and actions? What is the personal responsibility for an individual's actions and fate? What has caused Hurstwood's failure and Carrie's success? Can there be any moral lessons to be drawn from their fates?

SUGGESTED REFERENCES

Elias, Robert H. *Theodore Dreiser: Apostle of Nature.* Ithaca: Cornell UP, 1970.

---, ed. *Letter of Theodre Dreiser.* 3 vols. Philadelphia: U of Pennsylvania P, 1959.

Giles, Paul. "Dreiser's Style." *The Cambridge Companion to Theodore Dreiser.* Ed. Leonard Cassuto and Clare Virginia Edby. Cambridge: Cambridge UP, 2004. 47-62.

Gogol, Miriam ed. *Theodore Dreiser: Beyond Naturalism.* New York: New York University Press, 1995.

Hakutani, Yoshinobu, ed. *Theodore Dreiser and American Culture: New Readings.* Newark: U of Delaware P, 2000.

Pizer, Donald, ed. *New Essays on Sister Carrie.* Cambridge: Cambridge UP, 1991.

Salzman, Jack. *Theodore Dreiser: The Critical Reception.* New York: David Lewis, 1972.

West, James. *A Sister Carrie Portfolio.* Charlottsville: UP of Virginia, 1985.

Zayani, Mohamed. *Reading the Symptom: Frank Norris, Theodore Dreiser, and the Dynamics of Capitalism.* New York: Peter Lang, 1999.

Unit 11 F. Scott Fitzgerald

(1896 — 1940)

A GUIDE TO LITERARY TERMINOLOGY

"Jazz Age": *The Jazz Age refers to an era after the end of World War I (1918), through the Roaring Twenties, until the onset of the Great Depression (1930), which embodied the beginning of modern America. The age takes its name from jazz, a popular musical form in the United States which combines African and European musical styles. The Jazz Age and the writing borne of it are synonymous with the many attributes of the Roaring Twenties. Prohibition, women's suffrage, iconoclasm, material excess, Dixieland jazz, speakeasies, soaring stock markets, the rise of big business and organized crime, the pursuit of the American Dream, expatriation, the relaxation of sexual mores, the decline of Puritanism — all of these helped define the Jazz Age in American literature. The two most representative writers of the period were F. Scott Fitzgerald, who wrote* ***The Great Gatsby*** *(1925), and Sinclair Lewis, who wrote* ***Babbitt*** *(1922). These two novels were the most critically acclaimed works of the Jazz Age. Both writers were concerned with the corruptive influences of capitalism and conformity, and depicted their protagonists, Jay Gatsby and George F. Babbitt, as helpless victims of social and biological forces. Both detested the crassness, vulgarity, and hypocrisy of the society and kept themselves at a critical distance. Both had sounded their alarm that America's optimism, vitality, and individualism were dwindling and quickly becoming subordinated to the amoral pursuit of wealth.*

NOTES ON THE AUTHOR

F. Scott Fitzgerald was born in St. Paul, Minnesota to a family considered socially prominent but genteelly poor. With the financial aid of relatives he was sent to prep school and to Princeton where he neglected his studies but worked hard on musical comedies for the Triangle Club there. In his sophomore year, he began an epistolary romance with Ginevra King, who rejected him. In 1917, his senior year, he left Princeton and enlisted in the army, serving as a second lieutenant at staff headquarters. He began to write his first novel *The Romantic Egoist* while he was stationed at Fort Leavenworth, Kansas. He submitted the novel to Scribners, a publisher, in February1918, but it was rejected. While he was stationed in Alabama in 1918, he met and fell in love with Zelda Sayre at a country club dance. They were engaged in 1919, but Zelda broke the engagement when it appeared he would not be able to support a family. After he was discharged from the army in 1919, he obtained a job as an advertising writer. He rewrote *The Romantic Egoist*, changed the title to *This Side of Paradise*, and submitted it to Scribners again. In March 1920, it was published and became an immediate commercial success. A week later, he and Zelda got married.

In the early 1920s, F. Scott Fitzgerald and his wife Zelda Sayre became the symbolic couple of the Jazz Age which he had named and depicted in his story collection titled *Tales of the Jazz Age*. From 1920 to 1922, he published four books, *This Side of Paradise* (1920), *The Beautiful and Damned* (1922), *Flappers and Philosophers* (1922), and *Tales of the Jazz Age* (1922). Before and after the publication of *The Great Gatsby* (1925), he was better known as a spokesman for the young generation than he was a novelist. In 1924, the couple moved to the French Riviera, the setting of *Tender Is the Night* (1934), and stayed there for over two years, during which Fitzgerald began a friendship with Ernest Hemingway. Despite the wealth and fame brought by the success of his books, the Fitzgeralds had run into a debt because of their extravagant and glamorous lifestyle. In April 1930, Zelda had her first mental breakdown, which was followed by a diagnosis of schizophrenia and treatment in Switzerland from June 1930 to September 1931. She was confined to sanatoriums intermittently, both in Europe and the United States, until her death in 1948. Tortured by the illness of his wife and his own alcoholism, Fitzgerald died in 1940 at the age of 44 after a period of serious decline in health and in writing. Fitzgerald is regarded as one of the major American writers of the twentieth century. He wrote with an awareness of both history and his times, combining social observations with psychological insights to create enduring works that portray the emptiness of the pursuit of material riches and the American dreams of love and splendor.

SYNOPSIS OF THE WORK

This tragic story, told in a calm manner, is about Mrs. King, a convalescent schizophrenia patient who is going to travel with her husband to a Virginia beach resort. Unfortunately, Mr. King, on his way to the sanatorium to pick up his wife for the trip, is badly wounded in a traffic accident and dies two days later in the hospital. The doctors and nurses in the sanatorium are baffled about what to do when they discover that Mrs. King cannot accept the news of her husband's death.

They know she would surely have a mental breakdown if they insist on telling her the fact. Left with no better choice, they allow Mrs. King to wait for her husband every morning at the front gate.

The unvarnished realism of the story lends it poignancy and depth which sprang from Fitzgerald's own tragic personal experience. The writing of this short story was apparently affected by Zelda Sayre's mental illness. The story represented, to some extent, Fitzgerald's way to reconcile with the trauma caused by his wife's schizophrenia. In 1924, while the Fitzgeralds were living in France, Zelda began a relationship with a handsome French aviator. Scott threatened to leave Zelda unless she broke off the relationship. Zelda, in her autobiography, mentioned her husband's jealousy of the French aviator as one cause of her mental illness. She also blamed her husband for suppressing her creativity, which she thought contributed to the deterioration of her mental health.

SELECTED READINGS

The Long Way Out

I

We were talking about some of the older castles in Touraine[1] and we touched upon the iron cage in which Louis XI[2] imprisoned Cardinal La Balue[3] for six years, then upon oubliettes[4] and such horrors. I had seen several of the latter, simply dry wells thirty or forty feet deep where a man was thrown to wait for nothing; since I have such a tendency to claustrophobia[5] that a Pullman berth[6] is a certain nightmare, they had made a lasting impression. So it was rather a relief when a doctor told this story, that is, it was a relief when he began it, for it

1 Touraine: one of the traditional provinces of France. Its capital was Tours.

2 Louis XI: French King who ruled during the period between 1461 and 1483.

3 Cardinal La Balue: Jean Balue (1421—1491), a cardinal, was imprisoned in Loche from 1469 to 1480.

4 oubliette: a secret dungeon (地牢) with a trap door in the ceiling as its only means of entrance or exit.

5 claustrophobia: abnormal fear of being in a narrow or enclosed space (幽闭恐惧症).

6 Pullman berth: a Pullman is a type of train or railway carriage which is extremely comfortable and luxurious; a Pullman berth is a bed in a sleeping car.

seemed to have nothing to do with the tortures long ago. [1]

There was a young woman named Mrs. King who was very happy with her husband. They were well-to-do and deeply in love but at the birth of her second child she went into a long coma and emerged with a clear case of schizophrenia or "split personality." [2] Her delusion, which had something to do with the Declaration of Independence, [3] had little bearing on the case and as she regained her health it began to disappear. At the end of ten months she was a convalescent patient scarcely marked by what had happened to her and very eager to go back into the world.

She was only twenty-one, rather girlish in an appealing way and a favorite with the staff of the sanitarium[7]. When she became well enough so that she could take an experimental trip with her husband there was a general interest in the center. One nurse had gone into Philadelphia with her to get a dress, another knew the story of her rather romantic courtship in Mexico and everyone had seen her two babies on visits to the hospital. The trip was to Virginia Beach for five days.

It was a joy to watch her make ready, dressing and packing meticulously and living in the gay trivialities of hair waves and such things. She was ready half an hour before the time of departure and she paid some visits on the floor in her powder blue[8] gown and her hat that looked like one minute after an April shower. Her frail lovely face, with just that touch of startled sadness that often lingers after an illness, was alight with anticipation.

"We'll just do nothing," she said. "That's my ambition. To get up when I want to for three straight mornings and stay up late for three straight nights. To buy a bathing suit by myself and order a meal."

When the time approached Mrs. King decided to wait downstairs

---

7 sanitarium: an institution that provides medical treatment and rest, often in a healthy climate, for people who have been ill for a long time.

8 powder blue: pale grayish-blue.

instead of in her room and as she passed along the corridors with an orderly carrying her suitcase she waved to the other patients, sorry that they too were not going on a gorgeous holiday. The superintendent wished her well, two nurses found excuses to linger and share her infectious joy.

"What a beautiful tan you'll get, Mrs. King."

"Be sure and send us a postcard."

About the time she left her room her husband's car was hit by a truck on his way from the city, — he was hurt internally and was not expected to live more than a few hours. The information was received at the hospital in a glassed-in office adjoining the hall where Mrs. King waited. The operator, seeing Mrs. King and knowing that the glass was not sound proof, asked the head nurse to come immediately. The head nurse hurried aghast to a doctor and he decided what to do. So long as the husband was still alive it was best to tell her nothing, but of course she must know that he was not coming today.

Mrs. King was greatly disappointed.

"I suppose it's silly to feel that way," she said. "After all these months what's one more day? He said he'd come tomorrow, didn't he?"

The nurse was having a difficult time but she managed to pass it off until the patient was back in her room. Then they assigned a very experienced and phlegmatic nurse to keep Mrs. King away from other patients and from newspapers. By the next day the matter would be decided one way or another.

But her husband lingered on and they continued to prevaricate. A little before noon next day one of the nurses was passing along the corridor when she met Mrs. King, dressed as she had been the day before but this time carrying her own suitcase.

"I'm going to meet my husband," she explained. "He couldn't come yesterday but he's coming today at the same time."

The nurse walked along with her. Mrs. King had the freedom of the building and it was difficult to simply steer her back to her room, and the nurse did not want to tell a story that would contradict what the authorities were telling her. When they reached the front hall she signaled to the operator who fortunately understood. Mrs. King gave herself a last inspection in the mirror and said:

"I'd like to have a dozen hats just like this to remind me to be this happy always."

When the head nurse came in frowning a minute later she demanded:

"Don't tell me George is delayed?"

"I'm afraid he is. There is nothing much to do but be patient."

Mrs. King laughed ruefully. "I wanted him to see my costume when it was absolutely new."

"Why, there isn't a wrinkle in it."

"I guess it'll last till tomorrow. I oughtn't to be blue[9] about waiting one more day when I'm so utterly happy."

"Certainly not."

That night her husband died and at a conference of doctors next morning there was some discussion about what to do — it was a risk to tell her and a risk to keep it from her. It was decided finally to say that Mr. King had been called away and thus destroy her hope of an immediate meeting; when she was reconciled to this they could tell her the truth.

As the doctors came out of the conference one of them stopped and pointed. Down the corridor toward the outer hall walked Mrs. King carrying her suitcase.

Dr. Pirie, who had been in special charge of Mrs. King, caught his breath.

"This is awful," he said. "I think perhaps I'd better tell her now. There's no use saying he's away when she usually hears from him twice a week, and if we say he's sick she'll want to go to him. Any-

---

9 blue: sad.

body else like the job?"

II

One of the doctors in the conference went on a fortnight's vacation that afternoon. On the day of his return in the same corridor at the same hour, he stopped at the sight of a little procession coming toward him — an orderly carrying a suitcase, a nurse and Mrs. King dressed in the powder-blue colored suit and wearing the spring hat.

"Good morning, doctor," she said. "I'm going to meet my husband and we're going to Virginia Beach. I'm going to the hall because I don't want to keep him waiting."

He looked into her face, clear and happy as a child's. The nurse signaled to him that it was as ordered so he merely bowed and spoke of the pleasant weather.

"It's a beautiful day," said Mrs. King, "but of course even if it was raining it would be a beautiful day for me."

He looked after her, puzzled and annoyed — why are they letting this go on, he thought. What possible good can it do?

Meeting Dr. Pirie he put the question to him.

"We tried to tell her," Dr. Pirie said. "She laughed and said we were trying to see whether she's still sick. You could use the word 'unthinkable' in an exact sense here — his death is unthinkable to her."

"But you can't just go on like this."

"Theoretically no," said Dr. Pirie. "A few days ago when she packed up as usual the nurse tried to keep her from going. From out in the hall I could see her face, see her begin to go to pieces — for the first time, mind you. Her muscles were tense and her eyes glazed and her voice was thick and shrill when she very politely called the nurse a liar. It was touch and go there for a minute[10] whether we had

10 It was touch and go there for a minute: It was hard and risky to decide; touch and go: a risky, precarious, delicate situation.

a tractable patient or a restraint case[11] — and I stepped in and told the nurse to take her down to the reception room."

He broke off as the procession that had just passed and appeared again, headed back to the ward. Mrs. King stopped and spoke to Dr. Pirie:

"My husband's been delayed," she said. "Of course I'm disappointed but they tell me he's coming tomorrow and after waiting so long one more day doesn't seem to matter. Don't you agree with me, Doctor?"

"I certainly do, Mrs. King."

She took off her hat.

"I've got to put aside these clothes — I want them to be as fresh tomorrow as they are today." She looked closely at the hat. "There's a speck of dust on it, but I think I can get it off. Perhaps he won't notice."

"I'm sure he won't."

"Really I don't mind waiting another day. It'll be this time tomorrow before I know it, won't it?"

When she had gone along the young doctor said:

"There are still the two children."

"I don't think the children are going to matter. When she 'went under' she tied up this trip with the idea of getting well. If we took it away she'd have to go to the bottom and start over." [4]

"Could she?"

"There's no prognosis[12]," said Dr. Pirie. "I was simply explaining why she was allowed to go to the hall this morning."

"But there's tomorrow morning and the next morning."

"There's always the chance," said Dr. Pirie, "that some day he will be there."

The doctor ended his story here, rather abruptly. When we pressed

---

11 a restraint case: a case in which the patient had to be tied up.

12 prognosis: a prediction of the course of a disease.

him to tell what happened he protested that the rest was anticlimax — that all sympathy eventually wears out and that finally the staff of the sanitarium had simply accepted the fact.

"But does she still go to meet her husband?"

"Oh yes, it's always the same — but the other patients, except new ones, hardly look up when she passes along the hall. The nurses manage to substitute a new hat every year or so but she still wears the same suit. She's always a little disappointed but she makes the best of it, very sweetly too. It's not an unhappy life as far as we know, and in some funny way it seems to set an example of tranquility to the other patients. For God's sake let's talk about something else — let's go back to oubliettes."

NOTES ON THE TEXT

[1] The narrator "I" would like to listen to the doctor's story, which he thinks would release him from the horror of oubliettes in Europe. In the first paragraph, the author has set up a gloomy atmosphere in which the doctor's story, itself is no less easy to take, is to be told. The narrator's "release" is to be proved groundless as the doctor's story unfolds. The doctor, at the end of the story, cries out, "For God's sake let's talk about something else — let's go back to oubliettes."

[2] Schizophrenia is a mental disorder characterized by abnormal social behavior and failure to recognize what is real. People who suffer from it are unable to relate their thoughts and feelings to what is happening around them. They are often drawn from society. Symptoms include hallucinations, confused and unclear thinking, reduced social engagement and emotional depression. Split personality is a popular term to refer to "dissociative identity disorder," a psychological disorder in which two or more independent and distinct personality systems develop in the same individual. Each personality may alternately inhabit the person's conscious awareness to the exclusion of the others, but one is usually dominant.

[3] "The Declaration of Independence" was made in the Congress on July 4, 1776. The most famous statement in it reads: "We hold these truths to be self-evident, that all men are created equal, that they are endowed by their Creator with certain unalienable Rights, that among these are Life, Liberty and the pursuit of Happiness."

[4] "Went under" is a euphemism for having a breakdown. Here the speaker uses the drowning metaphor to describe a breakdown. "Go to the bottom and start over" suggests that she will

resume her symptoms as a schizophrenia patient and need to undergo another round of treatment in the hospital.

QUESTIONS FOR DISCUSSION

1. The story has two narrators, the narrator "I" (a first person limited perspective) and the doctor who tells the story (a third person omniscient perspective). What effects has Fitzgerald achieved by introducing two points of view and by putting one story within the frame of another?

2. In paragraph 1, the narrator says, "It (the story) seemed to have nothing to do with the tortures long ago." Notice that the author has deliberately put "the tortures long ago" in parallel with the torture of the present. Discuss the significance of this contrast. In what ways has this narrative pattern strengthened the thematic expression and emotional impacts of the story?

3. In the last paragraph the doctor says, "It's not an unhappy life as far as we know, and in some funny way it seems to set an example of tranquility to the other patients." How do you understand the doctor's words? In what sense is Mrs. King's life happy or unhappy? What is "funny" about such an example of tranquility? Has she really recovered from schizophrenia? Has her delusion disappeared?

4. At the very end of the story, the doctor says, "For God's sake let's talk about something else — let's go back to oubliettes." Why does he want to return to the topic of oubliettes? What emotional impact does the story have on the doctor himself and on us as readers?

SUGGESTED REFERENCES

Bruccoli, Matthew J. *Some Sort of Epic Grandeur: The Life of F. Scott Fitzgerald.* Columbia: U of South Carolina P, 2002.

---. *F. Scott Fitzgerald: A Descriptive Bibliography.* Pittsburgh: U of Pittsburgh P, 1987.

---. *Fitzgerald and Hemingway: A Dangerous Friendship.* New York: Carroll & Graf, 1994.

Bruccoli, Matthew and George Parker Anderson, eds. *F. Scott Fitzgerald's **Tender Is the Night**: A Documentary Volume.* Detroit: Bruccoli Clark Layman Thompson Gale, 2003.

Bryer, Jackson R., ed. *New Essays on F. Scott Fitzgerald's Neglected Stories.* Columbia: U of Missouri P, 1996.

---, ed. *F. Scott Fitzgerald: The Critical Reception.* New York: Franklin, 1978.

Kennedy, Gerald J. and Jackson R. Bryer, eds. *French Connections: Hemingway and Fitzgerald Abroad.* New York: St. Martin's Press, 1999.

Tate, Mary Jo. *F. Scott Fitzgerald A to Z: The Essential Reference to His Life and Work.* New York: Facts on File, 1998.

Unit 12 William Faulkner

(1897 – 1962)

A GUIDE TO LITERARY TERMINOLOGY

"Modernism": *Modernism was a literary trend covering roughly the beginning of World War I until about 1965. Modernist writers used experimental techniques such as stream-of-consciousness and opaque language to explore the psychological nature of the characters and to create a verisimilar reality, both physical and psychological. A central preoccupation of Modernism is with the inner self and consciousness. Modernists see decay and a growing alienation of the individual, instead of progress and growth. The machinery of modern society is perceived as impersonal, capitalist, and antagonistic to the artistic impulse. In fact, Modernism included a wide range of artistic movements including Symbolism, Impressionism, Futurism, Constructivism, Imagism, Expressionism, and Surrealism. It originated in Berlin, Vienna, Munich, Prague, Moscow, London and Paris, and later spread to New York and Chicago. Its most notable landmarks include Henry James's* ***The Ambassadors*** *(1903), Conrad's* ***Nostromo*** *(1904), T. S. Eliot's* ***The Waste Land*** *(1922) and James Joyce's* ***Ulysses*** *(1922).*

American Modernism reached its peak in the 1920s up to the 1940s. Famous American modernist writers include Ezra Pound, F. Scott Fitzgerald, John Steinbeck, Ernest Hemingway, and William Faulkner. They explored the psychological wounds and spiritual scars of the experiences of war and economic crisis. A related theme in American modernist literature is the loss of self and the need to build a self. Madness and its manifestations are another favorite modernist theme, as illustrated in Eugene O'Neill's ***The Emperor Jones****, Hemingway's* ***The Battler*** *and Faulkner's* ***That Evening Sun****.*

NOTES ON THE AUTHOR

William Faulkner was born William Cuthbert Falkner in New Albany, Mississippi. He added the "u" to his last name when he began to publish. When he was four or five, his family moved to Oxford, Mississippi, where he grew up and lived most of his life. The fictional county Yoknapatawpha, the setting for Faulkner's best known cycle of works, was based on Oxford. Yoknapatawpha becomes an emblem of the American South and its tragic history, due to Faulkner's portrait of its familial and historical "sagas." During the mid-1920s Faulkner lived for several months in New Orleans where he met Sherwood Anderson, who told him: "You're a country boy; all you know is that little patch up there in Mississippi where you started from." Faulkner was inspired by Anderson's words. He later discovered that "my own little postage stamp of native soil was worth writing about and that I would never live long enough to exhaust it, and that by sublimating the actual into the apocryphal I would have complete liberty to use whatever talent I might have to its absolute top. It opened up a gold mine of other people, so I created a cosmos of my own." Faulkner's central concern and theme, however, went far beyond Oxford, or Mississippi, or even America. It was, as he put it in his address in acceptance of the Nobel Prize, the universal theme of "the problem of the human heart in conflict with itself," the only subject that was "worth the agony and sweat" of the artist.

Faulkner began his writing as a poet and published his first book, a collection of verse entitled *The Marble Faun*, in 1924. His first two novels, *Soldier's Pay* (1925), a tale of postwar disillusionment, and *Mosquitoes* (1927), a satirical novel of ideas, are rather conventional. *Sartoris* (1929) is the first to be set in his fictional county of Yoknapatawpha, followed by a series of major modernist novels over the next seven years: *The Sound and the Fury*, his first major novel marked by radical technical experimentation including streams of consciousness, the convolution of temporal sequences, and multiple perspectives, *As I Lay Dying* (1930), *Sanctuary* (1931), *Light in August* (1932), and *Absalom, Absalom!* (1936). He revealed his concerns about racial prejudice and social injustice in the South in *Go Down, Moses* (1942), *Intruder in the Dust* (1948). The publication of *The Portable Faulkner* in 1946 brought him international recognition and financial health. He received the Nobel Prize for literature in 1950. His *Collected Stories* (1950) won the National Book Award. The first novel in the Snopes trilogy, *The Hamlet* (1940), deals with the rise to power of a poor white entrepreneur called Flem Snopes, and his eventual fall. The other two were *The Town* (1957) and *The Mansion* (1959). Faulkner died on July 6, 1962, in Byhalia, Mississippi.

Faulkner's novels explore the consequences of the dissolution of traditional values in the deep South and treat the decay and anguish in its society since the Civil War. He is arguably the greatest American novelist.

SYNOPSIS OF THE WORK

"A Rose for Emily" is set in Jefferson, Yoknapatawpha County, Mississippi, in the late nineteenth or early twentieth century. An unnamed narrator, assuming a first-person-plural "we" voice and representing the point of view of the townspeople, tells the story of an eccentric southern belle, Miss Emily Grierson. The story opens with Emily's funeral which the whole town take part in. Then as the narrator gradually unfolds the strange circumstances of Emily's life, the reader gets to know the odd relationship between Emily and her father, who manipulated her life and drove away all Emily's suitors, and a more mysterious one between Emily and a Yankee road worker named Homer Barron, her lover. After his father's death, Emily lives alone, with a Negro servant, in a dilapidated old mansion, lonely and impoverished. Her love affair with Homer Barron is considered out of place, due to what they each represent, one the old, declining tradition of the nobility in the American South, and the other the new, rising industrial forces in the American North.

When Homer Barron wants to desert her, Emily is seen purchasing arsenic, an act that the townspeople interpret as a suicide attempt. Then Homer Barron disappears from the town and is never heard from again. "We" assume he has returned north upon the completion of road construction. Though Emily does not commit suicide, the townspeople sympathize with her sad fate, but continue to gossip about her eccentricities. She never invites people to her house, and has lived a secluded life ever since. But her house has been "broken into" a few times: a "deputation" of the Board of Aldermen pay her a visit to talk about her taxes, but they are kicked out and told to see Colonel Sartoris, the old Mayor of Jefferson who remitted her taxes in 1894 and who died almost a decade ago (part I); four men sneak over to her house and sprinkle lime around to remove a bad smell from her house shortly after the disappearance of her sweetheart (part II); a Baptist minister calls upon her about the "disgrace" of her riding around in the buggy with Homer Barron, with no intention of marriage (part IV); curious townspeople come, upon her death, to inspect her house which has been closed to the townspeople for 40 years (part V). To their horror, they discover the skeleton of Homer Barron lying on Emily's bed in her upstairs room, which explains the stench from her house.

SELECTED READINGS

A Rose for Emily [1]

I

When Miss Emily Grierson died, our whole town went to her funeral: the men through a sort of respectful affection for a fallen monument, the women mostly out of curiosity to see the inside of her house, which no one save an old man-servant — a combined gardener and cook — had seen in at least ten years.

It was a big, squarish frame house that had once been white, decorated with cupolas and spires and scrolled balconies in the heavily lightsome style of the seventies, set on what had once been our most select street. But garages and cotton gins had encroached and obliterated even the august names of that neighborhood; only Miss Emily's house was left, lifting its stubborn and coquettish decay above the cotton wagons and the gasoline pumps — an eyesore among eyesores. And now Miss Emily had gone to join the representatives of those august names where they lay in the cedar-bemused cemetery among the ranked and anonymous graves of Union and Confederate soldiers who fell at the battle of Jefferson. [2]

Alive, Miss Emily had been a tradition, a duty, and a care; a sort of hereditary obligation upon the town, dating from that day in 1894 when Colonel Sartoris, [3] the mayor — he who fathered the edict that no Negro woman should appear on the streets without an apron — remitted her taxes, the dispensation dating from the death of her father on into perpetuity. Not that Miss Emily would have accepted charity. Colonel Sartoris invented an involved tale to the effect that Miss Emily's father had loaned money to the town, which the town, as a matter of business, preferred this way of repaying. Only a man of Colonel Sartoris' generation and thought could have invented it, and only a woman could have believed it.

When the next generation, with its more modern ideas, became mayors and aldermen, this arrangement created some little dissatisfaction. On the first of the year they mailed her a tax notice. February came, and there was no reply. They wrote her a formal letter, asking her to call at the sheriff's office at her convenience. A week later the mayor wrote her himself, offering to call or to send his car for her, and received in reply a note on paper of an archaic shape, in a thin, flowing calligraphy in faded ink, to the effect that she no longer went out at all. The tax notice was also enclosed, without comment.

They called a special meeting of the Board of Aldermen. A deputation waited upon her, knocked at the door through which no visitor had passed since she ceased giving china-painting lessons eight or ten years earlier. They were admitted by the old Negro into a dim hall from which a stairway mounted into still more shadow. It smelled of dust and disuse — a close, dank smell. The Negro led them into the parlor. It was furnished in heavy, leather-covered furniture. When the Negro opened the blinds of one window, they could see that the leather was cracked; and when they sat down, a faint dust rose sluggishly about their thighs, spinning with slow motes in the single sun-ray. On a tarnished gilt easel before the fireplace stood a crayon portrait of Miss Emily's father.

They rose when she entered — a small, fat woman in black, with a thin gold chain descending to her waist and vanishing into her belt, leaning on an ebony cane with a tarnished gold head. Her skeleton was small and spare; perhaps that was why what would have been merely plumpness in another was obesity in her. She looked bloated, like a body long submerged in motionless water, and of that pallid hue. Her eyes, lost in the fatty ridges of her face, looked like two small pieces of coal pressed into a lump of dough as they moved from one face to another while the visitors stated their errand.

She did not ask them to sit. She just stood in the door and listened quietly until the spokesman came to a stumbling halt. Then they could hear the invisible watch ticking at the end of the gold chain.

Her voice was dry and cold. "I have no taxes in Jefferson. Colonel Sartoris explained it to me. Perhaps one of you can gain access to the city records and satisfy yourselves."

"But we have. We are the city authorities, Miss Emily. Didn't you get a notice from the sheriff, signed by him?"

"I received a paper, yes," Miss Emily said. "Perhaps he considers himself the sheriff... I have no taxes in Jefferson."

"But there is nothing on the books to show that, you see. We must go by the —"

"See Colonel Sartoris. I have no taxes in Jefferson."

"But, Miss Emily —"

"See Colonel Sartoris." (Colonel Sartoris had been dead almost ten years.) "I have no taxes in Jefferson. Tobe!" The Negro appeared. "Show these gentlemen out."

II

So she vanquished them, horse and foot, just as she had vanquished their fathers thirty years before about the smell. That was two years after her father's death and a short time after her sweetheart — the one we believed would marry her — had deserted her. After her father's death she went out very little; after her sweetheart went away, people hardly saw her at all. A few of the ladies had the temerity to call, but were not received, and the only sign of life about the place was the Negro man — a young man then — going in and out with a market basket.

"Just as if a man — any man — could keep a kitchen properly," the ladies said; so they were not surprised when the smell developed. It was another link between the gross, teeming world and the high and mighty Griersons.

A neighbor, a woman, complained to the mayor, Judge Stevens, eighty years old.

"But what will you have me do about it, madam?" he said.

"Why, send her word to stop it," the woman said. "Isn't there a law?"

"I'm sure that won't be necessary," Judge Stevens said. "It's probably just a snake or a rat that nigger of hers killed in the yard. I'll speak to him about it."

The next day he received two more complaints, one from a man who came in diffident deprecation. "We really must do something about it, Judge. I'd be the last one in the world to bother Miss Emily, but we've got to do something." That night the Board of Aldermen met — three graybeards and one younger man, a member of the rising generation.

"It's simple enough," he said. "Send her word to have her place cleaned up. Give her a certain time to do it in, and if she don't..."

"Dammit, sir," Judge Stevens said, "will you accuse a lady to her face of smelling bad?"

So the next night, after midnight, four men crossed Miss Emily's lawn and slunk about the house like burglars, sniffing along the base of the brickwork and at the cellar openings while one of them performed a regular sowing motion with his hand out of a sack slung from his shoulder. They broke open the cellar door and sprinkled lime there, and in all the outbuildings. As they recrossed the lawn, a window that had been dark was lighted and Miss Emily sat in it, the light behind her, and her upright torso motionless as that of an idol. They crept quietly across the lawn and into the shadow of the locusts that lined the street. After a week or two the smell went away.

That was when people had begun to feel really sorry for her. People in our town, remembering how old lady Wyatt, her great-aunt, had gone completely crazy at last, believed that the Griersons held themselves a little too high for what they really were. None of the young men were quite good enough for Miss Emily and such. We had long thought of them as a tableau, Miss Emily a slender figure in white in the background, her father a spraddled silhouette in the foreground, his back to her and clutching a horsewhip, the two of them framed by the back-flung front door. So when she got to be thirty and was still single, we were not pleased exactly, but vindicated; even with insanity in the family she wouldn't have turned down all of her chances if they had really materialized.

When her father died, it got about that the house was all that was left to her; and in a way, people were glad. At last they could pity Miss Emily. Being left alone, and a pauper, she had become humanized. Now she too would know the old thrill and the old despair of a penny more or less.

The day after his death all the ladies prepared to call at the house and offer condolence and aid, as is our custom. Miss Emily met them at the door, dressed as usual and with no trace of grief on her face. She told them that her father was not dead. She did that for three days, with the ministers calling on her, and the doctors, trying to persuade her to let them dispose of the body. Just as they were about to resort to law and force, she broke down, and they buried her father quickly.

We did not say she was crazy then. We believed she had to do that. We remembered all the young men her father had driven away, and we knew that with nothing left, she would have to cling to that which had robbed her, as people will.

III

She was sick for a long time. When we saw her again, her hair was cut short, making her look like a girl, with a vague resemblance to those angels in colored church windows — sort of tragic and serene.

The town had just let the contracts for paving the sidewalks, and in the summer after her father's death they began the work. The construction company came with niggers and mules and machinery, and a foreman named Homer Barron, a Yankee — a big, dark, ready man, with a big voice and eyes lighter than his face. The little boys would follow in groups to hear him cuss the niggers, and the niggers singing in time to the rise and fall of picks. Pretty soon he knew everybody in town. Whenever you heard a lot of laughing anywhere about the square, Homer Barron would be in the center of the group. Presently we began to see him and Miss Emily on Sunday afternoons driving in the yellow-wheeled buggy and the matched team of bays from the livery stable.

At first we were glad that Miss Emily would have an interest, because the ladies all said, "Of course a Grierson would not think seriously of a Northerner, a day laborer." But there were still others, older people, who said that even grief could not cause a real lady to forget *noblesse oblige* — without calling it *noblesse oblige*. They just said, "Poor Emily. Her kinsfolk should come to her." She had some kin in Alabama; but years ago her father had fallen out with them over the estate of old lady Wyatt, the crazy woman, and there was no communication between the two families. They had not even been represented at the funeral.

And as soon as the old people said, "Poor Emily," the whispering began. "Do you suppose it's really so?" they said to one another. "Of course it is. What else could..." This behind their hands; rustling of craned silk and satin behind jalousies closed upon the sun of Sunday afternoon as the thin, swift clop-clop-clop of the matched team passed: "Poor Emily."

She carried her head high enough — even when we believed that she was fallen. It was as if she demanded more than ever the recognition of her dignity as the last Grierson; as if it had wanted that touch of earthiness to reaffirm her imperviousness. Like when she bought the rat poison, the arsenic. That was over a year after they had begun to say "Poor Emily," and while the two female cousins were visiting her.

"I want some poison," she said to the druggist. She was over thirty then, still a slight woman, though thinner than usual, with cold, haughty black eyes in a face the flesh of which was strained across the temples and about the eye-sockets as you imagine a lighthouse-keeper's face ought to look. "I want some poison," she said.

"Yes, Miss Emily. What kind? For rats and such? I'd recom —"

"I want the best you have. I don't care what kind."

The druggist named several. "They'll kill anything up to an elephant. But what you want is —"

"Arsenic," Miss Emily said. "Is that a good one?"

"Is... arsenic? Yes, ma'am. But what you want —"

"I want arsenic."

The druggist looked down at her. She looked back at him, erect, her face like a strained flag. "Why, of course," the druggist said. "If that's what you want. But the law requires you to tell what you are going to use it for."

Miss Emily just stared at him, her head tilted back in order to look him eye for eye, until he looked away and went and got the arsenic and wrapped it up. The Negro delivery boy brought her the package; the druggist didn't come back. When she opened the package at home there was written on the box, under the skull and bones: "For rats."

IV

So the next day we all said, "She will kill herself"; and we said it would be the best thing. When she had first begun to be seen with Homer Barron, we had said, "She will marry him." Then we said, "She will persuade him yet," because Homer himself had remarked — he liked men, and it was known that he drank with the younger men in the Elks' Club — that he was not a marrying man. Later we said, "Poor Emily" behind the jalousies as they passed on Sunday afternoon in the glittering buggy, Miss Emily with her head high and Homer Barron with his hat cocked and a cigar in his teeth, reins and whip in a yellow glove.

Then some of the ladies began to say that it was a disgrace to the town and a bad example to the young people. The men did not want to interfere, but at last the ladies forced the Baptist minister — Miss Emily's people were Episcopal [4] — to call upon her. He would never divulge what happened during that interview, but he refused to go back again. The next Sunday they again drove about the streets, and the following day the minister's wife wrote to Miss Emily's relations in Alabama.

So she had blood-kin under her roof again and we sat back to watch developments. At first nothing happened. Then we were sure that they were to be married. We learned that Miss Emily had been to the jeweler's and ordered a man's toilet set in silver, with the letters H. B. on each piece. Two days later we learned that she had bought a complete outfit of men's clothing, including a nightshirt, and we said, "They are married." We were really glad. We were glad because the two female cousins were even more Grierson than Miss Emily had ever been.

So we were not surprised when Homer Barron — the streets had been finished some time since — was gone. We were a little disappointed that there was not a public blowing-off, but we believed that he had gone on to prepare for Miss Emily's coming, or to give her a chance to get rid of the cousins. (By that time it was a cabal, and we were all Miss Emily's allies to help circumvent the cousins.) Sure enough, after another week they departed. And, as we had expected all along, within three days Homer Barron was back in town. A neighbor saw the Negro man admit him at the kitchen door at dusk one evening.

And that was the last we saw of Homer Barron. And of Miss Emily for some time. The Negro man went in and out with the market basket, but the front door remained closed. Now and then we would see her at a window for a moment, as the men did that night when they sprinkled the lime, but for almost six months she did not appear on the streets. Then we knew that this was to be expected too; as if that quality of her father which had thwarted her woman's life so many times had been too virulent and too furious to die.

When we next saw Miss Emily, she had grown fat and her hair was turning gray. During the next few years it grew grayer and grayer until it attained an even pepper-and-salt iron-gray, when it ceased turning. Up to the day of her death at seventy-four it was still that vigorous iron-gray, like the hair of an active man.

From that time on her front door remained closed, save for a period of six or seven years, when she was about forty, during which she gave lessons in china-painting. She fitted up a studio in one of the downstairs rooms, where the daughters and granddaughters of Colonel Sartoris' contemporaries were sent to her with the same regularity and in the same spirit that they were sent to church on Sundays with a twenty-five-cent piece for the collection plate. Meanwhile her taxes had been remitted.

Then the newer generation became the backbone and the spirit of the town, and the painting pupils grew up and fell away and did not send their children to her with boxes of color and tedious brushes and pictures cut from the ladies' magazines. The front door closed upon the last one and remained closed for good. When the town got free postal delivery, Miss Emily alone refused to let them fasten the metal numbers above her door and attach a mailbox to it. She would not listen to them.

Daily, monthly, yearly we watched the Negro grow grayer and more stooped, going in and out with the market basket. Each December we sent her a tax notice, which would be returned by the post office a week later, unclaimed. Now and then we would see her in one of the downstairs windows — she had evidently shut up the top floor of the house — like the carven torso of an idol in a niche, looking or not looking at us, we could never tell which. Thus she passed from generation to generation — dear, inescapable, impervious, tranquil, and perverse.

And so she died. Fell ill in the house filled with dust and shadows, with only a doddering Negro man to wait on her. We did not even know she was sick; we had long since given up trying to get any information from the Negro. He talked to no one, probably not even to her, for his voice had grown harsh and rusty, as if from disuse.

She died in one of the downstairs rooms, in a heavy walnut bed with a curtain, her gray head propped on a pillow yellow and moldy with age and lack of sunlight.

V

The Negro met the first of the ladies at the front door and let them in, with their hushed, sibilant voices and their quick, curious glances, and then he disappeared. He walked right through the house and out the back and was not seen again.

The two female cousins came at once. They held the funeral on the second day, with the town coming to look at Miss Emily beneath a mass of bought flowers, with the crayon face of her father musing profoundly above the bier and the ladies sibilant and macabre; and the very old men — some in their brushed Confederate uniforms — on the porch and the lawn, talking of Miss Emily as if she had been a contemporary of theirs, believing that they had danced with her and courted her perhaps, confusing time with its mathematical progression, as the old do, to whom all the past is not a diminishing road but, instead, a huge meadow which no winter ever quite touches, divided from them now by the narrow bottle-neck of the most recent decade of years.

Already we knew that there was one room in that region above stairs which no one had seen in forty years, and which would have to be forced. They waited until Miss Emily was decently in the ground before they opened it.

The violence of breaking down the door seemed to fill this room with pervading dust. A thin, acrid pall as of the tomb seemed to lie everywhere upon this room decked and furnished as for a bridal: upon the valance curtains of faded rose color, [5] upon the rose-shaded lights, upon the dressing table, upon the delicate array of crystal and the man's toilet things backed with tarnished silver, silver so tarnished that the monogram was obscured. Among them lay a collar and tie, as if they had just been removed, which, lifted, left upon the surface a pale crescent in the dust. Upon a chair hung the suit, carefully folded; beneath it the two mute shoes and the discarded socks.

The man himself lay in the bed.

For a long while we just stood there, looking down at the profound and fleshless grin. The body had apparently once lain in the attitude of an embrace, but now the long sleep that outlasts love, that conquers even the grimace of love, had cuckolded him. What was left of him, rotted beneath what was left of the nightshirt, had become inextricable from the bed in which he lay; and upon him and upon the pillow beside him lay that even coating of the patient and biding dust.

Then we noticed that in the second pillow was the indentation of a head. One of us lifted something from it, and leaning forward, that faint and invisible dust dry and acrid in the nostrils, we saw a long strand of iron-gray hair.

NOTES ON THE TEXT

[1] "A Rose for Emily" was first published in the April 30, 1930 issue of *Forum* and republished in 1931 in *These Thirteen*, a collection of Faulkner's short stories. Faulkner himself described the title of the story as "allegorical," saying, "The meaning was, here was a woman who has had a tragedy, an irrevocable tragedy and nothing could be done about it, and I pitied her and this was a salute ... to a woman you would hand a rose."

[2] Jefferson, the setting of this story, is Faulkner's fictional city in the fictional county of Yoknapatawpha which modeled on his hometown Oxford, Mississippi. The fact that Miss Emily is buried in a cemetery together with the Union and Confederate soldiers indicates not only her social status but also her association with the old tradition and history.

[3] It's interesting to note that Colonel John Sartoris models after Faulkner's own great-grandfather, William Clark Falkner, who was himself a colonel during the American Civil War. Faulkner published a novel entitled *Sartoris* in 1929, which portrays the decay of the Mississippi aristocracy after the American Civil War.

[4] The Episcopal Church is a branch of the Anglican Church in Scotland and the United States. Its American branch was formed from the remnants of the Church of England in the colonies after the Revolution War, and was finally given a constitution at a convention in Philadelphia in 1789.

[5] Notice that the word "rose" appears for the first time in the story, except in the title. It appears twice, as adjectives, in "rose color" and "rose-shaded light" in the same paragraph. A rose stands for love, but ironically it is found in a place that resembles a tomb.

QUESTIONS FOR DISCUSSION

1. In the very beginning (the first sentence) of the story, the narrator describes Miss Emily Grierson as a "fallen monument." In what sense is she a fallen monument? What does she symbolize in the story? What does her death signify? Why do the townspeople respect her?

2. Faulkner tells this story through a narrator using the first-person-plural perspective. Discuss the effects achieved by such a perspective from which Emily Grierson's mysterious life is revealed. How does the author bring in contrasting views and values between the new generations in Jefferson and Emily Grierson, the last of the aristocratic in town?

3. Gothic writers portray frightening scenarios, such as mysterious secrets, supernatural phenomenon, old castles laced with cobwebs, mad women, to create a breathless sense of horror and grotesqueness. Explore the gothic elements in this story and discuss their roles in the creation of a forbidding atmosphere in which an individual, representing the historical legacy of the old South, struggles against a repressive society.

4. How is the story structured? How does the author use foreshadowing to build suspense? What does that "long strand of iron-gray hair" suggest?

5. Emily's house is saturated with an atmosphere of decay and death. Find in the text some images related to death and decay and discuss their implications.

When her father dies, Emily does not admit he is dead. Nor does she tell anybody that Homer Barron is dead. What has caused Emily's denial of the deaths of her beloveds? Discuss the relationship between Emily's perception of death and her psychological state. Do you think she is mad? Why did Faulkner want to give a rose to her?

SUGGESTED REFERENCES

Bleikasten, André. *The Ink of Melancholy: Faulkner's Novels, from* ***The Sound and Fury*** *to* ***Light in August***. Bloomington: Indian UP, 1990.

Blotner, Joseph. *Faulkner: A Biography.* New York: Random House, 1974.

Brooks, Cleanth. *William Faulkner: The Yoknapatawpha Country.* New Haven: Yale UP, 1963.

Nebeker, Helen E. "Emily's Rose of Love: Thematic Implications of Point of View in Faulkner's 'A Rose for Emily.'" *The Bulletin of the Rocky Mountain Modern Language Association* 1970 (1): 3-13.

Parini, Jay. *One Matchless Time: A Life of William Faulkner.* New York: Harper Collins, 2004.

Singal, Daniel J. *William Faulkner: the Making of a Modernist.* Chapel Hill: U of North Carolina P, 1997.

Sullivan, Ruth. "The Narrator in 'A Rose for Emily.'" *The Journal of Narrative Technique* 1971(3): 159-78.

Wagner-Martin, Linda, ed. *William Faulkner: Six Decades of Criticism.* East Lansing: Michigan State UP, 2002.

Watkins, Floyd C. "The Structure of 'A Rose for Emily.'" *Modern Language Notes,* 1954 (7): 508-10.

Unit 13 Ernest Hemingway

(1899 – 1961)

A GUIDE TO LITERARY TERMINOLOGY

"The Lost Generation": *The phrase was popularized with the publication of Ernest Hemingway's* ***The Sun Also Rises*** *(1926), in which Hemingway used it in an epigraph that states, "You are all a lost generation." Hemingway borrowed this statement from American expatriate writer Gertrude Stein, who told him earlier that "all of you young people who served in the war...you are all a lost generation." The word "lost" means "disoriented, wandering, directionless," which indicates confusion and aimlessness. The Lost Generation was the generation of young writers disillusioned by the experience and aftermath of World War I. These writers felt that the traditional values they were brought up with were a sham, given the absurdity of the war and the devaluation of human life. They therefore rejected the hypocritical society that falsely advocated puritanical virtues. This generation of American writers included Ernest Hemingway, F. Scott Fitzgerald, T. S. Eliot, John Dos Passos, John Steinbeck, William Faulkner, Henry Miller, Hart Crane and William Slater Brown.*

NOTES ON THE AUTHOR

Ernest Miller Hemingway was born in Oak Park, Illinois, on July 21, 1899 to Dr. Clarence Hemingway, a respected physician, and Grace Hall Hemingway, a music teacher and talented singer. After graduating from high school in 1917 and working briefly as a reporter for *The Kansas City Star*, Hemingway enlisted with the World War I ambulance drivers in 1918 and worked in Italy. He was severely wounded on July 8 in the Italian frontline and taken to a Red Cross hospital in Milan for surgery and rehabilitation. During his convalescence in the hospital, he had an affair with a nurse, Agnes von Kurowsky, who rejected him shortly after agreeing to marry him. Hemingway was devastated by Agnes's rejection, which probably gave rise to his pattern of abandoning a wife before she abandoned him. Altogether he had four marriages in his life.

After Hemingway returned home in January 1919, he became a freelancer, staff writer, and foreign correspondent for *The Toronto Star*. He married Hadley Richardson in September 1921. The couple then moved to live in Paris from 1921 to 1926, where Hemingway, while covering events of Europe for *The Toronto Star* and writing fictions, met Gertrude Stein, Ezra Pound, James Joyce, Pablo Picasso,

Joan Miró — a group of expatriate modernist writer and artists whom Gertrude Stein referred to collectively as the "Lost Generation" — a term Hemingway had immortalized in the epigraph of his novel *The Sun Also Rises*. They decried the false ideals of patriotism which led young people to war and took the war as a symptom of the spiritually rotten modern world.

Hemingway published his first book, *Three Stories and Ten Poems*, in 1923, and a collection of short stories, *In Our Time* in 1925. By the time he published his first major novel *The Sun Also Rises* in 1926, he had become the spokesman for the "lost generation." The publication of his story collection *Men without Women* (1927) and *A Farewell to Arms* (1929) had established him as a prominent American writer. Hemingway did not write much during the 1930s. His next novel *For Whom the Bell Tolls* was not published until 1940. From 1940, he lived primarily in Cuba, the setting for his novella *The Old Man and the Sea* published in 1952 which made him an international celebrity and won the Pulitzer Prize in the same year. In October 1954, Hemingway received the Nobel Prize for Literature. Hemingway left Cuba in 1960 for a new last home in Ketchum, Idaho, where he, due to depression and serious deterioration of health, committed suicide on July 2, 1961.

SYNOPSIS OF THE WORK

"Soldier's Home" is a story about a young veteran's readjustment to life after he returns home from World War I. In 1917, while he was studying at a Methodist college in Kansas, Harold Krebs enlisted with the U. S. Marines and was sent to fight the war in Europe. After he returns home from Europe two years later, he feels alienated from his home and from the community in which he grew up. Traumatized by the war, he can no longer fit in with the conventional values of his hometown. People are not interested in what he says about the war when he tells them the truth. He feels he has to lie in order to get their attention. So he gives up talking about the war. Krebs likes to watch the girls in town, but he doesn't want to be involved in the complexity and politics of courtship. He would like to have one of them, but he doesn't want any consequences. His parents want him to find a job and get married, his sister wants him to come to her baseball match, but Krebs has to lie again in order not to hurt their feelings. He has indeed lost his trust and love of anybody, because of the war.

Harold Krebs is a representative of the "lost generation" of 1920s who, thwarted by the cruelty and absurdity of war, had been cut off from all sense of purpose, community identity, and historical connection. They had to face the pressure of living in a world without meaning.

SELECTED READINGS

Soldier's Home [1]

Krebs went to the war from a Methodist college [2] in Kansas. There is a picture which shows him among his fraternity brothers, all of them wearing exactly the same height and style collar. He enlisted in the Marines[1] in 1917 and did not return to the United States until the second division returned from the Rhine[2] in the summer of 1919.

There is a picture which shows him on the Rhine with two German girls and another corporal. Krebs and the corporal look too big for their uniforms. The German girls are not beautiful. The Rhine does not show in the picture.

By the time Krebs returned to his home town in Oklahoma the greeting of heroes was over. He came back much too late. The men from the town who had been drafted had all been welcomed elaborately on their return. There had been a great deal of hysteria[3]. Now the reaction had set in. People seemed to think it was rather ridiculous for Krebs to be getting back so late, years after the war was over.

At first Krebs, who had been at Belleau Wood, [3] Soissons, [4] the Champagne, [5] St. Mihiel [6] and in the Argonne [7] did not want to talk about the war at all. Later he felt the need to talk but no one wanted to hear about it. His town had heard too many atrocity stories

---

1 the Marines: The U. S. Marine Corps has been a component of the U. S. Department of the Navy since 1834. It is a branch of the U. S. Armed Forces responsible for providing power projection from the sea.

2 the Rhine: a European river that begins in the Swiss canton of Graubünden in the southeastern Swiss Alps, forms part of the Franco-German border, then flows through Germany and eventually empties into the North Sea in the Netherlands.

3 hysteria: a state of uncontrolled excitement, anger, or panic.

to be thrilled by actualities. Krebs found that to be listened to at all he had to lie, and after he had done this twice he, too, had a reaction against the war and against talking about it. A distaste for everything that had happened to him in the war set in because of the lies he had told. All of the times that had been able to make him feel cool and clear inside himself when he thought of them; the times so long back when he had done the one thing, the only thing for a man to do, easily and naturally, when he might have done something else, now lost their cool, valuable quality and then were lost themselves.

His lies were quite unimportant lies and consisted in attributing to himself things other men had seen, done or heard of, and stating as facts certain apocryphal[4] incidents familiar to all soldiers. Even his lies were not sensational at the pool room. His acquaintances, who had heard detailed accounts of German women found chained to machine guns in the Argonne forest and who could not comprehend, or were barred by their patriotism from interest in, any German machine gunners who were not chained, were not thrilled by his stories.

Krebs acquired the nausea in regard to experience that is the result of untruth or exaggeration, and when he occasionally met another man who had really been a soldier and they talked a few minutes in the dressing room at a dance he fell into the easy pose of the old soldier among other soldiers: that he had been badly, sickeningly frightened all the time. In this way he lost everything. [8]

During this time, it was late summer, he was sleeping late in bed, getting up to walk down town to the library to get a book, eating lunch at home, reading on the front porch until he became bored and then walking down through the town to spend the hottest hours of the day in the cool dark of the pool room. He loved to play pool.

In the evening he practiced on his clarinet[5], strolled down town,

---

4 apocryphal: not true; of questionable authenticity.
5 clarinet: a single-reed instrument with a straight tube（单簧管）.

read and went to bed. He was still a Hero to his two young sisters. His mother would have given him breakfast in bed if he had wanted it. She often came in when he was in bed and asked him to tell her about the war, but her attention always wandered. His father was non-committal.

Before Krebs went away to the war he had never been allowed to drive the family motor car. His father was in the real estate business and always wanted the car to be at his command when he required it to take clients out into the country to show them a piece of farm property. The car always stood outside the First National Bank building where his father had an office on the second floor. Now, after the war, it was still the same car.

Nothing was changed in the town except that the young girls had grown up. But they lived in such a complicated world of already defined alliances and shifting feuds that Krebs did not feel the energy or the courage to break into it. He liked to look at them, though. There were so many good-looking young girls. Most of them had their hair cut short. When he went away only little girls wore their hair like that or girls that were fast[6]. They all wore sweaters and shirt waists[7] with round Dutch collars. It was a pattern. He liked to look at them from the front porch as they walked on the other side of the street. He liked to watch them walking under the shade of the trees. He liked the round Dutch collars above their sweaters. He liked their silk stockings and flat shoes. He liked their bobbed hair and the way they walked.

When he was in town their appeal to him was not very strong. He did not like them when he saw them in the Greek's ice cream parlor. He did not want them themselves really. They were too complicated. There was something else. Vaguely he wanted a girl but he did not want to have to work to get her. He would have liked to have a girl but

6 fast: (of persons) devoted to pleasure, usually implying a greater or less degree of immorality; (of women) unrefined in habits and manners, disregardful of propriety or decorum.
7 shirt waist: a blouse with buttons down the fronts（松宽短罩衫）.

he did not want to have to spend a long time getting her. He did not want to get into the intrigue and the politics. He did not want to have to do any courting. He did not want to tell any more lies. It wasn't worth it.

He did not want any consequences. He did not want any consequences ever again. He wanted to live along without consequences. Besides he did not really need a girl. The army had taught him that. It was all right to pose as though you had to have a girl. Nearly everybody did that. But it wasn't true. You did not need a girl. That was the funny thing. First a fellow boasted how girls mean nothing to him, that he never thought of them, that they could not touch him. Then a fellow boasted that he could not get along without girls, that he had to have them all the time, that he could not go to sleep without them.

That was all a lie. It was all a lie both ways. You did not need a girl unless you thought about them. He learned that in the army. Then sooner or later you always got one. When you were really ripe for a girl you always got one. You did not have to think about it. Sooner or later it would come. He had learned that in the army.

Now he would have liked a girl if she had come to him and not wanted to talk. But here at home it was all too complicated. He knew he could never get through it all again. It was not worth the trouble. That was the thing about French girls and German girls. There was not all this talking. You couldn't talk much and you did not need to talk. It was simple and you were friends. He thought about France and then he began to think about Germany. On the whole he had liked Germany better. He did not want to leave Germany. He did not want to come home. Still, he had come home. He sat on the front porch.

He liked the girls that were walking along the other side of the street. He liked the look of them much better than the French girls or the German girls. But the world they were in was not the world he was in. He would like to have one of them. But it was not worth it. They were such a nice pattern. He liked the pattern. It was exciting. But he would not go through all the talking. He did not want one badly enough. [9]

He liked to look at them all, though. It was not worth it. Not now when things were getting good again. He sat there on the porch reading a book on the war. It was a history and he was reading about all the engagements he had been in. It was the most interesting reading he had ever done. He wished there were more maps. He looked forward with a good feeling to reading all the really good histories when they would come out with good detail maps. Now he was really learning about the war. He had been a good soldier. That made a difference.

One morning after he had been home about a month his mother came into his bedroom and sat on the bed. She smoothed her apron.

"I had a talk with your father last night, Harold," she said, "and he is willing for you to take the car out in the evenings."

"Yeah?" said Krebs, who was not fully awake. "Take the car out? Yeah?"

"Yes. Your father has felt for some time that you should be able to take the car out in the evenings whenever you wished but we only talked it over last night."

"I'll bet you made him," Krebs said.

"No. It was your father's suggestion that we talk the matter over."

"Yeah. I'll bet you made him," Krebs sat up in bed.

"Will you come down to breakfast, Harold?" his mother said.

"As soon as I get my clothes on," Krebs said.

His mother went out of the room and he could hear her frying something downstairs while he washed, shaved and dressed to go down into the dining-room for breakfast. While he was eating breakfast his sister brought in the mail.

"Well, Hare," she said. "You old sleepy-head. What do you ever get up for?"

Krebs looked at her. He liked her. She was his best sister.

"Have you got the paper?" he asked.

She handed him *The Kansas City Star* and he shucked off its brown wrapper and opened it to the sporting page. He folded *The Star* open and propped it against the water pitcher with his cereal dish to steady it, so he could read while he ate.

"Harold," his mother stood in the kitchen doorway, "Harold, please don't muss up the paper. Your father can't read his *Star* if it's been mussed."

"I won't muss it," Krebs said.

His sister sat down at the table and watched him while he read.

"We're playing indoor over at school this afternoon," his sister said. "I'm going to pitch."

"Good," said Krebs. "How's the old wing?"

"I can pitch better than lots of the boys. I tell them all you taught me. The other girls aren't much good."

"Yeah?" said Krebs.

"I tell them all you're my beau[8]. Aren't you my beau, Hare?"

"You bet."[9]

"Couldn't your brother really be your beau just because he's your brother?"

"I don't know."

"Sure you know. Couldn't you be my beau, Hare, if I was old enough and if you wanted to?"

"Sure. You're my girl now."

"Am I really your girl?"

"Sure."

"Do you love me?"

"Uh, huh."

---

8 beau: a man who is the lover of a girl or young woman.

9 You bet: an expression of emphatic agreement.

"Will you love me always?"

"Sure."

"Will you come over and watch me play indoor?"

"Maybe."

"Aw, Hare, you don't love me. If you loved me, you'd want to come over and watch me play indoor."

Krebs's mother came into the dining-room from the kitchen. She carried a plate with two fried eggs and some crisp bacon on it and a plate of buckwheat cakes.

"You run along, Helen," she said. "I want to talk to Harold."

She put the eggs and bacon down in front of him and brought in a jug of maple syrup for the buckwheat cakes. Then she sat down across the table from Krebs.

"I wish you'd put down the paper a minute, Harold," she said.

Krebs took down the paper and folded it.

"Have you decided what you are going to do yet, Harold?" his mother said, taking off her glasses.

"No," said Krebs.

"Don't you think it's about time?" His mother did not say this in a mean way. She seemed worried.

"I hadn't thought about it," Krebs said.

"God has some work for everyone to do," his mother said. "There can be no idle hands in His Kingdom."

"I'm not in His Kingdom," Krebs said.

"We are all of us in His Kingdom."

Krebs felt embarrassed and resentful as always.

"I've worried about you so much, Harold," his mother went on. "I know the temptations you must have been exposed to. I know how weak men are. I know what your own dear grandfather, my own father, told us about the Civil War and I have prayed for you. I pray for you all day long, Harold."

Krebs looked at the bacon fat hardening on his plate.

"Your father is worried, too," his mother went on. "He thinks you have lost your ambition, that you haven't got a definite aim in life. Charley Simmons, who is just your age, has a good job and is going to be married. The boys are all settling down; they're all determined to get somewhere; you can see that boys like Charley Simmons are on their way to being really a credit to the community."

Krebs said nothing.

"Don't look that way, Harold," his mother said. "You know we love you and I want to tell you for your own good how matters stand. Your father does not want to hamper your freedom. He thinks you should be allowed to drive the car. If you want to take some of the nice girls out riding with you, we are only too pleased. We want you to enjoy yourself. But you are going to have to settle down to work, Harold. Your father doesn't care what you start in at. All work is honorable as he says. But you've got to make a start at something. He asked me to speak to you this morning and then you can stop in and see him at his office."

"Is that all? " Krebs said.

"Yes. Don't you love your mother, dear boy?"

"No," Krebs said.

His mother looked at him across the table. Her eyes were shiny. She started crying.

"I don't love anybody," Krebs said.

It wasn't any good. He couldn't tell her, he couldn't make her see it. It was silly to have said it. He had only hurt her. He went over and took hold of her arm. She was crying with her head in her hands.

"I didn't mean it," he said. "I was just angry at something. I didn't mean I didn't love you."

His mother went on crying. Krebs put his arm on her shoulder.

"Can't you believe me, mother?"

His mother shook her head.

"Please, please, mother. Please believe me."

"All right," his mother said chokily. She looked up at him."I believe you, Harold."

Krebs kissed her hair. She put her face up to him.

"I'm your mother," she said. "I held you next to my heart when you were a tiny baby."

Krebs felt sick and vaguely nauseated.

"I know, Mummy," he said. "I'll try and be a good boy for you."

"Would you kneel and pray with me, Harold?" his mother asked.

They knelt down beside the dining-room table and Krebs's mother prayed.

"Now, you pray, Harold," she said.

"I can't," Krebs said.

"Try, Harold."

"I can't."

"Do you want me to pray for you?"

"Yes."

So his mother prayed for him and then they stood up and Krebs kissed his mother and went out of the house. He had tried so to keep his life from being complicated. Still, none of it had touched him. He had felt sorry for his mother and she had made him lie. He would go to Kansas City and get a job and she would feel all right about it. There would be one more scene maybe before he got away. He would not go down to his father's office. He would miss that one. He wanted his life to go smoothly. It had just gotten going that way. Well, that was all over now, anyway. He would go over to the schoolyard and watch Helen play indoor baseball.

NOTES ON THE TEXT

[1] "Soldier's Home" is a short story by Hemingway first collected in *In Our Time* published in 1925. It was based on Hemingway's own emotional experiences after the war and his readjustment. Hemingway returned home in January 1919 after he had recovered from a serious wound during World War I. He was not yet 20, but the war had changed him and his perceptions of war, love, patriotism, and the meaning of life.

[2] The establishment of a Methodist college was related to the Methodist ideals. The Methodists are Protestants who believe in the teachings of John Wesley (1703—1791) who argued for the notion of Christian perfection and against Calvinism, particularly, against its doctrine of predestination. He held that, in this life, Christians could achieve a state where the love of God "reigned supreme in their hearts," giving them outward holiness. Methodism is characterized by its emphasis on helping the poor and the average person, which has become a systematic approach to building the person, and the "church" and its missionary spirit. These ideals are put into practice by the establishment of hospitals, universities, orphanages, soup kitchens, and schools to follow Jesus's command to spread the Good News and serve all people.

[3] The Battle of Belleau Wood took place from June 1 to June 26 during the German 1918 Spring Offensive in World War I, near the Marne River in France. The battle was fought between the U. S. Second and Third Divisions and an assortment of German units.

[4] The Battle of Soissons was fought from July 18 to 22, 1918, between the French, with American assistance, and German armies. The battle ended with the French recapturing most of the ground lost to German Spring Offensive in may 1918. The Allies suffered 125,000 casualties (95,000 French, 13,000 British and 12,000 American), while the German suffered 168,000 casualties.

[5] The author probably refers to the First Battle of Champagne (December 20, 1914—March 17, 1915) in the Champagne region of France between the French Fourth Army and the German Third Army, and the Second Battle of Champagne (September 25, 1915—October 5, 1915) which was a French offensive against the invading German army. However, Harold Krebs couldn't have fought any of the two battles, for he enlisted in the U. S. Marine Corps long after they took place.

[6] The Battle of Saint-Mihiel was fought from 12 to 15 September 1918 during World War I, involving the American Expeditionary Force and French troops under the command of General John J. Pershing against German positions. The attack at the St. Mihiel Salient was part of Pershing's plan to break through the German lines and capture the fortified city of Metz. The attack on Metz, however, was not realized, as the Germans refortified their positions and the Americans then turned their efforts to the Meuse-Argonne Offensive.

[7] The battle of the Argonne Forest, also named Meuse-Argonne Offensive, was part of the final Allied offensive of World War I that stretched along the entire Western Front. It was

fought from September 26, 1918, until the Armistice on November 11, a total of 47 days. The battle was the largest in United States military history, involving 1.2 million American soldiers, and was one of a series of Allied attacks known as the Hundred Days Offensive, which brought the war to an end.

[8] The truth about Kreb's war experience is that he was "badly and sickly frightened all the time." This is a sign of cowardice which contradicts the conventional notions of heroism and courage. So, Kreb has "lost everything."

[9] As is shown in Hemingway's story collection *Men without Women*, and in other stories, such as "The Three-Day Below" from *In Our Time*, Hemingway's men prefer not to get married. Bill in "The Three-Day Below," for instance, says, "Once a man's married, he's absolutely bitched." He will be burdened by responsibilities, domesticity, and the pain locked in with a love that may easily be broken or lost.

QUESTIONS FOR DISCUSSION

1. While working as a young reporter for *The Kansas City Star*, Hemingway learned importance of writing as a rigorous craft of producing clarity, simplicity and strength of statement and expression. Hemingway's writing is characterized by simple declarative sentences stripped of adjectives or poetic adornment, or a sort of "journalistic objectivity." Find exemplary sentences from the text to illustrate his style. In what ways can this style help strengthen the theme of the story?

2. Discuss the disparity between what his hometown fellows expect of him and his own feelings about things such as war, religion, love, career, happiness, the meaning of life. In what sense is Krebs an antihero? What makes him lie (including his lies to his mother and his sister)?

3. For Hemingway, wounded in World War I, life was war, nasty, brutal and arbitrary. In the same token, the protagonist in this story, Krebs, has also experienced the cruelty of war in the battles of Belleau Wood, Soissons, Saint-Mihiel, and the Argonne Forest. Discuss what, apart from physical wounds, Krebs is attempting to overcome and recover from? Why is he unable to fit in with his home and with the values of his hometown where he was brought up? What has caused his loss of religious belief and his loss of purpose in life?

4. Why does Krebs want to read a book on the war? Does this suggest he is still haunted by his traumatic experiences during the war? At the end of the story, Krebs decides to go to the Kansas City to look for a job, but he will not go to his father's office. What does this ending of the story suggest?

5. Hemingway's heroes, or rather antiheroes, are usually men of solitude, who have to face reality alone and come to terms with the stark facts of life by themselves.

"Soldier's Home" is a story about the disillusionment of a war veteran grappling with its aftermath. How does Krebs react to the challenges from life? In what ways do you think Krebs has shown his "grace under pressure" and weathered the storm?

SUGGESTED REFERENCES

Baker, Carlos. *Ernest Hemingway: A Life Story.* New York: Charles Scribner's Sons, 1969.

Baker, Carlos. *Hemingway: The Writer as Artist.* Princeton: Princeton UP, 1972.

Donaldson, Scott, ed. *The Cambridge Companion to Ernest Hemingway.* New York: Cambridge UP, 1996.

Hemingway, Ernest and Carlos Baker, eds. *Selected Letters 1917-1961.* New York: Charles Scribner's Sons, 1981.

Oliver, Charles. *Ernest Heminway A to Z: The Essential Reference to the Life and Work.* New York: Checkmark Publishing, 1999.

Scholes, Robert. "New Critical Approaches to the Short Stories of Hemingway." *Decoding Papa:* ***A Very Short Story*** *as Work and Text.* Ed. Jackson J. Benson. Hurham, NC: Duke UP, 1990. 33-47.

Unit 14
Twentieth Century American Poets

Robert Lee Frost

(1915—2005)

A GUIDE TO LITERARY TERMINOLOGY

"Iambic Tetrameter": *Iambic tetrameter is a meter in poetry. It refers to a line consisting of four iambic feet. "Iambic" means the unit of sound is two syllables with the first unstressed and the second stressed. Each of these two syllable units is called a foot. Tetrameter means that each line of the poem contains four of these feet. Iambic tetrameter is a line comprising four iambs. Example:*

× / × / × / × /
Come live with me and be my love
(Christopher Marlowe, "The Passionate Shepherd to His Love")

But the meter in Robert Frost's "The Road Not Taken" is not the regular iambic tetrameter. It is different in that it has one syllable too many. Example:

× / × / × / × / /
Two roads diverged in a yellow wood

NOTES ON THE POET AND HIS POETRY

Though he was born in San Francisco and spent his childhood in the West, Robert Lee Frost came to be recognized as a New England poet. His family moved to Salem, New Hampshire, after his father's death in 1884. After graduation from high school as valedictorian and class poet, Frost tried to get a college education, first in Dartmouth College in 1892, but soon left, and then in Harvard for only two years (1897—1899). Afterwards he picked up some odd jobs while writing poetry. In 1912, he went to England, where he became acquainted with Ezra Pound and the "Georgian" group of poets that included Edward Thomas. It was also in London where he received his first acclaim as a poet. His first volume of poetry, *A Boy's Will* (1913), was published in England, followed by his second, *North Boston* (1914), and third, *Mountain Interval* (1916). Because of the outbreak of World War

I, he, together with his family, returned to the United States, settling on a farm near Franconia, New Hampshire. He taught and lectured in Amherst, Harvard, and the University of Michigan. His reputation as a poet grew with the publications of *New Hampshire* (1923), *West-Running Brooks* (1928), *Collected Poems* (1930), *A Further Range* (1936), *A Witness Tree* (1942), *Steeple Bush* (1974), and *In the Clearing* (1962). He won four Pulitzer Prizes (1924, 1931, 1937, and 1943), received honorary degrees from 44 colleges and universities, and was invited to read his poem "The Gift Outright" at the inauguration of President John F. Kennedy in 1961, at the age of 87. Despite his success, Frost was often haunted by personal misfortune. Two of his children died in infancy, a son took his own life, a daughter became mentally deranged.

Robert Frost wrote in the traditional forms, using rhyme, meter, and regular stanzas, despite the trend of American poetry toward free verse which he compared to "playing tennis without a net." In his writing, he preferred to use plain, colloquial expressions with the rhythms of the actual speech and the characteristics of New Englanders. But the simplicity of his poetic form and his frequent use of rural settings and farm life are often deceptive. His poems, for all their apparent simplicity, often explore the mysteries of darkness and irrationality in an indifferent world where the individuals remained lonely, helpless, and perplexed. They represent a wide range of human experience and reveal profound ideas; they are concerned with moral uncertainties, the mysteries and complexity of love, existence, and death.

SELECTED READINGS

The Road Not Taken [1]

Two roads diverged[1] in a yellow wood,
And sorry I could not travel both
And be one traveler, long I stood
And looked down one as far as I could
To where it bent[2] in the undergrowth; [2]

Then took the other, as just as fair,[3]

---

1 diverge: go in different directions from a common point; branch out.
2 bent: deviated from a straight line.
3 as just as fair: which is as proper and fair as the first road.

And having perhaps the better claim,
Because it was grassy and wanted wear[4];
Though as for that[5] the passing there[6]
Had worn them really about the same.

And both[7] that morning equally lay
In leaves no step had trodden black.[8]
Oh, I kept the first for another day!
Yet knowing how way leads on to way,
I doubted if I should ever come back.

I shall be telling this with a sigh [3]
Somewhere ages and ages hence[9]:
Two roads diverged in a wood, and I —
I took the one less traveled by,
And that has made all the difference. [4]

NOTES ON THE TEXT

[1] This poem was included in Frost's collection of poetry, *Mountain Interval*, published in 1916. It is one of Frost's best-known poems. Frost sent an advance copy to Edward Thomas, an English poet whom Frost befriended and took many walks together with while he stayed in England (1912—1915). Frost had intended the poem to be a gentle mock of indecision that Thomas showed whenever they came to a fork. But Thomas and many critics took it more seriously.

[2] The poem consist of four stanzas of iambic tetrameter (抑扬格四音步), but there are nine syllables per line instead of eight as required by tetrameter. The poem tells us that life always gives us two choices. But there is no certainty about which is better.

[3] Opinions differ as to the implication of the "sigh" here. It may be interpreted as one of regret

---

4 wanted wear: lacked wear; was not worn because few people had trodden on it.
5 Though as for that: though concerning the condition of the roads.
6 the passing there: the frequency of the roads being trodden on.
7 both: both roads.
8 In leaves no step had trodden black: in the fallen leaves that had not been trodden black by passers-by.
9 ages and ages hence: many years later. Hence: from now.

or one of self-satisfaction. In a 1925 reply letter to Crystine Yates, who asked him about the sigh, Frost replied, "It was rather private jest at the expense of those who might think I would yet live to be sorry for the way I had taken in life."

[4] The speaker has made it clear in the second and third stanzas that the two roads had equal claim; however, in the fourth stanza, which imagines his future retrospective reflection on his choice, he contradicts what he said earlier by emphasizing he took "the one less travelled by," which "has made all the difference." This poem is often misread. Students are encouraged to associate "taking the road less travelled by" with initiative and individualism. Or, more crudely, it is interpreted as an advice for them not to turn, like most people, toward sin or avarice, but to take "the road less travelled by." However, what the poet intends to show is perhaps self-deception. There is no discernible difference between the two roads. The irony is: people tend to look back and attribute more meaning to choices they made than they deserve.

QUESTIONS FOR DISCUSSION

1. What mood has the poet conveyed in the first stanza? Is it difficult for the narrator to make a choice? What is the risk involved if he takes one of the two roads?

2. Read the second and third stanzas carefully to find out if there was really any difference between the two roads. Why did the speaker choose the second road instead of the first one? In what sense was he justified in his choice?

3. What does the speaker's "sigh" in the fourth stanza suggest to you? There is an apparent disparity between what is said about the roads in the last stanza and in stanzas 3 and 4. How do you explain this?

4. By metaphorical extension, the nature scene of a forking path in the yellow woods can denote different possibilities in the complicated circumstances of the human world. The realization of one possibility would necessarily entail the failure in another. One can never "come back" again, because "way leads on to way." What attitude would you adopt when you're confronted with such a situation?

参考译文

未选择的路

顾子欣 译

黄色的树林里分出两条路，
可惜我不能同时去涉足，

我在那路口久久伫立，
我向着一条路极目望去，
直到它消失在丛林深处。

但我却选了另外一条路，
它荒草萋萋，十分幽寂，
显得更诱人、更美丽，
虽然在这两条小路上，
都很少留下旅人的足迹，

虽然那天清晨落叶满地，
两条路都未经脚印污染。
呵，留下一条路等改日再见！
但我知道路径延绵无尽头，
恐怕我难以再回返。

也许多少年后在某个地方，
我将轻声叹息把往事回顾，
一片树林里分出两条路，
而我选了人迹更少的一条，
从此决定了我一生的道路。

SELECTED READINGS

Stopping by Woods on a Snowy Evening [1]

Whose woods [2] these are I think I know.
His house is in the village though;
He will not see me stopping here
To watch his woods fill up with snow. [3]

My little horse must think it queer
To stop without a farmhouse near
Between the woods and frozen lake

The darkest evening of the year. [4]

He[10] gives his harness bells a shake
To ask if there is some mistake.
The only other sound's the sweep
Of easy wind and downy flake[11].[5]

The woods are lovely, dark, and deep, [6]
But I have promises to keep,
And miles to go before I sleep,
And miles to go before I sleep. [7]

NOTES ON THE TEXT

[1] "Stopping by Woods on a Snowy Evening" was written in 1922 and published in the *New Hampshire* volume (1923). It is Frost's most anthologized poem. Frost called it "my best bid for remembrance."

[2] Woods, following Dante's "dark forest," symbolizes the mystery of nature, death, and catastrophe. The image of woods often appears in Frost's poetry.

[3] Note that the poem follows a rhyme scheme of aaba, bbcb, ccdc, and dddd, with the third unrhyming line in each of the first three stanzas becoming the rhyme word of each succeeding stanza, which forms a chain rhyme similar to terzarima (a rhyming verse stanza form that consists of an interlocking three-line rhyme scheme) used in Dante's *Inferno*. In the last stanza, all end words rhyme and the final couplet consists of a repeated "And miles to go before I sleep." The intertwining and repetition of rhymes create a lingering musical quality. Note also that long vowels and diphthongs dominate in the poem, slowing down the pace and reinforcing a meditative mood.

[4] In this stanza, the narrator's perspective shifts to that of the personified little horse. "Frozen lake" denotes death; the "darkest evening of the year," together with the cold snow, indicates poet's frustration and depression.

[5] Note the contrast between the sound made by the shake of the little horse's bells, which denotes a call to life, and the sound of the snow flake, which is as quiet as death.

[6] In the line "The woods are lovely, dark, and deep," the loveliness consists in the depth and

10 He: my little horse.
11 downy flake: soothing, soft snow flakes.

darkness which make the woods so ominous. The theme of this poem, despite Frost's denial, is the temptation of death, even suicide, symbolized by the woods that are filling up with snow on the darkest evening of the year. The speaker is powerfully drawn to the woods.

[7] The dark woods filling up with snow is peaceful and appealing. The speaker's subconscious desire for death, tranquility and eternity is somehow interrupted by the shake of the little horse's bells, which reminds him of his "promises to keep." He therefore resists the temptation of sleep or death, and continues to travel down the road, to fulfill his earthly obligations.

QUESTIONS FOR DISCUSSION

1. The speaker stops to look at the dark woods during a journey. What does the journey symbolize? What does the woods symbolize? What is the theme of this poem?

2. Discuss how the poetic form, its rhyme scheme and the musical effects, help to create for the audience the impression of a journey in process.

3. In the poem the poet has created some contrasts, or rather pairs of opposites, e.g., noises and tranquility, nature (woods, snow, wind) and culture (village, promises), journey and sleep. Discuss the impact of the woods on the speaker. What makes it "lovely"? Why is he attracted to it on a snowy evening? What eventually has made him change his mind?

4. What similarity do snow and darkness share? How do they contribute to a sense of extinction?

5. Do you think the narrator is firm in his tone and attitude? Cite examples from the poem to support your opinion.

参考译文

雪夜林畔小驻

余光中 译

想来我认识这座森林，
林主的庄宅就在邻村，
却不会见我在此驻马，
看他林中积雪的美景。

我的小马一定颇惊讶：
四望不见有什么农家，

偏是一年最暗的黄昏，
寒林和冰湖之间停下。

它摇一摇身上的串铃，
问我这地方该不该停。
此外只有轻风拂雪片，
再也听不见其他声音。

森林又暗又深真可羡，
但我还要守一些诺言，
还要赶多少路才安眠，
还要赶多少路才安眠。

Ezra Pound

(1885－1972)

A GUIDE TO LITERARY TERMINOLOGY

"Imagism": *Imagism was an early twentieth-century movement in British and American Poetry which rejected the sentimentalism of the late-nineteenth-century poetry in favor of one that relied on concrete imagery. Its leading spokesman Ezra Pound, together with F. S. Flint, wrote an imagist "manifesto" published in* ***Poetry*** *magazine in 1913, in which they put forth guiding tenets for writing poems: conciseness of expression, concreteness of imagery, and rhythm composed "in sequence of the musical phrase, not in sequence of a metronome." Pound edited the first imagist anthology* ***Des Imagistes****, which was published in 1914. Afterwards, Amy Lowell assumed leadership of the movement. In a collection of imagist poems entitled* ***Some Imagist Poets*** *she edited, Lowell formally outlined the major objectives or criteria of the Imagists, who believed that poetry should: (1) regularly use everyday speech, but avoid clichés; (2) create new rhythms; (3) address any subject matter the poet desired; and (4) depict its subjects through precise, clear images. The imagist poets, above all, seek to render the poet's response to a visual impression as concisely and precisely as possible.*

NOTES ON THE POET AND HIS POETRY

Born on October 30, 1885, in Hailey, Idaho, Ezra Pound grew up in Pennsylvania and attended the University of Pennsylvania at the age of fifteen. In 1906 he graduated with an M. A. degree. He went to Europe in 1908 and spent most of his life there. He started the Imagist Movement in England and America, which flourished from 1909 to 1917, and had influenced many writers, including William Butler Yeats, James Joyce, Ernest Hemingway, Robert Frost, D. H. Lawrence, and T. S. Eliot. He published a series of short collections of poetry: *A Lume Spento* (1908), *Personae* (1909), *Exultations* (1909), *Canzoni* (1911), *Ripostes* (1912). He published his major works, *Homage to Sextus Propertius* in 1918 and *Hugh Selwyn Mauberley* in 1920. He is best known for his *Cantos*, a brilliant, though sometimes obscure, epic work which he began to write in 1915 and finished in 1969. It collects 117 cantos, or chapters.

In the Imagists' view, a poem should be written with economy of expression, and should produce a precise image and nothing more. They used free verse, new rhythms, and plain, conversational language. In 1914, Pound edited an anthology of the imagists' poetry entitled *Des Imagistes*, which includes the works of ten imagists, including William Carlos Williams, Hilda Dolittle, Amy Lowell and Ezra Pound. Pound had a lasting interest in Chinese philosophy and poetry. He regarded Chinese poetry as a model for American poets. His translation of classical Chinese poetry, *Cathay* (1915), had aroused many modern American poets' interest in Chinese poetry. T. S. Eliot called him "the man who discovered Chinese poetry for the contemporary age."

SELECTED READINGS

In a Station of the Metro [1]

The apparition[12] of these faces in the crowd; [2]
Petals on a wet, black bough. [3]

---

12 apparition: a phantom.

NOTES ON THE TEXT

[1] This poem was written in the form of the Japanese Haiku (俳句诗) and was first published in 1913. It is considered one of the leading poems of the Imagist poetry. "The metro" here refers to the subway in Paris. The poem originally consisted of thirty lines but was reduced to only fourteen words, which demonstrates the economy of expression and precision of imagery of the Imagist tradition.

[2] The poem consists of a set of images. In the first line, the word "apparition" captures the transience of "faces" coming and going in the metro station; it perhaps also signals the transience of human life.

[3] In the second line, "petals," which symbolize female beauty, contrast sharply with the bleakness of the "wet, black bough." Since the petals are detached from flowers and stuck to a bough, they also indicate the transience of life. By linking human faces in a crowd and petals on a bough, the poet calls attention to both the beauty and mortality of human life.

QUESTIONS FOR DISCUSSION

1. Pound once said of this poem, "In a poem of this sort, one is trying to record the precise instant when a thing outward and objective transforms itself, or darts into a thing inward and subjective." Discuss how the external images are created in the poem so that they may conjure up inward feelings or ideas without stating them explicitly.

2. Note that there is not any verb in this poem. It consists of only some phrases that form a set of images. This simple and economical style, which broke away from the verbose style of Victorian literature, was quite familiar in classical Chinese poetry. Cite some examples from Chinese poetry (e.g. Bai Juyi's portrayal of Yang Guifei in "玉容寂寞泪阑干, 梨花一枝春带雨") and discuss their similarities in form and style.

参考译文

在地铁车站

飞白 译

这几张脸在人群中幻景般闪现；
湿漉漉的黑树枝上花瓣数点。

SELECTED READINGS

A Pact [1]

I make a pact with you, Walt Whitman —
I have detested you long enough.
I come to you as a grown child
Who has had a pig-headed[13] father; [2]
I am old enough now to make friends.
It was you that broke the new wood, [3]
Now is a time for carving. [4]
We have one sap and one root —
Let there be commerce[14] between us.

NOTES ON THE TEXT

[1] This poem was published in 1916. It records Pound's changed attitude toward Whitman and the tribute he is now paying Whitman.

[2] "A pig-headed father" perhaps indicates the indoctrination of tradition. As the saying goes, "Like father, like son." But now, the poet has become an independent grown-up and is ready to accept Whitman's unorthodox way of writing poetry, that is, free verse. Note this poem itself is in free verse, following no regular meter or rhyme scheme.

[3] "Break the new wood" refers to Whitman's breaking the conventions of poetry by using free verse.

[4] In this line, the poet continues the metaphor of "breaking the new wood" in the previous line. After breaking the new wood, "Now is the time for carving." This suggests the poet's determination to follow Whitman's tradition of inventing new ways to write poetry.

QUESTIONS FOR DISCUSSION

1. Why did Pound want to make friends with Whitman?

2. Why does the poet use a legal term, "pact," and a formal business word, "commerce," to describe his new relationship with Whitman?

3. Discuss the significance of the image of trees (wood, sap, root) used in the poem.

13 pig-headed: stubborn.
14 commerce: exchange of ideas and experiences.

参考译文

合同

申奥 译

我跟你订个合同，惠特曼
长久以来我憎恨你。
我走向你，一个顽固父亲的孩子
已经长大成人了；
现在我的年龄已足够交朋友。
是你砍倒了新的丛林，
现在是雕刻的时候了。
我们有着共同的树液和树根——
让我们之间进行交易。

SELECTED READINGS

Salutation [1]

O generation of the thoroughly smug[15]
    and thoroughly uncomfortable, [2]
I have seen fishermen picnicking in the sun,
I have seen them with untidy families,
I have seen their smiles full of teeth
    and heard ungainly[16] laughter.
And I am happier than you are,

And they were happier than I am;
And the fish swim in the lake
    and do not even own clothing. [3]

15 smug: (disapproving) looking or feeling too pleased with oneself; self-righteously complacent; a self-satisfied person.
16 ungainly: awkward, clumsy, ungraceful.

NOTES ON THE TEXT

[1] Pound wrote this poem between 1913 and 1916, so he was addressing the generation of the early twentieth century.

[2] The generation of people the poet is speaking to consists of two groups, "the thoroughly smug" and "the thoroughly uncomfortable," the former being ignorant and the latter victims who could not adjust to the modern conditions of living. "The smug" here were probably the rich and successful business men who thought they could control the world.

[3] There is perhaps a semantic link between the "uncouth" fishermen and their family, who is "untidy," whose laughter "ungainly" and whose smiles "full of teeth," and the fish who "don't even own clothing." Both seem to be free from restraints. It's interesting to note the speaker says "I am happier than you are" and "they were happier than I am." The "you" is the generation the poet is addressing. The "they" are obviously the fishermen and their families. However, the reader can perhaps conclude that the fish swimming in water is the happiest of all.

QUESTIONS FOR DISCUSSION

1. Some of Pound's short poems are very ambiguous in meaning. Study the images of the poem and discuss how they combine to create meaning. Note that there can be different interpretations.

2. Who does the poet salute? What does the poet suggest in the poem?

参考译文

致敬

申奥 译

呵，整洁体面的一代人
和陷于困窘处境的一代人，
我看见渔民们在阳光下野餐，
我看见他们携带着邋遢的家属，
我看见他们露着满嘴牙齿微笑，
听到他们难听的笑声。
我比你们幸福，

他们比我幸福；
在湖水中游的鱼
甚至没有衣服。

SELECTED READINGS

The Garden [1]

Like a skein[17] of loose silk blown against a wall
She walks by the railing of a path in Kensington Gardens, [2]
And she is dying piece-meal[18]
    of a sort of emotional anaemia[19].

And round about there is a rabble[20]
Of the filthy, sturdy, unkillable infants of the very poor. [3]
They shall inherit the earth.

In her is the end of breeding. [4]
Her boredom is exquisite and excessive.
She would like someone to speak to her,
And is almost afraid that I
    will commit that indiscretion[21]. [5]

NOTES ON THE TEXT

[1] Once the private gardens of Kensington Palace, the Kensington Gardens are one of the Royal Parks of London, lying immediately to the west of Hyde Park. The garden was originally the western section of Hyde Park, which had been created by Henry VIII in 1536 to use as a hunting ground. It was separated from the remainder of Hyde Park in 1728 at the request of Queen Caroline and designed by Henry Wise in order to form a landscape garden, with the fashionable features including the Round Pond, formal avenues and a sunken Dutch garden.

[2] Pound depicts an aristocratic and decadent lady walking in the garden, with an air of arrogance despite her "emotional anaemia," which contrasts sharply with the vitality of the uncouth children depicted in the second stanza.

---

17 skein: a length of thread, especially wool or silk, wound loosely round on itself.
18 peace-meal: gradually; little by little.
19 anaemia: a medical condition in which somebody has too few red cells in their blood, making them look pale and feel weak.
20 rabble: the lowest or coarsest class of people.
21 indiscretion: an indiscreet act or remark; act or remark that is not morally acceptable.

[3] The "unkillable infants" possibly suggests the hatred of the lady for the children whom she wishes she could kill. However, she could do nothing about them except by not adding one of her own to their numbers.

[4] "The end of breeding" here has double meanings. It both signifies the lady's excessively high breeding and her sterility. The paradox can be explained by this: the lady is so high-bred that she would not possibly find a peer to mate with, hence sexually unproductive.

[5] The poet seems to be lamenting on the lady as perhaps the last aristocrat who will disappear soon, for she is not only "in the end of breeding," but also "dying peace-meal." Note that her high upbringing may also be indicated by her alertness to the speaker's possible "indiscretion."

QUESTIONS FOR DISCUSSION

1. Discuss the significance of the image of the lady in the garden. What kind of person is she? What is the poet's attitude toward the lady?

2. What does the poet intend to express or critique in this poem?

参考译文

花园

章智源 译

宛如松散的丝线飘在墙上，
她漫步在肯希顿花园的路旁。
她患了情感贫血症，
正奄奄一息走向死亡。

四周一阵喧闹，
是一群穷人家肮脏、结实、死不掉的孩子们。
他们将承传这片大地。

在她的身上是生育的终结，
她感到异常强烈的空虚。
她真想有人来找她说话，
可又担心我
行为失矩。

Langston Hughes

(1902 – 1967)

A GUIDE TO LITERARY TERMINOLOGY

"Harlem Renaissance": *Harlem Renaissance was a period of cultural, artistic and literary revival ushered in by African American artists in the 1920s and 1930s, during which black writers made themselves an important and exciting part of the American literary scene. In his introduction to an anthology entitled* ***The New Negro*** *(1925), which served as a manifesto for Harlem Renaissance, Alain Locke noted the concerted efforts of black writers, in contrast to the solitary efforts of earlier figures, to bring the African heritage to the foreground in their writings. Black writers and poets were influenced and inspired by jazz and its rhythm and blue syncopation, which had its roots in the music of southern blacks who had migrated north, and which contained the exuberant, free-riding style and form. A sudden increase in the number of published works by black writers also led to the rise of black-consciousness.*

Four major writers who established their reputation during this period were Claude McKay, Jean Toomer, Countee Cullen and Langston Hughes. Hughes, in his essay "The Negro Artist and the Racial Mountain" (1926), described the harmful attraction of white, middle-class values for blacks who were suppressing their "black selves" in an attempt to identify with white culture. His collection of poems ***The Weary Blues*** *(1926) embodies the spirit of the Renaissance with its celebration of black culture and folk traditions.*

NOTES ON THE POET AND HIS POETRY

Langston Hughes was an American poet, social activist, novelist, playwright, and the first prominent African-American writer in the American literary history. Among his contributions to American literature was the invention of a new literary form, the jazz poetry, which helped boost the Harlem Renaissance of the 1920s, a period when, as Hughes put it, "the negro was in vogue." However, Hughes held a different goal from other Harlem Renaissance writers, such as W. E. B. Du Bois, Jessie Redmon Fauset, and Alain LeRoy Lock, whom he had criticized as being overly accommodating and assimilating Eurocentric values to achieve social equality. His poetry depicts the lives of blacks in the lower social strata and criticizes prejudices based on skin-color and internal racism within the black community. Permeating in his work is the pride, resiliency, courage and humor of the African Americans, which manifest his theme that "black is beautiful." Hughes was a "people's poet" who extolled the African-American identity, expanded the African America's image of itself, and boosted a "black aesthetics."

He wrote 60 books, of which twelve are collections of poetry. His poetry collections include *The Weary Blues* (1926), *Fine Clothes to the Jew* (1927), *Harlem* (1942), *Montage of a Dream Deferred* (1951), *Ask Your Mama* (1961) and *The Panther and the Lash* (1967). Hughes's writing style is characterized by use of colloquialisms, strong rhythm, rhymes, images, and symbols.

SELECTED READINGS

Dreams [1]

Hold fast[22] to dreams
For if dreams die
Life is a broken-winged bird
That cannot fly. [2]

Hold fast to dreams
For when dreams go
Life is a barren field [3]
Frozen with snow.

NOTES ON THE TEXT

[1] For African Americans, who lived in misery then, having a dream was essential even though one was not sure if it could be realized. At least you could hope. It is worth noting that Hughes's poems about dreams (1920s) had exerted an influence on Martin Luther King's famous speech "I have a Dream" (1960s).

[2] In this metaphor, "a broken-winged bird" suggests the deprivation of the essential quality of a species. Not having a dream is then tantamount to not having one's soul, so to speak.

[3] In this metaphor, "a barren field" suggests sterility. A life without a dream is robbed of all its nourishment, fun and meaning.

22 fast: (adv.) tight, firmly.

QUESTIONS FOR DISCUSSION

1. What images does the poet use to demonstrate the consequences of not having dreams? What artistic effects do such images create?

2. Following the same images used by the poet, how would you describe the opposite situation when one does harbor dreams? Do you think dreams alone can help solve all the problems? If not, why should we still have dreams?

参考译文

梦想

紧紧抓住梦想
如果梦想死亡
生命就是一只折翅的鸟儿
不能飞翔。

紧紧抓住梦想
当梦想离去
生活就是一片荒芜的土地
与冰雪冻在一起。

SELECTED READINGS

A Dream Deferred [1]

What happens to a dream deferred?
Does it dry up
    like a raisin in the sun? [2]
Or fester[23] like a sore —
And then run?
Does it stink like rotten meat?
Or crust and sugar over —

23 fester: to become infected, to decay, deteriorate.

like a syrupy sweet?
Maybe it just sags[24]
like a heavy load.
Or does it explode?

NOTES ON THE TEXT

[1] This poem is also known in some editions as "Harlem," the capital of the African American life in the United States. The poem was published in 1951 — when frustration characterized the mood of American blacks. The language of "A Dream Deferred" is plain and frank. The narrator uses tropes to enable the reader to see and smell the frustration of African Americans. The poet expresses his indignation at a racist society which prevents the American blacks from having the opportunities to pursue their dreams freely and realizing them.

[2] The speaker's attitude is an advice-giving attitude. The poet doesn't want to postpone getting what they want. The poem is written in an informative caring tone to help people live the lives they dream of having. This phrase creates the image of a raisin that used to be a firm, moist, and healthy-looking grape that has become shriveled up into a raisin. This image gives an emotional effect of a dream deferred shriveling up and turning dark because the sun has baked it, so it dries up or loses its life-giving moisture.

Lorraine Vivian Hansberry (1930—1965), a black playwright, borrowed Hughes's phrase "a raisin in the sun" as the title of her famous play published and staged on Broadway in 1959, which received wide acclaim. Both Langston Hughess' "A Dream Deferred" and Lorraine Hansberry's "A Raisin in the Sun" focus on the effect of racism on African-Americans.

QUESTIONS FOR DISCUSSION

1. Different from the first poem, which depicts the disappearance of dreams, this poem talks about the deferment of dreams. What images does the poet use? What emotional impacts do they create? What is the difference between the images used in "Dreams" and this poem?

2. How do you compare the tone and mood of the two poems, i.e. "Dreams" and "A Dream Deferred"? What does the last word of the poem "explode" suggest?

3. Discuss the poet's reaction to the deferment of dreams in light of the historical context and the African Americans' actual condition of existence. What had led to his frustration and anger?

---

24 sag: sink downward.

参考译文

耽延的梦想

王道余 译

梦想若被耽延会怎样?
是否会风干
像太阳下的葡萄?
或者像伤口般溃烂——
流出脓浆?
是否会像腐肉一样恶臭?
或者会像带浆的甜点
结壳然后出糖?
也许它只会下坠
像一个重物。
它是不是还会爆炸?

SELECTED READINGS

Dream Variations [1]

To fling my arms wide
In some place of the sun,
To whirl and to dance
Till the white day is done.
Then rest at cool evening
Beneath a tall tree
While night comes on gently,
Dark like me — [2]
That is my dream!

To fling my arms wide
In the face of the sun,

Dance! Whirl! Whirl! [3]
Till the quick day is done.
Rest at pale evening...
A tall, slim tree...
Night coming tenderly
Black like me.

NOTES ON THE TEXT

[1] "Dream Variations" was first published in 1932, in a collection of poems entitled *The Dream Keeper and Other Poems*. The dream it depicts in the first stanza is very similar to the dream in the second stanza, not only in content, but also in form. However, the first stanza is less self-assured and more child-like, while the second stanza is more passionate and self-assured.

[2] The speaker feels safer and more relaxed as evening approaches, because he and the evening have something in common, that is, their darkness. This shows he is less unidentified during the night than during the day. Note also that in the second stanza, "dark" is replaced by "black," which indicates a more self-assured identification with African American community.

[3] Notice the use of onomatopoeia in this line, "Dance! Whirl! Whirl!" The pleasure and excitement of dancing is effectively conveyed by the short, powerful verbs.

QUESTIONS FOR DISCUSSION

1. What is the theme of this short poem? What impressions does the poem create? What techniques does Hughes use to create these impressions?

2. Why does the poet want to dance only during the day? What gives him pleasure and excitement?

3. Does he prefer the white day or the dark evening? Why?

4. What does the title of the poem suggest to you? Discuss how the poet creates in the poem musical effects by using rhythmic patterns, repetitions, and stanza organization.

参考译文

梦的变奏

张开我的双臂
在阳光下的某地，
旋转，跳舞
直到炽热的一天完毕。
然后在凉爽的傍晚休息
在一棵高树下
当夜晚温柔地降临，
像我一样黑——
那就是我的梦！

我张开我的双臂，
沐浴着太阳光辉，
跳啊！转啊！转啊！
直到迅捷的白昼离去。
在阴暗的黄昏中歇息……
挺拔而苗条的树……
黑夜温柔她来临
像我一样黑。

SELECTED READINGS

The Negro Speaks of River [1]

I've known rivers:
I've known rivers ancient as the world and older than the flow of
human blood in human veins.

My soul has grown deep like the rivers.

25 dusky: rather dark in color.

I bathed in the Euphrates [2] when dawns were young.
I built my hut near the Congo [3] and it lulled me to sleep.
I looked upon the Nile [4] and raised the pyramids above it.
I heard the singing of the Mississippi when Abe Lincoln
    Went down to New Orleans, and I've seen its
    Muddy bosom turn all golden in the sunset.

I've known rivers;
Ancient, dusky[25] rivers.

My soul has grown deep like the rivers.

NOTES ON THE TEXT

[1] "The Negro Speaks of Rivers" was first published in *The Crisis* in 1921, when he was an undergraduate at Columbia University. It became Hughes's signature poem, and was collected in his first book of poetry, *The Weary Blues* (1926).

[2] The Euphrates is the longest and one of the most historically important rivers of Western Asia. The Euphrates and the Tigris River have their sources within 50 miles of each other in eastern Turkey and travel southeast through northern Syria and Iraq to empty into the Persian Gulf. Hydrology is extremely important to the ecology of the area, which is called the Cradle of Civilization due to its ancient history.

[3] The Congo River is in Africa. It is the world's deepest river, with measured depths over 220 meters. It is the second largest river in the world by volume of water discharged.

[4] The Nile is the longest river in the world, stretching north from approximately 4,000 miles from East Africa to the Mediterranean. It is generally regarded as among the most culturally significant natural formations in human history.

QUESTIONS FOR DISCUSSION

1. Why does the poet, or the Negro, mention so many rivers? Where are they located respectively? What do the rivers symbolize in this poem?

2. In the third line of the poem, which is repeated in the last, the speaker compares the depth of his soul to the river. What is the purpose of this comparison?

3. Is the speaker proud of the historical and cultural heritage of the blacks? How does he express his pride in the poem?

4. "Jazz is a heartbeat," Hughes argued. Hughes learned a lot from African American music. His poems follow irregular meter and rhymes, which have achieved a kind of rhythms, spontaneity, and musicality comparable to jazz. Discuss the formal features of Hughes's poems and their links with jazz.

参考译文

黑人谈江河

我熟悉江河。
我熟悉像世界一样古老比人类脉管
里的血流年龄更高的江河。

我的灵魂已经成长得像江河一样深沉。
我曾在幼发拉底河中沐浴，当那些个
黎明都还年轻。
我曾在刚里河畔搭盖我的茅屋，它常
哼着催眠曲送我入睡。
我曾面对着尼罗河建造起一座座金字塔，
高耸在它的河岸上。
我曾听到密西西比河唱歌，当那位
亚伯·林肯南下新奥尔良，我看见它
浑浊的胸脯在夕阳中泛涌金波。

我熟悉江河，
古老的、忧悒的江河。

我的灵魂已经成长得像江河一样深沉。

Allen Ginsberg

(1926 – 1997)

A GUIDE TO LITERARY TERMINOLOGY

"The Beat Generation": *The Beat Generation refers to a group of American poets and novelists centered in San Francisco and New York who were active and influential in the latter half of the 1950s. The word "beat" has been interpreted as referring to both the feelings of oppression ("beaten down") and a desired, "beatific" state of vision or ecstasy. Feeling oppressed by the dominant culture, beat writers rejected the prevailing middle-class values, commercialism, conformity, and held anti-intellectual, antipolitical, and antiestablishment views. They shared an enthusiasm for the visionary states evoked by religious meditation, sexual experience, jazz or drugs. They also showed their discontent with the culture of a complacent and materialistic era by riding motorcycles and smoking marijuana.*

In their works, which express their alternative values, the Beats tend to use a very loose structure and slangs. They fashioned a literature that was more bold, straightforward, and expressive than anything that had come before. Allen Ginsberg and Jack Kerouac were the most prominent spokesmen for the movement. The Beat movement had tremendous influence on the idea of counterculture in the 1960s and the 1970s.

NOTES ON THE POET AND HIS POETRY

Allen Ginsberg was the founding father of the "Beat Generation," a group of American poets and novelists active in the late 1950s and early 1960s. His groundbreaking poems such as "Howl" and "Kaddish" had inspired the American counterculture of the second half of the twentieth century. Ginsberg was born in Newark, New Jersey, on June 3, 1926. When he attended Columbia University, he made friends with Jack Kerouac and William Burroughs. They three, together with Caleb Carr, Herbert Huncke, John Clellon Holmes and Neal Cassady, later became the nucleus of the "Beat Generation" writers. "Beat" referred loosely to their shared sense of spiritual exhaustion and rebellion against the general conformity, hypocrisy, and materialism of the American society. Beat writers were in favor of unfettered self-realization and self-expression, rejecting prevailing cultural, moral, and literary values. Different from conventional poets who wrote poetry as academic craftsmen, Ginsberg took it onto the podium and became a skilled public performer of his poems. He gave readings all over America and in other parts of the world as well, including China (1984). He played a portable harmonium when he read his poetry in front of an audience.

Allen Ginsberg published *Howl and Other Poems* in 1956. His finest work, "Kaddish," a long poem lamenting on his mother's insanity and death, was collected in *Kaddish and Other Poems* published in 1961. Other publications include *Reality Sandwiches* (1963), *Indian Journals* (1970), *The Fall of America* (1972), for which he was awarded National Book Award, *Mind Breathes* (1978), *Plutonian Ode* (1982), *Collected Poems* (1984), *White Shroud* (1986), and *Cosmopolitan Greetings* (1994).

SELECTED READINGS

America [1]

America I've given you all and now I'm nothing.
America two dollars and twenty-seven cents January 17, 1956. [2]
I can't stand my own mind.
America when will we end the human war?
Go fuck yourself with your atom bomb.
I don't feel good don't bother me.
I won't write my poem till I'm in my right mind.
America when will you be angelic?
When will you take off your clothes?
When will you look at yourself through the grave? [3]
When will you be worthy of your million Trotskyites? [4]
America why are your libraries full of tears?
America when will you send your eggs to India?
I'm sick of your insane demands.
When can I go into the supermarket and buy what I need with my
    good looks? [5]
America after all it is you and I who are perfect not the next world.
Your machinery[26] is too much for me.

26 machinery: the organization or structure of something.

You made me want to be a saint.
There must be some other way to settle this argument.
Burroughs is in Tangiers[27] I don't think he'll come back it's sinister. [6]
Are you being sinister or is this some form of practical joke?
I'm trying to come to the point.
I refuse to give up my obsession.
America stop pushing I know what I'm doing.
America the plum blossoms are falling. [7]
I haven't read the newspapers for months, everyday somebody goes on trial for murder.
America I feel sentimental about the Wobblies[28].
America I used to be a communist when I was a kid and I'm not sorry. [8]
I smoke marijuana[29] every chance I get. [9]
I sit in my house for days on end and stare at the roses in the closet.
When I go to Chinatown I get drunk and never get laid[30].
My mind is made up there's going to be trouble.
You should have seen me reading Marx.
My psychoanalyst thinks I'm perfectly right.
I won't say the Lord's Prayer.
I have mystical visions and cosmic vibrations.
America I still haven't told you what you did to Uncle Max[31] after he came over from Russia.

I'm addressing you.

---

27 Tangiers: a city in north Morocco.

28 the Wobblies: a nickname given to the Industrial Workers of the World, a socialist labor organization established in the U.S. in 1905.The Wobblies were harshly criticized by the United States government which largely shut down the group during World War I by prosecuting and politically embarrassing many of its leaders.

29 marijuana：大麻.

30 get laid: have sexual intercourse.

31 Uncle Max: here Ginsberg refers to Max Livergant, his uncle on his mother's side, who encountered hardships after immigrating to America for being both a communist and a Jew.

Are you going to let our emotional life be run by *Time Magazine*? [10]
I'm obsessed by *Time Magazine*.
I read it every week.
Its cover stares at me every time I slink past the corner candystore.
I read it in the basement of the Berkeley Public Library.
It's always telling me about responsibility. Businessmen are serious. Movie producers are serious. Everybody's body's serious but me.
It occurs to me that I am America.
I am talking to myself again.

Asia is rising against me.
I haven't got a chinaman's chance[32].
I'd better consider my national resources.
My national resources consist of two joints of marijuana millions of genitals an unpublishable private literature that goes 1,400 miles an hour and twenty-five-thousand mental institutions.
I say nothing about my prisons [11] nor the millions of underpriviliged who live in my flowerpots under the light of five hundred suns.
I have abolished the whorehouses of France, Tangiers is the next to go.
My ambition is to be President despite the fact that I'm a Catholic. [12]

America how can I write a holy litany[33] in your silly mood?
I will continue like Henry Ford my strophes are as individual as his automobiles more so they're all different sexes
America I will sell you strophes $2,500 apiece $500 down on your old strophe
America free Tom Mooney[34]

---

32 a chinaman's chance: very little chance, a dog's chance.
33 litany: a series of prayers to God for us in church services, spoken by a priest, etc., with set responses by church goers.
34 Tom Mooney: a labor leader in the early twentieth century who had been falsely imprisoned for a San Francisco bombing in 1916.

America save the Spanish Loyalists[35]
America Sacco Vanzetti[36] must not die
America I am the Scottsboro boys[37].
America when I was seven momma took me to Communist Cell meetings they sold us garbanzos a handful per ticket a ticket costs a nickel and the speeches were free everybody was angelic and sentimental about the workers it was all so sincere you have no idea what a good thing the party was in 1835 Scott Nearing[38] was a grand old man a real mensch[39] Mother Bloor[40] the Silk-strikers' Ewig-Weibliche[41] made me cry I once saw Israel Amter[42] plain. Everybody must have been a spy. [13]
America you don't really want to go to war.
America it's them bad Russians.
Them Russians them Russians and them Chinamen. And them Russians.
The Russia wants to eat us alive. The Russia's power mad. She wants to take our cars from out our garages.
Her wants to grab Chicago. Her needs a *Red Reader's Digest*. Her wants our auto plants in Siberia. Him big bureaucracy running our filling stations.
That no good. Ugh. Him makes Indians learn read. Him need big black niggers.

---

35 the Spanish Loyalists: the leftist army supported by the Soviet Union in the Spanish Civil War who fought the Fascist uprising supported by Nazi Germany.

36 Sacco Vanzetti: a reference to a famous legal case in which Ferdinando Nicola Sacco and Bartolomeo Vanzetti, two Italian born laborers with anarchist political views, were accused of murder and tried without due process. They were executed on August 23, 1927.

37 the Scottsboro boys: a reference to the Scottsboro Boys case, an alleged gang rape of two white girls by nine black teenagers on a Southern Railroad freight run on March 25, 1931. The boys were arrested, tried without adequate counsel, and hastily convicted on the basis of shallow evidence. All but one were sentenced to death.

38 Scott Nearing (1883—1983): an American radical economist who advocated pacifism, socialism, and simple living.

39 mensch: (German) human being.

40 Mother Bloor: Ella Reeve Bloor (1862—1951) was a leading figure in the Socialist Party of America in the early twentieth century who fought for workers' rights.

41 Ewig- Weibliche: (German) Eternal Female.

42 Israel Amter (1881—1954), a Marxist politician and founding member of the Communist Party USA. Amter is best remembered as one of the Communist Party leaders jailed in conjunction with the International Unemployment Day riot of 1930.

Hah. Her make us all work sixteen hours a day. Help. [14]
America this is quite serious.
America this is the impression I get from looking in the television set.
America is this correct?
I'd better get right down to the job.
It's true I don't want to join the Army or turn lathes in precision parts
 factories, I'm nearsighted and psychopathic anyway.
America I'm putting my queer shoulder to the wheel. [15]

NOTES ON THE TEXT

[1] "America" was written in 1956 when Ginsberg stayed in Berkeley, California. It was included in the original publication of *Howl and Other Poems*. "America" was one of the first widely read literary statements of the political unrest in the post-World War II United States.

[2] Here the poet laments on the spiritual poverty of the American life style, as if the meaning of life were a few dollars a day. The poem opens with the poet talking to the personified America, expressing the hopelessness of his life.

[3] The poet demanded that America see the deaths and destruction it caused.

[4] Trotskyite (托洛茨基分子), or Trotskyist, is someone who supports the revolutionary left-wing ideas of Leon Trotsky (1879－1940), a Marxist and leader of Russian Revolution. Here the poet, sardonically, accuses America of being no better than Trotskyites in terms of its equally brutal suppression of different political views.

[5] The question here is sarcastic. The poet mocks the corporatism of American life, which is symbolized by "the supermarket." Those with "good looks" have better commercial values and can therefore "buy" whatever they need with their "good looks."

[6] William Burroughs (1914－1997) was U. S. novelist, a member of the central group of the Beat Movement, and Allen Ginsberg's close friend. "Burroughs is in Tangiers" refers to his time spent in Tangiers where he was in a kind of exile from the United States because of legal problems related to the transport of illegal drugs from Mexico. Ginsberg strongly advocated the legalization of drugs. In this line, he warns America that if it continues to prosecute people like Burroughs for such petty crimes, the country will lose their "best minds."

[7] This line uses imagery from the East. In Eastern culture, the plum blossom is a symbol of peace. By saying that "the plum blossoms are falling" in America, Ginsberg implied that America's role as a leader of world peace was declining. Note that Ginsberg had been attracted to Eastern religion and culture throughout his life.

[8] Both Allen Ginsberg's parents had leftist political leanings, his father being a socialist, and his mother a communist. Their political views had surely influenced Allen's later outlook on

the world. Ginsberg's mother, Naomi Ginsberg, was from Russia. She retained her Communist view after immigrating to the United States. She took her sons to meetings of Communist Party in the 1930s. The historical context here is important: during the 1950s there was a strong anti-communist attitude in America, exemplified by Senator Joseph McCarthy's congressional hearings in which many Americans were accused of communist activities. By admitting in the poem that he was once a communist, Ginsberg risked being charged for treason.

[9] Ginsberg believed psychedelics could be of help in writing visionary poetry. In the 1950s, he experimented on various drugs to help him illicit visions. He claimed that some of his best poetry was written under the influence of drugs: the second part of "Howl" with peyote, "Kaddish" with amphetamines, and "Wales — A Visitation" with LSD. Ginsberg changed his attitude towards drugs after a journey to India in 1962, during which he learned about meditation and yoga. He regarded them as better ways to raise one's consciousness.

[10] Ginsberg here blamed America for seeing all events through the lens of the media (represented by *Time*) and for letting its "emotional life" be affected by the magazine. What he implied here was that the country was run by the media. Political and social decisions were not based on rationality and humanitarianism. Instead, they were made by leaders who catered to the taste of the media.

[11] Ginsberg was in jail a couple of times. In June 1949, Ginsberg was arrested for storing some stolen goods in his apartment. In 1967, he was arrested for taking part in a New York City antiwar demonstration.

[12] The poet says that he wants "to be President despite the fact that I'm a Catholic." This is an example of discrimination. Ginsberg himself was Jewish, but he makes this point because during this time it was widely assumed that a Catholic could not be elected President, though this assumption would fall only a few years later with the election of John F. Kennedy.

[13] Note that these unpunctuated sentences form a stream of consciousness. These lines reveal the poet's fond memories of a meeting in a Communist Party cell that his mother took him to when he was seven years old. "Everybody was angelic and sentimental about the workers it was all so sincere you have no idea what a good thing the party was..." The poet concludes, "Everybody must have been a spy," which is a sarcastic comment on America's paranoia over socialist or communist activities during this period and an indication of his sympathy for these persecuted angelic people.

[14] Here Ginsberg mocks the American ignorance by using forms of colloquial speech: wrong pronouns and incorrect verb tenses which suggest the ludicrousness of the fears of those who are uninformed and even illiterate.

[15] Putting one's shoulder to the wheel is an expression of hard work and labor. Yet this is contrasted by the poet's use of the word "queer," which denotes softness and an effeminate style. The suggestion is, even the outcasts, the weak, and the effeminate can make contribution. The word "queer" also means "homosexual." Here Ginsberg implicitly manifested his sexuality. He advocated different forms of sexual expression.

QUESTIONS FOR DISCUSSION

1. In this poem, Ginsberg makes use of the prophetic tradition of the Old Testament in which prophets, having visions from God, warned the people of Israel of their wayward faith and foretold of destruction and captivity. Discuss what the poet warns against and prophesizes in this poem.

2. In his conversations with his personified country, what are some of the most important topics the poet raises? Why is the poet not satisfied with his own status quo as well as that of his country? What are his criticisms of America?

3. Ginsberg experimented on the way of writing poetry. One of his unique features of writing is the use of unusually long lines in this poem. Cite some examples from the text and discuss their functions. How are they related, for instance, to the streams of consciousness? How are they intended to build up emotions?

4. Ginsberg relates the poem to music, saying that the key to understanding the structure of the poem is "in the jazz choruses." In what ways do you think the poem is similar with jazz?

参考译文

美国

文楚安 译

美国，我已给了你一切可我却一无所有。
美国今天是1956年1月17日，二美元二角七分
我无法再忍耐下去。
美国，什么时候我们才能停止人类间的战争?
用你自己的原子弹去揍你自己吧。
别打扰我我精神不振。
我不愿写诗除非我有好兴致。
美国，什么时候你才能天使般地可爱?
什么时候你才能脱下你的衣裳?
什么时候你能从坟墓那儿打量你自己?
什么时候你才不辜负你的难以计数的托洛茨基?
美国你的图书馆为何泪水汪汪?
美国你何时才能把鸡蛋送往印度?
我厌恶你那失去理智疯狂般的一厢情愿。

什么时候我才能到超级市场购买我中意的东西神情欢愉?
美国毕竟只有你和我现在才完美卓越而不期望于来世。
你的机器对我来说实在太多。
你使我想成为一个圣人。
这场争执必定会有其他办法来了结。
巴勒斯在坦吉尔，我想他不会回来真是另有心机。
你可也是别有用心或者这只不过是在耍弄某种可笑的把戏?
且让我回归正题。
我决不会因此就解除困窘。
美国别咄咄逼人，我明白我的作为。
美国，那丛梅花正在凋零。
数月来我没读报纸，每天总有人因为杀人而受审。
美国，我对沃布林成员深为同情。
美国，我年少时曾是共产主义者却从不后悔。
我抽大麻只要有机会。
我接连成天坐在家里凝视壁柜里的玫瑰。
每逢到唐人街我喝得烂醉从没倒地。
我已有预感会有麻烦缠身。
你一定看见我阅读马克思。
我的心理医生认为我压根儿没任何毛病。
我可不愿向上帝祈祷。
我怀着神秘的幻念感受到宇宙般无穷尽的振奋。
美国，我还没对你讲马克斯舅舅干了些什么当他从俄罗斯来到美国。

我在向你讲话。
你难道真愿意你的情感隐私让《时代》杂志控制吗?
《时代》杂志真让我入迷。
我每周都要读。
它的封面盯着我，每当我悄悄地从糖果店的一角路过。
我读它在伯克莱公共图书馆底层。
它总告诉我什么是责任感。商人们认真精明电影制片商非常务实。除了我人人都正儿八经。
我突然感到我就是美国。
我不过在自言自语。

亚洲正同我作对。
我没从任何中国人那儿得到过任何便利。
我得对我的国家资源从长计议。
我的国家资源包括两卷大麻成百万的阳具，从没出版的文学作品用喷气式飞机运载一小时跑一千四百英里，还有两万五千所精神病院。
我还没提到我的牢狱以及成百上千万穷苦百姓住在我的花坛上五百个太阳的光芒在他们头顶上闪耀。
我已经取缔关闭了法国妓院，下一个就该是坦吉尔。
我的抱负是当总统尽管我是天主教徒。

美国你如此傻里傻气，我怎能替你写一篇祷文?
我仍将写下去像亨利·福特我的诗行如同他的汽车都属于个人尽管性别不同。
美国，我愿将我的诗行卖给你每首两千五百美元，比你从前买的便宜五百美元。
美国，让汤姆·莫尼获得自由
美国，拯救西班牙忠于共和政府的人士
美国，萨柯和凡泽绝不能死去
美国，我就是被囚禁在斯科兹波洛镇的那些孩子中的一个!
美国，我七岁时妈妈带领我去参加共产党支部会他们卖给我们鹰嘴豆一张票一大把，一张票五美分人人都可以畅所欲言每个人都如天使般可爱对劳工满腔同情一切都那么真挚让你觉得还会有什么比这个党更好! 1935年斯柯特·尼尔是一个了不起的老头一个真正的孟什维克布洛尔大妈丝业公会罢工永恒的女性使我高呼我曾看见意第绪语演讲家伊萨里尔·阿麦塔平易近人。人人都准当过间谍。
美国，你并不真正想发动战争。
美国，那是他们可恶的俄国佬干的。
是他们俄国人还有他们中国人? 是他们俄国人。
俄国想活生生地把我们一口吞下。俄国当权者疯了，俄国人想从我们的车库中把汽车全抢走!
俄国想霸占芝加哥。她需要一份《红色读者文摘》。她想把我们的汽车制造厂迁到西伯利亚。用她庞大的官僚机器来运转我们的加油站。
那可不妙。唉。俄国要强迫印第安人学会阅读，他们需要身强力壮的黑鬼。
啊哈。俄国要迫使我们一天干活十六小时。呜呼救命。

美国，这一切可不是说着玩的。
美国，我看电视产生了这一切印象。
美国，你说说看这是否正确？
看来我还是最好去干自己的活儿。
我真的不想从军也不想在精密部件厂开车床，我可是近视眼而且心理变态怎么也躲得脱。
美国，恕我奇思怪论我对你可算是尽力而为了。

SUGGESTED REFERENCES

Robert Frost

Brower, Reuben A. *The Poetry of Robert Frost: Constellations of Intention.* New York: Oxford UP, 1963.

Faggen, Robert, ed. *The Notebooks of Robert Frost.* Cambridge: Harvard UP, 2007.

Meyers, Jeffrey. *Robert Frost: A Biography.* Boston: Houghton Mifflin, 1996.

Parini, Jay. *Robert Frost: A Life.* New York: MacMillan, 2000.

Ezra Pound

Albright, Daniel. *Quantum Poetics: Yeats, Pound, Eliot, and the Science of Modernism.* Cambridge: Cambridge UP, 1997.

Alexander, Michael. *The Poetic Achievement of Ezra Pound.* Berkeley: U of California P, 1979.

Barbarese, J. T. "Ezra Pound's Imagist Aesthetics: Lustra to Mauberley." *The Columbia History of American Poetry.* New York: Columbia UP, 1993. 307-8.

Dennis, Helen May. *A New Approach to the Poetry of Ezra Pound.* New York: Mellen, 1996.

Froula, Christine. *A Guide to Ezra Pound's Selected Poems.* New York: New Directions, 1982.

Grieve, Thomas F. *Ezra Pound's Early Poetry and Poetics.* Cambridge: U of Missouri P, 1997.

Homberger, Eric, ed. *Ezra Pound: The Critical Heritage.* London: Routledge & Kegan Paul, 1972.

Perloff, Marjorie. *The Dance of the Intellect: Studies in the Poetry of the Pound Tradition.* Evanston: Northwestern UP, 1996.

Tiffany, Daniel. *Radio Corpse: Imagism and the Crypt Aesthetic of Ezra Pound.* Cambridge: Harvard UP, 1995.

Langston Hughes

Bernard, Emily, ed. *Remember Me to Harlem: The Letters of Langston Hughes and Carl Van Vechten, 1925 — 1964.* New York: Knopf, 2001.

Berry, Faith. *Langston Hughes: Before and beyond Harlem.* Westport: Lawrence Hill & Co., 1983.

Leach, Laurie F. *Langston Hughes: A Biography.* Westport: Greenwood Publishing Group, 2004.

Rampersad, Arnold. *The Life of Langston Hughes, Volume 1: I, Too, Sing America.* Oxford: Oxford UP, 1986.

Rampersad, Arnold. *The Life of Langston Hughes, Volume 2: I Dream A World.* Oxford: Oxford UP, 1988.

Allen Ginsberg

Kraus, Michelle P. *Allen Ginsberg: An Annotated Bibliography, 1969—77.* Metuchen: Scarecrow, 1980.

Merrill, Thomas F. *Allen Ginsberg.* New York: Twayne, 1969.

Miles, Barry. *Ginsberg: A Biography, rev. ed.* London: Virgin Publishing, 2000.

Morgan, Bill. *The Works of Allen Ginsberg, 1941—1994: A Descriptive Bibliography.* Westport: Greenwood Press, 1995.

Portuges, Paul. *The Visionary Poetics of Allen Ginsberg.* Santa Barbara: Ross-Erikson, 1978.

Unit 15 Arthur Miller

(1915—2005)

A GUIDE TO LITERARY TERMINOLOGY

"Tragedy and the Common Man": *Throughout his writing career, Arthur Miller had been concerned with several distinct but related issues. In his early plays and in a series of essays published in the 1940s and 50s, Miller first outlined a form of tragedy that suits characters in moderm times, one that differed markedly from the traditional notion that only the nobility can be suitable subjects for tragedy. In "Tragedy and the Common Man", Miller claims that the "underlying struggle" of all such dramas "is that of the individual attempting to gain his 'rightful' position in society." Consequently, "the tragic feeling is invoked in us when we are in the presence of a character who is ready to lay down his life, if need be, to secure one thing — his sense of personal dignity." According to this view, even ordinary people — like Willy Loman, the protagonist of* ***Death of a Salesman*** *— can achieve true tragic stature. Mason Brown characterized* ***Death of a Salesman*** *as "a tragedy modern and personal, not classic and heroic."*

NOTES ON THE AUTHOR

Arthur Miller is widely regarded as one of the greatest American playwrights, whose works include oft-performed classics *Death of a Salesman* and *The Crucible*. Miller's plays are performed not only on Broadway, but also on the stages all over the world. They explore the grave questions of conscience, the torments and tragedies of ordinary men and women striving for dignity, respect, security in an increasingly industrialized and impersonal world. They examine misplaced and misunderstood values, rampant materialism, the conflicts between ideals and reality, between fathers and sons. They are emblematic of an age of change and redefinition in America after World War II.

Arthur Miller was born on October 17, 1915 in New York City, the son of a coat-manufacturer and a public school teacher. In 1928, his father's business failed and the family struggled to survive. The Great Depression taught the young Miller a lesson about the insecurity of modern existence. After graduation from high school, he worked in an auto-parts warehouse in order to save money for his studies at the University of Michigan. At the University, he washed dishes, fed experimental mice, and wrote plays to help pay the expenses. He won a university prize of 250 dollars for an autobiographical play titled *No Villain* when he was a sophomore, and won the same prize a second time for a play called *Honors at Dawn* when he was a junior. In his senior year, his play *They Too Arise*, which was a revision of his *No Villain*, won a nationwide playwriting contest, bringing Miller a prize of 1,250 dollars, a huge sum then.

After graduating from the University of Michigan in 1938, Miller returned to New York City and picked up some odd jobs as a script writer, a repairman for navy ships, and a screenplay writer. Miller's most important plays were written within a decade after World War II: *All My Sons* (1947), Miller's first success and winner of New York Drama Critics Award, *Death of a Salesman* (1949), winner of a Pulitzer Prize, *The Crucible* (1953), about the witch trials in Salem in 1692, *A View from the Bridge* and *A Memory of Two Mondays* (1955). His publications in the 1960s and 1970s include: *After the Fall* (1964), *The Price* (1968), *The Archbishop's Ceiling* (1976). His later plays incude: *The Ride Down Mount Morgan* (1991), *The Last Yankee* (1993), *Mr. Peters' Connections* (1998), and *Resurrection Blues* (2002).

In 1956, Miller married Marilyn Monroe and wrote a screenplay called *The Misfits* to star his wife. The film (1958) was a hit, but they were divorced in 1961. Afterwards Miller married Ingeborg Morath, to whom he remained married until his death in 2005. They raised a son and a daughter.

SYNOPSIS OF THE WORK

The Death of a Salesman is Miller's most critically acclaimed work which portrays the tragic story of the emotional collapse of Willy Loman, an aging salesman, husband and father who has come to symbolize the American Dream gone awry. Willy has worked for 35 years as a traveling salesman, but his job has given him neither financial security nor a sense of achievement or happiness. He wants to ask from his boss Howard Wagner for a New York position, for he is over 60 years old and finds it increasingly difficult to continue his work as a travelling salesman. Willy's elder son Biff plans to borrow money from his former employer Bill Oliver to get started in a sports goods business. However, instead of getting a new position in town, Willy is fired by his boss. Biff's request of a loan is also rejected. Both Biff and his younger brother Happy are in their thirties, unmarried and unsuccessful in career. The two sons invite their father to dinner the next day after Biff saw his boss. Though Willy loves his two sons, he is often angry with them because they have never amounted to anything.

At the restaurant, Willy refuses to hear bad news from Biff and gets angry when Biff tells him what happened. A bitter quarrel follows. Then Biff and Happy go home, leaving their frustrated father behind in the restaurant. Willy buys life insurance and kills himself by planning a car accident, hoping the insurance money can help Biff start his own business.

In the following selection, we witness what happens at the very end of the play, when Willy decides to commit suicide. Linda is Willy's wife. Ben, a successful self-made man as well as Willy's idol, is the ghost of his older brother from whom Willy often seeks advice.

SELECTED READINGS

The Death of a Salesman

(Excerpts from Act II)

[...]

(*Biff moves outside, Linda following. The light dies down on them and comes up on the center of the apron as Willy walks into it. He is carrying a flashlight, a hoe, and a handful of seed packets.* [1] *He raps the top of the hoe sharply to fix it firmly, and then moves to the left, measuring off the distance with his foot. He holds the flashlight to look at the seed packets, reading off the instructions. He is in the blue of night.*)

WILLY: Carrots... quarter-inch apart. Rows... one-foot rows. (*He measures it off.*) One foot. (*He puts down a package and measures off.*) Beets. (*He puts down another package and measures again.*) Lettuce. (*He reads the package, puts it down.*) One foot — (*He breaks off as Ben appears at the right and moves slowly down to him.*) What a proposition, ts, ts. Terrific, terrific. 'Cause she's suffered, Ben, [2] the woman has suffered. You understand me? A man can't go out the way, he came in, Ben, a man has got to add up to something. You can't, you can't — (*Ben moves toward him as though to interrupt.*) You gotta consider, now. Don't answer so quick. Remember, it's a guaranteed twenty-thousand-dollar proposition. [3] Now look, Ben, I want you to go through the ins and outs of this thing[1] with me. I've got nobody to talk to, Ben, and the woman has suffered, you hear me?

BEN (*standing still, considering*): What's the proposition?

WILLY: It's twenty thousand dollars on the barrelhead[2]. Guaranteed, gilt-edged[3], you understand?

BEN: You don't want to make a fool of yourself. They might not honor the policy[4].

WILLY: How can they dare refuse? Didn't I work like a coolie to meet every premium on the nose[5]? And now they don't pay off? Impossible!

BEN: It's called a cowardly thing, William.

WILLY: Why? Does it take more guts to stand here the rest of my life ringing up a zero? [4]

BEN (*yielding*): That's a point, William. (*He moves, thinking, turns.*) And twenty thousand — that is something one can feel with the hand, it is there.

WILLY (*now assured, with rising power*): Oh, Ben, that's the whole beauty of it! I see it like a diamond, shining in the dark, hard and rough, that I can pick up and touch in my hand. Not like — like an appointment![6] This would not be another damned-fool appointment, Ben, and it changes all the aspects. Because he[7] thinks I'm nothing, see, and so he spites me. But the funeral — (*Straightening up.*) Ben, that funeral will be massive! They'll come from Maine, Massachu-

---

1 go through the ins and outs of this: consider carefully the details of the proposition.

2 on the barrelhead: in cash.

3 gilt-edged: having gilded edges, as the pages of a book; of the highest quality or value.

4 policy: the document which shows the agreement that you have made with an insurance company (保单).

5 to meet every premium on the nose: to pay a sum of money regularly (to the insurance company) as required in the insurance policy; on the nose: exactly as prescribed in the policy.

6 Not like an appointment: Willy is referring to the appointment he has with his boss in which his request for a new position is turned down.

7 he: here it refers to Willy's son Biff.

setts, Vermont, New Hampshire! All the oldtimers with the strange license plates — that boy will be thunderstruck, Ben, because he never realized — I am known! Rhode Island, New York, New Jersey — I am known, Ben, and he'll see it with his eyes once and for all. He'll see what I am, Ben! He's in for a shock, that boy! [5]

BEN (*coming down to the edge of the garden*): He'll call you a coward.

WILLY (*suddenly fearful*): No, that would be terrible.

BEN: Yes. And a damned fool.

WILLY: No, no, he mustn't, I won't have that! (*He is broken and desperate.*)

BEN: He'll hate you, William. (*The gay music of the Boys is heard.*)

WILLY: Oh, Ben, how do we get back to all the great times? Used to be so full of light, and comradeship, the sleigh-riding in winter, and the ruddiness on his cheeks. And always some kind of good news coming up, always something nice coming up ahead. And never even let me carry the valises in the house, and simonizing, simonizing that little red car! Why, why can't I give him something and not have him hate me?

BEN: Let me think about it. (*He glances at his watch.*) I still have a little time. Remarkable proposition, but you've got to be sure you're not making a fool of yourself. (*Ben drifts off upstage and goes out of sight. Biff comes down from the left.*)

WILLY (*suddenly conscious of Biff, turns and looks up at him, then begins picking up the packages of seeds in confusion*):

Where the hell is that seed? (*Indignantly.*) You can't see nothing out here! They boxed in the whole goddam neighborhood!

BIFF: There are people all around here. Don't you realize that?

WILLY: I'm busy. Don't bother me.

BIFF (*taking the hoe from Willy*): I'm saying good-by to you, Pop. (*Willy looks at him, silent, unable to move.*) I'm not coming back any more.

WILLY: You're not going to see Oliver tomorrow?

BIFF: I've got no appointment, Dad.

WILLY: He put his arm around you, and you've got no appointment?

BIFF: Pop, get this now, will you? Everytime I've left it's been a fight that sent me out of here. Today I realized something about myself and I tried to explain it to you and I — I think I'm just not smart enough to make any sense out of it for you. To hell with whose fault it is or anything like that. (*He takes Willy's arm.*) Let's just wrap it up, heh? Come on in, we'll tell Mom. (*He gently tries to pull Willy to left.*)

WILLY (*frozen, immobile, with guilt in his voice*): No, I don't want to see her.

BIFF: Come on! (*He pulls again, and Willy tries to pull away.*)

WILLY (*highly nervous*): No, no, I don't want to see her.

BIFF (*tries to look into Willy's face, as if to find the answer there*): Why don't you want to see her?

WILLY (*more harshly now*): Don't bother me, will you?

BIFF: What do you mean, you don't want to see her? You don't want them calling you yellow[8], do you? This isn't your fault; it's me, I'm a bum. Now come inside!

(*Willy strains to get away.*) Did you hear what I said to you? (*Willy pulls away and quickly goes by himself into the house. Biff follows.*)

LINDA (*to Willy*): Did you plant, dear?

BIFF (*at the door, to Linda*). All right, we had it out. I'm going and I'm not writing any more.

LINDA (*going to Willy in the kitchen*): I think that's the best way, dear. 'Cause there's no use drawing it out, you'll just never get along. (*Willy doesn't respond.*)

BIFF: People ask where I am and what I'm doing, you don't know,

8 call you yellow: call you a coward.

and you don't care. That way it'll be off your mind and you can start brightening up again. All right? That clears it, doesn't it? (*Willy is silent, and Biff goes to him.*) You gonna wish me luck, scout? (*He extends his hand.*) What do you say?

LINDA: Shake his hand, Willy.

WILLY (*turning to her, seething with hurt*): There's no necessity to mention the pen at all, y'know.

BIFF (*gently*): I've got no appointment, Dad.

WILLY (*erupting fiercely*): He put his arm around...?

BIFF: Dad, you're never going to see what I am, so what's the use of arguing? If I strike oil[9] I'll send you a check. Meantime forget I'm alive.

WILLY (*to Linda*): Spite, see?

BIFF: Shake hands, Dad.

WILLY: Not my hand.

BIFF: I was hoping not to go this way.

WILLY: Well, this is the way you're going. Good-by.

(*Biff looks at him a moment, then turns sharply and goes to the stairs.*)

WILLY (*stops him with*): May you rot in hell if you leave this house!

BIFF (*turning*): Exactly what is it that you want from me?

WILLY: I want you to know, on the train, in the mountains, in the valleys, wherever you go, that you cut down your life for spite!

BIFF: No, no.

WILLY: Spite, spite, is the word of your undoing! And when you're down and out, remember what did it. When you're rotting somewhere beside the railroad tracks, remember, and don't you dare blame it on me!

BIFF: I'm not blaming it on you!

WILLY: I won't take the rap[10] for this, you hear?

9 strike oil: become rich overnight.

10 rap: the act of criticizing or blaming.

(*Happy comes down the stairs and stands on the bottom step, watching.*)

BIFF: That's just what I'm telling you!

WILLY (*sinking into a chair at a table, with full accusation*): You're trying to put a knife in me — don't think I don't know what you're doing!

BIFF: All right, phony! Then let's lay it on the line[11]. (*He whips the rubber tube* [6] *out of his pocket and puts it on the table.*)

HAPPY: You crazy...

LINDA: Biff! (*She moves to grab the hose, but Biff holds it down with his hand.*)

BIFF: Leave it there! Don't move it!

WILLY (*not looking at it*): What is that?

BIFF: You know goddam well what that is.

WILLY (*caged, wanting to escape*): I never saw that.

BIFF: You saw it. The mice didn't bring it into the cellar! What is this supposed to do, make a hero out of you? This supposed to make me sorry for you?

WILLY: Never heard of it.

BIFF: There'll be no pity for you, you hear it? No pity!

WILLY (*to Linda*): You hear the spite!

BIFF: No, you're going to hear the truth — what you are and what I am!

LINDA: Stop it!

WILLY: Spite!

HAPPY (*coming down toward Biff*): You cut it now!

BIFF (*to Happy*): The man don't know who we are! The man is gonna know! (*To Willy*) We never told the truth for ten minutes in this house!

---

11 lay it on the line: talk about this frankly.

HAPPY: We always told the truth!

BIFF (*turning on him*): You big blow, are you the assistant buyer? You're one of the two assistants to the assistant, aren't you?

HAPPY: Well, I'm practically —

BIFF: You're practically full of it! We all are! And I'm through with it. (*To Willy.*) Now hear this, Willy, this is me.

WILLY: I know you!

BIFF: You know why I had no address for three months? I stole a suit in Kansas City and I was in jail. (*To Linda, who is sobbing.*) Stop crying. I'm through with it. (*Linda turns away from them, her hands covering her face.*)

WILLY: I suppose that's my fault!

BIFF: I stole myself out of every good job since high school!

WILLY: And whose fault is that?

BIFF: And I never got anywhere because you blew me so full of hot air[12] I could never stand taking orders from anybody! That's whose fault it is!

WILLY: I hear that!

LINDA: Don't, Biff!

BIFF: It's goddam time you heard that! I had to be boss big shot in two weeks, and I'm through with it.

WILLY: Then hang yourself! For spite, hang yourself!

BIFF: No! Nobody's hanging himself, Willy! I ran down eleven flights with a pen in my hand today. And suddenly I stopped, you hear me? And in the middle of that office building, do you hear this? I stopped in the middle of that building and I saw — the sky. I saw the things that I love in this world. The work and the food and time to sit and smoke. And I looked at the pen and said to myself, what the hell am I grabbing this for? Why am I trying to become what I don't want to be?

---

12 hot air: empty, exaggerated talk.

What am I doing in an office, making a contemptuous, begging fool of myself, when all I want is out there, waiting for me the minute I say I know who I am! Why can't I say that, Willy? (*He tries to make Willy face him, but Willy pulls away and moves to the left.*)

WILLY (*with hatred, threateningly*): The door of your life is wide open!

BIFF: Pop! I'm a dime a dozen[13], and so are you!

WILLY (*turning on him now in an uncontrolled outburst*): I am not a dime a dozen! I am Willy Loman, and you are Biff Loman!

(*Biff starts for Willy, but is blocked by Happy. In his fury, Biff seems on the verge of attacking his father.*)

BIFF: I am not a leader of men, Willy, and neither are you. You were never anything but a hard-working drummer who landed in the ash can like all the rest of them! I'm one dollar an hour, Willy. I tried seven states and couldn't raise it. A buck an hour! Do you gather my meaning? I'm not bringing home any prizes any more, and you're going to stop waiting for me to bring them home!

WILLY (*directly to Biff*): You vengeful, spiteful mut[14]!

(*Biff breaks from Happy. Willy, in fright, starts up the stairs. Biff grabs him.*)

BIFF (*at the peak of his fury*): Pop, I'm nothing! I'm nothing, Pop. Can't you understand that? There's no spite in it any more. I'm just what I am, that's all.

(*Biff's fury has spent itself, and he breaks down, sobbing, holding on to Willy, who dumbly fumbles for Biff's face.*)

WILLY (*astonished*): What're you doing? What're you doing? (*To Linda.*) Why is he crying?

BIFF (*crying, broken*): Will you let me go, for Christ's sake? Will you take that phony dream and burn it before something happens? (*Strug-*

---

13 a dime a dozen: a person of not much importance, cheap and ordinary.

14 mut: a mongrel (杂种狗), (applied to a person) a term of contempt or abuse.

gling to contain himself, he pulls away and moves to the stairs.) I'll go in the morning. Put him — put him to bed. (*Exhausted, Biff moves up the stairs to his room.*)

WILLY (*after a long pause, astonished, elevated*): Isn't that — isn't that remarkable? Biff — he likes me!

LINDA: He loves you, Willy!

HAPPY (*deeply moved*): Always did, Pop.

WILLY: Oh, Biff! (*Staring wildly.*) He cried! Cried to me. (*He is choking with his love, and now cries out his promise.) That boy — that boy is going to be magnificent!*

(Ben appears in the light just outside the kitchen.)

BEN: Yes, outstanding, with twenty thousand behind him.

LINDA (*sensing the racing of his mind, fearfully, carefully*): Now come to bed, Willy. It's all settled now.

WILLY (*finding it difficult not to rush out of the house*): Yes, we'll sleep. Come on. Go to sleep, Hap.

BEN: And it does take a great kind of a man to crack the jungle. [7]

(*In accents of dread, Ben's idyllic music starts up.*)

HAPPY (*his arm around Linda*): I'm getting married, Pop, don't forget it. I'm changing everything. I'm gonna run that department before the year is up. You'll see, Mom. (*He kisses her.*)

BEN: The jungle is dark but full of diamonds, Willy.

(*Willy turns, moves, listening to Ben.*)

LINDA: Be good. You're both good boys, just act that way, that's all.

HAPPY: 'Night, Pop. (*He goes upstairs.*)

LINDA (*to Willy*): Come, dear.

BEN (*with greater force*): One must go in to fetch a diamond out.

WILLY (*to Linda, as he moves slowly along the edge of kitchen, toward the door*): I just want to get settled down, Linda. Let me sit alone for a little.

LINDA (*almost uttering her fear*): I want you upstairs.

WILLY (*taking her in his arms*): In a few minutes, Linda. I couldn't sleep right now. Go on, you look awful tired. (*He kisses her.*)

BEN: Not like an appointment at all. A diamond is rough and hard to the touch.

WILLY: Go on now. I'll be right up.

LINDA: I think this is the only way, Willy.

WILLY: Sure, it's the best thing.

BEN: Best thing!

WILLY: The only way. Everything is gonna be — go on, kid, get to bed. You look so tired.

LINDA: Come right up.

WILLY: Two minutes.

(*Linda goes into the living-room, then reappears in her bedroom. Willy moves just outside the kitchen door.*)

WILLY: Loves me. (*Wonderingly.*) Always loved me. Isn't that a remarkable thing? Ben, he'll worship me for it!

BEN (*with promise*): It's dark there, but full of diamonds.

WILLY: Can you imagine that magnificence with twenty thousand dollars in his pocket?

LINDA (*calling from her room*): Willy! Come up!

WILLY (*calling into the kitchen*): Yes! Yes. Coming! It's very smart, you realize that, don't you, sweetheart? Even Ben sees it. I gotta go, baby. 'By! 'By! (*Going over to Ben, almost dancing.*) Imagine? When the mail comes he'll be ahead of Bernard again! [8]

BEN: A perfect proposition all around.

WILLY: Did you see how he cried to me? Oh, if I could kiss him, Ben!

BEN: Time, William, time!

WILLY: Oh, Ben, I always knew one way or another we were gonna make it, Biff and I!

BEN (*looking at his watch*): The boat. We'll be late. (*He moves slowly off into the darkness.*)

WILLY (*elegiacally, turning to the house*): Now when you kick off, boy, I want a seventy-yard boot[15], and get right down the field under the ball, and when you hit, hit low and hit hard, because it's important, boy. (*He swings around and faces the audience.*) There's all kinds of important people in the stands, and the first thing you know... (*Suddenly realizing he is alone.*) Ben! Ben, where do I...? (*He makes a sudden movement of search.*) Ben, how do I...?

LINDA (*calling*): Willy, you coming up?

WILLY (*uttering a gasp of fear, whirling about as if to quiet her*): Sh! (*He turns around as if to find his way; sounds, faces, voices, seem to be swarming in upon him and he flicks at them, crying.*) Sh! Sh! (*Suddenly music, faint and high, stops him. It rises in intensity, almost to an unbearable scream. He goes up and down on his toes, and rushes off around the house.*) Shhh!

LINDA: Willy?

(*There is no answer. Linda waits. Biff gets up off his bed. He is still in his clothes. Happy sits up. Biff stands listening.*)

LINDA (*with real fear*): Willy, answer me! Willy!

(*There is the sound of a car starting and moving away at full speed.*)

LINDA: No!

BIFF (*rushing down the stairs*): Pop!

(*As the car speeds off, the music crashes down in a frenzy of sound, which becomes the soft pulsation of a single cello string. Biff slowly returns to his bedroom. He and Happy gravely don*[16] *their jackets. Linda slowly walks out of her room. The music has developed into a dead march. The leaves of day are appearing over everything. Charley and Bernard, somberly dressed, appear and knock on the kitchen door. Biff and Happy slowly descend the stairs to the kitchen as Charley and Bernard enter. All stop a moment when Linda,*

---

15 boot: a quick hard kick.

16 don: put on.

in clothes of mourning, bearing a little bunch of roses, comes through the draped doorway into the kitchen. She goes to Charley and takes his arm. Now all move toward the audience, through the wall-line of the kitchen. At the limit of the apron, Linda lays down the flowers, kneels, and sits back on her heels. All stare down at the grave.)

NOTES ON THE TEXT

[1] The opening scene in this selection depicts Willy attempting to plant some vegetables in his garden at night. He has bought some seeds. Planting seeds represent for Willy a chance to prove the worth of his labor — that is, his ability to bring food to the family. It is also a symbol of Willy's efforts to cultivate and nurture his sons. Willy is now suffering from serious psychological crisis, because he regards himself as a failure in both his career and his responsibility as a father.

[2] Ben is Willy's older brother who was a ruthless, but successful businessman, a diamond tycoon. His way of doing business is: "Never fight fair." In the jungle of the business world, Ben always came out on top. Willy sees Ben as a symbol for success; the irony is: Billy himself is the opposite type. Willy wants his sons to follow Ben's example. Although Ben is dead now, he often appears, as a ghost, in Willy's hallucinations.

[3] Twenty-thousand-dollar proposition here refers to a life insurance policy. Willy plans to commit suicide in order to get the money for his son Biff, to help him start a business of his own.

[4] "Ring up a zero" means making no money at all. By now Willy has lost his job and doesn't make any money.

[5] In one of his hallucinations, Willy imagines his funeral to be attended by many people, which will prove his importance to his son Biff. He has longed to be well-known and wealthy, but unfortunately he has never achieved this goal, not even after his death. Notice that Willy's mental state is declining. In derangement, he talks with the ghost of his deceased brother.

[6] In an earlier scene Linda finds a rubber tube connected to the gas pipe in the basement, which signals Willy's suicide attempt.

[7] Ben frequently boasts, "When I was 17 I walked into the jungle, and when I was 21 I walked out. And by God I was rich."

[8] Bernard is the son of Willy's next-door neighbor, Charley, who is successful in business and willing to help Willy. Bernard is clearly presented in the play as the opposite of Biff, despite the fact that Bernard takes Biff as his idol. Bernard eventually becomes one of the country top lawyers. His success is difficult for Willy to accept because his own sons do not measure up.

QUESTIONS FOR DISCUSSION

1. The plot of a play is often driven by dramatic conflicts. Discuss how the conflict between Willy and Biff help develop the plot of the play and how they eventually come to reconciliation at the end of play.

2. Find examples from the text that indicate Willy's mental derangement. Discuss how Willy's hallucinations are related to his miserable experiences as a failure.

3. What role does Ben, or rather Ben's ghost, play in Willy's decision to commit suicide? Ben thus says of a diamond, "Not like an appointment at all. A diamond is rough and hard to the touch." How do you understand the meaning of Ben's words? How do they reflect Willy's own obsession with success?

4. How do you comment on Willy's last effort to help his son Biff? What can we learn about the reality of the American Dream from the tragic fate of Willy?

SUGGESTED REFERENCES

Bigsby, Christopher, ed. *The Cambridge Companion to Arthur Miller.* New York: Cambridge UP, 1997.

Moss, Leonard, *Arthur Miller.* Boston: Twayne Publishers, 1980.

Bloom, Harold, ed. *Arthur Miller's Death of a Salesman: Contemporary Literary Views.* New York: Chelsea House Publishing, 1995.

Bigsby, Christopher. *Arthur Miller.* Cambridge: Harvard UP, 2009.

Griffin, Alice. *Understanding Arthur Miller.* Columbia: U of South Carolina P, 1996.

Mason, Jeffrey D. *Stone Tower: The Political Theater of Arthur Miller.* Ann Arbor: U of Michigan P, 2008.

Otten, Terry. *The Temptation of Innocence in the Dramas of Arthur Miller.* Columbia: U of Missouri P, 2002.

Unit 16 Joseph Heller

(1923—1999)

A GUIDE TO LITERARY TERMINOLOGY

"Black Humor": *The phrase was first used by André Breton, a French surrealist theoretician, in his 1935* ***Anthology of Black Humor (Anthologie de l'humour noir)*** *to depict a subgenre of comedy and satire in which laughter arises from cynicism and skepticism. In black humor, topics and events that are usually regarded as taboo are treated in an unusually humorous or satirical manner while retaining their seriousness. Bruce Jay Friedman, in his anthology entitled* ***Black Humor****, brought the concept of black comedy to the United States. The term came to prominence in the 1950s and 1960s, when it was used to describe a type of humor that combines a sense of the absurdity of life with farce. The goal of serious black humor in literature is to express the ultimate senselessness and futility of contemporary life. Joseph Heller's* ***Catch-22*** *is a classic example of serious fiction that engages in black humor. Yossarian, the protagonist of* ***Catch-22****, thus contemplates the question whether an insane bombardier can be grounded:*

There was only one catch and that was Catch-22, which specified that a concern for one's own safety in the face of dangers that were real and immediate was the process of a rational mind. Orr was crazy and could be grounded. All he had to do was ask; and as soon as he did, he would no longer be crazy and would have to fly more missions. Orr would be crazy to fly more missions and sane if he didn't, but if he was sane he had to fly them. If he flew them he was crazy and didn't have to; but if he didn't want to he was sane and had to. Yossarian was moved very deeply by the absolute simplicity of this clause of Catch-22 and let out a respectful whistle.

NOTES ON THE AUTHOR

Joseph Heller is best known for his novel *Catch-22*, which presents a satirical vision of war, stripping it of all heroism, glory, and honor and replacing it with a nightmarish picture of violence, bureaucracy, and lunacy. The novel provoked a great deal of controversy upon its initial publication in 1961. Millions of copies were sold and the word "catch-22" has entered the English lexicon to describe a situation in which there is no way out because of a set of inherently illogical rules or conditions.

Joseph Heller was born in Coney Island in Brooklyn, New York, to poor Jewish parents who immigrated to the United States from Russia. After graduating from high school in 1941, he joined the U. S. Army Air Corps in the following year. He was sent to the Italian Front two years later as a bombardier, where he flew 60 combat missions. The event that directly inspired him to write *Catch-22* occurred on August 15, 1944 over Avignon, France, during Heller's 37th bombing mission. Heller later said that the details of the Avignon mission on which Snowden dies — on Yossarian's 37th mission — correspond "perhaps ninety percent to what I did experience." After the war, Heller took the advantage of the GI Bill to earn his B. A. from New York University in 1948 and his M. A. from Columbia University in 1949. Then he spent a year at St Catherine's College, Oxford on Fulbright Scholarship. After teaching at Pennsylvania State University for two years (1950—1952), Heller returned to New York and took a series of advertising and marketing jobs. In 1953, he began writing *Catch-22*, which was published in 1961, when he was 38. Over the remaining 38 years of his life, he wrote six novels — *Something Happened* (1974), *Good as Gold* (1979), *God Knows* (1984), *Picture This* (1988), *Closing Time* (1994), *Portrait of an Artist, As an Old Man* (2000), an anti-war play titled *We Bombed in New Haven* (1968), and two memoirs.

SYNOPSIS OF THE WORK

Catch-22, one of the greatest literary works of the twentieth century, tells the story of Captain John Yossarian, a bombardier of the American Air Force based in Pianosa, an island in the Mediterranean Sea, west of Italy in World War II. Most people would regard the war as just and fair and the veterans as great heroes, but in the novel Joseph Heller treats the war as sheer madness. He condemns both war and the military bureaucracy that carry out systematic slaughter of human lives. The satirical tone of the novel and its fractured narrative structure reflect the lunatic nature of the military enterprise Yossarian finds himself hopelessly stuck in. Yossarian, whose instinctual alertness and resistance to all lofty causes in the name of patriotism provide the counterforce to death and mortality, embodies life. His fear of death and love of life are manifested in his design of one strategy after another to stay alive. Tired from flying endless missions (the required number is always raised by Colonel Cathcart when Yossarian gets close to it), Yossarian tries to stay in the military hospital by faking a liver condition. While in the hospital, Yossarian has to censor letters sent by enlisted men to their families and friends, a job he finds thoroughly monotonous and meaningless. He plays games with the letters by blacking out parts of them and by signing someone else's name such as "Washington Irving."

After leaving the hospital, Yossarian decides to go crazy so as to avoid flying more combat missions. It is then that he encounters the absurd logic of catch-22, according to which only a crazy person can be exempted from combat and anyone who seeks exemption from combat cannot be considered crazy. Joseph has scattered miniature versions of catch-22 throughout the novel. The same irrational, self-negating, and paradoxical logic works for the required number of mission: by continually raising the number of missions, the rule has, in effect, negated itself and becomes absurd and futile. Another instance is: Yossarian finds his commanding officers more dangerous than the German enemies they are supposed to fight. He claims, "The enemy is anybody who's going to get you killed, no matter which side he's on, and that includes Colonel Cathcart." Colonel Cathcart, however, is only one of the numerous indifferent and self-serving officers, including Peckem, Dreedle, and Scheisskopf, who may get Yassarian and his fellow airmen killed any time. Yossarian has been scared by the deaths of many of his comrades. The death of a young airman named Snowden — who was blown apart by antiaircraft fire and who died painfully in Yossarian's arms — haunts Yossarian throughout the novel. The gruesome death of his friends, Nately, McWatt, Mudd, Kid Sampson, Dobbs, Chief White Halfoat and Hungry Joe, has hardened his hatred of military life. Eventually, when Colonel Cathcart offers him a chance to go home on condition that he like and praise Cathcart on his return home, he at first agrees, but in the end decides to desert the Air Corps altogether and go to Sweden.

SELECTED READINGS

Catch-22

(Chapter I "The Texan")

It was love at first sight.

The first time Yossarian saw the chaplain he fell madly in love with him. [1]

Yossarian was in the hospital with a pain in his liver that fell just short of[1] being jaundice. The doctors were puzzled by the fact that it

1 fall short of: fail to satisfy (未达到).

wasn't quite jaundice. If it became jaundice they could treat it. If it didn't become jaundice and went away they could discharge him. But this just being short of jaundice all the time confused them.

Each morning they came around, three brisk and serious men with efficient mouths and inefficient eyes, accompanied by brisk and serious Nurse Duckett, one of the ward nurses who didn't like Yossarian. They read the chart at the foot of the bed and asked impatiently about the pain. They seemed irritated when he told them it was exactly the same.

"Still no movement?" the full colonel demanded.

The doctors exchanged a look when he shook his head.

"Give him another pill."

Nurse Duckett made a note to give Yossarian another pill, and the four of them moved along to the next bed. None of the nurses liked Yossarian. Actually, the pain in his liver had gone away, but Yossarian didn't say anything and the doctors never suspected. They just suspected that he had been moving his bowels[2] and not telling anyone.

Yossarian had everything he wanted in the hospital. The food wasn't too bad, and his meals were brought to him in bed. There were extra rations of fresh meat, and during the hot part of the afternoon he and the others were served chilled fruit juice or chilled chocolate milk. Apart from the doctors and the nurses, no one ever disturbed him. For a little while in the morning he had to censor letters, but he was free after that to spend the rest of each day lying around idly with a clear conscience. He was comfortable in the hospital, and it was easy to stay on because he always ran a temperature of 101. He was even more comfortable than Dunbar, who had to keep falling down on his face in order to get his meals brought to him in bed.

After he had made up his mind to spend the rest of the war in the hospital, Yossarian wrote letters to everyone he knew saying that he was in the hospital but never mentioning why. One day he had a better

2 move one's bowels: to pass solid waste out of the body.

idea. To everyone he knew he wrote that he was going on a very dangerous mission. "They asked for volunteers. It's very dangerous, but someone has to do it. I'll write you the instant I get back." And he had not written anyone since.

All the officer patients in the ward were forced to censor letters written by all the enlisted-men patients, who were kept in residence in wards of their own. It was a monotonous job, and Yossarian was disappointed to learn that the lives of enlisted men were only slightly more interesting than the lives of officers. After the first day he had no curiosity at all. To break the monotony he invented games. Death to all modifiers,[3] he declared one day, and out of every letter that passed through his hands went every adverb and every adjective. The next day he made war on articles. He reached a much higher plane of creativity the following day when he blacked out everything in the letters but a, an and the. That erected more dynamic intralinear tensions, he felt, and in just about every case left a message far more universal. Soon he was proscribing parts of salutations and signatures and leaving the text untouched. One time he blacked out all but the salutation "Dear Mary" from a letter, and at the bottom he wrote, "I yearn for you tragically. R. O. Shipman, Chaplain, U. S. Army." R. O. Shipman was the group chaplain's name. [2]

When he had exhausted all possibilities in the letters, he began attacking the names and addresses on the envelopes, obliterating whole homes and streets, annihilating entire metropolises with careless flicks of his wrist as though he were God. Catch-22 required that each censored letter bear the censoring officer's name. Most letters he didn't read at all. On those he didn't read at all he wrote his own name. On those he did read he wrote, "Washington Irving."[4] When that grew monotonous he wrote, "Irving Washington." Censoring the

3 Death to all modifiers: delete all the modifiers.

4 Washington Irving (1783 – 1859): American author, essayist, biographer, historian, and diplomat of the early nineteenth century.

envelopes had serious repercussions, produced a ripple of anxiety on some ethereal military echelon that floated a C. I. D. man[5] back into the ward posing as a patient. They all knew he was a C. I. D. man because he kept inquiring about an officer named Irving or Washington and because after his first day there he wouldn't censor letters. He found them too monotonous.

It was a good ward this time, one of the best he and Dunbar had ever enjoyed. With them this time was the twenty-four-year-old fighter-pilot captain with the sparse golden mustache who had been shot into the Adriatic Sea[6] in midwinter and not even caught cold. Now the summer was upon them, the captain had not been shot down, and he said he had the grippe. In the bed on Yossarian's right, still lying amorously on his belly, was the startled captain with malaria in his blood and a mosquito bite on his ass. Across the aisle from Yossarian was Dunbar, and next to Dunbar was the artillery captain with whom Yossarian had stopped playing chess. The captain was a good chess player, and the games were always interesting. Yossarian had stopped playing chess with him because the games were so interesting they were foolish. Then there was the educated Texan from Texas who looked like someone in Technicolor and felt, patriotically, that people of means — decent folk — should be given more votes than drifters, whores, criminals, degenerates, atheists and indecent folk — people without means.

Yossarian was unspringing rhythms in the letters[7] the day they brought the Texan in. It was another quiet, hot, untroubled day. The heat pressed heavily on the roof, stifling sound. Dunbar was lying motionless on his back again with his eyes staring up at the ceiling like a doll's. He was working hard at increasing his life span. He did it by

---

5 C. I. D. man: a member of the Criminal Investigation Department.

6 shot into the Adriatic Sea: (his plane) was shot down and dropped into the Adriatic Sea, but he survived. Adriatic Sea: 亚得里亚海, 地中海的一个大海湾，在意大利与巴尔干半岛之间。

7 unspringing rhythms of the letters: make the letters incomplete and lack of coherence by removing some words from them.

cultivating boredom. Dunbar was working so hard at increasing his life span that Yossarian thought he was dead. They put the Texan in a bed in the middle of the ward, and it wasn't long before he donated his views.

Dunbar sat up like a shot. "That's it," he cried excitedly. "There was something missing — all the time I knew there was something missing — and now I know what it is." He banged his fist down into his palm. "No patriotism," he declared.

"You're right," Yossarian shouted back. "You're right, you're right, you're right. The hot dog, the Brooklyn Dodgers. Mom's apple pie. That's what everyone's fighting for. But who's fighting for the decent folk? Who's fighting for more votes for the decent folk? There's no patriotism, that's what it is. And no matriotism[8], either."

The warrant officer on Yossarian's left was unimpressed. "Who gives a shit?"[9] he asked tiredly, and turned over on his side to go to sleep.

The Texan turned out to be good-natured, generous and likable. In three days no one could stand him. [3]

He sent shudders of annoyance scampering up ticklish spines, and everybody fled from him — everybody but the soldier in white, who had no choice. The soldier in white was encased from head to toe in plaster and gauze. He had two useless legs and two useless arms. He had been smuggled into the ward during the night, and the men had no idea he was among them until they awoke in the morning and saw the two strange legs hoisted from the hips, the two strange arms anchored up perpendicularly, all four limbs pinioned strangely in air by lead weights suspended darkly above him that never moved. Sewn into the bandages over the insides of both elbows were zippered lips through which he was fed clear fluid from a clear jar. A silent zinc pipe rose from the cement on his groin and was coupled to a slim rubber hose that carried waste from his kidneys and dripped it efficiently into a clear, stoppered jar on the floor. When the jar on the floor was

8 matriotism: this word is created by Yossarian to ridicule "patriotism;" the prefix "patri-", which means "father," is the opposite of "matri-", which means "mother."
9 Who gives a shit?: Who cares?

full, the jar feeding his elbow was empty, and the two were simply switched quickly so that the stuff could drip back into him. All they ever really saw of the soldier in white was a frayed black hole over his mouth. [4]

The soldier in white had been filed next to the Texan, and the Texan sat sideways on his own bed and talked to him throughout the morning, afternoon and evening in a pleasant, sympathetic drawl. The Texan never minded that he got no reply.

Temperatures were taken twice a day in the ward. Early each morning and late each afternoon Nurse Cramer entered with a jar full of thermometers and worked her way up one side of the ward and down the other, distributing a thermometer to each patient. She managed the soldier in white by inserting a thermometer into the hole over his mouth and leaving it balanced there on the lower rim. When she returned to the man in the first bed, she took his thermometer and recorded his temperature, and then moved on to the next bed and continued around the ward again. One afternoon when she had completed her first circuit of the ward and came a second time to the soldier in white, she read his thermometer and discovered that he was dead.

"Murderer," Dunbar said quietly.

The Texan looked up at him with an uncertain grin.

"Killer," Yossarian said.

"What are you fellas talkin' about?" the Texan asked nervously.

"You murdered him," said Dunbar.

"You killed him," said Yossarian.

The Texan shrank back. "You fellas are crazy. I didn't even touch him."

"You murdered him," said Dunbar.

"I heard you kill him," said Yossarian.

"You killed him because he was a nigger," Dunbar said.

"You fellas are crazy," the Texan cried. "They don't allow niggers in here. They got a special place for niggers."

"The sergeant smuggled him in," Dunbar said.

"The Communist sergeant," said Yossarian.

"And you knew it." [5]

The warrant officer on Yossarian's left was unimpressed by the entire incident of the soldier in white. The warrant officer was unimpressed by everything and never spoke at all unless it was to show irritation.

The day before Yossarian met the chaplain, a stove exploded in the mess hall and set fire to one side of the kitchen. An intense heat flashed through the area. Even in Yossarian's ward, almost three hundred feet away, they could hear the roar of the blaze and the sharp cracks of flaming timber. Smoke sped past the orange-tinted windows. In about fifteen minutes the crash trucks from the airfield arrived to fight the fire. For a frantic half hour it was touch and go.[10] Then the firemen began to get the upper hand. Suddenly there was the monotonous old drone of bombers returning from a mission, and the firemen had to roll up their hoses and speed back to the field in case one of the planes crashed and caught fire. The planes landed safely. As soon as the last one was down, the firemen wheeled their trucks around and raced back up the hill to resume their fight with the fire at the hospital. When they got there, the blaze was out. It had died of its own accord, expired completely without even an ember to be watered down, and there was nothing for the disappointed firemen to do but drink tepid coffee and hang around trying to screw the nurses.

The chaplain arrived the day after the fire. Yossarian was busy expurgating all but romance words from the letters when the chaplain sat down in a chair between the beds and asked him how he was feeling. He had placed himself a bit to one side, and the captain's bars[11]

---

10 it was touch and go: it was uncertain whether the fire could be controlled.

11 captain's bars: 上尉领章。

on the tab of his shirt collar were all the insignia Yossarian could see. Yossarian had no idea who he was and just took it for granted that he was either another doctor or another madman.

"Oh, pretty good," he answered. "I've got a slight pain in my liver and I haven't been the most regular of fellows, I guess, but all in all I must admit that I feel pretty good."

"That's good," said the chaplain.

"Yes," Yossarian said. "Yes, that is good."

"I meant to come around sooner," the chaplain said, "but I really haven't been well."

"That's too bad," Yossarian said.

"Just a head cold[12],"the chaplain added quickly.

"I've got a fever of a hundred and one," Yossarian added just as quickly.

"That's too bad," said the chaplain.

"Yes," Yossarian agreed. "Yes, that is too bad."

The chaplain fidgeted. "Is there anything I can do for you?" he asked after a while.

"No, no." Yossarian sighed. "The doctors are doing all that's humanly possible, I suppose."

"No, no." The chaplain colored faintly. "I didn't mean anything like that. I meant cigarettes... or books... or... toys."

"No, no," Yossarian said. "Thank you. I have everything I need, I suppose — everything but good health."

"That's too bad."

"Yes," Yossarian said. "Yes, that is too bad."

The chaplain stirred again. He looked from side to side a few times, then gazed up at the ceiling, then down at the floor. He drew a deep breath.

---

12 head cold: a common cold affecting the nasal passages and resulting in congestion and sneezing and headache（普通伤风感冒）.

"Lieutenant Nately sends his regards," he said.

Yossarian was sorry to hear they had a mutual friend. It seemed there was a basis to their conversation after all.

"You know Lieutenant Nately?" he asked regretfully.

"Yes, I know Lieutenant Nately quite well."

"He's a bit loony, isn't he?"

The chaplain's smile was embarrassed. "I'm afraid I couldn't say. I don't think I know him that well."

"You can take my word for it," Yossarian said. "He's as goofy as they come."

The chaplain weighed the next silence heavily and then shattered it with an abrupt question. "You are Captain Yossarian, aren't you?"

"Nately had a bad start. He came from a good family."

"Please excuse me," the chaplain persisted timorously. "I may be committing a very grave error. Are you Captain Yossarian?"

"Yes," Captain Yossarian confessed. "I am Captain Yossarian."

"Of the 256th Squadron?"

"Of the fighting 256th Squadron," Yossarian replied. "I didn't know there were any other Captain Yossarians. As far as I know, I'm the only Captain Yossarian I know, but that's only as far as I know."

"I see," the chaplain said unhappily.

"That's two to the fighting eighth power,"[13] Yossarian pointed out, "if you're thinking of writing a symbolic poem about our squadron."

"No," mumbled the chaplain. "I'm not thinking of writing a symbolic poem about your squadron."

Yossarian straightened sharply when he spied the tiny silver cross on the other side of the chaplain's collar. He was thoroughly astonished, for he had never really talked with a chaplain before.

"You're a chaplain," he exclaimed ecstatically. "I didn't know you were a chaplain."

---

13 two to the eighth power: 2的8次方。

"Why, yes," the chaplain answered. "Didn't you know I was a chaplain?"

"Why, no. I didn't know you were a chaplain." Yossarian stared at him with a big, fascinated grin. "I've never really seen a chaplain before."

The chaplain flushed again and gazed down at his hands. He was a slight man of about thirty-two with tan hair and brown diffident eyes. His face was narrow and rather pale. An innocent nest of ancient pimple pricks lay in the basin of each cheek. Yossarian wanted to help him.

"Can I do anything at all to help you?" the chaplain asked.

Yossarian shook his head, still grinning. "No, I'm sorry. I have everything I need and I'm quite comfortable. In fact, I'm not even sick."

"That's good." As soon as the chaplain said the words, he was sorry and shoved his knuckles into his mouth with a giggle of alarm, but Yossarian remained silent and disappointed him. "There are other men in the group I must visit," he apologized finally. "I'll come to see you again, probably tomorrow."

"Please do that," Yossarian said.

"I'll come only if you want me to," the chaplain said, lowering his head shyly. "I've noticed that I make many of the men uncomfortable."

Yossarian glowed with affection. "I want you to," he said. "You won't make me uncomfortable."

The chaplain beamed gratefully and then peered down at a slip of paper he had been concealing in his hand all the while. He counted along the beds in the ward, moving his lips, and then centered his attention dubiously on Dunbar.

"May I inquire," he whispered softly, "if that is Lieutenant Dunbar?"

"Yes," Yossarian answered loudly, "that is Lieutenant Dunbar."

"Thank you," the chaplain whispered. "Thank you very much. I must visit with him. I must visit with every member of the group who is in the hospital."

"Even those in other wards?" Yossarian asked.

"Even those in other wards."

"Be careful in those other wards, Father," Yossarian warned. "That's where they keep the mental cases. They're filled with lunatics."

"It isn't necessary to call me Father," the chaplain explained. "I'm an Anabaptist[14]."

"I'm dead serious about those other wards," Yossarian continued grimly. "M. P.s[15] won't protect you, because they're craziest of all. I'd go with you myself, but I'm scared stiff: Insanity is contagious. This is the only sane ward in the whole hospital. Everybody is crazy but us. This is probably the only sane ward in the whole world, for that matter." [6]

The chaplain rose quickly and edged away from Yossarian's bed, and then nodded with a conciliating smile and promised to conduct himself with appropriate caution. "And now I must visit with Lieutenant Dunbar," he said.

Still he lingered, remorsefully. "How is Lieutenant Dunbar?" he asked at last.

"As good as they go," Yossarian assured him. "A true prince. One of the finest, least dedicated men in the whole world."

"I didn't mean that," the chaplain answered, whispering again. "Is he very sick?"

"No, he isn't very sick. In fact, he isn't sick at all."

"That's good." The chaplain sighed with relief.

"Yes," Yossarian said. "Yes, that is good."

---

14 Anabaptist: a member of Anabaptism, a Protestant movement in the sixteenth century that believed in the primacy of the Bible, baptized only believers, not infants, and believed in complete separation of church and state.

15 M. P.: military police.

"A chaplain," Dunbar said when the chaplain had visited him and gone. "Did you see that? A chaplain."

"Wasn't he sweet?" said Yossarian. "Maybe they should give him three votes."

"Who's they?" Dunbar demanded suspiciously.

In a bed in the small private section at the end of the ward, always working ceaselessly behind the green ply board partition, was the solemn middle-aged colonel who was visited every day by a gentle, sweet-face woman with curly ash-blond hair who was not a nurse and not a Wac[16] and not a Red Cross girl but who nevertheless appeared faithfully at the hospital in Pianosa[17] each afternoon wearing pretty pastel summer dresses that were very smart and white leather pumps with heels half high at the base of nylon seams that were inevitably straight. The colonel was in Communications, and he was kept busy day and night transmitting glutinous messages from the interior into square pads of gauze which he sealed meticulously and delivered to a covered white pail that stood on the night table beside his bed. The colonel was gorgeous. He had a cavernous mouth, cavernous cheeks, cavernous, sad, mildewed eyes. His face was the color of clouded silver. He coughed quietly, gingerly, and dabbed the pads slowly at his lips with a distaste that had become automatic.

The colonel dwelt in a vortex of specialists who were still specializing in trying to determine what was troubling him. They hurled lights in his eyes to see if he could see, rammed needles into nerves to hear if he could feel.

There was a urologist for his urine[18], a lymphologist for his lymph[19], an endocrinologist for his endocrines[20], a psychologist for

16 Wac: Women's Army Corps.
17 Pianosa: a small island in Italy.
18 urine：尿。
19 lymph: 淋巴。
20 endocrine: 内分泌腺。

his psyche, a dermatologist for his derma[21]; there was a pathologist for his pathos[22], a cystologist for his cysts[23], and a bald and pedantic cetologist[24] from the zoology department at Harvard who had been shanghaied[25] ruthlessly into the Medical Corps by a faulty anode in an I. B. M. machine and spent his sessions with the dying colonel trying to discuss Moby Dick with him. [7]

The colonel had really been investigated. There was not an organ of his body that had not been drugged and derogated, dusted and dredged, fingered and photographed, removed, plundered and replaced. Neat, slender an erect, the woman touched him often as she sat by his bedside and was the epitome of stately sorrow each time she smiled. The colonel was tall, thin and stooped. When he rose to walk, he bent forward even more, making a deep cavity of his body, and placed his feet down very carefully, moving ahead by inches from the knees down. There were violet pools under his eyes. The woman spoke softly, softer than the colonel coughed, and none of the men in the ward ever heard her voice.

In less than ten days the Texan cleared the ward. The artillery captain broke first, and after that the exodus[26] started. Dunbar, Yossarian and the fighter captain all bolted the same morning. Dunbar stopped having dizzy spells, and the fighter captain blew his nose. Yossarian told the doctors that the pain in his liver had gone away. It was as easy as that. Even the warrant officer fled. In less than ten days, the Texan drove everybody in the war back to duty — everybody but the C. I. D. man, who had caught cold from the fighter captain and come down with pneumonia.

---

21 derma：皮肤。
22 pathos：痛苦。
23 cyst：囊肿。
24 cetologist: a zoologist who studies whales.
25 shanghai: to induce or compel someone to do something.
26 exodus: a departure of a large number of people from a place at the same time; Exodus: the departure of the Israelites from Egypt (see the Bible).

NOTES ON THE TEXT

[1] According to Heller, he initiated the writing of *Catch-22* by pondering the two lines: "It was love at first sight. The first time he saw the chaplain, [Yossarian] fell madly in love with him." Over the next few hours, he began to sketch his ideas about characters, plot, tone, and themes on note cards. Within a week, he sent his agent the first chapter which was published in 1955 as "Catch-18", in Issue 7 of *New World Writing*. After writing on and off for eight years, he finished and published the whole novel in 1961.

[2] Here Yossarian is playing basically a language game with the letters he is forced to censor. Yossarian's game with the letters can be read as a parody of the military's more destructive game with human lives, of which many of Yossarian's fellow airmen are victims. Notice Heller's use of military words here: "Death to all modifiers;" "he made war on articles." Yossarian's game signals both his boredom and his ridicule of the military authorities' distortion of the communicative function of language, which is exemplified by the illogical law of Catch-22. As Yossarian has realized, Catch-22 is but a trap made up of words to keep him and other bombardiers flying combat missions. What is upsetting about Catch-22 is that men are put in real danger based on some unreal and unreliable words.

[3] Note that the Texan cannot be "good-natured, generous and likable" and makes enemies with everybody at the same time. The paradox here has become Joseph Heller's signature expression in the novel. It carries in it the same kind of logical irrationality as Catch-22. Other examples in the chapter are: "Dunbar was working so hard at increasing his life span that Yossarian thought he was dead." "The captain was a good chess player, and the games were always interesting. Yossarian had stopped playing chess with him because the games were so interesting they were foolish." "If it became jaundice they could treat it. If it didn't become jaundice and went away they could discharge him. But this just being short of jaundice all the time confused them." The logical confusion created by this pattern of expression reinforces one of the themes of the novel — i.e. the absurdity of war and the inhumanity of military bureaucracy.

[4] The soldier in white looks more like an inanimate object than a living human being. He does not have a name, nor does he have a recognizable face. His body is bandage-wrapped all over except his mouth and remains completely still. Most bizarre of all, the liquid that dripped out of his body into a jar is injected back into his body when the jar is full. The soldier in white represents the way the soldiers are treated as interchangeable objects. Months after his death, he is replaced by another, identical soldier in white.

[5] Here Dunbar and Yossarian are making fun of the Texan, who believes "patriotically" that "people of means" (WASP) should be given more votes than "people without means" (non-WASP). It is apparent that Dunbar and Yossarian hate the Texan for his prejudice against people of lower social class. That explains why they accuse the Texan of murdering the

soldier in white whom they claim to be a "nigger."

[6] Yossarian and a few of his friends, including Dunbar and Orr, are depicted as the only sane people in the novel. Throughout the novel, Heller intends the sane to look insane and vice versa. As Heller himself said of his novel, "Everyone in my book accuses everyone else of being crazy. Frankly, I think the whole society is nuts — and the question is: What does a sane man do in an insane society?" In this case, Yossarian and Dunbar may sound crazy, they are actually saner than the Texan.

[7] It is worthy of notice that the error made by the IBM machine in selecting doctors is as bizarre as the error in time, or anachronism (the IBM machine didn't exist during World War II). In a 1977 essay on *Catch-22*, Heller stated that the "antiwar and antigovernment feelings in the book" were a product of the Korean War and the 1950s rather than World War II itself. In other words, Heller's criticisms are not intended for World War II but for the Cold War and McCarthyism. Heller uses anachronisms like loyalty oaths and computers (IBM machines) to situate the novel in the context of the 1950s. The principal themes of the novel have much more to do with the 1950s: the bureaucratic absurdities, the sometimes life-denying logic of capitalism, and the pressures to conform. An example of this is Heller uses Milo Minderbinder to make a scathing attack on American capitalism.

QUESTIONS FOR DISCUSSION

1. Discuss the question of patriotism as the Texan and Yossarian understand it. What are the differences in their perception of patriotism? What has led to such differences?

2. Cite some examples from the text that demonstrate bureaucratic absurdity at work and discuss how they reflect the American reality of the 1940s and 1950s.

3. The events and situations depicted in the text seem to be disparate and disjointed. However, Heller does achieve some kind of stylistic, structural and thematic unity in the text. Explain how he is capable of achieving such unity in the text.

4. Heller uses the Catch-22 paradox and self-negating sentences to communicate his vision of the world. Find as many such paradoxical expressions in the text as possible and explain their significance in conveying the author's thoughts and feelings.

SUGGESTED REFERENCES

Bloom, Harold, ed. *Joseph Heller's **Catch-22***. Philadelphia: Chelsea House Publishers, 2007.

Craig, David M. *Tilting the Mortality: Narrative Strategies in Joseph Heller's Fiction.* Detroit: Wayne State

UP, 1997.

Merrill, Robert. *Joseph Heller.* Boston: Twayne, 1987.

Nagel, James, ed. *Critical Essays on Joseph Heller.* Boston: G. K. Hall, 1984.

Pinker, Sanford. *Understanding Joseph Heller.* Columbia: U of South Carolina P, 2009.

Potts, Stephen W. ***Catch-22**: Antiheroic Antinovel.* Boston: Twayne Publishers, 1989.

Seed, David. *The Fiction of Joseph Heller: Against the Grain.* New York: St. Martin's Press, 1989.